Reference Librarianship and Justice

Reference Librarianship and Justice

Edited by

Kate Adler, Ian Beilin, and Eamon Tewell

Library Juice Press
Sacramento, CA

Published by Library Juice Press in 2018

Library Juice Press
PO Box 188784
Sacramento, CA 95818

http://libraryjuicepress.com

This book is printed on acid-free paper.

Library of Congress Cataloging-in-Publication Data

Names: Adler, Kate, 1979- editor. | Beilin, Ian, 1968- editor. | Tewell,
    Eamon, editor.
Title: Reference librarianship & justice : history, practice & praxis /
    edited by Kate Adler, Ian Beilin, and Eamon Tewell.
Other titles: Reference librarianship and justice
Description: Sacramento, CA : Library Juice Press, 2018. | Includes
    bibliographical references and index.
Identifiers: LCCN 2018035330 | ISBN 9781634000512 (alk. paper : acid-free
    paper)
Subjects: LCSH: Reference services (Libraries)--Social aspects. | Reference
    services (Libraries)--United States--Case studies. | Libraries and
    society--United States. | Social justice--United States.
Classification: LCC Z711 .R44445 2018 | DDC 025.5/2--dc23
LC record available at https://lccn.loc.gov/2018035330

Table of Contents

Leaky Ceilings, Staplers, and Nazis: Collocating Reference Work and Social Justice

Maria T. Accardi

"I really want you to understand me," he said.

A student—I'll call him Hector—had approached me at the reference desk seeking assistance. He needed to find sources on a specific type of classical music. Complicating things was that his professor insisted on his using print sources only. I get so angry when students tell me things like this, because this outdated perspective places unneeded obstacles in a student's path for no valid reason I can think of. In this case, Hector's path was impeded by his professor's antediluvian view that the only "good" sources available were printed on paper. His professor was obviously wrong, and Hector knew it, and I knew it. He had wanted to use Oxford Music Online, which is precisely where I was going to direct him before learning of his restriction. I tried to not display my anger too obviously, though. I want to empathize with students but I don't want to appear to be critical of their professor. I'm a person, though, and maybe sometimes that criticism leaks out a bit, but I try to keep it in check.

"That must be frustrating," I told Hector. He agreed.

Hector told me more about this classical music term he was researching. I was unfamiliar with the term in question, so Hector defined it for me, but I was still a little unclear. I had a pretty good music education in high school and college, and this, coupled with my own actual interest in classical music, makes me reasonably well-informed about the subject. But

I just wasn't connecting with Hector for some reason. I couldn't follow his explanation. So I Googled the term and found the Wikipedia entry, displaying it on the patron-facing monitor of the reference desk dual monitor setup. We read through the entry together, and I made a joke about consulting Wikipedia. Hector said that he found Wikipedia to be very useful when it came to classical music, and I agreed. We talked through the subject a bit more, and he cited examples of this kind of music. Then I started to catch on. I understood what he was talking about.

"I really want you to understand me," he said again. And I did. I looked directly at him, made eye contact, and I felt warm. I allowed this warmth to soften my facial expression and body language. We were connected. It was one of those moments where everything felt exactly right, where we were two human beings in relationship to one another. The energy of our encounter shifted somehow. We had been speaking cordially and warmly; now our interaction felt more electric, alive. Hector then started to tell me about the leaky ceiling in his apartment, how he had reported it to the maintenance office, how he hoped it would be repaired by the time he got home. As he narrated his tale, I could see the leaky ceiling, hear the water dripping, feel the anxiety of wondering if and when it would be repaired. We had moved beyond a sterile transmission of information. We were two people, connected. I wasn't sure why or how Hector had drifted from talking about classical music to talking about his leaky ceiling in his apartment and wondered if I had missed a transition. I would like to think that he felt free to talk about his personal concerns because I made an effort to humanize our conversation, to indicate that I cared about him as a person, because he thought I seemed nice and helpful and friendly.

I admit that this is not the kind of encounter I had in mind when I was grudgingly constructing a reference desk staffing schedule this past summer. A few years ago, due to some internal organization of roles among the librarians at my institution, I had the coordination of reference folded into my ever expanding grab-bag of responsibilities. I was now the Coordinator of Instruction *and* Reference, and at first, I was very excited about this development. I have ideas about reference services and staffing, a vision, strategies I'd like to explore. However, given the demands of my role as instruction coordinator, it soon became clear that my role in coordinating reference would purely be administrative. In short, the thankless chore of creating the reference desk staffing schedule was now my job. I realize how churlish and ungracious this attitude sounds, but this is how I felt at the time.

The reference desk at my library is staffed only by faculty librarians with master's degrees, and there is a librarian sitting at the desk for as long as the library is open, and this includes evenings and weekends while school is in session. I have complicated feelings about this staffing model, but until I have the time or energy to do otherwise, this is the model we use. Creating the summer schedule is an especially trying task that has to take into account the many absences of librarians taking time off. Rather than creating a standard schedule that is the same for the whole summer session, just as I do in fall and spring semesters, I essentially have to create an entirely new schedule for each week in order to accommodate everyone's vacation plans. This logistical challenge becomes especially vexing when I considered the fact that summer enrollment was down ten percent from the previous year, which was also down from the previous year, which means the library was nearly empty during the summer sessions. It seemed absurd to expend so much energy and angst trying to staff a desk that hardly anyone needed.

However, I recently reconsidered this perspective of what constitutes a "need" for a librarian sitting at the reference desk. This semester, after having taken myself out of the rotation for about a year, I resumed a once-weekly evening reference shift. I'm the Monday night librarian, which means I sit at the desk from 5 pm to 10 pm in a state of constant readiness and approachability, just in case someone needs me. Thus far, people have needed me for printing help, refilling staplers, and pointing out the bathrooms. I expect that this sounds familiar to many academic librarians who sit at a reference desk. I was recounting my first evening shift of the semester to my therapist, who remarked wryly, "Right, and you got a master's degree so you can help people print." He was making a joke, and, to be candid, he was echoing words I have previously said myself. But suddenly, as he said these words, something shifted inside of me. The shift was initially wordless, just an intuitive sense that something was changing inside of me, and then, when I talked it through with my wife, I realized: No, I *didn't* get a master's degree so I could help people print. But I *did* get a master's degree so that I could be a helpful, friendly person who could make a difference of some kind in the lives of college students. This is exactly why I went to library school. My route to academic librarianship was circuitous, but the teaching experience I gained as a master's student in English, specifically when I took my English 102 students to the library for instruction, illuminated a previously unimagined career pathway, a way of working with students and helping them access the information they need to be successful in personal, academic, and other settings.

So, yes, I honestly really and truly did get a master's degree so I could be a helpful person in the lives of college students. I just never imagined it would involve refilling so many staplers. In the early years of my career, I became interested in the literature on student retention and what role the library might play in helping students complete their degrees. I felt—and still feel—uneasy about the research linking things like student GPA and frequency of library use, because I am opposed to surveilling and policing and tracking student behavior. I think it is creepy and immoral. I did, however, feel a sort of intuitive resonance with the research that pointed to the impact of having helpful adults actively involved in the life of college students.[1] This strikes me as infinitely more meaningful and powerful, this emphasis on relationships, on actual human beings connecting and seeing each other, than it is to count how many times a student walked into a library and then correlate it to their GPA. I'm paraphrasing, but this is the general idea, and it is the one that is most in alignment with my philosophy of librarianship, a worldview and approach that sees social justice as the ultimate goal of my work and practice and praxis.

It is hard, though, to continue to find meaning and purpose in *just* being a helpful grownup refilling the stapler when there are actual literal Nazis marching in the streets of Charlottesville, Virginia. While I was working on the draft of this foreword you're reading, a literal actual white supremacist Nazi drove his car into a crowd of anti-fascist protesters and killed a woman. As someone who considers feminism and social justice as organizing principles of my philosophy of librarianship, I consider myself pretty conscious and enlightened and aware of the injustice and oppression that are baked into the very bones of our world, but even so, everything I'd already drafted for this introduction I was asked to write suddenly seemed astonishingly trivial. Those in position of privilege profess shock and disbelief that violent and disgusting acts of emboldened white supremacists could be possibly be happening in the United States of America in 2017. Those whose lives are regularly imperiled emotionally, physically, psychically and in all other ways because they are not white, straight, cis, or able-bodied are saying, "How is this a surprise?"

And yet, *isn't* it a surprise that it has somehow become controversial to assert that Nazis do not belong in libraries or anywhere? The libraryland blogosphere appears to be experiencing intermittent noxious eruptions of "but free speech!", as if "free speech" excuses and justifies the emotional and physical violence experienced by those whose very humanity

---

1   Maurie Caitlin Kelly, "Student retention and academic libraries," *College and Research Libraries News* 56, no. 11 (Dec. 1995): 757–59.

and existence actual literal Nazis in the year 2017 want to erase. Based on my cursory reading of a Wikipedia article about volcanoes, it doesn't look like there's much you can do about this geographical phenomenon. I don't think you can stop volcanoes from erupting, so here is where my extended metaphor no longer coheres: we absolutely can and must stop the toxic sludge that the "but free speech! Libraries should be neutral!" perspective promotes. Our profession is polluted by this perspective, which seeks to reinforce and undergird the white supremacist status quo at the expense of the vulnerable. It is immoral to remain silent and allow this to persist while people are suffocating on the toxic ash of white supremacy.

Mere days before I wrote the above words, mere days before actual literal Nazis marched through though the streets of Charlottesville, Virginia, my library had its annual staff retreat, and I found myself in a heated and lively discussion with my colleagues about neutrality. Librarians are supposed to be neutral, right? We should present all sides of all arguments. If a patron approaches the reference desk asking a question about something we find personally repugnant or troubling, we should somehow ignore our own beliefs and perspectives and treat that interaction like a sterile, dehumanized transaction of information, right? I presented an argument so impassioned against such rhetoric that later a few colleagues approached me to make sure we were cool, that I wasn't mad at them or anything. I wasn't mad, I reassured them. I'm just a person with lots of feelings and my own bias and point of view. To ask me to somehow dissociate myself with those feelings and biases and point of view is akin to asking me to somehow be disembodied or dehumanized.

A few days later, however, after watching live footage of Nazis bearing torches and shouting Nazi slogans on a college campus, I realized that this is more than just a matter of disagreement. This is where I need to draw a distinct and definitive line. The issue of neutrality isn't one where reasonable people can agree to disagree. This is a moral issue, one that is not up for debate. The right of human beings to exist is not debatable. I don't care if this goes against the widely held view of the library as the intellectual heart of campus, as the bastion of intellectual freedom. Do not tell me that Nazis need the library, as though being exposed to more enlightened viewpoints will magically make them less hateful, because they don't and they won't. I would argue that those who need the library, its collections, and the people who keep the literal and virtual doors open, are people whose voices are usually silenced rather than amplified, whose factual existence is somehow regarded as some theoretical intellectual debate.

I acknowledge that it's perhaps easier for me to espouse such apparently contrary views because I'm an academic librarian. Teaching and learning are at the core of what we do at the reference desk. It's expected and normal for a librarian to treat the reference encounter as more than just the sterile exchange of information; we're *supposed* to find teachable moments. My library genealogy includes working as a library page and circulation clerk in public libraries in high school and college, but I've never worked at a public library reference desk, as some of those who have contributed to this volume. I've never worked in a special library. I've never provided reference services by mail to people who are incarcerated, and neither have I been placed on house arrest because I've been accused of inciting ethnic hatred against Russians via my reference work, as described in one of the chapters in this volume. I have immense privilege. I'm empowered by academic freedom. Librarians at my institution are tenure-track faculty, and I have tenure. I was recently promoted to full-rank librarian, the equivalent of full professor for librarians at Indiana University. All of this is to say that I know that I have privilege and freedom to make such claims, but I also have to note how mindboggling it seems that making such claims is so politically fraught that I need the protection of privilege.

Privilege means that I have an obligation to take risks, to try to bring about social change, to attempt to correct and write over the harm done to the people I encounter in my daily life the library. Here is where my current experience in psychotherapy has illustrated, and continues to illustrate, the power of corrective emotional experience, and I think it provides a useful parallel to envision the work we do in reference. As theorized by psychoanalyst Franz Alexander, "The patient, in order to be helped, must undergo a corrective emotional experience suitable to repair the traumatic influence of previous experiences. It is of secondary importance whether this corrective experience takes place during treatment in the transference relationship, or parallel with the treatment in the daily life of the patient."[2] In other words, the positive experience of the therapeutic relationship, especially if infused with the empathetic, nonjudgmental acceptance theorized by Carl Rogers as "unconditional positive regard,"[3] helps to heal the damage of past trauma by kind of writing over it with a more positive experience. It's almost like when you save a file with the same name as a preex-

---

2   Franz Alexander et al., *Psychoanalytic Therapy: Principles and Application* (Lincoln: University of Nebraska Press, 1946), 65.

3   Carl Rogers, *On Becoming a Person* (Boston: Houghton Mifflin, 1961), 283.

isting file and Word asks you if you want to overwrite it. Similarly, I think we can see the work of advancing social justice through reference as a way of correcting and overwriting negative, demeaning, and dehumanizing experiences faced by our patrons with more positive, humanizing, and affirming ones. It means that the vulnerable are centered and protected and valued. It means that the relationship that happens at the reference desk or elsewhere is valid and important and a means of bringing about social justice. It means that libraries collect and make accessible materials that represent marginalized communities and subjects. And, yes, it means that I will refill the staplers, and refill them with joy, and also listen, with a warm and receptive heart, while Hector talks about his leaky ceiling.

Reference work as social justice work strikes me as a natural alliance, a partnership that links similar items together. I'm reminded of how I explain to students the way in which call numbers collocate similar items, although I seldom actually use the word "collocate," because jargon can have a distancing effect. It makes intuitive and practical sense for reference and social justice to sit side-by-side on the shelf. The essays in this volume outline ways of engaging in social justice work through reference, describing how these concepts sit side-by-side on the shelf, and as I read them and re-read them and contemplate them, I see the work described herein coalescing around two broad axes: people and things. (I told you this was broad.) By *people*, I mean, of course, the *people*, the human beings we interact with, the relationships built through an approach to reference governed by an ethic of care, of seeing an information-seeker as a whole person, and seeing ourselves, as librarians, as whole people as well. And by *things*, I mean the materials, the collections, the information that people seek in order to meet whatever need they might have. I realize how reductive this might sound, and I don't mean to oversimplify, but this strikes me as the very essence of reference work. Without people and without things, we have nothing to do, nowhere to sit, no way of meeting anyone's needs, no one to benefit from the refilled staplers.

In other words, as described in this book, reference work advances the work of social justice through collecting and making accessible materials pertaining to groups who would normally be erased or dismissed, as well as through the people involved in doing such work, such as approaching reference work through a lens that seeks to humanize what is sometimes a dehumanizing process, the vulnerability of having a need and asking someone to help meet that need. The essays in this book describe ways of prioritizing access and use, collecting and preserving oral histories, providing materials to those who have little to no access to information sources, approaching pedagogy in ways that value the whole person, insisting on the importance of the interpersonal and relationship-building, and valuing alternative ways of knowing and seeing the world.

If I were called upon to define a social justice orientation to reference work, I think my definition would be informed by all of the above. The contributors to this volume are engaging in the important and necessary work of social justice through librarianship and these are voices we need to pay attention to. We need to let these voices shape our perspectives and influence our own work. My definition would be also be informed, in part, by Paulo Freire's *unveiling of reality*: "Whereas banking education anesthetizes and inhibits creative power, problem-posing education involves a constant unveiling of reality. The former attempts to maintain the *submersion* of consciousness; the latter strives for the *emergence* of consciousness and *critical intervention* in reality."[4] What is the reality that I seek to unveil when I'm sitting at the reference desk, or ordering books for the collection, or teaching library instruction sessions, or, yes, refilling the stapler? The reality I want to unveil is that the world is unjust but we *can* make it more just, and that work begins when we insist on what is moral and what is right, and when we see each other, face-to-face—in person, through the snail mail, in an online chat box, in an email—as human beings in relationship to one another.

I want to note here that I think about words a lot more than maybe is normal. I was an English major, and I'm a big etymology nerd—high school Latin will do that to a person—and so when I was recently thinking about the term "reference interview," I looked up the etymology of the word "interview" and I was so delighted and fascinated to see that it comes from Latin via French, meaning "to see one another."[5] This is such a beautiful image, isn't it? But does an interview ever really happen this way? Think about the last time you talked to a patron at the reference desk, or at the circulation desk, or any kind of desk in the library. Did you really *see* the patron? And did the patron really see *you*? What would it mean to truly see each other when interacting with a patron? I think to truly see each other, "to respect and care for the souls of students,"[6] to borrow the

---

4   Paulo Freire, *Pedagogy of the Oppressed* (New York: Continuum, 2000), 81.

5   "Interview." Merriam-Webster.com. Accessed November 6, 2017. https://www.merriam-webster.com/dictionary/interview.

6   bell hooks, *Teaching to Transgress: Education as the Practice of Freedom* (New York: Routledge, 1994).

language of bell hooks, means aligning the emotionally vulnerable parts of yourself to the corresponding parts of the patron. It means remembering what it felt like to be in a library and maybe not understanding where anything was or how to read a call number and what a call number is anyway. It means feeling incredibly stressed about your leaky ceiling, the seemingly unreasonable demands of your professor, and all of the other aspects of your life, and inevitably giving short shrift to one of those areas.

The work of social justice through the work of reference is one that is necessarily more energy consuming. You need more bandwidth. It takes more emotional and intellectual energy to refill a stapler with joy than it is to do it perfunctorily. Similarly, it takes significantly more emotional and intellectual energy to argue that no, Nazis are not welcome in the library, and then still have the emotional and intellectual energy to help Hector navigate his information need and manage his anxiety about his leaky ceiling. This work is hard, but it is necessary. Let these essays fortify you with the energy you need to stifle the volcanoes of white supremacy and other bilious forms of hatred. It means that you may also need to seek the kindness and support of like-minded people, to nurture your own soul, your own unique path and goals and gifts and talents, just as tenderly and compassionately as you would the anxious patron who is walking up to you at the reference desk right here, right now, and maybe, this time, you will finally see one another.

This is what I want this foreword to tell you. I really want you to understand me.

Works Cited

Alexander, Franz. *Psychoanalytic Therapy: Principles and Application.*
    Lincoln: University of Nebraska Press, 1946.

Freire, Paulo. *Pedagogy of the Oppressed.* New York: Continuum, 2000.

hooks, bell. *Teaching to Transgress: Education as the Practice of Freedom.*
    New York: Routledge, 1994.

"Interview." Merriam-Webster.com. Accessed November 6, 2017.
    https://www.merriam-webster.com/dictionary/interview.

Kelly, Maurie Caitlin. "Student Retention and Academic Libraries,"
    College and Research Libraries News 56, no. 11 (Dec. 1995): 757–59.

Rogers, Carl R. *On Becoming a Person: A Therapist's View of Psychotherapy.*
    Boston: Houghton Mifflin, 1961.

Introduction

Kate Adler, Ian Beilin, and Eamon Tewell

The call for this book announced our belief that reference librarianship is too often overlooked by our profession, collapsed into other hybrid titles and disappearing desks. We sought to make a claim for this unique and increasingly precarious place. Maria T. Accardi, in her moving foreword to this book, reminds us that reference is possibly the most humane thing that we do in the library. It is perhaps the least efficient, and yet, potentially the most powerful. While there may be anecdotal and statistical observations of an overall decline in reference desk "traffic,"[1] and that many of the questions received at reference desks are directional or procedural, less or certain types of activity should not be used as excuses to trivialize or abolish reference. To do so is to acquiesce to a neoliberal numbers game. Meaningful exchanges, nuanced dialogue, and substantive work continue to occur through reference. This unique space is worth fighting for, and in looking at the contours of its long history and the complicated and varied work we do today, this book is a rallying cry. In the end, we have not had to make this claim ourselves. We have been lucky to have a chorus of deep-

---

1 Rachel Applegate, "Whose Decline? Which Academic Libraries are 'Deserted' in Terms of Reference Transactions?" *Reference & User Services Quarterly* vol. 48, no. 2 (2008): 176–89.

ly thinking, lively, and passionate librarians and archivists to make this argument with.

One could pinpoint reference librarianship's inauguration in North America to the autumn of 1876, when Samuel S. Green, a librarian at Worcester Public Library, published a foundational article in *Library Journal*.[2] In this cheerful article, Green examines the relationship between librarians and patrons and recommends a "pleasant talk" with users. Librarians can stimulate a love of learning and direct investigators to the best sources of information, he tells us. Green also writes that through "pleasant conversation… you find out what books users in the library actually need," and that one of the best "means of making the library popular is to mingle freely with its users, and help them in every way."[3] Critical pedagogy has advanced a more complicated framework for thinking about dialogue, and scholarship on critical reference has sought to think through dialogue in the context of Library and Information Science (LIS).[4] From a critical perspective, dialogue is a guiding principle for reference. Yet in the North American context, the reference exchange is bound up with the history of librarianship's whiteness and its status as a feminized, if nonetheless male-dominated at the highest levels, "helping" profession.

The archetype of a feminized benevolent librarian that, in Gina Schlesselman-Tarango's formation "turns on colonial notions of white benevolence," is located primarily in the reference librarian. Schlesselman-Tarango calls upon the Legacy of Lady Bountiful, a representation of a benevolent educator who is "white, female, cisgender, heterosexual, able-bodied, and white middle class," to think about some of the ways in which librarianship, as a feminized, "civilizing," missionary profession, is constructed through colonialism, patriarchy and white supremacy.[5] In the North American context, the public library itself is entangled in complicated histories of Gilded Age and Progressive Era philanthropy, benevolence, and

---

2   Robert Wedgeworth, *World Encyclopedia of Library and Information Services* (Chicago: American Library Association, 1993): 703.

3   Samuel S. Green, "Personal Relations Between Librarians and Readers," *Library Journal* 1, no. 2 (1876): 74–81.

4   Kate Adler, "Radical Purpose: The Critical Reference Dialogue at a Progressive Urban College," *Urban Library Journal* 19 no. 1 (2013); John J. Doherty, "Reference Interview or Reference Dialogue?" *Internet Reference Services Quarterly* 11, no. 3 (2006): 97–109.

5   Gina Schlesselman-Tarango, "The Legacy of Lady Bountiful: White Women in the Library," *Library Trends* 64, no. 4 (2016): 667–86.

capitalism.[6] LIS has in recent years increased its efforts to trouble the view that the library is "an egalitarian institution providing universal access to information for the general public," in Todd Honma's words. As Honma points out in his 2005 essay "Trippin' Over the Color Line," "such idealized visions of mythic benevolence tend to conveniently gloss over the library's susceptibility in reproducing and perpetuating racist social structures."[7] More recently, Fobazi Ettarh has demonstrated how the traditions of service that have helped uphold white supremacy have been, and continue to be, integral to the practice of "vocational awe" that structures and guides the library profession today. Ettarh reminds us that, "Librarianship, like the criminal justice system and the government, is an institution. And like other institutions, librarianship plays a role in creating and sustaining hegemonic values, as well as contributing to white supremacy culture."[8] As librarianship's public face, reference is the key ambassador of such a legacy and practice. Indeed, Lady Bountiful haunts reference practice most of all. Honma and others have done rigorous work disaggregating and unpacking LIS's culpability in reifying entrenched power structures. However, the essays in this collection evoke the possibility—in all its texture and complexity—that another world is possible, and it is already and always happening.

Anthropologist David Graeber contends that anthropology as a discipline is particularly well poised to imagine an anarchist, collectivist vision, since after all, "most actually-existing self-governing communities, and actually-existing non-market economies in the world have been investigated by anthropologist[s]."[9] So too librarians, particularly those aligned with critical or social justice projects, are especially well suited to imagine the role of the library in supporting such a vision. Libraries, after all, are

6   Lua Gregory and Shana Higgins, "In Resistance to a Capitalist Past: Emerging Practices of Critical Librarianship," in *The Politics of Theory and the Practice of Critical Librarianship*, ed. Karen P. Nicholson and Maura Seale (Sacramento: Library Juice Press, 2018), 21–38.

7   Todd Honma, "Trippin' Over the Color Line: The Invisibility of Race in Library and Information Studies," *InterActions: UCLA Journal of Education and Information Studies* 1, no. 2 (2005): 2. Retrieved from https://escholarship.org/uc/item/4nj0w1mp.

8   Fobazi Ettarh, "Vocational Awe and Librarianship: The Lies We Tell Ourselves," *In the Library with the Lead Pipe*, January 10, 2018. Retrieved from http://www.inthelibrary-withtheleadpipe.org/2018/vocational-awe/.

9   David Graeber, *Fragments of an Anarchist Anthropology* (Chicago: Prickly Paradigm Press, 2006), 11.

one of the few not fully market-drenched spaces we have. Graeber suggests that "one obvious role for a radical intellectual is to… look at those who are creating viable alternatives, try to figure out what might be the larger implications of what they are (already) doing and then offer those ideas back, not as prescriptions but as contributions, possibilities."[10] Nothing is as instructive as looking to what we have always done.

Radical, progressive, and unequivocally political librarianship has a long and inspiring history. There are individual librarians who rallied against injustice, and in the process changed what we knew librarianship to be: intellectual freedom fighters like Zoia Horn and Judith Krug, those who worked tirelessly to support marginalized and oppressed communities, like Regina Andrews, Clara Breed, Dr. Elfreda Chatman, and Miriam Braverman, alternative publishers like Celeste West, and radical catalogers like Sandy Berman. There are organizations that fight for these same aims, and have been doing so for some time. The American Library Association's Social Responsibilities Round Table was founded in 1969, and has since provided a means for librarians to engage with social issues within ALA. The Progressive Librarians Guild and their journal *Progressive Librarian*, established in 1990, seeks to align librarianship's actions with its stated values of supporting democracy and countering the commodification of information. Radical Reference has been operating chapters across the U.S. and in Canada, initially forming to provide assistance to activists and demonstrators at the 2004 Republican National Convention, and taking a grassroots approach to the intersection of information workers and activism.[11] Many other radical and progressive library-oriented groups exist internationally, including the Radical Librarians Collective based in the U.K. and *Bibliotek i Samhälle* (Libraries in Society) in Sweden. These groups apply methods and strategies that range from direct action to working within professional associations, and each have played a major role in reaching towards social justice in librarianship.

It is with histories like these in mind that we have divided this book into three sections: History, Practice, and Praxis. These subjects are braided together and woven through one another and their entanglement produces new meanings. Theory, as Marx notes in so many words, is a tool.

---

10   Graeber, 12.

11   Melissa Morrone and Lia Friedman, "Radical Reference: Socially Responsible Librarianship Collaborating with Community," *The Reference Librarian* 50, no. 4 (2009): 371–96.

It is not an end in and of itself. It is a lens. It clarifies our thinking, sharpens our language and demands more from our practice. It is the practice that brings us to the table. Practice is the application of theory, however utopian or realist that theory might be, while the long shadow of history hangs over it all. In librarianship—including critical librarianship—as in social movements, and in politics more generally, an informed engagement of history is often missing. Yet we are reminded, again and again, that we neglect history at our own peril. Tyranny and exploitation, though they may be differently adorned, are not new. Many librarians today are asking ourselves urgent, existential questions about our ethical responsibilities in a climate wherein information is increasingly and maliciously fabricated. It may feel to some in the United States that the world has careened out of orbit sharply, violently, overnight. However, that is a perspective of only the most enfranchised among us; the world we inhabit has been a long time coming. Authoritarian regimes that trade in propaganda are not new, and if we are to strategize resistance we must turn toward history.

We can look to the actions of librarians during the period of Martial Law in the Philippines as Iyra S. Buenrostro and Johann Frederick A. Cabbab do in their chapter "Unbound: Recollections of Librarians During Martial Law in the Philippines." Indeed, how might we understand the experience of incarceration in the United States if we read it in conjunction with the history of tyrannical and repressive political regimes? How might we understand the work of librarians in prisons—as several chapters in this book detail—differently when we think about it through the work of librarians in the Philippines, or the work of librarians in Ukraine under Soviet Rule, as Megan Browndorf explores in "'I Did What I Was Told to Do': Ukrainian Reference Librarianship and Responding to Volatile Expectations"? These questions of time, place, and the shifting meaning of social justice are also explored in Jeff Hirschy's chapter, which examines archival memory and the role of libraries, archives, and museums in moving beyond deeply embedded master narratives of segregation.

The majority of the chapters in the Dispatches from the Field section take up prison librarianship, and in different ways the authors agitate the idea that mere access to information can empower. Chapters like Joshua Finnell's "2596 Girls School Road: The Indiana Women's Prison Far-Away Reference Desk" complicate the easy notion of the library as straightforward institution of pure good, although they do not overturn our faith in what it is that libraries and librarians can do. Prison libraries, perched at a complex nexus of exile and enlightenment[12] and the librarians who do daily, mindful work in these draconian settings, illustrate for us and actively engage the question of what libraries and librarians can possibly do to foster empowerment in the most totalitarian of settings. In Finell's chapter, Emily Jacobson's "Reference by Mail to Incarcerated People," Hannah Lee and Danielle Ball's "Reference Behind Bars: Social Contract and Information Needs of Prison Inmates," and "Dispatches From the Field of Prison Librarianship" by Erin Rivero, Marisa Hernandez, Stephanie Osorio and Vanessa Villarreal, we see myriad examples of librarians wrestling with these questions every day.

Elsewhere, authors consider the question of empowerment as well. Haruko Yamauchi's rigorous and illuminating study of library school students during the War on Poverty in the late 1960s and early 1970s adds new depth to the open question of what role libraries and librarians can or should play in an effort to "empower" a community to which they do not belong. It is a question that haunts not only libraries but the entire field of not-for-profit social service work. Lady Bountiful's spirit is here, too. When we turn toward Julia Marden's "The Case for Critical Data Reference in Public Libraries," we see new layers of possibility of personal and community engagement through library work. Meanwhile, Rachael Dreyer's chapter "Hiding in Plain Sight: Reference Archivists as Social Justice Actors" explores another setting and focus: the many possibilities for archivists to employ social justice principles in their practice and facilitate access to the collections they oversee.

Practice implies honing and expertise, and this volume speaks powerfully about the craft and substance of reference. Veronica I. Arellano-Douglas highlights how reference work can apply the concept of intersubjective mutuality to develop a more compassionate and understanding practice, as a contrast and response to the pressures of our work environments. Carrie Forbes and Jennifer Bowers apply the principles of *sentipensante* pedagogy to reference consultations in their chapter "Social Justice, Sentipensante Pedagogy, and Collaboration," combining this theory with methods from the education and social work fields to provide new perspectives that can guide critical reference practice. The interpersonal nature of reference, imbued with power dynamics and shifting identities, is highlighted in these and a number of other contributions, including

---

12 Brenda Vogel, *The Prison Library Primer: A Program for the Twenty-First Century* (Lanham, MD: Scarecrow Press, 2009).

Shawn(ta) Smith-Cruz's analysis of Audre Lorde's identity, practice, and the implications for reference. As Smith-Cruz writes: "[I]n-between spaces create strange friction at the reference desk, for example, a space that holds two or more co-existing bodies negotiating boundaries and hierarchical roles which will contextualize the exchange of information at bay." Smith-Cruz's "Lesbian Librarianship For All: A Manifesto" presents an autobiographical manifesto that asks us to recognize our positions as simultaneously experiencing power and marginalization, and as implicated in upholding the violence of capitalism while seeking ways to enact change. This chapter and others in the Praxis section illustrate that theory is lived experience, and it can and does encompass activism, thus broadening traditional academic conventions and the theorists often invoked in critical librarianship discourse.

It is our hope and our belief that the chapters collected in this volume are an important addition to building a language and a set of priorities around critical reference practice and its theoretical underpinnings. It is our hope too that this book reminds us of the deep import of rigorous historical work within LIS and in social movements more broadly. If this title is a rallying cry, it is also perhaps an acknowledgment of the role of the radical intellectual and a claim for librarianship's place within that history. If we were each to use our profession, regardless of what it is, as a standpoint from which to call for a more just world and a more rigorous engagement with it, perhaps we could all be better off. This collection of research, manifestos, ideas, and inspirations is one demonstration of that possibility.

Reference and Justice, Past and Present

Ian Beilin

Librarianship seems to be increasingly oriented toward its own future, and discussions revolving around the topic often get fraught with anxiety regarding the "value" or purpose of libraries and librarians. Very often the solution to the library's perceived challenges is to find ways to better meet patrons', or the general public's, information needs, beyond the "traditional" library. Yet when these needs are identified and acknowledged as going beyond the boundaries of what was once considered part of librarianship (for example, teaching coding or 3D printing skills), calls for reform often rest on assumptions of a past in which librarians were focused on a narrower set of priorities. The chapters in this section, which provide a perspective on the past, as well as a perspective beyond North America (abroad, to the Philippines and Ukraine, specifically), demonstrate that libraries and librarians have always acted to respond to the information (and other) needs of patrons and the public, and that information workers, with or without a professional training, have played a critical role in struggles for justice, particularly under conditions in which the repressive and destructive powers of state and capital attempt to restrict or abolish access to information. Information workers have always met vital needs, and will continue to do so, with or without the library.

Historically, libraries and reference work have been so closely associated that it is difficult to separate them as distinct concepts. While libraries have been identified or at least associated with collections, reference often functions in some kind of relation to those collections. But in the sense of providing help with getting access to and finding information, reference is bigger and broader than libraries, if libraries are thought of in strictly institutional terms. Reference can be conducted without the aid of a library or outside of a library, and it can be, and often is, conducted by someone other than a professionally trained librarian.[1] In this sense reference is perennial and permanent, wholly independent of libraries and lasting as long as there is a need for access to information. This section on the history of reference (and this book as a whole) embraces such a broad conception of reference, though most of the examples described, both historically and in the present, take place either in libraries and archives, or were undertaken by professionally trained librarians and archivists.

As Kate Adler notes in her introduction to the Practice section of this book, there are many critical frameworks to look toward in building a reference service oriented toward justice. In a similar fashion, there are multiple stories, narratives, and traditions from the past, both within and beyond libraries, that can help do the same. The intertwined histories of reference and the struggle for justice reach into the present, even if the historical conditions, regimes, and people may have changed. What this section highlights is the specific role that library reference and library reference workers play in the struggle for justice. The chapters focus on moments of political and social crisis, and the vital roles that library and archive workers played in providing information (reference) services during these crises. They demonstrate

---

1   This can be a controversial subject among some librarians, as reference work is often seen, as
    well as officially designated in some cases, as the exclusive (rightful) work of library degree-
    holding professionals. At some academic libraries, university and union rules mandate that
    only library faculty may work the reference desk. This has the positive effect of guaranteeing
    a good wage even for adjuncts who provide reference (labor that is often devalued, even
    within the library context), but it has the negative one of further entrenching librarian elitism
    and privilege and driving a deeper wedge between librarians and 'staff' and student workers.
    For an excellent and prominent recent example of reference work outside the library, see
    the documentation and writings related to the Occupy Wall Street Library, the library that
    "founded itself," in the words of Jaime Taylor: https://peopleslibrary.wordpress.com/; Jessa
    Lingel, "Occupy Wall Street and the Myth of the Technological Death of the Library," *First
    Monday* 17:8 (Aug. 6, 2012). See also the contributions to Melissa Morrone, ed., *Informed
    Agitation: Library and Information Skills in Social Justice Movements and Beyond*, Library Juice
    Press, 2013. For another example of reference services beyond library confines, see the work
    of the network of collectives, Radical Reference: http://radicalreference.info/. On the ques-
    tion of who should provide reference inside the library, see Brett Bodemer, "They CAN and
    they SHOULD: Undergraduates Providing Peer Reference and Instruction," *College &
    Research Libraries* 75, no. 2 (2014): 162–78; and Lauren Wallis, "Information of My Own:
    Peer Reference and Feminist Pedagogy," in Maria T. Accardi, ed., *The Feminist Reference
    Desk: Concepts, Critiques, and Conversations*, Library Juice Press, 2017, 189–201.

the critical importance of reference work under such conditions, but they also show how the lessons learned from these experiences inform everyday reference work, particularly in the state of permanent crisis in which we find ourselves in 2018. The challenges faced by librarians in Soviet and post-Soviet Ukraine, the struggles against martial law under Marcos in the Philippines, against white supremacy in Birmingham, Alabama, and against racism and poverty in the urban northeast in the 1960s and 1970s: none of these are isolated or distant experiences. They are all relevant today, and the struggles described in each of these chapters are ongoing. Another point that these chapters emphasize is the varying degrees of documentation of the struggles of the past, as there are for any historical event or period. The crucial role of archivists, not only in preserving historical memory, but in making it accessible and useful, is also a part of the stories told here, and the distinction between reference work and archival work is also one that is challenged or dissolved, particularly under the strains of acute political and social crisis.

The ideology of library neutrality, still a structuring feature of librarianship in North America, has served to obscure, minimize, or even deny the many ways in which librarians in the past were activists, both inside and outside of their libraries. While much of the language of American librarianship, at least at the institutional level, embraces certain 'core values', which may include social justice commitments, the idea of a politically committed librarianship has been misrepresented or feared as partisanship. The present vulnerability of libraries throughout North America and Europe to funding cuts, ideological attacks, and physical attacks or even elimination, have led some librarians to fear and decry the active involvement of institutions in the struggles against racism, sexism, homophobia, transphobia, anti-Semitism, classism, and fascism. The initial reaction of the American Library Association to the 2016 Presidential election results was a telling example of this impulse. But the intensified sense of crisis and danger posed by that election also mobilized many others to embrace a more politically committed, activist, and explicitly non-neutral librarianship.[2] While the roles of librarians and libraries continue to be debated, it is clear that any position is a political one, and that reference librarianship, because it is situated at the point of contact between library/librarian and patron/user, may be the most political.

---

2   See for example the chapters in Alison Lewis, *Questioning Library Neutrality: Essays from Progressive Librarian*, Library Juice Press, 2008; Chris Bourg, "Never Neutral: Libraries, Technology, and Inclusion," *The Feral Librarian*; and Nicole Pagowsky and Niamh Wallace, "Black Lives Matter! Shedding Library Neutrality Rhetoric for Social Justice," *College & Research Libraries News* 76, no. 4 (2015): 196–214.

Works Cited

Bodemer, Brett. "They CAN and they SHOULD: Undergraduates Providing Peer Reference and Instruction." *College & Research Libraries* 75, no. 2 (2014): 162–78.

Bourg, Chris. "Never Neutral: Libraries, Technology, and Inclusion." *The Feral Librarian*. January 28, 2015. https://chrisbourg.wordpress.com/2015/01/28/never-neutral -libraries-technology-and-inclusion/.

Lewis, Alison. *Questioning Library Neutrality: Essays from Progressive Librarian*. Library Juice Press, 2008.

Lingel, Jessa. "Occupy Wall Street and the Myth of the Technological Death of the Library." *First Monday* 17, no. 8 (Aug. 6, 2012). http://firstmonday.org/ojs/index.php/fm/article/view/3845/3280.

Morrone, Melissa, ed. *Informed Agitation: Library and Information Skills in Social Justice Movements and Beyond*. Library Juice Press, 2013.

Occupy Wall Street Library. https://peopleslibrary.wordpress.com/.

"Open Letter to ALA President Julie Todaro re: Recent ALA Statements." *Librarian in Black*. November 20, 2016. http://librarianinblack.net/librarianinblack/ alastatements/.

Pagowsky, Nicole and Niamh Wallace. "Black Lives Matter! Shedding Library Neutrality Rhetoric for Social Justice." *College & Research Libraries News* 76, no. 4 (2015): 196–214.

Radical Reference. http://radicalreference.info/.

Wallis, Lauren. "Information of My Own: Peer Reference and Feminist Pedagogy," in Maria T. Accardi, ed. *The Feminist Reference Desk: Concepts, Critiques, and Conversations*. Library Juice Press, 2017, 189–201.

Urban Information Specialists and Interpreters: An Emerging Radical Vision of Reference for the People, 1967–1973

Haruko Yamauchi

Struggle for Social Relevance

Public librarians in the United States were not oblivious to the turmoil of social change in the 1960s. In the wake of the civil rights movement, the 1964–68 War on Poverty, and the widespread influence of works such as Michael Harrington's 1962 book *The Other America: Poverty in the United States* and the problematic Moynihan Report of 1965—which simultaneously advocated for and pathologized the low-income African American family—librarians questioned their role in low-income communities of color.[1]

---

1   Kathleen Weibel, "The Evolution of Library Outreach 1960–1975 and Its Effect on Reader Services. Occasional Paper Number 16," (Urbana-Champaign: University of Illinois Graduate School of Library Science, 1982): 3–5; Christina Copenhaver and Joanne Boelke, "Library Service to the Disadvantaged, A Bibliography," (Minneapolis: ERIC Clearinghouse on Library and Information Sciences, 1968).

Increasingly, public libraries created programs to reach "underpriv-ileged" (or "unserved") communities, and in 1968 the American Library Association (ALA) opened an Office for Service to the Disadvantaged.[2] Most of these programs focused on the deficits of patrons, not the failings of the economic, social, and political systems in which they lived. Many library articles during this period assumed that the problem to be solved was that the "disadvantaged" were unaware of or had incorrect knowledge about services available to them.[3] From this viewpoint, low-income ur-ban residents were seen to have needed reference services relevant to daily problems because they lacked the "ability to cope in the complex metrop-olis," and those disadvantaged by "age, poverty, handicaps, racial and cul-tural discrimination, unemployment, and undereducation" were primari-ly hampered by their own low literacy, relatively little contact with outside institutions, and an over-reliance on mass media and local rumor for in-formation.[4] In 1975, a wide-ranging review of the relevant contemporary literature posited that low-income people sought to fulfill ever-changing ("kinetic") crisis information needs more than long-term ("potential") in-formation needs (such as knowing the names of one's government repre-sentatives) because of their inability to plan for the future.[5]

An alternate interpretation of low-income communities' demand for urgent information, of course, would be that their lives were in more constant crisis than people with greater racial, social, economic, and ed-ucational privilege. Some library studies did acknowledge that people needed guidance because an increasingly convoluted array of service agencies with unclear, overlapping mandates was creating confusion.[6] Regardless of how they framed the problem, more public librarians recog-nized that low-income urban communities of color were not being served

---

2   Ford, Barbara J. "Libraries, Literacy, Outreach and the Digital Divide." *American Library Association.*

3   Thomas Childers and Joyce A. Post, *The Information-Poor in America.* (Metuchen, N.J.: Scarecrow Press, 1975), 7, 32, 40.

4   Rosemary Du Mont, *Reform and Reaction*, 117; Childers and Post, *The Information-Poor*, 7, 32, 40.

5   Ibid, 36–7.

6   Jane E. Stevens, "Urban Information Centers and Their Interface with the National Program for Libraries and Information Service", (Washington, D.C.: National Commission on Libraries and Information Science, 1975): 6, 17. http://files.eric.ed.gov/fulltext/ED114102.pdf

adequately by libraries, and that reference services that addressed daily problems would be helpful. Several conferences were held throughout the mid-1960s to mid-1970s for librarians to discuss "library service to the unserved."[7]

This chapter will examine how the library profession, particularly within the context of LIS education, acted on its growing desire during this era to enable librarians to be more relevant and responsive to low-income, primarily African American, urban communities. It will first describe the dominant trends within library discourse, based on library writings of the time (particularly conference proceedings and articles in *Library Journal*), and how ideas shifted over the course of roughly a decade starting in the mid-1960s. It will then give a brief overview of the urban librarian training programs that emerged in the early 1970s. The latter half of the article, based on archives of internal and external correspondence, statements presented at conferences, library publication articles, reports to funders, published essays by the program directors, and press releases, will examine in greater detail the case of three related projects spearheaded by Mary Lee Bundy, which were among the earliest and most radical efforts. The first two projects were related, and belonged to the University of Maryland: a field training for library students, and then a program for "urban information interpreters" which sought to recruit African American librarians and emphasized political awareness and action-research projects in its curriculum. The third project was an independent publishing venture for social justice reference sources. Finally, this chapter will discuss the Maryland urban librarian program's unfortunate demise amidst increasingly rancorous conflict between the program leaders and their community partner, university administrators, and federal funder. The chapter concludes by seeking to draw lessons from the successes and failures of these early programs.

---

7   Theodore Samore, *Progress in Urban Librarianship: A Seminar on Community Information Needs and the Designing of Library Education Programs to Meet These Needs* (Milwaukee: Wisconsin University School of Library Science, 1974); Virginia H. Mathews, "Narrative Evaluation Report on the Institute for Strengthening Librarians' Capability to Elicit and Respond to the Felt Needs of Minority/Culturally Isolated/Disadvantaged Persons and Groups in the Southwest," (Washington, DC: Bureau of Libraries and Educational Technology, 1972). Note that the 1974 Wisconsin conference was a sequel to an earlier conference at the same university in 1967.

From Information and Referral to Information Power

One way to disseminate information about jobs, housing, health care, childcare, welfare, and other services was the creation of Information and Referral (I&R) centers, sometimes called neighborhood information centers. I&R centers began to appear in U.S. cities in the late 1950s, and gained steam throughout the 1960s. The roots of I&R services were in the Social Service Exchange that had once existed among social welfare agencies, which were developed in an earlier wave of response to harsh social conditions in the 1870s. I&R centers therefore had evolved independently of libraries.[8]

Public librarians, however, took notice of the growing I&R center movement, given that they shared the same patron and client base. Prompted not only by admiration, but also by fear of irrelevance as non-library information systems grew stronger, they began to question how library reference services might learn from I&R centers.[9] Libraries were filled with professionals well-equipped to collect, organize, and distribute information, but not necessarily trained or willing to take on I&R roles that included elements of interpreting legal texts or offering personal counseling.[10] Many did not want to give patrons direct advice or refer to sources beyond books, even as some librarians began to point out that the most current information might now be obtained via a telephone call or non-traditional publication.[11] Despite trepidation about librarian reticence, training, logistics, and budgets, some urban libraries began to incorporate I&R methods into their reference work. They created telephone hotlines and systemat-

---

8   Nicholas Long, "Information and Referral Services: A Short History and Some Recommendations," in *Libraries and Neighborhood Information Centers: Papers Presented at an Institute Conducted by the University of Illinois Graduate School of Library Science,* October 24–27, 1971, edited by Carol L. Kronus and Linda Crowe, (Urbana, IL: University of Illinois Graduate School of Library Science, 1972): 3, 10; Stevens, *Urban Information Centers,* 3.

9   James Welbourne, "Training Urban Information Specialists," in Kronus and Crowe, *Libraries and Neighborhood Information,* 108.

10   Dorothy Sinclair, "Linking New and Traditional Library Services," in Kronus and Crowe, *Libraries and Neighborhood Information,* 76–78; Estabrook, "Emerging Trends in Community Library Services," *Library Trends,* 28 (Fall 1979): 162.

11   Mary Lee Bundy and Paul Wasserman, "Professionalism Reconsidered," *College & Research Libraries,* 29, no. 1 (January 1968), 9–10.

ically referred patrons to service agencies.[12] Libraries also acquired pamphlets, directories, and contact information for local agencies as part of their reference collections. However, many I&R-like reference projects to publicize local services relied on ephemeral federal funding and were therefore short-lived.[13]

The I&R center model of reference, and its aim to increase individuals' access to services, with the library serving as a neutral conduit, could hardly be called radical. Librarians were generally reluctant to criticize service agencies for fear of jeopardizing their collaboration, and a 1973 model for I&R centers explicitly stated that the model was "not intended to bring about any *direct change* in the delivery of human services, since that is unrealistic." [emphasis added].[14] However, the I&R model signaled a shift to reference that prioritized the daily needs of residents in low-income neighborhoods. Next in the evolution would be the construction of reference as a way to energize communities toward collective change, with both librarian and patron taking on a critical stance regarding service providers.

While libraries experimented with the I&R model, a more radical vein began to emerge within certain segments of librarianship. In 1969, ALA recognized the Social Responsibilities Round Table (SRRT), founded by a small but rapidly growing contingent of librarians who saw an urgent need for libraries to respond to the intense social changes of the time.[15] SRRT founders attacked the idea of library neutrality, which they critiqued as an excuse to avoid confronting social injustice.[16] Librarians of color—although severely underrepresented—also began to create their own affiliates: the Black Caucus in 1970, the Asian/Pacific American Librarians Caucus (now "Association") in 1975, and REFORMA in 1976.[17]

---

12   Ibid., 10.

13   Stevens, *Urban Information Centers*, 10–15, 25; Estabrook, "Emerging Trends," 151, 159; Major Owens, "A Model Library for Community Action," *Library Journal* 95, no. 9 (1970): 1704.

14   Long, "Information and Referral Services," 10.

15   Kenneth Duchac, "A Plea for Social Responsibility," [reprint; original August 1968], *Library Journal* 117, no. 8 (1992): S6.

16   Wayne Wiegand, "Tunnel Vision and Blind Spots: What the Past Tells Us About the Present," *The Library Quarterly*, 69, no. 1 (1999): 19.

17   Although REFORMA's purpose is serving Spanish-speaking *patrons*, it has also drawn in Latino librarians.

One influential figure in librarianship at this time was Major Owens, a librarian with the Brooklyn Public Library in the 1950s and 1960s. An activist both within and beyond libraries, Owens oversaw New York City's antipoverty program from 1968–1973, served as a member of the United States House of Representatives for his Brooklyn district from 1983–2006, and was called the "librarian *in* Congress".[18] Owens decried in unstinting terms the failure of the public library to be relevant to social needs, particularly those of low-income minority neighborhoods. In a stirring 1970 *Library Journal* article, Owens described how libraries could directly supply "information power" to communities, insisting that true change could not come "case by case, with individual and family counseling... [t]he only answer is community action, total effort."[19]

This kind of collective power would mean, for example, knowing when annual appropriations were decided and the names of local officials and their respective roles in the budgeting process, with librarians providing straightforward explanations of city fiscal matters.[20] Owens envisioned information as a tool of righteous persuasion in the hands of a progressive-minded community, and explained why librarians had to play an active role:

> Comparative statistics which show the cost of a hand grenade vs. the cost of milk for school children or the cost of a super bomber vs. the cost of a low-income project are the kinds of things that the community will need as weapons to battle for a greater share of the funds needed to improve their lives. These bits of information become weapons in the community arsenal. While the average librarian would be able to secure all of this material within a relatively few hours, most community action personnel or the residents themselves would have to search for days or weeks, or are completely unaware of the fact that they can get such information.[21]

---

18   American Library Association, "Memorial Resolution for Major Owens," *ALA Memorial #2*. (Philadelphia: ALA Midwinter Meeting, 2014): 1–2; Joseph Fried, "Major Owens, 77, Education Advocate in Congress, Dies," *New York Times*, October 22, 2013, A27; John N. Berry III, "Major Owens," *Library Journal* 138, no. 21 (2013): 10; New York Library Association, "Major Owens Remembered," *Bulletin of the New York Library Association*, 62, no. 1 (February 2014).

19   Owens, "A Model Library," 1703.

20   Ibid.

21   Ibid.

The New Urban Library Education

Several Library and Information Science (LIS) programs emerged to train librarians to bring this kind of information power to communities. Major Owens, with Miriam Braverman, founded the Community Media Librarian Program (COMLIP) at Columbia University's library school in 1973.[22] Other programs in this vein included the Urban Library Services Program at Case Western University (1972–1974); the Inner City Library Institute at the University of Wisconsin-Milwaukee (1971–1974); a "Research-Action-Teaching" series of activities at Syracuse University (underway at least by 1971); and the Community Information Specialist Program at the University of Toledo (1972–1978).[23] The University of Maryland at College Park ran two related initiatives, to be discussed in greater detail below: an initial venture called the High John Library (1967–1968), and the Urban Information Specialist Program (UISP) in 1970–1971.

These new urban LIS programs varied in how they framed their goals. At Syracuse, the assumption was that low-income residents often "misinterpret[ed] the social agencies' purpose," and that what they needed most was information such as "finding a job, getting the furnace fixed, getting insurance, finding a daycare center, finding a doctor."[24] They disregarded the long-term potential information needs that Owens would have said were crucial—such as understanding their rights and how local government worked—as "luxuries when one is cold and hungry."[25] In contrast, the Maryland UISP asserted that new kinds of reference services could go beyond immediate individual crises to "secure the citizen's right to partic-

---

22   Miriam Braverman, "The Community Media Librarian Program of Columbia University," in Samore, *Progress*, 25; Mary Lee Bundy, "The Social Relevancy of Library Education: An Accounting," in *Activism in American Librarianship*, 1962–1973, Mary Lee Bundy and Frederick J. Stielow, Eds., (New York: Greenwood Press. 1987): 94.

23   Brenda Dervin, "The Research-Action-Teaching Effort at Syracuse University's School of Library Science," In Samore, *Progress*, 129; Laurence L. Sherrill, "Insight before Outreach: UWM Trains for Inner City Library Service," *Wisconsin Library Bulletin*, 28, no. 2 (March–April 1972), 79–80; Finding Aid of the Inner City Library Service Institute Records, 1971–1974; Goldwyn, A.J. "The Urban Library Services Program (1972–1974) at Case Western Reserve University," in Samore, *Progress*, 27; Miles W. Martin, "The Community Information Specialist Program," in Samore, *Progress*, 32; Bundy, "Social Relevancy," 92.

24   Dervin, "Research-Action-Teaching Effort," 131–32.

25   Ibid.

ipate in institutional decision making affecting their welfare, and to encourage the poor to participate and to make change."[26]

Most of the new programs included both traditional courses in reference work and courses about inner city social issues. Syracuse's version of the latter was called "Minorities: Library and Information Centers" and was intended to " 'blow the students' minds."[27] Implicit in such phrasing was the expectation that students in the new urban programs would continue to be mostly White and middle class, as was typical of traditional LIS programs, and this held true for the most part. The programs also required fieldwork in libraries and/or social service agencies. These encounters often brought out middle-class White students' discomfort with and ignorance of the communities they wanted to serve, and sometimes revealed that library schools were not well prepared to navigate partnerships with other institutions, as several were caught off guard by logistical and territorial conflicts.

Case Western asserted that potential students who merely "wanted to 'help' people but who had no contact with urban poverty were not accepted." However, the tone of final student reports belie the depth of that claim.[28] Their students worked twelve hours a week at a social agency and four hours at a public library.[29] Dissatisfied with the work in the agencies, they requested and were allowed to take over the running of a library branch, with faculty convincing the library to replace existing staff with people who "had to some degree the same ideas and goals" as the students, even though the students were only to stay one year.[30] One student later recalled with surprise that residents were not happy to lose their familiar

---

26   Mary Lee Bundy, Robert Bundy, Andrew Jones, William Miles, Robert Morris, and James Welbourne, *Urban Information Specialist Project: An Educational Program to Prepare Community Information Workers in the Urban Setting*, (College Park, MD: School of Library and Information Services, University of Maryland, 1971): 8.

27   Ibid., 133.

28   Benjamin F. Head, "Urban Library Services Program at Case Western Reserve University: My Education, Experiences and Attitude," in Samore, *Progress*, 82; A.J. Goldwyn, "The Urban Library Services Program (1972–1974) at Case Western Reserve University," in Samore, *Progress*, 27.

29   Roger Mae Johnson, "Field Work in Public Library Training—The Only Way to Go," in Samore, *Progress*, 72–3.

30   Goldwyn, "The Urban Library Services Program," 31; Head,"Urban Library Services Program," 84.

staff, nor to see changes made without consulting the community, such as removing a long-standing wrought iron fence because students deemed it unattractive.[31] In his account, this student glosses over these conflicts before concluding with satisfaction, "I have been able to learn how to handle myself in many inner-city situations which is really saying a lot… I have had much personal growth."[32]

At Syracuse, students worked five hours a week at a local information center, met with community leaders, and went with staff to "the jail, to welfare homes, to burned-out houses, to family crises."[33] Much time was spent discussing students' "personal problems of coping across such cultural differences."[34] Students recorded journal entries such as: "Four hours at the neighborhood center and I'm dead, emotionally and physically. Everything is crisis." Another wrote: "[e]verything here is very personality oriented and somehow I just don't fit;" and, with a dawning insight, "neighborhood people must run the Center. They live in the community. They know where the hidden streets are."[35] Students at the University of Wisconsin—Milwaukee mostly found their fieldwork helpful, but some complained of a lack of preparation, feeling rejected by patrons for not sharing the same ethnic background (Chicano), and a lack of trust between the university and the agency. Library staff gave mixed reviews of the students' work, and requested clearer roles and expectations for the placements.[36] One Syracuse faculty member—who had begun to question whether some community problems were attributable not to community ignorance, but rather to a lack of resources and to agencies' failures to fulfill their promises—reflected that while it was hard for middle-class newcomers to understand the neighborhood, the neighborhood was all too familiar with the "establishment point of view."[37]

---

31   Ibid., 85.

32   Ibid., 86.

33   Ibid.

34   Ibid., 134.

35   Ibid.

36   David M. Logsdon, "An Evaluation of the UWM School of Library and Information Science Inner City Institute Program: Summary Report," in Samore, *Progress*, 109–26.

37   Ibid., 134, 136.

Some of the new urban programs tried to recruit more students of color and students from working-class backgrounds. Columbia's COMLIP did not require a bachelor's degree for admission if an applicant had shown "an active involvement that resulted in a contribution to the community," and was notable in that thirteen of their initial sixteen students were minorities (twelve Black and one Puerto Rican).[38] But few LIS students were like Mary Suttle, who was both a library student and local resident, and understood that her community saw the library as "a non-communicative animal," "an alien in the community," and a place for middle class people who had extra leisure time.[39]

The naïveté and unexamined privilege of middle-class White students in urban library programs would later be derided by one of the founders of the University of Maryland UISP, Mary Lee Bundy, as a "wasteful use of public funds for Whites to 'research' information needs of urban people, only to 'discover' what any urban resident already knows."[40] Bundy's critiques of librarian training would eventually show her to be among the most radical of the influential LIS leaders of her time. She problematized library reference that would reproduce, without critical comment, information about services that came from the agencies providing the service, as such institutions restricted what they let people know in order to avoid scrutiny. While acknowledging the importance of disseminating information, Bundy stressed that merely learning about opportunities "does not multiply the number of opportunities… [i]nforming a man of his rights does not ensure he will receive them."[41]

> The man going on trial in a domestic case does not want to know the law; he wants to know how to ensure that his case comes before a judge who understands his culture. Someone considering taking advantage of a low-moderate income housing program wants some realistic advice on what he is actually getting himself into. People in a

---

38   Braverman, "Community Media Librarian Program," in Samore, *Progress*, 26.

39   Mary Suttle, "Urban Library Training Program: Fieldwork," in Samore, *Progress*, 76; Mary Suttle, "Determining Community Information Needs: A Personal Statement." In Samore, *Papers*, 19.

40   Urban Information Specialists, *Community Information Programs: Nine Proposals*, (College Park, MD: Urban Information Interpreters, Inc., 1975), 8.

41   Mary Lee Bundy, "Urban Information and Public Libraries: A Design for Service," *Library Journal* 97, no. 2 (1972): 162–64.

tenement trying to force a landlord to make improvements may need help in finding out who he is and how to force him to make changes, not the law, which is on [the landlord's] side anyway.[42]

In Bundy's view, in order be relevant and effective, librarians would have to go beyond the I&R ideal of increasing patrons' access to information to becoming "information interpreters" who were unabashed advocates and active consultants to community-based organizations. Such information workers would do things like unearth policy-makers' voting records, the public and private interests of city council members, and the names of slumlords, all to support action for social justice.[43]

High John the Conqueror

Despite the radicalism of Bundy's later writing, her first attempt to integrate fieldwork into library education in 1967 fell into many of the same traps as the other urban LIS programs, i.e., White students' discomfort with and ignorance of a low-income African American neighborhood, conflict between the library school and their community partner, and a short, grant-dependent life.

The 1967 project was known by the name of the library that served as a lab for the Maryland School of Library Information Services (SLIS) students: High John, after the African American folk hero High John the Conqueror.[44] As with the other urban library programs, the goal was to have students learn first-hand by working in a "deprived" community, in this case Fairmount Heights, Maryland, just outside of Washington, D.C. Eight SLIS students took a course in "Library Service to The Disadvantaged" and worked four hours a week at High John, while four of their classmates worked twenty hours a week at the library, took a research methods seminar, and were considered research assistants. The tuition of these four students was waived, and each was paid $2,700/year ($19,692 in 2017 dollars).[45]

---

42   Ibid., 166.

43   Ibid., 163, 166.

44   "High John," *Library Journal* 93, no. 2 (1968): 147.

45   Ibid., 148; Bundy and Moses, "A New Approach", 4; United States Bureau of Labor Statistics. *CPI Inflation Calculator.* http://data.bls.gov/cgi-bin/cpicalc.pl

The project was originally meant to last three years, with the Prince George's County library system contributing $20,000 for the first year, and the SLIS providing $88,000 in grant money from the federal Office of Education (OE) for the first 18 months.[46] The branch that became High John had previously operated between 1948–1961 before being closed "due to lack of business" and replaced by a bookmobile.[47] The building was a rambling house which had its reference collection in the dining room, adult section in a former bedroom, children's books tossed into a big box, and a staff room with no door, into and out of which children wandered at will.[48]

High John was less reflective of Bundy's later racial critiques than of other values of the new generation in the 1960s, such as individual liberty and an escape from traditional norms. An unnamed reporter for *Library Journal* felt that the "principal factor about High John is its looseness," and there was no traditional cataloging, nor any fines.[49] Richard Moses, of Baltimore's Enoch Pratt Free Library, who oversaw the fieldwork and taught the research seminar, said that "[a]nyone can do anything he wants in the library, as long as he doesn't interfere with anyone else's freedom. That's about as close to a rule as we can get."[50] Although the library did have an "information center" for referrals to local agencies, I&R-style, there was no well-defined or revolutionary view of reference.

In a striving-to-be-hip account penned for the ALA *Bulletin* ("Those things? Tokens, man. Tokens? Yeh. You pay for your books with 'em"), Moses indicates that High John was always more about the library students' experience than the community they purported to serve. By his account, the library school had wanted to create "a laboratory library to give the middle class librarian-to-be a taste and a talent for working with 'those people'— a

---

46   "High John,"148; Mary Lee Bundy and Richard Moses, "A New Approach to Educational Preparation for Public Library Service: An Experimental Program in Library Education for Work with a Specialized Clientele," (Washington, DC: Bureau of Research, Office of Education, U.S. Department of Health, Education, and Welfare, 1969): 1. http://files.eric.gov/fulltext/ED027929.pdf.

47   Elizabeth B. Hage, "More High John," *Library Journal* 95, no. 18 (1970): 3416.

48   Ibid, 149–51.

49   Ibid, 151.

50   Ibid.

real so-called library 'poverty program.'"[51] All of the initial twelve students were White (eleven were women), and once on the ground "were clearly suffering from cultural shock" in the poor Black community.[52] Students grew frustrated with the time it took to build relationships in the neighborhood, and after incidents of broken windows and stolen equipment, some expressed fear and refused to work in the evenings.[53] They were also flustered by the children and teens' rambunctiousness and felt that Moses and the one professional librarian in the branch—both of whom interacted with more ease with patrons—had created an environment they couldn't handle. When Moses withdrew from day-to-day operations of the library, he admitted he hadn't prepared students well enough to take over.[54] In response to the White students' "culture shock" (the sole Black student joined in the second semester), the SLIS added two class sessions on "exploring [students'] personal prejudices, guilt and anxiety," after which the students tellingly reported that they felt the hours spent processing their own feelings was "more valuable than all of the others put together."[55]

High John soon ended, with bitter feelings. As with some of the other urban programs, the UMD SLIS ran into conflict with their partner over territory, logistics, and restore original: differing interpretations of what had happened and what it meant. SLIS Dean Paul Wasserman fretted that their experiment had only reached what he jarringly called "the white Negroes— the ones who are after the usual middle class values" and not the truly deprived.[56] The *Library Journal* reporter thought that Mary Lee Bundy, as project director, and Wasserman had not been concerned by what would happen to the people of Fairmount Heights after they left, a sentiment vigorously seconded by Elizabeth Hage, the county library director, who charged that

---

51 Richard B. Moses, "Jottings from High John: Random Paragraphs Toward a Sometime Article," *ALA Bulletin*, 62, no. 4 (April 1968): 378–79.

52 "High John," 152.

53 Ibid.

54 Ibid, 153.

55 Mary Lee Bundy and Richard Moses, "A New Approach to Educational Preparation for Public Library Service: An Experimental Program in Library Education for Work with a Specialized Clientele," (Washington, DC: Bureau of Research, Office of Education, U.S. Department of Health, Education, and Welfare, 1969): 11–12. http://files.eric.ed.gov/fulltext/ED027929.pdf

56 "High John", 153.

when the grant money was cut off after 18 months, the University of Maryland "dropped the project like a hot cake," leaving the county to pick up the tab to continue services.[57] Hage went on to describe the "bitter disillusionment [of] a community that had grown to regard the branch as a bright spot in an otherwise poverty ridden and long neglected area."[58] She and two of the SLIS leaders got into a public scrape with extended tit-for-tat postmortems of the project, both published in *Library Journal*, each accusing the other of failing the community.[59] One SLIS professor admitted that the library had been unwisely chosen without community input, and instead based on "criteria developed by liberal, white librarians with only marginal knowledge of the community," and he cautioned that any future projects must be truer collaborations in order to succeed.[60] With an unresolved, broken relationship with the public library, the UMD SLIS moved on to its next iteration of librarian training, this time with a stronger definition of social justice goals.

The Urban Information Specialist Program: Ideals

The Urban Information Specialist Program (UISP) explicitly declared that the librarian in the role of "information interpreter" should strive not to be a neutral facilitator of access to services, but rather a conscious advocate whose "stance with agencies obliged to provide information is an aggressive one."[61] The information interpreter should seek to increase community knowledge and skills, because a "community's prospects for control over its own life situation is heightened or reduced by the extent to which it has information needed to make judgments and then to act on them."[62] As librarians were to be active interpreters of information, patrons were also expected to be decision makers capable of using their own discernment. For instance, a course on the

---

57   Ibid; Hage, "More High John," 3416.

58   Ibid.

59   Robert B. Croneberger and James C. Welbourne, Jr. ,"Triumph & Tragedy: A Play in Two Acts," *Library Journal* 95, no. 9 (1970): 1705–1708; Hage, "More High John," 3416–3418.

60   John C. Colson, "The Agony of Outreach: Some Reconsiderations Based on the High John Project," *Library Journal* 98, no. 17 (1973): 2818, 2820.

61   Welbourne, *First Year*, 23.

62   Ibid, 19, 23.

media offered not only an analysis of media bias, but strategies for community residents to get media outlets to fairly represent their point of view.[63]

James Welbourne—who had been part of High John, was hired by the SLIS to increase Black student recruitment, and would later become UISP director—noted that the difficulties at High John had taught them that the typical library student was not suited for this kind of work and stressed the importance of admitting students with previous life and work experience in "the ghetto community."[64] More explicitly than most other LIS program administrators, Welbourne and Bundy were staunch critics of institutionalized racism within education, and expressed frustration that Black students were under pressure by skeptical White educators to prove their academic qualifications, that Black students found themselves in an educational system that "rules out the values, interests, and needs of [their] people."[65] The UISP explicitly sought to recruit more Black students, increased financial aid, and waived the requirement of a bachelor's degree for admission. Eleven of the seventeen students accepted to the UISP were Black and six White, resulting in the admission of more Black students than any library school other than Atlanta University (as Welbourne noted, this milestone was "a result more of the failure of other library schools than [of] the success of Maryland.")[66]

---

63 Welbourne, "Training Urban Information Specialists," 106.

64 James Welbourne, *The Urban Information Specialist Program: First Year*, (College Park, MD: University of Maryland School of Library and Information Services, 1971); John Colson to Charles E. Bishop, November 22, 1970, School of Library and Information Services—Urban Information Specialist Program. Office of the Chancellor Records, Series 4.1, Special Collections, Hornbake Library, University of Maryland Libraries, College Park, MD.

65 Mary Lee Bundy and James Welbourne, "Notes on Institutional Racism to Guide a Discussion with the Faculty of the School of Library and Information Services, on October 29, 1970", School of Library and Information Services—Urban Information Specialist Program. Office of the Chancellor Records, Series 4.1, Special Collections, Hornbake Library, University of Maryland Libraries, College Park, MD.

66 Bundy et al., *Urban Information Specialist Project*, 6, 11; James Welbourne, *The Urban Information Specialist Program: First Year*, (College Park, MD: University of Maryland School of Library and Information Services, 1971): 3; Welbourne, James, "Statement Prepared for the Caucus of Black Librarians at the American Library Association's 89th Convention, Detroit 1970: A Black Position Paper on White Racism in Library Education," included as attachment to memorandum from Mary Lee Bundy to J. Colson, J. Donohue, Robert Haro, Larry Heilprin, Jerry Kidd, James Liesener, E. Colson, E. Warner, and Paul Wasserman, July 6, 1970, School of Library and Information Services—Urban Information Specialist Program. Office of the Chancellor Records, Series 4.1, Special Collections, Hornbake Library, University of Maryland Libraries, College Park, MD.

UISP Student Proposals

Rather than working part-time at a library or social agency, UISP students took an applied research methods course and then designed summer projects in which they were expected to "articulate a ghetto problem, design a solution, and write a proposal for testing it during the summer months."[67] Instead of taking place in a library, projects could be tied to an inner-city college, a labor union, or any other group where community members could be reached.[68]

In the introduction to a published collection of the UISP students' action-research proposals, the author (unnamed, but most likely Mary Lee Bundy) located the roots of the problems of poverty outside the community, condemning the employment market, the public educational system, exploitation by landlords, "a punitive and coercive criminal justice system," and pervasive anti-Black racism.[69] Black people were "continually spied on by the various agencies which attempt to control them, and their leaders, followed and watched. Mind control by means of brain operations in(sic) only the next step... The potential of urban based information centers in overcoming this adverse information situation, are(sic) several."[70] Each of the proposals challenged traditional reference work either in terms of purpose, source of information, method of dissemination, and/or the librarian's role as interpreter.

Teen researchers. Cheryl Marshall proposed training teenagers as community researchers in two low-income neighborhoods in Montclair, New Jersey. The teens would receive training on people's rights to information, the "dynamics of poverty and racism," and "ways of gaining access to desired information." The teens would conduct five weeks of research via questionnaires and interviews with officials, as well as "'rapping' [with the] 'man in the streets'" (without taking notes, because of an endemic distrust of surveys). The researchers would learn the rights one had if ar-

---

67   Ibid, 104; Welbourne, *The Urban Information Specialist Program*, 5–6.

68   Ibid., 22.

69   Urban Information Specialists, *Community Information Programs*, 3.

70   Ibid., 1–2. Given revelations of the era, including FBI surveillance of Black militant groups, and the exposé in 1972 of forty years of deception and exploitation through the Tuskegee Study, speculation about mind-control surgery may not have struck politically aware readers as far-fetched.

rested, how to file complaints, and how bail worked. They would not only look up housing codes, but translate them into clear language, and ask tenants whether or not code violations were in fact usually corrected. Finally, they would write and publish a manual with their findings and distribute it within the city.[71]

Consciousness-raising for Black high school students. Alfred Nero proposed a "re-educational" program for the young people in his neighborhood of Bedford-Stuyvesant in Brooklyn, where he wanted to create a "street-oriented community base" for information interpreters to "reach and teach in non-traditional, non-academic ways" about welfare rights, health, and above all, Black history and pride. Although he wanted information interpreters to tell people about practical matters such as job opportunities and legal assistance, his project focused on consciousness-raising, including the study of African religions and Black history, in order to "restore the essence of respect and pride in Blackness which present educational programs attempt to obliterate." Although his principles were strongly outlined, pragmatic considerations were skimpy: he allowed for only two weeks of outreach, and although he intended to implement telephone reference for elderly shut-ins, hospital patients, and incarcerated people, he outlined no plan to let these groups know about the program.[72]

Union information service. Although it was not published with the other proposals, and thus fewer details survive, one student proposed that an information center be attached to the union for which she was an organizer, in order to respond "to the needs which the public library was not answering" and serve as a place for organizing.[73]

Welfare rights information center. Anthony Miller's proposal, the most developed of those published, directly connected reference to social action groups and explicitly raised the purpose of collective action over individual benefit. The National Welfare Rights Organization (NWRO), which existed from 1966–1975, included over 300 local groups in its network. Members were welfare or ex-welfare recipients, while organizers were either from the community or arrived via student organizing, the civil rights movement, or programs such as the Peace Corps and VISTA. Information

---

71   Cheryl Marshall, "A Project to Retrieve Community Information for Dissemination to Community Workers through the Use of Teenage Researchers," in Urban Information Specialists. *Community Information Programs*, 11, 16–18, 20.

72   Ibid., 25–28.

73   Welbourne, "Training Urban Information Specialists," 105.

interpreters in the proposed center would seek out data to directly support local WRO actions. Reference sources would include census data, newsletters, interviews with community people, lists of social agencies and activist groups, NWRO literature, city council minutes, news clippings, and more. Blurring the line between organizer and librarian, the information interpreter in Miller's plan was also charged with framing collective solutions. Miller noted that although welfare recipients had "a painfully clear picture of what the problems are and how they affect his or her family," they often had less detailed analyses of systemic causes and potential collective solutions.[74]

All the student proposals set very ambitious goals for a summer-long project. Unfortunately, no documentation has apparently survived that chronicles the results.

UISP: Reflections on the First Year, Dashed Hopes for the Second

In 1971, James Welbourne issued a public report on the UISP's first year, intended to serve as an advocacy tool. The program was in danger of not being funded again and his team wanted to rally support from the library field. While touting the ideals of the program, Welbourne also admitted challenges, the overarching one being how to translate the program's ideals into reality in order to "make the connection between information access and the solution of ghetto problems." They had found that some course content had been too theoretical, and recommended tying readings to more concrete cases the following year. Welbourne also alluded to White students whose disenchantment with the political establishment neither guaranteed their commitment to inner city communities, nor inoculated them from "expectancy of favored treatment because of their race," and described conflict within the SLIS because some faculty could not adjust when "a white liberal project became, as it should have, a ghetto, largely black oriented project."[75]

Unfortunately, the UISP did not have a chance to address their self-identified challenges in a second year. Instead, a long, bitter battle

---

74   Anthony Miller, "A Project to Design a Model for a Welfare Rights Information Center." In Urban Information Specialists, *Community Information Programs*, 36, 38–39, 44, 48, 56.

75   Welbourne, *First Year* 1, 28, 30–34.

within the SLIS over funding and administration shut it down. Hefty files of memos and letters from all parties are thick with blame in all directions. Did the UISP die because the SLIS administrators were still in the "help the unserved" mentality, unwilling to evolve to an empowerment mind-set? Did they kill it, as Bundy and Welbourne would later charge, out of sheer racist opposition to its goals?[76] Welbourne had already accused the SLIS of deliberately hiring less qualified White candidates over Black candidates, and of undermining its own efforts to increase Black recruitment.[77] Two condescending racial insults can be found in existing correspondence, one from a faculty member who called Welbourne "a poor Black who has been misused—befuddled and egged into 'racist' attacks" by Bundy, and a patronizing remark from the vice chancellor describing Welbourne as "an able and increasingly militant Black" (as for Bundy, both men described her on separate occasions as "brilliant but erratic", with the faculty member also calling her "an acid-tongued middle-aged spinster").[78]

In addition, we cannot know about microaggressions in faculty meetings, or insulting tones of voice, or too-easily provoked skepticism about the program based on its leaders' identities, or even how much more passionately the university's letters of support might have been written in

---

76 Mary Lee Bundy, "The Disgrace at Maryland: A Paper Presented at the Urban Information Specialist Program Evaluation Conference," August 24–25, 1971; Welbourne, "A Charge with Regard to the School of Library and Information Services," n.d.; Bundy and Welbourne, "Notes on Institutional Racism"; James Welbourne, "Statement Prepared for the Caucus of Black Librarians at the American Library Association's 89th Convention, Detroit 1970: A Black Position Paper on White Racism in Library Education, With Particular Reference to the Black Recruitment Program at the School of Library and Information Services at the University of Maryland," attachment to July 6 1970 letter from Mary Lee Bundy to J. Colson, J. Donohue, Robert Haro, Larry Heilprin, Jerry Kidd, James Liesener, E. Olson, E. Warner, and Paul Wasserman, School of Library and Information Services—Urban Information Specialist Program. Office of the Chancellor Records, Series 4.1, Special Collections, Hornbake Library, University of Maryland Libraries, College Park, MD.

77 James Welbourne to George Callcott, July 30, 1970; Welbourne, "Statement Prepared for the Caucus of Black Librarians", School of Library and Information Services—Urban Information Specialist Program. Office of the Chancellor Records, Series 4.1, Special Collections, Hornbake Library, University of Maryland Libraries, College Park, MD.

78 Lawrence Heilprin to Charles Bishop, June 8, 1971; George Callcott to Louis Kaplan, September 10, 1971, School of Library and Information Services—Urban Information Specialist Program. Office of the Chancellor Records, Series 4.1, Special Collections, Hornbake Library, University of Maryland Libraries, College Park, MD.

the program's defense had it been led by White men, or had it not included so many Black students. The daily manifestations of racism against women and men of color, and of sexism against women of all races, often pass without being documented, and there is no reason to believe that the SLIS was so far ahead of its time as to be ahead of our own time as well, into some utopian era free of all consciously or unconsciously perpetuated patriarchy and White supremacy.

That said, within the reams of surviving correspondence among university administrators, except for the quotes above, there are no other explicit racial insults, and there is consistently stated support for the goals of the UISP both within the department and from the federal funders, who praised the goal of increasing minority recruitment and of developing more relevant information programs for urban communities as the two strongest aspects of the UISP proposal.[79]

What is heavily documented in the SLIS correspondence is the administrators' exasperation with UISP leaders on a personal level (particularly with Bundy), and accusations that Welbourne and Bundy were overly antagonistic to their peers, insulting to the institution upon which their program depended for survival, and even guilty of placing "personal aggrandizement" above the hard work of planning and maintaining a sustainable program.[80] One professor claimed the UISP's charges of racism were offered as excuses to avoid criticism of the program, while another expressed support for the program's goals while denouncing the "gross verbal abuse" and "threats of political and academic reprisal" aimed at any faculty who questioned the specifics of the program.[81]

When it came to the funds requested by the UISP for its second year, Burton Lamkin, the federal officer responsible for handling their grant,

---

79 Ray Fry to Wilson Elkins, n.d. [received June 24, 1971], School of Library and Information Services—Urban Information Specialist Program. Office of the Chancellor Records, Series 4.1, Special Collections, Hornbake Library, University of Maryland Libraries, College Park, MD

80 John Colson to Charles Bishop, December 16, 1970, School of Library and Information Services—Urban Information Specialist Program. Office of the Chancellor Records, Series 4.1, Special Collections, Hornbake Library, University of Maryland Libraries, College Park, MD

81 J.S. Kidd to Charles Bishop, December 3, 1970; Colson to Bishop, December 16, 1970; Heilprin to Bishop, June 8, 1971, School of Library and Information Services—Urban Information Specialist Program. Office of the Chancellor Records, Series 4.1, Special Collections, Hornbake Library, University of Maryland Libraries, College Park, MD

noted that the amount requested was one-third of his office's entire national budget for library employment grants, even though two previously funded projects under Bundy's leadership had failed to comply with basic reporting requirements and data retention.[82] A hastily revised budget from Welbourne (shifting most budget "cuts" from the government to the university) included the hiring of Bundy's brother and questionably high expenses for 60 day-trips for Bundy and another faculty member.[83] An SLIS administrator later said that Lamkin had privately blamed the "irresponsible leadership" of the UISP for his unwillingness to fund them at the levels requested.[84]

The tone of negotiations deteriorated. Bundy demanded that an acting dean save the UISP although the library school "neither deserves nor has earned the right to have" it.[85] Welbourne made unfounded promises to potential UISP faculty that the university would pay their salaries if the grant were to fall through and called on a local congressman to denounce the University, even though he knew it had supported the grant's renewal.[86] The UISP issued a press release charging racism as the sole reason that

82 Burton Lamkin to Charles Bishop, March 29, 1971, School of Library and Information Services—Urban Information Specialist Program. Office of the Chancellor Records, Series 4.1, Special Collections, Hornbake Library, University of Maryland Libraries, College Park, MD

83 James C. Welbourne to George Callcott, November 30, 1970; Welbourne, "A Charge", School of Library and Information Services—Urban Information Specialist Program, Office of the Chancellor Records, Series 4.1, Special Collections, Hornbake Library, University of Maryland Libraries, College Park, MD

84 George H. Callcott to Margaret E. Chisholm, August 16, 1971, School of Library and Information Services—Urban Information Specialist Program. Office of the Chancellor Records, Series 4.1, Special Collections, Hornbake Library, University of Maryland Libraries, College Park, MD.

85 Mary Lee Bundy to James W. Liesener, July 14, 1971, School of Library and Information Services—Urban Information Specialist Program. Office of the Chancellor Records, Series 4.1, Special Collections, Hornbake Library, University of Maryland Libraries, College Park, MD.

86 George Callcott to James Welbourne, August 9, 1971; Mitchell, Parren J. press conference statement included as attachment in James Welbourne to C.E. Bishop, June 14, 1971, School of Library and Information Services—Urban Information Specialist Program, Office of the Chancellor Records, Series 4.1, Special Collections, Hornbake Library, University of Maryland Libraries, College Park, MD

the program was not refunded.[87] Welbourne's tone, once courteous, began to echo Bundy's, calling the UISP the "only sound intellectual and professional part" of the SLIS, as the rest of the library school was—he said he was quoting another, unnamed, faculty member—"a bag of shit."[88]

By the end of the summer, the OE had offered a reduced amount of funding, the SLIS had insisted on more control over the UISP as a condition of renewal, and the UISP had rejected both. Bundy asked for and received a sabbatical, and Welbourne was hired back for one year with no promise of further renewal.[89]

The ugly implosion of the UISP, which had held so much promise in its outstandingly bold foray into community-action-based reference and its incisive critique of White middle-class librarianship, is a disappointment for contemporary progressive librarians in search of inspiration from history. The fight left each side exhausted and obstinate. The aftermath dragged on into the next school year, but Bundy moved on to her next project, publishing reference works for social change.

Publishing for Radical Reference: Urban Information Interpreters, Inc.

Urban Information Interpreters, Inc. (UIII), formed in 1971 while the UISP was struggling to survive, was, briefly, a publisher of radical reference materials. Institutional tax documents and board minutes show that although UIII referred to itself in the collective, it was very much Mary Lee Bundy's project, with some participation from her brother Robert Bundy,

---

87   "Press Release: Black Faculty and Students of the Urban Information Specialist Program Charge White University of Maryland Officials with Racism and Violations of Civil Rights", August 27, 1971, School of Library and Information Services—Urban Information Specialist Program, Office of the Chancellor Records, Series 4.1, Special Collections, Hornbake Library, University of Maryland Libraries, College Park, MD

88   James C. Welbourne to George Callcott, July 30, 1971, School of Library and Information Services—Urban Information Specialist Program, Office of the Chancellor Records, Series 4.1, Special Collections, Hornbake Library, University of Maryland Libraries, College Park, MD

89   Margaret Chisholm to James C. Welbourne, August 24, 1971; James W. Liesener to James C. Welbourne, May 3, 1971, School of Library and Information Services—Urban Information Specialist Program, Office of the Chancellor records, Special Collections and University Archives, University of Maryland Libraries, College Park, MD.

a man named Irving Gilchrist, and, in the beginning, James Welbourne.[90] The introduction to the UIII-published collection of UISP student proposals declared that "[t]here is no rationale to support Whites controlling funding for urban information programs, or managing them once in operation," and renounced any role for library schools in "preparing Whites as urban information workers, i.e., to work with the 'disadvantaged' [because] White professionals will be trusted to protect the White system… We are saying to White professionals, managers and federal bureaucrats… You are not competent to make these decisions and should remove yourselves from any involvement in urban information affairs."[91] This separatist argument would have been more straightforward if the main author of all the UIII works had not been a White woman (and the main federal bureaucrat handling the UISP request, Burton Lamkin, had not been an African American man, who was himself a demographic-breaking research librarian).[92] There is no record of Bundy ever addressing the questions raised by her own spearheading of urban information efforts, including those raised by the UISP's proposed second year budget, which would have given her, a White woman, a considerably higher salary than James Welbourne, the Black man who had taken over as director since the first semester: her $23,638 to his $16,500 (in 2017 dollars, $142,180 to $99,246).[93]

Regardless of any contradictions we might discern between her espoused ideology and certain of her own actions, Bundy's reference publication project was unquestionably the result of an immense amount of dedicated research and work, and extended her vision of reference's potential for fueling social change. She proposed transforming library reference collections, turning departments of "fine arts, social science, business and

---

90   Urban Information Interpreters, Inc. Archives, Special Collections, Hornbake Library, University of Maryland Libraries.

91   Urban Information Specialists, *Community Information Programs*, 9–10

92   "Speaking of People," *Ebony* 15, no. 12 (October 1960): 6.

93   James Welbourne to Charles Bishop, August 16, 1971, School of Library and Information Services—Urban Information Specialist Program, Office of the Chancellor records, Special Collections and University Archives, University of Maryland Libraries, College Park, MD. Note that the average professor's salary in 1972 ranged from $12,032–$19,191. "Average Salary of Full-Time Instructional Faculty on 9-month Contracts in Institutions of Higher education, By Academic Rank, Sex, and Control and Type of Institution: 1970–71 to 1994–95" [table]; United States Bureau of Labor Statistics, CPI Inflation Calculator.

technology" into departments of "welfare, housing, health, education, labor, the system of justice, and politics and government," and intended to publish the kind of reference work that could live in such departments.[94] UIII included a mission statement in the front of several of their books, which read in part:

> U.I.I.I.'s principal attack on poverty, racism and repression in the social system, is through information access [and] serves an educational function by providing education in a range of relevant information skills for community organizers and others involved in effecting social change.

> U.I.I.I. is, and intends to be, at the fore of changes which will enhance the power of people over institutions and so the prospects for meaningful change in the political and economic circumstances of the urban poor.[95]

UIII publications included directories and bibliographies meant to serve community-based groups as well as librarians. For librarians in the Internet age, it takes effort to recall or comprehend how hard it was in the early 1970s for small activist groups to find one another, particularly when few would have had the budget or time for extensive travel or research beyond their own urgent, immediate campaigns. Although other superficially similar directories had been published, they focused on service providers, not activist groups, which often could only find each other by word of mouth, a kind of networking which had much greater geographical limitations at the time.[96]

Publications included *The National Prison Directory* (two volumes, 1975 and 1979), *The Guide to the Literature of Social Change* (1977), *The National Children's Directory* (1977), *The National Civil Rights Directory* (1979), and nine shorter works (possibly mimeographed pamphlets; it is

---

94 Bundy, "Urban Information and Public Libraries," 166.

95 Urban Information Interpreters and Mary Lee Bundy, *The National Prison Directory: a Prison Reform Organizational and Resource Directory* (College Park, MD: Urban Information Interpreters, 1979), front matter.

96 Bundy, Mary Lee, and Irvin Gilchrist, *The National Civil Rights Directory: An Organizations Directory* (College Park, MD: Urban Information Interpreters, 1979).

unclear if any exemplars survive) published between 1972–1973 that were "relevant to the development of urban information service."[97]

The prison directories compiled information about 700 prison reform groups that held a sweeping range of goals, including the abolition of the death penalty, a moratorium on prison construction, community based alternatives to imprisonment, sexual assault in prisons, and the fight against repressive legislation in Congress. Groups ranged from COYOTE (advocating for sex workers' rights), to I&R centers focused on criminal justice, to prison committees that belonged to the Black Panther Party, the National Council of Churches, and state Bar associations.[98]

The National Children's Directory defined children as a powerless, oppressed group, noting that poor, minority, female, and/or gay children faced additional discrimination and disadvantages. In addition to listing entities from students' rights groups to organizations fighting sex stereotypes in children's media to manuals explaining how to start one's own school, to the child labor branch of the US Department of Labor, the book included a bibliography of over 300 reference sources "prepared especially for citizen action groups" and essays on children's rights.[99]

The Guide to the Literature of Social Change noted the shift in the 1970s away from street protests toward organizing people so that they could leverage existing laws and use litigation, watchdogging, and electoral politics to effect change. As such, the book presented "publications that serve to guide people in their efforts to form groups and to develop their programs, sustain themselves economically and successfully undertake social change action."[100] The book was meant as an acquisitions tool for reference librarians, and as a means for groups to connect to each other. It listed publications from full-length books about community organizing strate-

97   Urban Information Specialists, *Community Information Programs*, front matter.

98   Urban Information Interpreters, Mary Lee Bundy and Kenneth R. Harmon eds., *The National Prison Directory: Organizational Profiles of Prison Reform Groups in the United States: Base Volume.* (College Park, MD: Urban Information Interpreters,1975): 17–27.

99   Urban Information Interpreters, Mary Lee Bundy and Rebecca Glen Whaley eds., *The National Children's Directory.* College Park, MD: Urban Information Interpreters. 1977): 1–4, 37–38.

100   Urban Information Interpreters, *Guide to the Literature of Social Change, Vol. 1,* (College Park, MD: Urban Information Interpreters, Inc., 1977): 1.

gies to small pamphlets like one from the People's Law School in San Francisco explaining how to access local government records.[101]

The National Civil Rights Directory—which included a range of groups from the Puerto Rican Studies Department of John Jay College, to county-level human rights commissions, to Boricua College, to Pacifica radio station WBAI—decried the "myth that things are getting better for racial minorities in the United States," given endemic police brutality and other forms of racial injustice.[102]

One difficulty in compiling these directories must have been how quickly groups formed, changed, and died. Comparing the two volumes of the prison book, one can see that many groups had gone defunct in the intervening four years, while others had changed addresses or were absorbed into other institutions.[103] Some groups were also reluctant, in an age of COINTELPRO harassment of activists, to be listed in a directory "which could readily be used by those interests with a stake in perpetuating inequality."[104] As valuable as the directories might have been in this era, updating and publishing them with a small team (especially one with a poor track record of managing funds) was not a sustainable venture, and like the UISP and High John before it, UIII had a relatively short life.

Implications for Today

Over the past decade, an increasingly intersectional critique of librarianship and library school education, and their complicity with White supremacy, patriarchy, neoliberalism, and other forms of oppressive hegemony has emerged.[105] A full discussion of advances made (and not made)

---

101   Urban Information Interpreters, *Guide to the Literature of Social Change*, 2, 5–7, 10.

102   Bundy and Gilchrist, *National Civil Rights Directory*, i.

103   Urban Information Interpreters, *National Prison Directory*, 1.

104   Bundy and Gilchrist, *National Civil Rights Directory*, i, iii.

105   See: regular Twitter discussions using the hashtag #critlib; the 2016 Symposium on Critical Library Pedagogy held in Tucson, Arizona; critlib unconferences held before the 2015 and 2017 national ACRL conferences; books published by Library Juice Press; online journals such as *In the Library with the Lead Pipe*; etc.

since the 1970s is beyond the scope of this chapter.[106] However, the experiences of the urban library education programs of the early 1970s yield some direct lessons to those of us who yet believe that information can be power, that a collective benefit yields more lasting change than solving individual problems, and that we should examine how LIS programs can inculcate the idea of socially transformative reference.

Institutional collaboration. Current notions of the importance of marrying theory to action in praxis may encourage us to bring back to LIS education the idea of ideologically framed fieldwork, perhaps in community-based organizations. The urban LIS programs of the 1970s found that collaborations with public libraries and service agencies were, however, fraught with questions of territory and authority. Library schools and students often made the mistake of charging into existing institutions in a directive capacity, if not outright replacing local staff, and collaborative initiatives reliant on external grant funding were by nature short-lived, leaving students hanging and communities shortchanged. Any LIS program that would place students into local institutions should proceed with complete respect for their partners and a clear and realistic plan for long-term sustainability.

Student experience of fieldwork. Middle class White students had a difficult time functioning in low-income minority neighborhoods, and although students in some programs reported that the fieldwork prepared them well, the benefit was less clear to the agencies and communities they were meant to serve. Increased recruitment of students of color—a challenge that continues four decades later—might help reduce overt cultural conflicts, although an awareness of intersectionality and of the spectrum of individual experience and personality should also preclude the assumption that all library students of color will be instantly culturally competent in all communities of color. Any LIS programs placing any students in the field should work with their partners to determine how placements will benefit the community, not only the students, and establish clear expectations for students' roles and responsibilities, with both support and a plan of corrective action if students fail to interact appropriately or contribute positively.

---

106   Current scholarship on social justice in LIS education includes Nicole A. Cooke's recently published *Information Services to Diverse Populations: Developing Culturally Competent Library Professionals* as well as the anthology *Teaching for Justice: Implementing Social Justice in the LIS Classroom.*

Creating a radical program within an existing LIS school. Although the UISP founders' post-mortem message was that their program was simply killed by racism, an analysis of the existing correspondence suggests that—whatever implicit or explicit racism existed at the University—there was also a deep unwillingness on the part of the program's directors to fulfill promises made in exchange for money or to compromise on any budget or administrative item. Any question of the program's methods or accounting was immediately denounced as an ideological attack. Publicly demonizing the flawed institutional hand that feeds you may generate some personal satisfaction, but may also lead to a short life for the program. As progressive or radical librarians driven by our ideals, we must be self-reflective enough to recognize that possessing a just aim does not bless every decision we make as perfect, nor does it exempt us from treating colleagues with the respect we demand for ourselves, nor immunize us against the self-interest that can infect any human being, no matter how brilliant or righteous.

Information power reference beyond libraries. Librarianship no longer fears being made obsolete by I&R centers, but by Google and the open web. The role that Major Owens outlined for librarians—finding and organizing information that non-professionals could not—has become less clear in an age in which non-librarians are also adept at finding and compiling information. Still, our libraries, with their public platforms, can share and amplify the work of others, from grassroots political strategy groups like Indivisible to mass movements like Black Lives Matter. In this age of the Trump administration and a host of movements organizing for resistance across the country, we should take every opportunity to help disseminate information that can further the collective struggle for increasing social justice.

Works Cited

American Library Association. "Memorial Resolution for Major Owens." *ALA Memorial #2*. Philadelphia: ALA Midwinter Meeting. 2014. http://www.ala.org/aboutala/sites/ala.org.aboutala/files/content/governance/council/council_documents/2014_mw_council_documents/M_2_Major%20Owens%20(F)_0.pdf

"Average Salary of Full-Time Instructional Faculty on 9-month Contracts in Institutions of Higher education, By Academic Rank, Sex, and Control and Type of Institution: 1970–71 to 1994–95" [table]. https://nces.ed.gov/programs/digest/d96/d96t229.asp

Berry III, John N. "Major Owens." *Library Journal* 138 , no 21 (2013): 10.

Braverman, Miriam. "The Community Media Librarian Program of Columbia University." In Samore, Progress. 25–6.

Bundy, Mary Lee. "The Disgrace at Maryland: A Paper Presented at the Urban Information Specialist Program Evaluation Conference". August 24–25, 1971. Unpublished. School of Library and Information Services—Urban Information Specialist Program. Office of the Chancellor Records, Series 4.1, Special Collections, Hornbake Library, University of Maryland Libraries, College Park, MD

———. "The Social Relevancy of Library Education: An Accounting." In *Activism in American Librarianship, 1962–1973*. Mary Lee Bundy and Frederick J. Stielow, Eds. New York: Greenwood Press. 1987. 83–97.

———. "Urban Information and Public Libraries: A Design for Service." *Library Journal* 97, no. 2 (1972): 161–69.

Bundy, Mary Lee, Robert Bundy, Andrew Jones, William Miles, Robert Morris, and James Welbourne. *Urban Information Specialist Project: An Educational Program to Prepare Community Information Workers in the Urban Setting*. College Park, MD: School of Library and Information Services, University of Maryland. 1971.

Bundy, Mary Lee, and Irvin Gilchrist. *The National Civil Rights Directory: An Organizations Directory*. College Park, MD: Urban Information Interpreters. 1979.

Bundy, Mary Lee and Richard Moses. "A New Approach to Educational Preparation for Public Library Service: An Experimental Program in Library Education for Work with a Specialized Clientele." Interim report. Washington: Bureau of Research, Office of Education, U.S. Department of Health, Education, and Welfare. 1969. http://files.eric.ed.gov/fulltext/ED027929.pdf

Bundy, Mary Lee and Paul Wasserman. "A Departure in Library Education." *Journal of Education for Librarianship*, 8, no. 2 (Fall 1967). 124–32.

Bundy, Mary Lee and Paul Wasserman. "Professionalism Reconsidered." *College & Research Libraries*, 29, no. 1 (January 1968). 5–26.

Bundy, Mary Lee and James Welbourne, "Notes on Institutional Racism to Guide a Discussion with the Faculty of the School of Library and Information Services, on October 29, 1970". Unpublished. School of Library and Information Services—Urban Information Specialist Program. Office of the Chancellor Records, Series 4.1, Special Collections, Hornbake Library, University of Maryland Libraries, College Park, MD.

Childers, Thomas, and Joyce A. Post. *The Information-Poor in America.* Metuchen, N.J.: Scarecrow Press. 1975. http://hdl.handle.net/1860/736.

Colson, John C. "The Agony of Outreach: Some Reconsiderations Based on the High John Project." *Library Journal* 98, no. 17 (1973): 2817–20.

Copenhaver, Christina and Joanne Boelke. "Library Service to the Disadvantaged, A Bibliography." Minneapolis: ERIC Clearinghouse on Library and Information Sciences. 1968. http://files.eric.ed.gov/fulltext/ED026103.pdf

Croneberger, Robert B. and James C. Welbourne, Jr. "Triumph & Tragedy: A Play in Two Acts." *Library Journal* 95, no. 9 (1970): 1705–08.

Dervin, Brenda. "The Research-Action-Teaching Effort at Syracuse University's School of Library Science." In Kronus and Crowe, *Libraries and Neighborhood Information Centers.* 129–37.

Duchac, Kenneth. "A Plea for Social Responsibility." [reprint; original August 1968]. *Library Journal* 117, no. 8 (1992): S6–S8.

Du Mont, Rosemary. *Reform and Reaction: The Big City Public Library in American Life.* Westport, CT: Greenwood Press, 1977.

Estabrook, Leigh. "Emerging Trends in Community Library Services." *Library Trends*, 28 (Fall 1979): 151–64.

Finding Aid of the Inner City Library Service Institute Records, 1971–1974. http://digicoll.library.wisc.edu/cgi/f/findaid/findaid-idx?c=wiarchives;cc=wiarchives;view=reslist;rgn=main;didno=uw-mil-uwmac0056;subview=standard

Ford, Barbara J. "Libraries, Literacy, Outreach and the Digital Divide." *American Library Association.* http://www.ala.org/offices/olos/olosprograms/jeanecoleman/00ford

Fried, Joseph. "Major Owens, 77, Education Advocate in Congress, Dies." *New York Times*, October 22, 2013, A27.

Goldwyn, A.J. "The Urban Library Services Program (1972–1974) at Case Western Reserve University." In Samore, *Progress*, 27–31.

Hage, Elizabeth B. "More High John." *Library Journal* 95, no. 18 (1970): 3416–18.

Head, Benjamin F. "Urban Library Services Program at Case Western Reserve University: My Education, Experiences and Attitude." In Samore, *Progress*, 82–6.

"High John." *Library Journal* 93, no. 2 (1968): 147–55.

Johnson, Roger Mae. "Field Work in Public Library Training—The Only Way to Go." In Samore, *Progress*, 72–5.

Kronus, Carol L. and Linda Crowe, eds. *Libraries and Neighborhood Information Centers: Papers Presented at an Institute Conducted by the University of Illinois Graduate School of Library Science*, October 24–27, 1971. Urbana, IL: University of Illinois Graduate School of Library Science, 1972.

Logsdon, David M. "An Evaluation of the UWM School of Library and Information Science Inner City Institute Program: Summary Report". In Samore, *Progress*, 109–26.

Long, Nicholas. "Information and Referral Services: A Short History and Some Recommendations." In Kronus and Crowe, *Libraries and Neighborhood Information Centers*, 1–14.

Marshall, Cheryl. "A Project to Retrieve Community Information for Dissemination to Community Workers through the Use of Teenage Researchers." In *Urban Information Specialists, Community Information Programs*, 10–20.

Martin, Miles W. "The Community Information Specialist Program." In Samore, *Progress*, 32–3.

Mathews, Virginia H. "Narrative Evaluation Report on the Institute for Strengthening Librarians' Capability to Elicit and Respond to the Felt Needs of Minority/Culturally Isolated/Disadvantaged Persons and Groups in the Southwest." Washington, DC: Bureau of Libraries and Educational Technology, 1972.

Miller, Anthony. "A Project to Design a Model for a Welfare Rights Information Center." In *Urban Information Specialists, Community Information Programs*. 36–57.

Moses, Richard B. "Jottings from High John: Random Paragraphs Toward a Sometime Article." *ALA Bulletin*, 62, no. 4 (April 1968): 377–80.

Nero, Alfred. "A Proposal to Design a Re-educational Program Geared to Implement the Information Needs of Black Inner City High School Youth." In *Urban Information Specialists, Community Information Programs*, 21–28.

New York Library Association. "Major Owens Remembered." *The Bulletin of the New York Library Association*, 62. no. 1 (February 2014).

Owens, Major. "A Model Library for Community Action." *Library Journal* 95, no. 9 (1970): 1702–04.

Samore, Theodore, ed. *Progress in Urban Librarianship: A Seminar on Community Information Needs and the Designing of Library Education Programs to Meet These Needs*. Milwaukee: Wisconsin University School of Library Science, 1974.

School of Library and Information Services—Urban Information Specialist Program, October 1970–June 1971. Office of the Chancellor Records, Series 4.1, Special Collections, Hornbake Library, University of Maryland Libraries, College Park, MD.

School of Library and Information Services—Urban Information Specialist Program, December 1970–March 1972. Office of the Chancellor Records, Series 4.1, Special Collections, Hornbake Library, University of Maryland Libraries, College Park, MD.

Sherrill, Laurence L. "Insight before Outreach: UWM Trains for Inner City Library Service." *Wisconsin Library Bulletin*, 28, no. 2 (March–April 1972): 79–80.

Sinclair, Dorothy. "Linking New and Traditional Library Services." In Kronus and Crowe. *Libraries and Neighborhood Information*, 73–90.

"Speaking of People." *Ebony*, 15, no. 12 (October 1960): 6.

Stevens, Jane E." Urban Information Centers and Their Interface with the National Program for Libraries and Information Service." Washington, D.C.: National Commission on Libraries and Information Science, 1975. http://files.eric.ed.gov/fulltext/ED114102.pdf

Suttle, Mary. "Urban Library Training Program: Fieldwork." In Samore, *Progress*, 76.

Suttle, Mary. "Determining Community Information Needs: A Personal Statement." In Samore, *Progress*, 19.

United States Bureau of Labor Statistics. *CPI Inflation Calculator*. http://data.bls.gov/cgi-bin/cpicalc.pl.

Urban Information Interpreters. *Guide to the Literature of Social Change*, Vol. 1. College Park, MD: Urban Information Interpreters, Inc., 1977.

Urban Information Interpreters. *The National Children's Directory*. College Park, MD: Urban Information Interpreters, 1977.

Urban Information Interpreters, and Mary Lee Bundy. *The National Prison Directory: a Prison Reform Organizational and Resource Directory*. College Park, MD: Urban Information Interpreters, 1979.

Urban Information Interpreters, Mary Lee Bundy, and Kenneth R. Harmon. *The National Prison Directory: Organizational Profiles of Prison Reform Groups in the United States: Base Volume*. College Park, MD: Urban Information Interpreters, 1975.

Urban Information Specialists. *Community Information Programs: Nine Proposals*. College Park, MD: Urban Information Interpreters, Inc., 1973.

Weibel, Kathleen. "The Evolution of Library Outreach 1960–1975 and Its Effect on Reader Services. Occasional Paper Number 16." Urbana-Champaign: University of Illinois Graduate School of Library Science, 1982.

Welbourne, James. "Statement Prepared for the Caucus of Black Librarians at the American Library Association's 89th Convention, Detroit 1970: A Black Position Paper on White Racism in Library Education, with particular reference to the black recruitment program at the School of Library and Information Services at the University of Maryland." Unpublished. School of Library and Information Services—Urban Information Specialist Program. Office of the Chancellor Records, Series 4.1, Special Collections, Hornbake Library, University of Maryland Libraries, College Park, MD

— — —. "Training Urban Information Specialists." In Kronus and Crowe, *Libraries and Neighborhood Information Centers*, 100–09.

— — —. *The Urban Information Specialist Program: First Year*. College Park, MD: University of Maryland School of Library and Information Services, 1971. http://files.eric.ed.gov/fulltext/ED051830.pdf

Wiegand, Wayne. "Tunnel Vision and Blind Spots: What the Past Tells Us About the Present." *The Library Quarterly*, 69, no. 1 (1999): 1–32.

Unbound: Recollections of Librarians During Martial Law in the Philippines

Iyra S. Buenrostro and Johann Frederick A. Cabbab

Documents and materials in libraries and archives are the backbone from which official and normative histories are established. The story of how these documents and materials are gathered in the case of a dictatorial regime, under which terror, censorship and widespread confiscation of subversive materials were commonplace, is particularly fascinating and instructive. In writing and understanding experiences as evidence where "seeing is the origin of knowing," the stories and recollections of individuals must gain attention, as these are the dimensions of human life that are often omitted or overlooked in conventional or official histories.[1]

The University of the Philippines Diliman Main Library is more than a repository of knowledge—it is a democratic space. The unassuming walls of this six-decade old building have been a sanctuary and stronghold for freedom and democracy. Listening to the recollections of librarians who worked at the University of the Philippines (UP) Diliman underscores the importance of experience as evidence of the past. Their stories of social involvement reveal how they silently served the country by saving it from oblivion.

---

1   Joan W. Scott, "The Evidence of Experience", *Critical Inquiry 17,* no. 4 (1991): 776.

The Downward Spiral

Ferdinand E. Marcos won the 1965 Presidential elections and served as the tenth president of the Republic of the Philippines. He duplicated this feat in 1969 for a second term amidst claims by political rivals of electoral fraud. By his side was his First Lady, Imelda R. Marcos. They are two of the main protagonists in the period of Philippine history that has been described as a Conjugal Dictatorship.[2] What followed Marcos' reelection plunged the country into crisis.

Prior to Marcos ascending to the presidency, the power and wealth in the Philippines were concentrated in about two dozen families and clans. Between them they owned 85% of the wealth of the country and wielded tremendous influence and sway with whoever was seated in power.[3] In the years they were in Malacañang,[4] Ferdinand and Imelda sought to destroy these families, and also blocked their ambitions of absolute power. They installed their own group of cronies who would be beholden only to them.[5] One indicator of this was that, in her numerous trips abroad, First Lady Imelda R. Marcos' notoriety as a social-climbing jetsetter from an impoverished country was slowly being established. The Philippines fell into debt, inflation rose signaling the increase in the prices of commodities, and the Philippine peso was devalued. By 1970, there were massive violent demonstrations, protests and strikes led by students in alliance with other sectors such as workers, peasants and the urban poor. They protested against graft and corruption in the government, regression of the economy, high oil prices, and the fraudulent re-election of Ferdinand Marcos. This period of unrest from January to March 1970 became known as the "First Quarter Storm".[6]

---

2   Primitivo Mijares, Marcos' official pressman, used the term "Conjugal Dictatorship" to describe how Ferdinand and Imelda Marcos ruled the country. For further reading, see Primitivo Mijares, *The Conjugal Dictatorship of Ferdinand and Imelda Marcos* (San Francisco: Union Square Pub., 1976).

3   Myles A. Garcia, Thirty Years Later... *Catching Up with the Marcos-Era Crimes* (Quezon City: MAG Publishing, 2016), 1–2.

4   The presidential palace located in Manila.

5   Myles A. Garcia, Thirty Years Later... *Catching Up with the Marcos-Era Crimes* (Quezon City: MAG Publishing, 2016), 1.

6   Jose F. Lacaba, *Days of Disquiet, Nights of Rage: The First Quarter Storm & Related Events* (Manila: Anvil Pub., 2003), xi–xxvi.

In a continuing act of defiance, students, faculty members and residents of the University of the Philippines Diliman, together with transport workers, staged an uprising and barricaded themselves inside the campus from February 1 to 9, 1971, to protest the increase in oil prices and for the removal of the military presence inside the university. This would be known as "The Diliman Commune." Later that year, on August 21, 1971, hand grenades were lobbed at the stage of the Plaza Miranda campaign rally of the Liberal Party (Marcos' political opposition). The bombing led to deaths and several injuries which included prominent politicians critical of the administration. The First Quarter Storm, the Diliman Commune, the Plaza Miranda Bombing and the rise of the communist movement were said to have triggered the declaration of martial rule or *Batas Militar* in the Philippines.[7]

In the Eye of the Storm

Rod was an activist and library student assistant in UP Tarlac during the First Quarter Storm. Being a student activist came with certain risks, one of which was being hunted down by the military. Rod was not spared from this, and his father told him not to return home to the province for his own safety and instead to find a place to hide. Rod relocated to Quezon City, where he found solace in kindred spirits at the University of the Philippines Diliman Main Library where he started to work as a library aide. Life in Diliman in 1971 wasn't pleasant, though. Rod settled in the Employee's' Village. Occasionally the residents would be rounded up by military forces in the middle of the night during a "*sona*," or police lineup, where suspected undesirables were picked out and detained for further questioning or even torture.[8]

Vyva was a librarian from the cataloging section of the Main Library. She was also a graduate student at the Institute of Library Science which was housed in the same building. She lived in Makati but stayed on cam-

---

7   For further discussion of this period, see Jose F. Lacaba, *Days of Disquiet, Nights of Rage: The First Quarter Storm & Related Events* (Manila: Anvil Pub., 2003). See also Nathan Gilbert Quimpo, "Watching the Storm," in *Subversive Lives: A Family Memoir of the Marcos Years*, eds. Susan F. Quimpo and Nathan Gilbert Quimpo (Mandaluyong City, Manila: Anvil Pub., 2012), 45–58.

8   The University of the Philippines, then and now, is a hotbed of militant activism in the Philippines. For further reading, see Bienvenido Lumbera et al., eds., *Serve the People: Ang Kasaysayan ng Radikal na Kilusan sa Unibersidad ng Pilipinas* (Quezon City: IBON Foundation, Inc., 2008).

pus during the week at the Sanggumay Dorm, a dormitory for female graduate students. On September 21, 1972, she attended a Freedom Party near Palma Hall. The event featured political songs, pocket rallies, vigils, and teach-ins. This was where the Diliman Republic made up of faculty, staff and students could congregate. A taxi driver, who was plying the university's main road, called out to them as they crossed the street. He shouted "Nag-declare na raw ng Martial Law! (There's a rumor that Martial Law has been declared!)" then sped off.

Vyva's brother picked her up by car the next morning. Traveling from Diliman to Makati would entail traversing EDSA (Epifanio de los Santos Avenue), Metro Manila's main thoroughfare. On the way home they encountered tanks and army jeeps on the road. An army jeep with horns blaring wanted to pass them but Vyva's brother wasn't immediately able to give way. A soldier on the jeep aimed his armalite rifle at them as a means of intimidation as they overtook their car.

Sally was an Administrative Officer of the library. On a midnight on one of the days leading up to the declaration of Martial Law, she heard the campus emergency siren. Then the military stormed the dorms on campus. They were there, ready, lurking in the shadows even before the official announcement came on national television. The cover of darkness at midnight was when they started patrolling and policing the streets of Diliman.

Rosalie trod up the steps of the library on her way to the *Filipiniana*[9] section where she worked. She passed by Sally who was assigned to Readers Services from time to time. Rosalie had availed of her allotted leaves on and off for the past couple of months due to a delicate pregnancy. Today was Monday, September 25, 1972, and as she walked up the steps, she noticed an eerie silence unusual for the lively campus of the State University. Today there were uncharacteristically few library patrons. There were no newspapers delivered to the front desk. Martial Law in the Philippines had already been declared.

Martial Law in the Philippines

Proclamation No. 1081 was the infamous presidential proclamation imposing Martial Law in the Philippines. It was dated September 21, 1972, though it was supposedly signed by then President Ferdinand E. Marcos

---

9   Materials, both published and unpublished, by or about the Philippines and Filipinos.

on the 17th. President Marcos himself formally announced Martial Law *(Batas Militar)* on the 23rd on live television at around eight in the evening.[10] The military was authorized to arrest personalities including journalists, political activists and militant students who were overtly against his administration. All public utilities were taken over by the government, supreme power was granted to the military, curfew and strict censorship were likewise implemented, and all types of media—from newspapers, magazines, student publications to mass media outfits—were either stringently controlled or closed down.[11] With the emergency powers granted to the president by the 1935 Constitution, President Marcos put the country under military rule and claimed that this act along with his own version of utopia—the *New Society*—would save the republic.[12] However, the supposed reform and democratic revolution led to thousands of human rights violations, marking the period of Martial Law from 1972 to 1981 and the years leading up to the EDSA People Power Revolution in 1986 as the darkest years of the country's recent history. According to Amnesty International, approximately 70,000 people were imprisoned, 34,000 were tortured, and 3,240 were killed during this period.[13] Appalling physical and psychological tortures were inflicted on victims in undisclosed detention

10   Based on President Marcos' diary dated September 14, 1972, on this day he already informed the military that he would proceed with the proclamation of Martial Law. Days before the public announcement of martial rule, opposition leader Sen. Benigno Aquino, Jr. exposed in his privilege speech the impending imposition of Martial Law as reported by his anonymous informant from a top-secret military plan called "Oplan Sagittarius." Primitivo Mijares, Marcos' former pressman, recounted that Marcos told a convention of historians that he signed the proclamation on September 17. Marcos was said to have strong numerological beliefs that he made September 21 the official date of the proclamation document, because 21 is divisible by 7—his lucky number. This "Marcos Style" to "shoot first, explain later" was common during his presidency. For further reading on Marcos' dictatorship, read Primitivo Mijares, *The Conjugal Dictatorship of Ferdinand and Imelda Marcos* (San Francisco: Union Square Pub., 1976).

11   "Infographic: The Day Marcos Declared Martial Law." Official Gazette, accessed November 20, 2016, http://www.gov.ph/featured/ infographic-day-marcos-declared-martial-law-september-23-1972/

12   Roberto T. Tiglao, "The Consolidation of the Dictatorship", in *Dictatorship and Revolution: Roots of People Power,* eds. Aurora Javate-De Dios, Petronilo BN. Daroy and Lorna Kalaw-Tirol (Manila: Conspectus, 1988), 26–69.

13   Michael Charleston B. Chua, "Tortyur: human rights violations during the Marcos regime," 2012, accessed November 1, 2016, https://bangkanixiao.files.wordpress. com/2012/10/chua-tortyur-human-rights-violations-during-the-marcos-regime.pdf.

centers or *safe houses*. They included electric shocks, beatings, water cures, Russian roulette, sexual assaults such as rape, and other forms of psychological and mental tortures.[14]

On January 17, 1981, President Marcos lifted Martial Law with the issuance of Proclamation No. 2045, but still remained as the country's absolute authority. The subsequent events, specifically the assassination of opposition leader Benigno Aquino, Jr. in 1983, the fraudulent outcome of the Snap Elections in 1986, and the withdrawal of support of Defense Secretary Juan Ponce Enrile and General Fidel Ramos for the Marcos government triggered the church and more people to step up against the dictatorial government. On February 22 to 25, 1986, the peaceful People Power Revolution, also known as the EDSA Revolution, ended the two-decade dictatorship. Corazon Aquino, widow of Senator Benigno Aquino, Jr., became the president and liberal democracy was reinstated.[15]

But the struggle for social justice did not stop there. The economy of the Philippines was left in shambles from the billions of debt and plundered wealth by the Marcoses. Issues of human rights violations were far from resolved. A Truth Commission could have helped in the healing and reconciliation process, but the Philippines was one of the few countries where a truth commission did not work in the face of its transition from a dictatorial to democratic regime.[16] The success of a truth commission is a reflection of "national will" and a "national commitment to fully understand and learn from the country's difficult, sometimes very controversial and often quite painful history."[17] Unfortunately, until now, no justice had been given to those who died and suffered under this oppressive regime. Not a single perpetrator has been prosecuted.

---

14 For a more graphic discussion of the torture methods used under the Marcos regime, see Don Kevin Hapal, "Worse than Death: Torture Methods During Martial Law," *Rappler*, February 23, 2016, accessed November 16, 2016, http://www.rappler.com/nation/121365-torture-martial-law-marcos-regime.

15 For the full chronology of events from 1968 to 1987, refer to Aurora Javate-De Dios, Petronilo BN. Daroy and Lorna Kalaw-Tirol, eds., *Dictatorship and Revolution: Roots of People Power* (Manila: Conspectus, 1988): 865–72.

16 Kenneth Christie, *The South African Truth Commission* (Basingstoke: Macmillan, 2000), 58.

17 Priscilla Hayner, "Truth Commissions: A Schematic Review", *International Review of the Red Cross* 88, 862 (2006): 296.

Fast forward to 2016. The recently concluded Philippine presidential elections, in which the late dictator's son Ferdinand "Bongbong" Marcos Jr. ran and lost for Vice-President, saw a lot of mud slung by social media campaign teams. The "troll" tactics and marketing strategies started with a lot of disinformation (deliberately providing wrong information), which eventually led to a lot of misinformation (providing wrong information) on all sides. This resulted in a portion of the population knowing that Martial Law existed and that atrocities had happened, and another portion that denied evils committed by the Martial Law men. Somewhere in the middle are those who are still uncertain of what happened during Martial Law. This is where librarians can help a divided nation. It could be done through the establishment and verification of the truth and the facts that support it. This can only be accomplished through a display of bravery and implicit activism.

Librarians and Silent Activism

Sally started out as an Administrative Officer of the UP Main Library before transitioning to library work. She recalls that besides Rod there were many other activist librarians in the UP Main Library during Martial Law. They came from different parts of the country: Bicol, Pampanga, etc. Some were part-time library assistants who had flexible working hours, which worked to the benefit of the activist movement, since military personnel could not pinpoint them as participants of mass actions based on work absences. Rod, though, laments (but does not regret) the time he went AWOL to attend one of these mass actions, as this led to him to be disqualified for monetary benefits given to university employees who served forty years. He also remembers how the declaration of Martial Law put a damper on Diliman activism and momentarily silenced the madding or maddening crowd. It depends on which side of the martial law fence one was on, either the maddening crowd was driving a Marcos insane or the madding crowd is being driven insane because of a Marcos. With Martial Law it was probably both.

The Coming of Change

The University of the Philippines is and will always be considered a microcosm of Philippine society. Housed within its walls are academics from different disciplines, from all parts of the country, from different racial and indigenous descents, and from all walks of life. Differences aside, this melting pot of the best minds that the country offers has always been guided by the spirit of Oneness, a "One University." Academics, who from day one have sworn their lives to serve the country and its people, and are guided by the principles of honor and excellence. The struggle of the country has also been the struggle on campus. Change came immediately during Martial Law. Terror, oppression, and intimidation came from the government, producing the people's fight for freedom and democracy.

"We have to clock in by eight o'clock in the morning and we had to adjust our travel times and leave from our homes earlier," narrates Rosalie. "We lived in Cubao and going to work took us so much time because all public and private vehicles were flagged down at the University Avenue entrance." Checkpoints had been set up there after the declaration of Martial Law. "The soldiers would board our buses and jeepneys for searches and checking of our IDs. It was scary." Sally adds, "even walking around was terrifying."[18]

"I don't know, personally I was never afraid for my life, but I was angry and frustrated. There's nothing else left to feel because your hands are tied," explains Vyva. "I joined some organizations where we talked about these things but we could only meet in small groups." She remembered what happened to her friends: "Some of my friends were arrested... and tortured... It's hard to describe, you feel it well up inside, the anger accumulates but at the same time you feel helpless..." Then she offers a sigh of past exasperation, "what can one person do?"[19]

"You have no idea who you can trust. It was a dictatorship. On the onset there will be peace and order, for those who aren't politicized that was all they saw, peace and order." Vyva then continues describing the then prevailing atmosphere in the library: "I would think in general, as to those who worked in the library at that time, there were no Judases. Though we all went about with our jobs with caution."[20]

Rosalie and Sally recall when then-University Librarian Marina Dayrit mulled over a mass leave of absence by the librarians. The building would be closed down, no one would report for duty, and there would be no service. "We already had leave forms," recalls Sally. "We did not want the library to be ransacked... and raided by outsiders and the military."

---

18   Interview with Rosalie B. Faderon, June 14, 2016.

19   Interview with Vyva Victoria M. Aguirre, June 14, 2016.

20   Interview with Vyva Victoria M. Aguirre, June 14, 2016.

The president of the university at that time, Salvador P. Lopez, intervened. He said, "go back to work, do not go on mass leave." The librarians complied, even if a lot of them dreaded the worst.[21] "The problem," Vyva pointed out, "was that the raids aren't always direct ones. There were moles in the university. If they find or see something they thought was subversive, like books and other printed materials, they reported it immediately to the military. Then the military comes."[22]

The University has always been a spawning ground for future leaders, with the campus dorms serving as jump-off points for activism. Vyva recalls advisories suggesting that dormers not keep leaflets and books in their rooms lest the dorms be raided. She recalls the incident when residents of the Sampaguita Residence Hall, the dorm for female upperclassmen, were on the receiving end of one of these raids and were flushed out with tear gas.[23] Sally remembers the effect this had on the residents of Sanggumay Residence Hall where one could literally hear papers being torn and flushed down the toilet.[24]

As the initial shock subsided, the situation started to escalate on campus and in the library. It started with the card catalogs, which weren't spared. "Ms. Dayrit asked that all the card catalogs be placed in the social science reading room and padlocked," narrates Sally. "There were people who were outsiders who infiltrated the campus and brought with them ink, purple ink. They would splash the ink on the catalog cards making them unreadable."[25]

Although the threat came in the form of terror and intimidation, this did not stop the librarians and members of the UP community from doing their duty to the country and future generations. Their commitment to providing service did not change; this meant they had to ensure that their current and future users were provided with the necessary tools to learn, which necessitated different forms of selection, acquisition, and dissemination.

---

21 Interview with Salvacion M. Arlante, June 21, 2016.

22 Interview with Vyva Victoria M. Aguirre, June 14, 2016.

23 Interview with Vyva Victoria M. Aguirre, June 14, 2016.

24 Interview with Salvacion M. Arlante, October 22, 2015.

25 Interview with Salvacion M. Arlante, October 22, 2015.

The Hidden Collection

"Everybody was surprised," says Rosalie, "a few weeks after, some faculty members… they had personal copies of papers… radical ones." She remembers faculty members from the political science, history and Filipino departments of the University, these were people that they knew. "They were so afraid that these will be discovered in their possession."[26] Fear led academics to dispose of their documents. Some buried them deep in the ground, others took them home to their residences.

Fortunately, many academics donated their materials to the library. "One of our library staff members, Valerio Nofuente, used to be with the Filipino Department before he transferred to the library. They would usually talk to him regarding depositing their materials," added Rod. "He was active and tireless in collecting these materials. I remember he was also a writer and married to one of our librarians."[27] The materials collected consisted of papers, folders, and even envelopes. In addition, Vyva recalls that the 1973 Constitutional Convention had no complete records because of the declaration of Martial Law and the delegates had taken their notes and records home with them. Some of these were eventually deposited with the librarians and the library ended up with a number of 1973 Constitutional Convention records made up of loose sheets. The library accepted these and other materials under the veil of secrecy.[28] Sally added that "these papers came from different sources like the *Hukbong Bayan Laban sa Hapon* (HUKBALAHAP or Nation's Army Against the Japanese Soldiers) led by Luis Taruc, the Communist Party of the Philippines (CPP), student organizations, *Samahan ng Demokratikong Kabataan* (SDK or Association of Democratic Youth), *Kabataang Makabayan* (KM or Nationalist Youth), etc. This is why we called them the Philippine Left Papers. Later on they became the Radical Papers."[29]

Personal papers were not the only targets during Martial Law. Library books were also on the hit list. "During those years I remember that books from shelves were confiscated because of censorship," related Vyva. "There were news stories that the military raided libraries and took

---

26   Interview with Rosalie B. Faderon, June 14, 2016.

27   Interview with Rodolfo Y. Tarlit, October 22, 2015.

28   Interview with Vyva Victoria M. Aguirre, June 14, 2016.

29   Interview with Salvacion M. Arlante, June 21, 2016.

down books that can be classified as subversive." Vyva remembers specific books such as Karl Marx's *Das Kapital* and *Quotations from Chairman Mao Tse-tung* (aka *The Little Red Book)* as some of those banned.[30] Sally adds that Clinton L. Rossiter's *Marxism: The View from America* as well as other books about Communism, Marxism, etc. were also banned.[31] "We just heard that there were some books here in the library that were considered 'censored'," narrates Rosalie. "The book *Philippine Society and Revolution* by Amado Guerrero," she says, referring to the nom de guerre of Jose Maria (Joma) Sison, founder of the Communist Party of the Philippines, "this was sort of revealing and critical of the existing government. It was removed from the reserve section."[32] Vyva adds, "that book by Jose Maria Sison was available anywhere before Martial Law. But when Martial Law was declared, copies became scarce since it was classified as subversive literature." Vyva remembers Ms. Dayrit's directive to pull out the subversive materials: "The library had the foresight of pulling out these materials from the open shelves and storing them in the stock room so that they would not be confiscated."[33] Sally recalls that they had to photocopy some books before storing the originals since some student leaders borrowed them.[34] By then the military had started raiding printing presses, and then the raids on newspapers came, so libraries were sure to be targeted next. "It was Martial Law, there were no announcements of government orders," says Vyva, "The military and police forces just swoop down on you. You have no idea of the law because there was no law."[35]

Another directive by University Librarian Marina Dayrit involved *"polyeto"*. These Martial Law handbills, leaflets and pamphlets were originally thought of as having fleeting usefulness but were deemed by the library to have future research, historical and institutional value. As activism spread, so did the handbills. They were left on tables in the library in the hopes that others would read them. Sally remembers individual sheets, and even tied bundles, being left in different places in the library. Some were even

---

30   Interview with Vyva Victoria M. Aguirre, June 14, 2016.

31   Interview with Salvacion M. Arlante, October 22, 2015.

32   Interview with Rosalie B. Faderon, June 14, 2016.

33   Interview with Vyva Victoria M. Aguirre, June 14, 2016.

34   Interview with Salvacion M. Arlante, June 21, 2016.

35   Interview with Vyva Victoria M. Aguirre, June 14, 2016.

sent by mail. No one knew where and who they came from. Ms. Dayrit instructed everyone to collect them all. The librarians took it one step further: when they saw one, they would pick it up and pocket it, even if it was in the trash. Rod remembers that Ms. Dayrit would instruct them to go to different places and collect these handbills. Ms. Dayrit would say, "go to *Mendiola*.[36] Go to that teach-in. Go to that gathering. Go to that demonstration."[37] On these expeditions it was suggested that they not wear white. When water cannons come into play, the dye mixed with the water would stain white shirts and make demonstrators readily identifiable.[38] The librarians would ask for copies of the handbills at these events. Students would hand them freshly printed ones or help them collect samples strewn on the streets. Being caught in possession of these handbills was dangerous and were grounds for incarceration, so most of the time the male library staff, which included Rod, were sent out to do the task. Being able to jump over gates and fences became a necessary skill to avoid capture. "Our collection processes were great," says Sally. "Even if it entailed us joining rallies and demonstrations and scavenging through trash just to get soiled materials. We took them back to the library and cleaned them up. It took a lot of effort, a lot of commitment."[39] The librarians recognized that these materials would be needed if someone was going to write about this period in Philippine history. They had to be stored somewhere, and the library then decided that they be collected under lock and key in the rare book section of the library.

The Problem with Accountability

Adding to and securing the collection was not the only problem for librarians. What was in the institution was relatively easy to address, but what was not in the library's possession was another matter. Library books on loan to faculty, staff and students which were considered banned were confiscated by the police and military. Sally recounts how she accompanied University President Lopez and University Librarian Dayrit to places like

---

36 An iconic street for mass actions and protests near the Malacañang Palace, the President's official residence.

37 Interview with Rodolfo Y. Tarlit, June 21, 2016.

38 Interview with Salvacion M. Arlante, June 21, 2016.

39 Interview with Salvacion M. Arlante, June 21, 2016.

the Quezon City Jail to bail out students. They were also there to retrieve books which were confiscated. "The books had 'UP Library' stamped on them," narrates Sally. "If we don't ask for them back we won't see them again. I think they burn them in one big pile at Camp Aguinaldo.[40]"[41]

Sally recalls a forum with Colonel Noe S. Andaya, the Chief of the Office for Community Relations of the Armed Forces of the Philippines, where they discussed the military's incursion into the University. She asked about what happened to the books confiscated from faculty members. "You see Colonel," she explained, "the books, if they are overdue, they are charged against the faculty members. But if they are not returned, the librarian is accountable for every single item because this is a government institution. We must request for relief from property accountability. How can we request for relief from property accountability if we cannot justify that the books were lost because they were confiscated by the military?"[42]

This was a big problem for librarians. "If you exceed the allowable excess of five percent of the size of the collection in losses," explains Sally, "it will be charged against your salary. That was the rule, and that was an agreement between the Commission on Audit (COA) and the library and the librarians. That is why no one wanted to be the head of a library if you'll have losses that exceed five percent. That's five percent! That's a big chunk of your retirement benefits." This was finally resolved upon the intervention of University President Lopez and the military. The Commission on Audit agreed to accept affidavits executed by the faculty, staff and students signifying that the books they borrowed were confiscated resulting in the librarians being relieved from property accountability.[43]

Till the End

Until the day Marcos was overthrown, the university remained the bed of activism. "The Metrocom[44] would charge forward," relates Rosalie. "The area spanning the Beta Way and the AS building was a battleground. All

---

40   Military headquarters of the Armed Forces of the Philippines (AFP).

41   Interview with Salvacion M. Arlante, October 22, 2015 and June 21, 2016.

42   Interview with Salvacion M. Arlante, June 21, 2016.

43   Interview with Salvacion M. Arlante, June 21, 2016.

44   Philippine Constabulary Metropolitan Command.

the benches and classroom chairs were fashioned into makeshift barricades. Pillboxes and molotov cocktails were the explosive of choice. I remember (eminent physicist and former Diliman Chancellor) Dr. Roger Posadas on the rooftops throwing pillboxes."[45] Sally adds, "yes, I remember they asked us to donate our pantyhoses in order for them to manufacture molotov."[46] Despite that library services remained regular until 1986 during the EDSA Revolution. "There were many rallies and classes were always suspended," Rosalie recalls, she had already taken up teaching duties at the Institute of Library Science at that time. "The administration had to take steps to salvage the semester. Students got 'P' or pass, no numerical marks. Quite problematic for those running for honors."[47]

"What do we do now?" Sally asked rhetorically. With a wave of her hand she answered her own question, "so we started. We looked at the inventory of what we collected and thought of what needs to be done. We were trying to get some funds already. We wondered if we have enough to come out with a microfilm index. So we started microfilming, but we couldn't do more, so we get funds."[48] She notes that researchers do ask for this collection. She ends with the thought that maybe other institutions be given duplicate copies in case what the library has is lost or damaged.[49]

Martial Law is described in recent history as the period when this freedom of information was missing. "We cannot have freedom of information under a dictatorship," relates Vyva, "The purpose of freedom of information is transparency, right? But how do you expect a dictatorship to be transparent? There were no copies of documents during Martial Law. We couldn't provide copies to researchers asking us for presidential decrees and Malacañang records. Plus, there were a lot of laws that were confidential." She further elaborates, "we always hear 'ignorance of the law excuses no one from compliance therewith.' But how can you comply with a law that is confidential? As a librarian and even as a lawyer, I really think censorship is a very negative thing. There's a purpose for transparency, it prevents corruption. It prevents your own government from stealing from you,

---

45　Interview with Rosalie B. Faderon, June 14, 2016.

46　Interview with Salvacion M. Arlante, October 22, 2015.

47　Interview with Rosalie B. Faderon, June 14, 2016.

48　In collaboration with Cornell University and the University of Wisconsin, these papers were organized, indexed and microfilmed in 1996.

49　Interview with Salvacion M. Arlante, June 21, 2016.

or even killing people, etc. But if you have a dictatorship… No, you have none of that, you have nothing."

"Our library is a repository of history," Vyva continues. "If you're not brave or courageous enough as a librarian to preserve this as much as possible, then there will come a time when people won't know about the truth." She ends by retelling a quote from Mahatma Gandhi: "Freedom is so ingrained in our consciousness that not even a repressive government will be able to curtail that freedom. Like they say, 'you can imprison my body but you cannot imprison my mind.'"[50]

A New Day

The historic EDSA People Power in 1986 that deposed the dictator and his family from their seat of power was a new beginning—a turning point for the Philippines in reclaiming democracy. This new beginning was filled with promises, expectations as well as uncertainty. The restoration of democracy was not an easy feat. Being left with a disintegrated economy and the death of a generation of brilliant young minds who could have been the future leaders of the country, the Philippines seemed to have never recovered from the aftermath of the Marcos regime. At present, the Filipinos have divided views towards this period of Philippine history. Some would argue that it would be better to simply move on and focus on the present circumstances. Some would straightforwardly disagree as they recurrently call for justice and reparations for the victims, and fervently campaign for social justice. For the librarians of the University of the Philippines Diliman, it appears that they recognize both. They see the importance of moving on from the nation's wounded past but this could not be done without collective healing and understanding of what transpired during the Martial Law years.

The stories recounted by the librarians of UP Diliman illustrate the transformative role of librarians in making the library a space not only for gathering materials but also for future historical inquiries and truth-seeking initiatives. The audacity of librarians amidst the reign of terror helped save a portion of history that could have been lost and totally forgotten. In a situation where all were living in fear, the librarians had the foresight of what should be done, remembered and understood by the future genera-

---

50   Interview with Vyva Victoria M. Aguirre, June 14, 2016.

tions. The librarians extended their responsibilities beyond the walls of the library and put themselves in danger just to keep and collect these materials that would later be useful in uncovering slivers of reality of the country's recent dark past. While it is true that it is impossible to construct a complete memory of the past, what the librarians did decades ago was a preparation for the future—the day when people's hands are not tied anymore as they speak and stand up freely for their freedom and their rights. When narratives in the pages of history have come unbound, someone has to piece them back together.

All the librarian respondents for this chapter have now retired from the University. Besides working at the UP Main Library, they became professors who served as full-time faculty and senior lecturers at the University of the Philippines School of Library and Information Studies (formerly the Institute of Library and Information Science and, before that, the Institute of Library Science). Prof. Rosalie B. Faderon became Dean of the School of Library and Information Studies before retiring. Prof. Vyva Victoria M. Aguirre also became Dean of the School of Library and Information Studies. She served as Commissioner of the Presidential Commission on Good Government, an agency created to recover the Marcos' ill-gotten wealth, under Chairperson Haydee Yorac. She is also a lawyer, law professor and Thesis and Program Coordinator at the De La Salle University College of Law. Prof. Rodolfo Y. Tarlit, a member of the Board of Trustees of the Martial Law Memorial Commission, became the University Librarian of the University of the Philippines Library System before retiring. Prof. Salvacion M. Arlante also became the University Librarian of the University of the Philippines Library System. She is currently the Library Department Head and Programme Head of the LIS Department of the School of Education, Liberal Arts, Music, and Social Work of Centro Escolar University, Manila.

Works Cited

Christie, Kenneth. *The South African Truth Commission. Basingtoke: Macmillan*, 2000.

Chua, Michael Charleston B. "Tortyur: Human Rights Violations during the Marcos Regime." 2012. https://bangkanixiao.files.wordpress.com/2012/10/chua- tortyur-human-rights-violations-during-the-marcos-regime.pdf (accessed November 1, 2016).

Garcia, Myles A. *Thirty Years Later... Catching Up with the Marcos-Era Crimes.* Quezon City: MAG Publishing, 2016.

Hapal, Don Kevin. "Worse than Death: Torture Methods During Martial Law." *Rappler,* February 23, 2016. http://www.rappler.com/nation/121365-torture-martial-law-marcos-regime (accessed November 16, 2016).

Hayner, Priscilla. "Truth Commissions: A Schematic Review." *International Review of the Red Cross* 88, no. 862 (2006): 295–310.

Javate-De Dios, Aurora , Daroy, Petronilo BN., and Kalaw-Tirol, Lorna, eds., *Dictatorship and Revolution: Roots of People Power.* Manila: Conspectus, 1988.

Lumbera, Bienvenido, Taguiwalo, Judy, Tolentino, Rolando, Guillermo, Ramon, and Alamon Arnold, eds. *Serve the People: Ang Kasaysayan ng Radikal na Kilusan sa Unibersidad ng Pilipinas.* Quezon City: IBON Foundation, Inc., 2008.

Lacaba, Jose F. *Days of Disquiet, Nights of Rage: The First Quarter Storm & Related Events.* Manila: Anvil Pub., 2012.

Mijares, Primitivo. *The Conjugal Dictatorship of Ferdinand and Imelda Marcos.* San Francisco: Union Square Pub., 1976.

Official Gazette. "Infographic: The Day Marcos Declared Martial Law." http://www.gov.ph/featured/infographic-day-marcos-declared-martial-law-september-23-1972/ (accessed November 20, 2016).

Quimpo, Nathan Gilbert. "Watching the Storm." In *Subversive Lives: A Family Memoir of the Marcos Years*, edited by Susan F. Quimpo and Nathan Gilbert Quimpo. Manila: Anvil Pub., 2012.

Scott, Joan W. "The Evidence of Experience." *Critical Inquiry* 17, no. 4 (1991): 773–97.

Tiglao, Roberto T. "The Consolidation of the Dictatorship." In *Dictatorship and Revolution: Roots of People Power,* edited by Aurora Javate-De Dios, Petronilo BN. Daroy and Lorna Kalaw-Tirol, 26–69. Manila: Conspectus, 1988.

"I Did What I Was Told to Do": Ukrainian Reference Librarianship and Responding to Volatile Expectations

Megan Browndorf

On October 29, 2015, Russian authorities placed Natalya Sharina, the head of the Library of Ukrainian Literature in Moscow, under house arrest and accused her inciting ethnic hatred against Russians.[1] In December the Russian Investigations Committee searched two other homes of library employees.[2] In March 2017, Moscow closed the library and marked the collection for a new center of Slavonic culture. Moscow says that "there was no political element" to the library's situation, but Sharina's legal team claims political motivation. Amnesty International has designated Sharina a "prisoner of conscience."[3] In June 2017, a judge found Sharina guilty of extremism, and an added charge of embezzlement, and sentenced her to

---

1 Nadia Beard, "Natalia Sharina: Russian Police Detain Ukrainian Library Director for 'Inciting Ethnic Hatred'," *The Indepenedent,* October 29, 2015, http://www.independent. co.uk/news/world/europe/natalia-sharina-russian-police-detain-ukrainian-library-director-for-inciting-ethnic-hatred-a6714011.html.

2 "Russian Investigators Search Homes of Ukrainian Library Staff," *BBC Monitoring Former Soviet Union–Political,* December 14, 2015.

3 Andrew Osborn, "Disappearing Books: How Russia is Shuttering its Ukrainian library," *Reuters,* March 15, 2017, http://www.reuters.com/article/ us-ukraine-crisis-russia-library-idUSKBN16M0PW.

four years in prison—which her lawyer stated he would appeal, up to the European Court of Human Rights, if necessary.[4]

Whether or not this particular instance of tension between Russia and Ukraine is politically motivated, it represents the politicized nature of the library. Every resource a reference librarian collects, shares, and suggests to library users, in a politically charged context, has the potential to become—wittingly or unwittingly—a political act. Using the case of Ukrainian libraries in World War II, this chapter focuses on the unwitting element of political acts in reference librarianship. How does reference librarianship operate in an environment where the definition of "justice" is unclear and professional expectations change drastically and quickly? This question is particularly pertinent in totalitarian environments where the government reaction to any action is often, as Hannah Arendt argues, purposefully arbitrary.[5]

The collections that librarians were charged to protect and the relationships they built with patrons were artificial and problematic in the first place. But the destruction of these collections and relationships under the Nazis were also problematic. The argument of this chapter is that in the face of injustice in the library context, a simply defined and just response does not always exist. Beyond following orders, neither support of the Communists nor support of the Nazis was inherently just or the right response for Ukrainian librarians. Indeed as was Sharina's experience, any response was the wrong response and complicated any moralism that one could attach to most actions.

Flux defined Ukraine before, during, and after World War II. Millions of people were caught in this flux, among them reference librarians. Some of the librarians most affected by this were those working in the public scientific libraries, developed in the years leading up to the war by the Soviet state to be centers of scholarship for the masses. These were most often women, often without professional training, instead learning their trade through experience and political education. The flux of the period left these reference librarians to navigate ambiguous choices in an effort to balance personal morality, professional practice, and the effects of Soviet and Nazi power.

---

4   Andrew Osborn, "Head of Moscow's Ukrainian Library Convicted of Incitement Against Russians," *Reuters,* June 5, 2017, http://www.reuters.com/article/us-ukraine-crisis-russia-library-idUSKBN18W12T.

5   Hannah Arendt, *Origins of Totalitarianism* (New York: Houghton Mifflin Harcourt, 1973): 451–61.

While there is a significant personal element to these decisions, this chapter instead focuses on the environment in which these decisions had to be made. This chapter considers the expectations placed upon reference librarians and the opportunities open to them, and is based primarily on official documents with some supporting insights from librarians and library users. Although I make some effort to discuss the personal implications of this environment, it is the environment of the impossible situation that the history and documents allow me to discuss. This research has been developed from analysis of official Soviet documents, both from Moscow and the Ukrainian Soviet Socialist Republic, documents from the Vernadskii library in Kyiv and the library in Kharkiv, and interviews from the Harvard's Soviet Social System Interview Project.[6] These sources are limited to the official expectations for libraries throughout Ukraine's system, the two largest libraries at the time, and individuals who emigrated to the United States. Because this chapter grew out of research on the official narrative in the post-war recovery in Ukraine, the most significant absences are that of smaller libraries and personal insights from librarians and patrons, which I hope to be able to study in the future.

The chapter is divided into three parts. The first section provides the context of Ukrainian and Soviet library history. The next sections consider the periods before, during, and after WWII and the interactions among Soviet, Nazi, and local forces. The last section uses the case study of Ukrainian libraries during World War II to complicate "justice" in an environment where power is fluid.

The Ukrainian Soviet Library: The Environment Before the War

To understand Ukraine during this period, knowledge of changes in geography and nationality relations are essential. The Ukrainian People's Republic was formed in 1917 in the aftermath of World War I during the early years of the Russian Civil War. It included most of what is modern Ukraine, with the exception of Galicia, where L'viv is located, in the

---

6   From the Harvard Project on the Soviet Social System Website: "The digital collection consists chiefly of summary transcripts of 705 interviews conducted with refugees from the USSR during the early years of the Cold War. A unique source for the study of Soviet society between 1917 and the mid-1940s, the HPSSS includes vast amounts of one-of-a-kind data on political, economic, social and cultural conditions." http://hcl.harvard.edu/collections/hpsss/index.html.

West. In 1921, nearing the end of the Civil War, the contested territories of the non-functioning Ukrainian People's Republic were divided among newly forming states. The Eastern portion was subsumed into the Soviet Union as the Ukrainian Soviet Socialist Republic, Volhynia in the West went to Poland (and Galicia remained with Poland) and Bukovina in the South went to Romania. It was not until 1939, through the Molotov-Ribbentrop agreement, that Galicia and Volhynia joined the Ukrainian Soviet Socialist Republic and then, in 1940, the Soviet Union annexed what is now Ukrainian Bukovina.

While the entirety of the Ukrainian Soviet Socialist Republic had diverse populations, Galicia, Volhynia, and Bukovina had uniquely significant non-Ukrainian populations. For example, in the final Romanian census of Romania-controlled Ukraine in 1930, the Ukrainian majority stood at only 32%. Meanwhile, 62% of the population was split among Romanians (28.5%), Russians (12.8%), Bulgarians (11.1%) and Jews (8.4%).[7] L'viv in Galicia had long been a center of Polish intellectual culture and had a diverse population that sat at 16% Ukrainian at the close of the war.[8] While these territories had long been ethnically diverse, this was largely an effect of interwar Romanianization in Bukovina and Polonization in Galicia and Volhynia.[9] In the Ukrainian Soviet Socialist Republic, there had first been intense Ukrainization and then under Stalin, Russianization.

In this geographic flux, and through the often violent changes of nationality relationships in Soviet Ukraine, libraries played an instrumental role. Lenin's wife, the librarian Nadezhda Krupskaia, pushed libraries as "the most economical means of bringing the book to the masses."[10] During the early days of the Soviet Union, the Extraordinary Commission for the Liquidation of Illiteracy (*Cheka Likbez*) set up libraries, reading rooms, and bookmobiles throughout Russia, Ukraine and the Soviet republics.[11]

---

7   Piotr Eberhardt, *Ethnic Groups and Population Changes in Twentieth-Century Central-Eastern Europe,* trans. Jan Owsinski (New York: M.E. Sharpe, 2003): 214.

8   William Jay Risch, *The Ukrainian West: Culture and the Fate of Empire in Soviet Lviv* (Boston: Harvard University Press, 2011): 31.

9   George Shevelov, *The Ukrainian Language in the First Half of the Twentieth Century (1900–1941): Its State and Status* (Boston: Harvard University Press, 1989): 175–99.

10   Quoted in Boris Raymond, *Krupskaia and Soviet Russian Librarianship, 1917–1939* (Metuchen, NJ: Scarecrow Press, 1979): 46.

11   Charles E. Clark, *Uprooting Otherness: The Literacy Campaign in NEP-Era Russia* (Selinsgrove: Susquehanna University Press, 2000): 117.

The liquidation of private libraries and the installation of those collections in public libraries and universities played both the practical role of quickly growing Soviet libraries, pulling them under centralized control, and the symbolic role of asserting the collective ownership of the once noble classes' property.[12] The library was a means through which to quickly and efficiently improve literacy, class-consciousness, and industrial and agricultural productivity.[13]

Libraries also served as tools of cultural education and control. The *Glavpolitprosvit*[14] sent lists to libraries of materials deemed appropriate and of those materials which needed to be protected or culled from the collection and sent to central libraries. The practice of censorship was a significant and expected part of librarianship throughout the Soviet period, particularly so under Stalin. Communist cultural commissions required libraries to actively work toward "the cultural growth of the worker and farmer and [toward] addressing the question of socialist reconstruction of the economy."[15] This meant censorship and reader education in the form of literary evenings and readers' advisory. One librarian from Kharkov, who eventually emigrated from Ukraine to the United States, described the organizational structure of her work as "control at every point."[16]

In Ukraine, nationality politics further complicated this element of reader education and control. Throughout the development of the library system, libraries supported Ukrainian literature and language collections as part of a broader policy of Ukrainization. The goal was to educate a largely illiterate, mostly Ukrainian-speaking, populace and endear them to Marxism-Leninism and the Soviet system.[17] Under Stalin, in the 1930s,

12 Liubov Andreevna Dubrovina and Oleksii Semenovych Onyshchenko, *Bibliotechna sprava v Ukraini v XX stolitti* (Kyiv: NAN Ukrainy, 2009): 119.

13 Clark, *Uprooting Otherness*: 34, 125–26.

14 This is the "Committee on Enlightenment" which bore the responsibility for library considerations and policies.

15 "Postanovlenie TsK VKP(b) 'Ob uluchshenii bibliotechnoi raboty,'" October 30, 1929, in Kniga i Knizhnoe Delo 1917–1941: 257–58.

16 Harvard Project on the Soviet Social System, Schedule A, Vol. 31, Case 306/(NY)1106, http://nrs.harvard.edu/urn-3:FHCL:962276, accessed August 8, 2017.

17 Raymond, *Krupskaia and Soviet Russian Librarianship*: 168; Maria Haigh, "Making Ukrainians in the Library: Language, Libraries, and National Identity," *The Canadian Journal of Information and Library Science* 33, no. 3/4 (2009): 148; Matthew Pauly, *Breaking the Tongue* (Toronto: University of Toronto, 2015): 5.

this policy reversed quickly and sharply toward a policy of Russification.[18] Successful collectivization rendered concessions to Ukrainian language and culture unnecessary and all central administration of the state and intellectual culture happened in Russian.[19] Stalin purged supporters of the Ukrainization policy at all levels. In 1939 Western Ukraine was partitioned off from Poland and came under Soviet jurisdiction through the Molotov-Ribbentropp pact. Quickly, through the end of 1939 and 1940, the *Glavpolitprosvit* integrated collections and libraries from these regions into the larger Soviet system. All known private libraries were collectivized. Eastern Ukraine and Russia sent politically appropriate material in Russian and Ukrainian to these libraries to reshape the collections from their largely Polish holdings.[20] Foreign language collections became centralized in newly formed large institutions such as the new Lviv National Scientific Library (named for Vasyl Stefanyk). The Ossolineum in L'viv, a center of Polish letters and one of the largest collections of Polish language materials, was absorbed into what would become the Vasyl Stefanyk Lviv National Scientific Library of Ukraine (Stefanyka).[21]

The Occupied Ukrainian Library

Under Soviet rule, the library was still intended to serve the needs of the reader, but only when the needs of the reader aligned with those that the

---

18 This change toward Russification was widespread throughout the Soviet Union under Stalin. In the early Soviet period, *korenizatsiia* ("rooting" or "indigenization") prioritized national consciousness among the various Soviet nationalities, particularly in places—such as Ukraine—that had long been ethnically diverse. In the mid 1930s Stalin purged much of the proponents of *korenizatsiia* throughout the Soviet Union and Russian language and culture became the "first among equals." See Terry Martin, *Affirmative Action Empire* (Ithaca: Cornell University Press, 2001) for more about nationalities policy during this period.

19 Martin, *Affirmative Action Empire:* 352–67.

20 "Iz otcheta l'vovskogo obkoma KP(b)U na pervoi oblastnoi partkonferentsii—o rabote bibliotek," April 23 1940, in Kniga i knizhnoe delo 1917–1941: 409. "Iz spravki komiteta po delam kul'turno-prosvetitel'nykh uchrezhdenii pri sovete ministrov USSR o rabote kul'turno-prosvetitel'nykh uchrezhdenii v zapadnykh oblastiakh USSR—o rabote bibliotek," December 9, 1949, in Kniga i Knizhnoe Delo 1941–1984: 96.

21 Tarik Cyril Amar, *The Paradox of Ukrainian Lviv: A Borderland City between Stalinists, Nazis, and Nationalists* (Ithaca: Cornell University Press, 2015): 71.

state determined. Some reference librarians did find ways to help readers navigate politically difficult instances. One user described a librarian in Kyiv giving them a pre-revolutionary history book for their work to use without signing for the material.[22] Another stated that some researchers acquired lists of unfavorable materials from librarians they knew well. The sharing of these lists, which were supposed to remain confidential, could allow an individual to navigate a continually shifting canon of acceptable literature.[23] Still, as early as the 1920s, the ideological reality of the librarian was that of a "worker for the masses" who was "responsible before the Party and the proletarian state for all his work, for every book given out ."[24] "Counterrevolutionary sabotage" had been recorded in 1929 in libraries at Dnepropetrovsk, Kharkiv, and Odessa.[25] However, it would be easier to not follow directives in regard to shaping the library outside of large cities and libraries such as the ones in Kharkiv and Kyiv as most objectionable material had been sent to the larger libraries during centralization.

Collections and access during the Soviet period, before Nazi occupation in Ukraine, served the needs and desires of the state and party. Professional dissent within the library was not an option as the entire purpose of the library was to serve the needs of the state. The role of reference librarians was to serve as arms of political education. While not all were party members, each library employed party members to ensure allegiance and professional advancement was not possible without party membership.[26]

For the Nazis, however, libraries were not an instrument of educational control since Germany deemed any education of the population in Eastern Europe, particularly for Slavs, unnecessary. The Reich Minister for the Eastern Occupied Territories, Alfred Rosenberg, divided the library materials into three groups—valuable materials to be sent back to Germany, Western European language literature to remain in collections, and material to be

---

22 Harvard Project on the Soviet Social System, Schedule A, Vol. 2, Case 11 (interviewer J.R. Type A3), http://nrs.harvard.edu/urn-3:FHCL:939734: 33 (accessed August 8, 2017).

23 Harvard Project on the Soviet Social System, Schedule A, Vol. 31, Case 306/(NY)1106, http://nrs.harvard.edu/urn-3:FHCL:962276, accessed August 8, 2017: 11.

24 Evgeny Dobrenko, *The Making of the State Reader: Social and Aesthetic Origins of Soviet Literary Culture* (Berkeley: Stanford University Press, 1997): 233.

25 Ibid., 232.

26 Harvard Project on the Soviet Social System, Schedule A, Vol. 31, Case 306/(NY)1106, http://nrs.harvard.edu/urn-3:FHCL:962276, accessed August 8, 2017: 18.

destroyed. Specifically earmarked for destruction were Ukrainian and Russian Soviet imprints, Marxist, "Bolshevist," Jewish, and agitprop materials.[27]

Those librarians who had not evacuated were integral to these efforts. The aforementioned librarian from Kharkiv had been left behind to take care of the library. She described her work: "Every day I got the keys from the German commandant and every evening I brought them back to him. I did what I was told to do."[28] Just as in the Soviet period, the room for protest or any efforts to undermine Nazi efforts was minimal. Furthermore, what a "just" protest could look like for these librarians was complex as was the response to the Nazi invasion itself among Ukrainians. Some greeted the Nazis as liberators. Some saw the Nazis as a potentially instrumental way to regain autonomy. Some simply bemoaned the destruction of their life's work.[29] One librarian, another from the Kharkiv library, protested the Nazis' final burning of books on a bridge in the city before they retreated and was told that it "wasn't her concern" and to "go home."[30] In Kyiv's libraries, librarians, mostly women, performed the physical labor of consolidating remaining collections at a single point and the "classics of Marxism-Leninism" were burned for warmth.[31]

The Unoccupied Soviet Ukrainian Library

This book examines the intersection of justice and reference librarianship. I use the case of the reference librarian in occupied Ukraine to illustrate that justice is not simply an act of socially informed decision making. Did the

---

27 "Rozporiadzhennia Shtandortkomendatruy Kharkova Shhodo 'chistki bibliotek' robochoiu hrupoiu pid kerivyntstvom shtabu Rozenberha," September 10, 1942, in Bibliotechni fondi Kharkova v roki druhoi svitovoi viiny: dolia kul'turnyx skarbiv ukrainy pid chas druhoi svitovoi viiny arkhivy, biblioteky, muzei: (Kyiv: Povernuti imena, 1997): 46–7.

28 Harvard Project on the Soviet Social System, Schedule A, Vol. 31, Case 306/(NY)1106, http://nrs.harvard.edu/urn-3:FHCL:962276: 3 (accessed August 8, 2017).

29 Liubov Andreevna Dubrovina and Oleksii Semenovych Onishchenko, *Istoriia natsional'noi biblioteky ukrainy imeni V.I. Vernads'koho: 1941–1964* (Kyiv: Naukova Dumka, 2003): 65.

30 *Bibliotechni fondi Kharkova v roki druhoi svitovoi viiny: dolia kul'turnyx skarbiv ukrainy pid chas druhoi svitovoi viiny arkhivy, biblioteky, muzei* (Kyiv: Povernuti imena, 1997): 97

31 Karel Berkhoff, *Harvest of Despair: Life and Death in Ukraine Under Nazi Rule* (Boston: Harvard University Press, 2008): 158.

reference librarian who destroyed propagandistic volumes under the Nazis perform a dissident act against the Soviet state? Did the reference librarian who saved volumes from destruction fight against the Nazi cultural policies? Anger at the Soviet state—anger which was anti-communist, anti-Soviet, and/or anti-Russian in nature—and anti-Semitism both played roles in some of the reactions to Nazi occupation in the Ukrainian libraries, as it did in the whole of Ukraine. Still librarians mostly "did what [they were] told to do."

That said, as part of a general Soviet distrust of Ukraine, the Soviet state cast suspicion on all librarians who had worked with the Nazis. The Kharkiv librarian, who emigrated to the United States, left Ukraine as the Germans did specifically because an NKVD[32] man had come by and made clear that she would be targeted after the Soviet army returned.[33] A part of the reaction against librarians who had stayed and survived the occupation was based on what the Soviets perceived as lackluster stewardship of the collections.[34] However, another part was because the reference librarian in particular played the role of propaganda intermediary. Their work was to lead library users to the correct literature and thus was inherently political.[35] Librarians were to know the accepted political culture and through reference interactions share that line. The Soviet Union under Stalin did not trust those Ukrainian librarians who had worked with the Germans with that duty.

In response to this distrust, the Soviet Union tightened control over library practice and education throughout Ukraine. What was truly a restructuring in order to more closely control collections and the operations of librarians—reference and otherwise—was passed off as a rebuilding

---

32   The NKVD (*Narodnyi Komissariat Vnutrennikh Del*) was the Soviet secret police organ from 1934–1946 and was the primary means through which the purges in the 1930s occurred.

33   Harvard Project on the Soviet Social System, Schedule A, Vol. 31, Case 306/(NY)1106, http://nrs.harvard.edu/urn-3:FHCL:962276: 5 (accessed August 8, 2017).

34   "Prikaz komiteta po delam kul'turno-prosvetitel'nykh uchrezhdenii pri sovnarkome USSR," May 16, 1945, in *Kniga i Kniznoe Delo 1941–1984*: 31.

35   Harvard Project on the Soviet Social System, Schedule A, Vol. 31, Case 306/(NY)1106, http://nrs.harvard.edu/urn-3:FHCL:962276: 34 (accessed August 8, 2017).

back to a pre-war state, especially in Western Ukraine.[36] Education became paramount as a way of increasing control over librarians in Ukraine. Although the calls for better education mentioned the techniques and tools of librarianship, it was the political education that was key. The Soviet Union solidified a hierarchical structure of responsibility, which made librarians at town libraries subordinate to regional libraries and then subordinate to the central library in Kyiv.[37]

Libraries and the Possibilities and Impossibilities of Justice

In the Soviet Union under Stalinism, a reference librarian would risk livelihood and even life by taking actions that supported a vision of justice that differed from Soviet power. These actions occurred, but they had to be small and personal or otherwise were exceedingly difficult. Reference librarians had to serve as one of the many faces of censorship in the Soviet Union. When the Nazis occupied Ukraine, these librarians did what they had always done—culled the collections according to orders. But when the Soviet Union returned to Ukraine and the work of reestablishing control over the libraries began, Soviet power decided that collaboration with the Nazis was equal to dissent. Regardless of any feelings of justice or injustice, librarians did not decide what actions the state would read as in support or against the state's interests. Thus the environment made even the action of existing complex.

I began this chapter with the story of the Ukrainian Literature Library in Moscow because it illustrates an important trend in libraries historically operating with Ukrainian collections in Russia and the Soviet Union. The mere act of attempting to operate can be read as a statement by power, even when it is not intended to be an active support of "justice." The work of the reference librarian in an autocratic environment can unwittingly support the struggle against injustice or wittingly support injustice simply through how their work is read by power.

However, I want to end this chapter by highlighting the purposeful decisions that Ukrainian librarians continue to make to support what

---

36 Margaret A. Browndorf, "World War II and the Building of the Ukrainian Library," in *Libraries: Traditions and Innovations: Papers from the Library History Seminar XIII,* eds. Melanie A. Kimball & Katherine Wisser (Boston: De Gruyter Saur, 2017): 108–23.

37 Dubrovina and Onyshchenko, *Bibliotechna sprava v Ukraini v XX stolitti* (Kyiv: NAN Ukrainy, 2009): 119.

they see as the correct decision for their communities. Among many community supports, a few protesters set up a library in the middle of 2014's Euromaidan protests as a learning space with donated books, where Kyiv librarians volunteered.[38] Librarians opened the doors of the National Parliamentary Library in Kyiv as a clinic referred to as "Medical Point One" in the midst of the violence.[39] There was room for these librarians to act in a way that they believed supported the just approach, and they did so.

Chances for librarians to make decisions to support justice exist and librarians do take advantage of them. However, what the fight looks like, when it happens, and whether or not a librarian is engaged in that fight is not always under their control. The conscious actions of these librarians during the Euromaidan protests can be contrasted with the "extremism" ascribed to Natalya Sharina at the beginning of this chapter. Both were read as support of Ukrainian autonomy from Russia—intent was, and for Sharina, remains, irrelevant. The totalitarian obsession with dissent can mean that actions are unintentionally in support or in contest of power. While plenty of self-defined dissidents existed in Ukraine through World War II and following, the Soviet Union was the determining factor of what was and was not a dissenting act, in libraries as in the rest of the country.

The story of reference librarianship before, during, and after the Nazi occupation of Ukraine was one of constantly changing expectations, which made any successful active measures toward "justice" nearly impossible. Under the occupation, librarians had the choice of standing up to the Nazis in order to support collections they themselves may not even completely have valued or to destroy their own collections. Regardless of the decisions they made at that point, the reference librarian's role as intermediary meant the Glavpolitprosvit wanted complete certainty over their loyalty. Volatility of expectations proscribed the choices of the reference librarians during this period, and as such significantly proscribed any conscious anti-authoritarian activism that may have been possible.

---

38   Jim Heintz, "Ukraine Protest Library a Break From the Tensions," *Associated Press,* February 10, 2014, https://www.yahoo.com/news/ukraine-protest-library-break-tensions-110813394.html; Anna Chebotariova, "Voices of Resistance and Hope: On the Motivations and Expectations of Euromaidaners," in *Ukraine's Euromaidan: Analyses of a Civil Revolution,* ed. David R. Marples and Frederick V. Mills (Stuttgart: ibidem-Verlag, 2015): 169.

39   Jack Stubbs, "Kiev Protestors Shun State Hospitals for Volunteer Clinics," *Reuters,* January 27, 2014, http://www.reuters.com/article/ukraine-medics-idUSL5N0L10ZC20140127.

Works Cited

Amar, Tarik Cyril. *The Paradox of Ukrainian Lviv: A Borderland City Between Stalinists, Nazis, and Nationalists.* Ithaca: Cornell University Press, 2015.

Arendt, Hannah. *Origins of Totalitarianism.* New York: Houghton Mifflin Harcourt, 1973.

Beard, Nadia. "Natalia Sharina: Russian Police Detain Ukrainian Library Director for 'Inciting Ethnic Hatred'." *The Independent.* October 29, 2015. Retrieved from http://www.independent.co.uk/news/world/europe/natalia-sharina-russian-police-detain-ukrainian-library-director-for-inciting-ethnic-hatred-a6714011.html.

Berkhoff, Karel. *Harvest of Despair: Life and Death in Ukraine Under Nazi Rule.* Boston: Harvard University Press, 2008.

Bibliotechni fondi Kharkova v roki druhoi svitovoi viiny: dolia kul'turnyx skarbiv ukrainy pid chas druhoi svitovoi viiny arkhivy, biblioteky, muzei. Kyiv: Povernuti imena, 1997.

Browndorf, Margaret A. "World War II and the Building of the Ukrainian Library." In *Libraries: Traditions and Innovations: Papers from the Library History Seminar XIII,* ed. Melanie A. Kimball and Katherine Wisser, 108–23. Boston: De Gruyter Saur, 2017.

Chebotariova, Anna. "Voices of Resistance and Hope: On the Motivations and Expectations of Euromaidaners." In *Ukraine's Euromaidan: Analyses of a Civil Revolution,* ed. David R. Marples and Frederick V. Mills, 163–78. Stuttgart: ibidem-Verlag, 2015.

Dobrenko, Evgeny. *The Making of the State Reader: Social and Aesthetic Origins of Soviet Literary Culture.* Berkley: Stanford University Press, 1997.

Dubrovina, Liubov Andreevna, and Oleksii Semenovych Onishchenko. *Bibliotechna sprava v Ukraini v XX stolitti.* Kyiv: NAN Ukrainy, 2009.

— — —. *Istoriia natsional'noi biblioteky ukrainy imeni V.I. Vernads'koho: 1941–1964.* Kyiv: Naukova Dumka, 2003.

Eberhardt, Piotr. *Ethnic Groups and Population Changes in Twentieth-Century Central-Eastern Europe.* Translated by Jan Owsinski. New York: M.E. Sharpe, 2003.

Haigh, Maria. "Making Ukrainians in the Library: Language, Libraries, and National Identity." *The Canadian Journal of Information and Library Science* 33, no. 3/4 (2009): 141–58.

Harvard Project on the Soviet Social System. Schedule A, Vol. 2, Case 11 (interviewer J.R. Type A3). http://nrs.harvard.edu/urn-3:FHCL:939734. Accessed August 8, 2017.

Harvard Project on the Soviet Social System. Schedule A, Vol. 31, Case 306/(NY)1106. http://nrs.harvard.edu/urn-3:FHCL:962276. Accessed August 8, 2017.

Heintz, Jim. "Ukraine Protest Library a Break From the Tensions." *Associated Press.* February 10, 2014. Retrieved from https://www.yahoo.com/news/ukraine-protest-library-break-tensions-110813394.html.

Kniga i Knizhnoe Delo v Ukrainskoi SSR: Sbornik dokumentov i materialov 1917–1941. Kyiv: Naukova Dumka, 1985.

Kniga i Knizhnoe Delo v Ukrainskoi SSR: Sbornik dokumentov i materialov 1941–1984. Kyiv: Naukova Dumka, 1986.

Martin, Terry. *Affirmative Action Empire: Nations and Nationalism in the Soviet Union, 1923–1939.* Ithaca: Cornell University Press, 2001.

Osborn, Andrew. "Disappearing Books: How Russia is Shuttering its Ukrainian Library." *Reuters.* March 15, 2017. Retrieved from http://www.reuters.com/article/us-ukraine-crisis-russia-library-idUSKBN16M0PW.

— — —. "Head of Moscow's Ukrainian Library Convicted of Incitement Against Russians." *Reuters.* June 5, 2017. Retrieved from http://www.reuters.com/article/us-ukraine-crisis-russia-library-idUSKBN18W12T.

Pauly, Matthew. *Breaking the Tongue: Language, Education, and Power in Soviet Ukraine, 1923–1934.* Toronto: University of Toronto, 2015.

Raymond, Boris. *Krupskaia and Soviet Russian Librarianship, 1917–1939.* Metuchen, NJ: Scarecrow Press, 1979.

Risch, William Jay. *The Ukrainian West: Culture and the Fate of Empire in Soviet Lviv.* Boston: Harvard University Press, 2011.

"Russian Investigators Search Homes of Ukrainian Library Staff." *BBC Monitoring Former Soviet Union—Political.* December 14, 2015.

Shevelov, George. *The Ukrainian Language in the First Half of the Twentieth Century (1900–1941): Its State and Status.* Boston: Harvard University Press, 1989.

Stubbs, Jack. "Kiev Protesters Shun State Hospitals for Volunteer Clinics." *Reuters.* January 27, 2014. Retrieved from http://www.reuters.com/article/ukraine-medics-idUSL5N0L10ZC20140127.

Social Justice and Birmingham Collecting Institutions: Education, Research and Reference Librarianship

Jeff Hirschy

In Birmingham, Alabama there are many collecting institutions that manage the history, narratives, and stories of that city. Two of the main ones, especially when it comes to the Civil Rights Movement, the movement's aftermath, and Birmingham's relationship with social justice, are the Birmingham Public Library Department of Archives and Manuscripts (BPLDAM) and the Birmingham Civil Rights Institute (BCRI). The goals of each institution revolve around telling the complete story of the history of Birmingham. This means not falling back on a master narrative like that of Jim Crow and white supremacy but moving towards the goal of a pluralistic historical narrative and society.[1]

A "collecting institution" is any library, archive, or museum that has been tasked with preserving and providing access to the historical, cultural, and sociality records of the community they serve. Each institution, if designed correctly, can help facilitate a search for social justice. In this search, reference librarians and archivists play the most important role. These two positions create the library guides and finding aids that help facilitate the

---

[1] The education and research opportunities surrounding both institutions have led to the construction of websites like http://kidsinbirmingham1963.org. This website tells the stories of the children who went through the events of Birmingham in 1963.

two most important social justice functions of libraries and archives: education and research.[2]

The BPLDAM was founded in 1976 in the aftermath of the Civil Rights Movement, which took place in Birmingham during the 1950's and 1960's.[3] For the first time in Birmingham's then 100-year history, a collecting institution in Birmingham wanted to collect all of Birmingham's history. This desire is expressed in the mission statement of the Department of Archives and Manuscripts:

> The Birmingham Department of Archives and Manuscripts collects government records, business records, maps, photographs, letters, diaries, scrapbooks, and other primary material documenting the history and development of Birmingham, Jefferson County and the surrounding area of Alabama known as the Birmingham District. The Archives collects material statewide relating to the Episcopal Church in Alabama, the Civil Rights Movement in Alabama, Jewish history and life in Alabama, LGBTQ history and life in Alabama, and the Environmental Movement in Alabama.[4]

The Department of Archives and Manuscripts was joined by the BCRI sixteen years later, in 1992. During those sixteen years, the people of Birmingham, its government, and activists struggled over what would be included in the Institute and why they even wanted to build an Institute in the first place. In the eyes of some, Birmingham had embraced multiple narratives after 1963 so there was no need to return to the events of the Civil Rights Movement and the Jim Crow Era. Those who believed this thought that Birmingham had already completed its transformation from prison to

---

2 Examples of this are "The Modern Civil Rights Movement: Primary Sources: Government Documents" Library Guide (guides.lib.ua.edu/c.php?g=431886&p=2945712) at the University of Alabama, and the "Alabama. Tenth Judicial Circuit Court *State of Alabama vs. Robert E. Chambliss* Trial Transcript, 1977" Finding Aid (www.bplonline.org/resources/archives/aids/AR85.pdf) located at the Birmingham Public Library Department of Archives and Manuscripts.

3 "Birmingham Public Library–Central–Archives." Birmingham Public Library–Central–Archives. Accessed August 16, 2016. http://www.bplonline.org/locations/central/archives/.

4 Ibid.

temple of liberty and did not need to be guided or even to remember.[5] This opinion did not prevail and the Civil Rights Institute opened in 1992 with a strong emphasis on education, research, and the continued fight for civil rights in Birmingham and the wider world. It is reflected in the organization's mission statement:

Mission

To enlighten each generation about civil and human rights by exploring our common past and working together in the present to build a better future.

Vision

We stand strong as THE CORNERSTONE of the civil rights story, a living memorial with an on-going mission.

Values

The Birmingham Civil Rights Institute is committed to:

- Persevering and telling the Birmingham story
- Being a good steward of archival and financial resources
- Creating programs that encourage cultural awareness
- Championing civil and human rights by facilitating an atmosphere of dialogue and understanding[6]

History of Birmingham, Alabama

Before the founding of both institutions, Birmingham's collecting institutions served the city's Jim Crow master narrative of white supremacy. Both BPLDAM and BCRI broke from the city's long history of social, historical, political, economic, and physical abuse of all those who fell outside the master narrative. The reasons why Birmingham needed and still needs col-

---

5 Jimerson, Randall C. *Archives Power: Memory, Accountability, and Social Justice.* Chicago: Society of American Archivists, 2009. Pg. 6–9.

6 "About BCRI | Birmingham Civil Rights Institute." About BCRI | Birmingham Civil Rights Institute. Accessed July 28, 2016. http://www.bcri.org/Information/AboutBCRI.html.

lecting institutions like BPLDAM and BCRI can be traced to the very beginning of Birmingham's history.[7]

In the aftermath of the Civil War, the white peoples of Alabama and the American South were beaten and angry. They had lost their war for "freedom," their slaves, and the civilization they had built before the war. Everything that had made the South "great" in their eyes had been destroyed by the victorious Union Army. For those angry and defeated white men, the only thing left to do was to rebuild their civilization and get it as close to the one they had had before the war. They were going to reconstruct the master narrative that supported that civilization as best they could.[8]

A master narrative is the set of rules that guide a society or collecting institution in what they protect, cultivate, and preserve.[9] Before the Civil War, the master narrative of Alabama was the story of the rich white planter class that drove the state's economy and ran the government. That narrative was destroyed by the Civil War and was the narrative the survivors of that war would attempt to rebuild in the aftermath. During the Reconstruction Period (1865–1877), white southerners realized if they were going to reconstruct their master narrative they needed to expand their economy to successfully compete with the rest of the country.[10]

To construct this new world, Alabama and the South needed industrial cities on par with the great industrial cities of the North. In 1871, John Turner Milner was on such a quest in central Alabama.[11] Milner, the Chief Engineer of the North and South Railroad, had been assigned the task of picking the crossing of his railroad, the North and South, and the Chattanooga and Alabama Railroad.[12] The hope of Milner and of both companies was that the site chosen would give birth to a great southern in-

---

7   Birmingham's story, like that of many cities of the South, was built on white supremacy and power. For example, see Douglas Blackman's *Slavery by Another Name: The Re-Enslavement of Black Americans from the Civil War to World War II.*

8   This want would form what became known as "The Lost Cause" movement. For more see Tony Horowitz's *Confederates in the Attic: Dispatches from the Unfinished Civil War.*

9   The US Constitution is an example of a master narrative.

10   Eric Foner, *Reconstruction: America's Unfinished Revolution, 1963–1877*, New York: Harper Perennial Modern Classics, 2014.

11   Dorothea O Warren, *The Practical Dreamer: A Story of John T. Milner, His Family And Forebears*, Birmingham, AL: The Southern Family Press, 1959, 154.

12   Ibid., 150–54.

dustrial city. After searching for several months, Milner selected the Jones Valley as the crossing point.[13] The Jones Valley had several things going in its favor. It was close to water, and it had large deposits of iron ore, coal, and limestone, which were all the necessary materials to produce steel and drive the growth and development of a large industrial city.[14]

And a city did rise there. Birmingham, Alabama was founded in 1871, but it was founded upon a master narrative that would preach the exclusion of large portions of its citizens for the next 100 years.[15] One of the reasons that Birmingham was able to expand so quickly after its formation was because of the assistance, once again, of John T. Milner. The system that Milner helped found and run was a new form of slavery. Instead of agricultural slaves, African-American men became industrial slaves. African-American men were arrested for petty crimes like jaywalking and sent to work in Birmingham's steel mills, factories, and mines.[16] This new form of slavery helped to implement and continue the master narrative that Birmingham was built on. That master narrative, or the only allowed narrative, was the white man's narrative. The history of white wealthy southerners was the only history that mattered. Anything other than their Jim Crow brand of history was forgotten because it was not "important."

Education, Research, and Social Justice

In his book, *Archives Power: Memory, Accountability, and Social Justice*, Randall C. Jimerson describes three different types of collecting institutions: the temple, the prison, and the restaurant.[17] Temple institutions are collecting institutions where the archivist or librarian preserves the "original" interpretation of items or collections. Prison institutions are institutions where the archivist or librarian serves an oppressive higher power. Restaurant institutions are institutions where the archivist or librarian serves as a guide to the user, allowing them to make their own decisions

---

13   Ibid., 157–159.

14   Ethel Armes, *The Story of Coal and Iron in Alabama*. Tuscaloosa, AL: University of Alabama Press, 2011.

15   Blackmon, 39.

16   Ibid., 39–48.

17   Jimerson, 6–9.

and let the collections and items speak for themselves. Like South Africa, before and after apartheid, Birmingham Alabama's collecting institutions traveled the transformational and evolutionary road from prison institutions to restaurant institutions starting in 1963.[18] This would not have been possible without the archivists and reference librarians who helped ensure their collecting institutions played strong roles in the relationship between their collecting institutions and facilitating social justice. No longer would it be just the story of Birmingham's white citizens. Birmingham would walk down the road of cultural and informational liberation from the Jim Crow prisons it had found itself in for most of its history. This is where the BPLDAM and BCRI enter the story. They helped, and continue to help, guide the city of Birmingham and all those who visit, or read about it, through educational and research opportunities towards social justice.[19]

To guide Birmingham and its collecting institutions towards social justice, these two institutions needed to create need tools. The two main tools created by the reference librarians and archivists in Birmingham, like those of other communities, were library guides and finding aids. Library guides are lists of resources compiled by reference librarians to assist in research.[20] Finding aids are documents used in archives to describe specific collections and tell researchers if a collection might be useful to their research.[21]

The BPLDAM holds multiple collections that examine many aspects and sections of Southern history and culture. Each one of these collections is supported by strong finding aids and library guides that guide users through each collection and offer them additional resources to investigate. Before the formation of the Department in 1976, there was no such support; in fact, there was barely any support at all for information that didn't support the Jim Crow master narrative of white supremacy.

---

18 A description of the South African journey and the continuing journey South African collection institutions are still on see *Archives and Justice: A South African Perspective* by Verne Harris.

19 For example, the Birmingham Civil Rights Institute creates curriculum guides that provide educators with lesson plans based around the events of the Civil Rights Movement. (http://www.bcri.org/education_programs/curriculumguide.html). At the Birmingham Library, subject guides have been created to guide users in their searches for various information. (http://www.bplonline.org/virtual/subjects/)

20 Southern Illinois University. "What is a LibGuide?" libguides.lib.siu.edu/training

21 Society of American Archivists. "Finding Aid." www2.archivists.org/glossary/terms/f/finding-aid.

Today's Department of Archives and Manuscripts holds many of the collections and records that were used to serve the master narrative of Jim Crow and segregation.[22] These collections and records exalt the "glories" of the white citizens and white history of Birmingham while they erased any other perspective and culture from the history of the city. After the founding of the Department and the gathering of those collections and records under the umbrella of that Department, the same collections and records that once served the master narrative of white supremacy became free to speak the truth to all current and future generations.

One collection that was given a voice by reference librarians and archivists was the Birmingham Police Surveillance Files (BPSF). This collection also went through the transformation from supporting Jim Crow to serving as a tool for social justice. These files, dated 1941–1972, contain information collected about civil rights meetings, demonstrations, and organization efforts. They also have information related to white supremacists, pornography, voting rights, and Rev. Fred Shuttlesworth.[23] Most of these documents were generated by the Birmingham Police Department when Bull Connor ran that department.[24]

Whatever narratives this collection naturally generated were suppressed during the first decades of its existence. During those years, the collection was suppressed by the overarching master narrative of Birmingham of the mid-twentieth century. It was enslaved to the master narrative that Bull Connor and his supporters preached.

After it was placed in the BPLDAM this collection had the chance to finally speak without the overarching and overbearing power of a master narrative suppressing it. When this weight was lifted, the collection came to life. Instead of telling the story of the "glories" of Jim Crow Birmingham, it told of the horrors. It told the story of a police force which beat, oppressed, and terrorized its own citizens because those citizens wanted equal rights.[25] In the United States of the twentieth century, a country that was

---

22 "Birmingham Public Library–Central–Archives." Birmingham Public Library–Central–Archives. Accessed April 16, 2016. http://www.bplonline.org/locations/central/archives/.

23 http://encore.bham.lib.al.us/iii/encore/record/C__Rb1490380?lang=eng

24 Ibid.

25 "About BCRI | Birmingham Civil Rights Institute." About BCRI | Birmingham Civil Rights Institute. Accessed April 16, 2016. http://www.bcri.org/Information/AboutBCRI.html.

fighting the Cold War as a bastion of freedom and liberties, a police force imprisoned, beat, surveilled, and killed citizens in the name of a fascistic racist master narrative.

Like the liberated records of apartheid South Africa, the files of the BPSF collection can inform, educate, and warn users in the present and future of the horrors of the past and the lessons to be learned from them. They can be used by organizations like Black Lives Matter to show potential allies that the issue of police brutality and its effects is not a new problem but a long-term American problem. Collections like the BPSF can help people, for example, white Americans, see this issue in a new light and hopefully realize it finally needs to stop. In collections like the BPSF, the finding aid, library guide, and reference librarian all play a very important role. The reference librarian makes sure that the documents describing the documents, collections, or items are accurate and accessible to the public and researchers. Without reference librarians or archivists to describe them, the items contained within collecting institutions could be labeled wrongly or fail to live up to their potential as a tool in the search for social justice.

The BPLDAM and BCRI are both restaurant institutions. Unfortunately for the people of Birmingham, it took nearly 105 years to realize that all narratives working together would produce the strongest society. For those 105 years, the master narrative was that of the rule and continued advancement of the white Birminghamians and their white civilization. All other narratives were "enemies" of the white master narrative and were not supposed to matter to the average citizen, historian, or librarian. This helped perpetuate 105 years of racial strife, violence, and oppression. Birmingham could never realize its true potential with only one part of its story being told.

After the opening of the doors of prison collecting institutions in the 1970s, Birmingham and its collecting institutions finally had a chance to examine what had happened in the first 105 years. The original master narrative was collapsing. From average citizens to reference librarians and archivists, there was a growing desire to include the narratives of forgotten groups, like Catholics, women, and African Americans, who had been the "other" during the reign of Jim Crow. What would replace it would be up to new collecting institutions. The original master narrative had to collapse so new narratives could grow and evolve.

The collecting institutions of the new post-Jim Crow Birmingham would be led by the BPLDAM and BCRI. Both institutions place an emphasis on supporting and growing Birmingham's new pluralistic narrative and apply the historical lessons of Birmingham to the present and the world. They educate the public and allow for research into Birmingham's past so that narratives and their lessons can be learned by present and future generations. This is seen in the mission statement of each institution.

Education and research are the most important social justice tools of both institutions. Both education and research function as figurative transmission towers for the memories and lessons of the past. They are the vehicles through which a collecting institution can help a society to struggle toward justice locally, nationally and internationally.

After telling the story of Birmingham's struggle for civil rights, the Institute warns its visitors that the struggle is not over. In a series of panels on their display floor and in the educational information they provide to teachers, schools, and the public to continue educating after their visit, the Civil Rights Institute tells visitors about some of the civil rights and social justice struggles that have taken place since the events in Birmingham.[26] Both the panels and the educational material remind visitors that the struggle for civil rights and social justice is not over. The Institute wants to be always moving, always growing, and always learning.

Contemporary movements can learn from the educational opportunities at both the BPLDAM and BCRI. Collections like the Birmingham Police Surveillance Files Collection and the public museum portion of BCRI show visitors and users that many of the issues facing minority groups in the United States are not problems that have developed in the last few decades. They show instead that these problems are long-term problems that have plagued the United States for a large part of its history. Organizations like Black Lives Matter and researchers and authors like Diane McWhorter use these items and structures to inform the public and potential allies of the true history of the United States. Educating the public about the long-term injustice that is present in the structures of American life and society can go a long way in helping to facilitate social justice.

Along with educational opportunities, another way local collecting institutions can facilitate social justice is through research opportunities and the production of secondary works based upon the collections contained in collecting institutions. Research is an important way to present the ideas and lessons, especially social justice lessons, contained in collecting institutions to the wider world. Research conducted in the BPLDAM has produced books like Diane McWhorter's *Carry Me Home: Birmingham,*

---

26   To learn more about the exhibits offered at the Birmingham Civil Rights Institute see: http://www.bcri.org/Exhibitions/PermanentGallery.html.

Alabama: The Climactic Battle of the Civil Rights Movement. Carry Me Home was born from the records and collections stored at the Department of Archives and Manuscripts. McWhorter, who is originally from Birmingham, used the record and collections of the archive, and her own personal stake in her project, to tell the story of Birmingham's eventful year of 1963.[27]

For researchers like McWhorter, finding aids and library guides are important research tools. Both describe and explain collections, documents, and items allowing researchers to get a sneak peek and determine whether the collections, documents, and items support their research. Because of the library guides and finding aids, the reference librarian and the archivist play an important part, if not the most important part, in the research component of the potential relationship between collecting institutions and the search for social justice. In McWhorter's case, the finding aid of the Birmingham Police Surveillance Files or a library guide on Jefferson County, Alabama (the county Birmingham is in) helped her with the initial research of her book.[28]

Because McWhorter was a small child in 1963 living in Mountain Brook, Alabama, she did not fully realize what was happening at Birmingham's heart. She knew there was a conflict, and she had family members on one side but she didn't know what they were fighting for at the time. She wrote *Carry Me Home* to tell the story of Birmingham and her family in 1963 as a way to answer all her questions.[29]

What she discovered was that the events of 1963 were the result of decades of racial and political intrigue in Birmingham and Alabama.[30] What she found was a raging battle over the master narrative of Jim Crow that started in the 1940s and would finally end in 1963. She discovered that her family played a role in this intrigue and had supported the master narrative of Jim Crow. Her father and uncle were minor members of the Big Mules,[31] Birmingham and Alabama businessmen who controlled the politics, cultural, and business in the city and state. Starting in the 1940s, the Big Mules cultivated, organized, and assisted forces that would support their domination and fight against any threat to it and the narrative that

---

27 McWhorter. Pg. xv-xvi.

28 http://www.bplonline.org/resources/archives/collections.aspx?q=10

29 McWhorter. Pg. xvi.

30 Ibid. Pg. 150.

31 Ibid. Pg. 400.

told its story.[32] They cultivated the likes of Bull Connor and Asa Carter to lead the fight against outside influences and forces. The Big Mules did not want change and fought it at any cost.

According to McWhorter, the only reason the Big Mules eventually broke and gave in to the demands of the Civil Rights Movement was the fact that it was beginning to affect their pocketbooks. The images circling the globe of Bull Connor's police department beating children gave Birmingham a black eye and painted it into the same corner occupied by Nazi Germany and Pol Pot's Cambodia. This, and not their changed belief system or rejection of Birmingham's master narrative, was part of the reason that 1963 was a victory for civil rights. McWhorter's analysis in *Carry Me Home Alabama* should serve as a warning. The victory won in Birmingham in 1963 was not the final battle in the war but just another battle. The liberation is incomplete and the war is ongoing. In 2015, an Indian man was badly beaten by police officers in Northern Alabama. According to the man's family, the only reason he was beaten was because he didn't speak English and was not white. The officers reported he was belligerent and didn't answer their questions. Whatever the reasons that he was beaten, it was a case of police brutality and overreach.[33] This man's civil rights were taken away from him by officers doing their best impression of Bull Connor's police force from the 1960s.

This sense of continuing struggle is the most important lesson one can take from *Carry Me Home,* and it is one of the most important lessons one can take from any of the collections, or works produced by them, in the BPLDAM. Most of these collections were created in a time and place where they served, even if not designed for it, the master narrative of Jim Crow. They serve only the white civilization and the system of supremacy designed to support and glorify the White Man.

But now, because of the Department of Archives and Manuscripts, all the collections, documents, and items in both institutions serve multiple narratives and provide lessons for present and future generations to examine, learn about, and apply to their own situations. These documents serve as guides to the public looking to find information about their community's past, the press using history as warnings for the future, and researchers searching for lessons in the remnants of the past. Overall, they serve as signposts to follow in any search for social justice in any collecting institution.

---

32   Ibid. Pg. 450.

33   "Grandpa Partially Paralyzed after Encounter with Police." CNN, http://www.cnn.com/2015/02/12/us/alabama-police-beating/ (accessed April 16, 2016).

The Future

With the assistance of archivists and reference librarians, the Birmingham Public Library Department of Archives and Manuscripts and Birmingham Civil Rights Institute use education and research opportunities to help Birmingham and the wider world search for, or work towards, social justice. It would not be possible for these collecting institutions to help their community work towards justice, or even for such a relationship to exist, if not for the guides created by archivists and reference librarians. The finding aid of the Birmingham Police Surveillance Files Collection guide the user through that collection and allows anyone to pull the valuable social justice lessons out of those files. This, along with library guides based around topics such as social justice and civil rights, allow both institutions to put a strong foot forward in providing both educational and research opportunities. Without these guiding documents, these social lessons might be lost in the mists of history.

However, just because library guides and finding aids help collecting institutions in fostering social justice through education and research opportunities, it does not mean that restaurant collecting institutions are always on an upward trajectory towards a liberated information promised land. Restaurant collecting institutions like the BPLDAM and BCRI still have their problems.

Like any restaurant collecting institution, Birmingham's two main collecting institutions can "forget" parts of the history they have been assigned to preserve. Take for example the story of African-American radio hosts in mid-twentieth century Birmingham. Radio was one of two professions, the other being the clergy, where African-Americans could establish themselves and advance during the period. During the Civil Rights Movement, some of these radio hosts played an important role in rallying protesters and marchers. But this role is forgotten by the BCRI and would not be remembered at all if not for the effort of a Bob Friedman, a transplant from New York City, who has spent the last 27 years interviewing these hosts and preserving their memories and thoughts at his Birmingham Black Radio Museum.[34] Without Friedman, this important part of Birmingham's history would be lost forever.

Hopefully, such lacunae will be corrected in not just the Civil Rights Institute, but all collecting institutions with an interest in fostering so-

---

34   For more information see http://thebbrm.org/

cial justice. As more information is discovered and organized at both institutions, the archivists and reference librarians at both institutions will continue to produce library guides and finding aids that will guide users towards the social justice lessons contained in the collections of both institutions. Access to all of the educational and research opportunities contained within these institutions or any strong collection is an important in any collecting institution facilitating social justice. Every narrative, to the best of the institution's ability needs to be represented and access needs to be open and complete. If this happens, both the Birmingham Public Library Department of Archives and Manuscripts and the Birmingham Civil Rights Institute will continue to be strong living restaurant institutions, growing in their abilities to present education and research opportunities and continuing to help Birmingham and the wider world work towards social justice.

Works Cited

"About BCRI | Birmingham Civil Rights Institute." About BCRI | Birmingham Civil
    Rights Institute. Accessed April 16, 2016.
    http://www.bcri.org/Information/AboutBCRI.html.

"Alabama Museums Association." Alabama Museums Association. Accessed April 16, 2016.
    http://www.alabamamuseums.org/museums/view_museum.php?museum=112.

Amnesty International. https://www.amnesty.org/en/countries/.

Arendt, Hannah. *Eichmann in Jerusalem: A Report on the Banality of Evil.*
    New York: Penguin Classics, 2006.

Bascomb, Neal. *Hunting Eichmann: How a Band of Survivors and a Young Spy Agency
    Chased Down the World's Most Notorious Nazi.* New York: Mariner Books, 2009.

BHAM Wiki. "Eleanor Bridges." http://www.bhamwiki.com/w/Eleanor_Bridges.

"Birmingham Public Library–Central–Archives." Birmingham Public Library–Central–
    Archives. Accessed April 16, 2016. http://www.bplonline.org/locations/central/
    archives/.

Birmingham Public Library. "Civil rights files and related material, 1941–1981 (bulk
    1963–1972) (bulk 1963–1972)." http://encore.bham.lib.al.us/iii/encore/record/C__
    Rb1490380?lang=eng.

Blackmon, Douglas A. *Slavery by Another Name: The Re-Enslavement of Black Americans
    from the Civil War to World War II.* New York: Anchor Books, 2008.

Burton, Antoinette M. *Archive Stories: Facts, Fictions, and the Writing of History.* Durham,
    NC: Duke University Press, 2005.

Carson, Clayborne, David J. Garrow, Gerald Gill, Vincent Harding, and Darlene Clark
    Hine, eds. *The Eyes On The Prize Civil Rights Reader: Documents, Speeches, And
    Firsthand Accounts From The Black Freedom Struggle.* New York: Penguin Books, 2013.

Caswell, Michelle. *Archiving the Unspeakable: Silence, Memory, and the Photographic Record
    in Cambodia.* Madison, WI: University of Wisconsin Press, 2014.

Clark, Alexandra. *Hidden History of Chattanooga.* London: The History Press, 2008.

Chappell, David. *Inside Agitators: White Southerners in the Civil Rights Movement.*
    Baltimore: Johns Hopkins University Press, 1996.

Committee, Church. *The FBI, COINTELPRO, And Martin Luther King Jr.: Final Report of
    The Select Committee To Study Governmental Operations With Respect To Intelligence
    Activity.* St. Petersburg: Red and Black Publishers, 2011.

Encyclopedia Britannica. "Aeneas." http://www.britannica.com/topic/Aeneas.

Digital Archive of the Guatemalan National Police Historical Archive (AHPN)." Digital Archive of the Guatemalan National Police Historical Archive (AHPN). Accessed April 16, 2016. https://ahpn.lib.utexas.edu/.

Duff, Wendy, Andrew Flinn, Karen Suurtamm, and David Wallace. "Social Justice Impact of Archives: A Preliminary Investigation." Archival Science 13, no. 4 (2013): 317–48.

Eskew, Glenn T. *But for Birmingham: The Local and National Movements in the Civil Rights Struggle.* The University of North Carolina Press, 1997.

"George Wallace", http://www.pbs.org/wgbh/amex/wallace/sfeature/quotes.html.

Gilliland, Anne. "Neutrality, social justice and the obligations of archival education and educators in the twenty-first century." Archival Science 11, no. 3 (November 2011): 193–202.

Gilmore, Kim. "The Birmingham Children's Crusade of 1963." Bio.com. Accessed April 16, 2016. http://www.biography.com/news/black-history-birmingham-childrens-crusade-1963-video.

"Grandpa Partially Paralyzed after Encounter with Police." CNN. Accessed April 16, 2016. http://www.cnn.com/2015/02/12/us/alabama-police-beating/.

Hampton, Henry, Steve Fayer, and Sarah Flynn. *Voices of Freedom: An Oral History of the Civil Rights Movement from the 1950's Through the 1980's.* New York: Bantam, 1991.

Hayner, Priscalla B. *Unspeakable Truths: Transitional Justice and the Challenge of Truth Commissions.* New York: Routledge, 2011.

ITCJ. "What is Transitional Justice?" https://www.ictj.org/about/transitional-justice.

Jimerson, Randall C. *Archives Power: Memory, Accountability, and Social Justice.* Chicago: Society of American Archivists, 2009.

— — —. "Archives for All: Professional Responsibility and Social Justice." American Archivist (2006).

— — —. "Embracing the Power of Archives." American Archivist 69 (2006): 19–32.

John Benjamins Publishing Company. "Considering Counter-Narratives: Narrating, Resisting, Making Sense." https://benjamins.com/#catalog/books/sin.4/main.

Jovanovic, Spoma. *Democracy, Dialogue, and Community Action: Truth and Reconciliation in Greensboro.* Little Rock: University of Arkansas Press, 2012.

MacMillan, Margaret. *Dangerous Games: The Uses and Abuses of History.* New York: Modern Library Classics, 2008.

McWhorter, Diane. *Carry Me Home: The Climactic Battle of the Civil Rights Revolution.* New York: Simon & Schuster Paperbacks, 2012.

Meredith, Martin. *Coming to Terms: South Africa's Search for Truth.* New York: Public Affairs, 1999.

"Missing and Murdered Indigenous Women in Canada Could Number 4,000." The Guardian. 2016. Accessed April 16, 2016. http://www.theguardian.com/world/2016/feb/17/missing-and-murdered-indigenous-women-in-canada-could-number-4000.

National Association of Social Workers. "Social Justice." http://www.naswdc.org/pressroom/features/issue/peace.asp.

Nelson Mandel Centre of Memory. "Nelson Mandela Digital Archive Project." http://archive.nelsonmandela.org/.

Parker, Geoffrey. *Global Crisis: War, Climate Change & Catastrophe In The Seventeenth Century.* New Haven, CT: Yale University Press, 2013. Pg. xxix-xxx.

Raiford, Leigh, and Renee Romano, eds. *Civil Rights Movement in American Memory.* Athens, GA: University of Georgia Press, 2006.

Rieder, Jonathan. *Gospel of Freedom: Martin Luther King, JR.'s Letter From Birmingham Jail And The Struggle That Changed A Nation.* New York: Bloomsbury, 2013.

Roberts, Gene, and Hank Klibanoff. *The Race Beat: The Press, The Civil Rights Struggle, and The Awakening Of A Nation.* New York: Vintage Books, 2006.

Roberts, J.M., and Odd Arne Westad. *The Penguin History of the World.* New York: Penguin Books, 2013. Pg. 53–4.

Schwartz, Joan M., and Terry Cook. "Archives, Records, and Power: The Making of Modern Memory." Archival Science (2002): 1–19.

South Asian American Digital Archive. "SAADA and the Community-Based Archives Model: What Is a Community-Based Archives Anyway?" https://www.saada.org/tides/article/20120418-704.

The WikiLeaks Files: The World According to US Empire. New York: Penguin Random House, 2015.

Von Ranke, Leopold, and Georg S. Iggers. *The Theory and Practice of History.* New York: Routledge, 2010.

Ward, Brian E. *Radio and the Struggle for Civil Rights in the South.* Gainesville, FL: University Press of Florida, 2006.

Warren, Dorothea O. *The Practical Dreamer: A Story of John T. Milner, His Family And Forebears.* Birmingham, AL: The Southern Family Press, 1959.

Weld, Kristen. *Paper Cadavers: The Archives of Dictatorship in Guatemala.* Durham, NC: Duke University Press Books, 2014.

Welsh, Frank. *A History of South Africa.* New York: Harper Collins Publishers, 2000.

Wikipedia. "Memory Institutions." https://en.wikipedia.org/wiki/Memory_institution.

Wilson, Bobby M. America's *Johannesburg: Industrialization and Racial Transformation in Birmingham.* New York: Rowman & Littlefield Publishers, 2000.

Towards a Critical (Affective) Reference Practice: Emotional, Intellectual and Social Justice

Kate Adler

The vision for *Reference Librarianship and Justice* grew out of a conviction that if we are guided by a commitment not only to social justice, but also to emotional justice and to intellectual justice, and if we engage in authentic dialogue with our patrons and with our communities that, perhaps, reference librarians can do something genuinely unique, meaningful and *interesting*. The essays in this book and in this section give me faith that we can and that this vision is being realized every day.

The notion that a mindful critical reference practice might partner in nudging us slowly toward a more just society is somewhat high-minded. Yet if we heed the lessons that abound all around us, nuts-and-bolts lessons of social justice movements, and on-the-ground lessons from one another, there is so very much to draw from and so much reason for optimism. There are multiple critical frameworks to look toward; frameworks that can help us articulate, interrogate and ultimately intervene upon myriad interlocking regimes of power that commit daily violence. Critical theories of race and anti-colonialism, of disability, women of color feminism, critical pedagogy and queer theory can all help us to sharpen and deepen a mindful and critical practice.

It is my view that that there is woven into the fabric of librarianship a deep ethical core, one that is essential and powerful though it may be layered with utopian longings. Critical librarianship has worked to interrogate the realities that those longings smack up against. White supremacy and inequalities of power and access are threaded into our catalogs, our collections, and our practices. Still, libraries (can) continue to be "so mainstream yet so…socialist," so quietly remarkable.[1] A Critical Reference Librarianship, tethered and committed to social justice work, is its own very specific kind of remarkable intervention, as this book explores.

I join others who have argued that a critical reference practice should be understood as affective care work that assists in the learning process within an educational setting. Affective labor, as feminist scholars have explored, is often rendered invisible within a capitalist, industrial framework. Stripped of all pretension, what we do involves sitting (literally or metaphorically) with *another human being*, listening (literally or metaphorically) to *another human being*. I feel this every day in my own work at a small, urban college, where our average age is 35 and 97% of our students are people of color; where most are women and the vast majority of them low-income. When our students research homelessness in New York City, it may be that they themselves are currently homeless, or have lived on the edge of homelessness, or have moved away from that edge and are now working in a homeless shelter. As Paulo Freire and others have taught us, our students and patrons bring a whole lot of life, and a whole lot of expertise, to the table. At my school, when students research domestic violence, or single motherhood, or asthma in the South Bronx, or re-entry programs for formerly incarcerated people, these may be significant issues in their own lives. Research help and affective care work can be interwoven.

As Maria Accardi so eloquently describes in her introduction to this book, in the reference process we sit with another human being and perhaps we *connect*, and perhaps we have a moment wherein we *understand* one another a little, and perhaps also we understand some of the ideas and research questions we are grappling with together. Unlike many other types of service points—in social work or medical work—the reference dialogue is based on curiosity and ideas; it is driven by intellectual inquiry. In the process of searching for articles or facts about a subject or talking through an idea, we can intervene, together, at the fissure points of epistemological violence within information systems. David James Hudson, Gina Schlesselman-Tarango, and others have yoked theories of white-

---

1   Melissa Morrone, ed., *Informed Agitation: Library and Information Skills in Social Justice Movements and Beyond* (Sacramento: Library Juice Press, 2014), 4.

ness to critical LIS practice, where "whiteness is…the production of shared norms…underwritten by physical and epistemological violence."[2] Critical theories of race, feminism, queerness, classification and whiteness all teach us to be mindful of what Hudson calls "epistemological violence." This is a violence that is insidious, as it hinges on the capacity of power to "render itself natural and unquestionable."[3] That is, there is a kind of violence that is enacted at the nexus of power and knowledge that monopolizes access to information and regimes of truth and yet, there are always cracks in these systems, points of fissure where we can intervene.

It is my hope that a critical reference practice can render visible so much of what has been obscured in the context of the library. The appearance of neutrality is always a red flag. Undergirding the semblance of neutrality are complex, violent, systemic regimes of power and hegemony. In the case of the library catalog there are hierarchies of classification, discipline, and knowledge. As Melissa Adler has observed, the techniques employed by classifying books and "making them accessible are necessarily constraining and bound by relations of power."[4] Yet, as Emily Drabinski notes, "[n]either changing the language nor changing the structure can eliminate fundamental limitations of classification systems."[5]

Reference librarians can, if we are mindful to do so, front-line intervene on the very structures in which we are embedded. This, to me, is the only intellectually honest way to navigate the ethical binds presented by interlocking power structures. Framed as we are by neoliberal racial capitalism, we are implicated in these structures and are at risk of reifying them. We may not be able to completely transcend complex, knotty, enmeshed power structures but we can partner with our students and patrons to "grapple with problems"[6] of classification in library catalogs and power dynamics embedded in information systems. Since Emily Drabinski wrote

---

2   David James Hudson, "The Whiteness of Practicality," in *Topographies of Whiteness: Mapping Whiteness in Library and Information Studies*, ed. Gina Schlesselman-Tarango (Sacramento: Library Juice Press, 2017), 205.

3   Ibid., 214.

4   Melissa Adler, *Cruising the Library: Perversities in the Organization of Knowledge* (New York: Fordham University Press, 2017), x.

5   Emily Drabinski, "Teaching the Radical Catalog," in *Radical Cataloging: Essays at the Front*, ed. K.R. Roberto (Jefferson, NC: McFarland & Co., 2008), 202.

6   Ibid., 205.

her widely cited "Teaching the Radical Catalog," with the adoption of the *Framework for Information Literacy for Higher Education* the Association of College and Research Libraries (ACRL) has moved toward a conceptualization of "information literacy"[7] and the research process that creates room for a more critical reference practice. ACRL's *Framework* speaks to the relational and contextual nature of information, of authority and of the process of research. In particular, the frame "Scholarship as Conversation" gestures toward what I have elsewhere described as a "Critical Reference Dialog,"[8] borrowing from Paulo Freire's seminal work, *Pedagogy of the Oppressed*. In Freire's vision of critical pedagogy, dialogue requires faith, humanity, humility and courage. Dialogue, in this sense, is what lies at the heart of the profoundly human moment that Accardi speaks of in her introduction. It is the emotional justice, the attention to affective labor, and to a larger good that is a pre-condition for a truly critical reference practice; or at least for a practice in the service of social good.

This section is concerned with questions of practice. We operate in the long shadow of Marx's old thesis: "The philosophers have only interpreted the world, in various ways; the point is to change it."[9] Steve Garner, a foundational thinker in the study of whiteness, tells us that analyzing whiteness is only effective if deployed to anti-racist ends; it must stay focused on the unique set of power relations that constitute racism.[10] In this spirit, I would argue that critical librarianship is only effective if it is cast toward anti-racist, anti-ableist, queer, and feminist, et al. objectives. In her recent book, *Living a Feminist Life,* Sara Ahmed writes that "feminism is at stake in how we generate knowledge" and that feminism "develops in dialog with others."[11] This is true of any critically engaged life. And certainly, the practice of a Critical Reference Librarianship is forged in dialog.

---

7   I'm choosing to use scare quotes here to gesture towards the fact that this is not an unproblematic term, even as its been re-engaged by ACRL, it is still a phrase that performs a set of disciplinary techniques in tandem with a litany of standards and "assessment" protocols, that can be hallmarks of the neoliberal university.

8   Adler, K. (2013). Radical Purpose: The Critical Reference Dialogue at a Progressive Urban College. *Urban Library Journal* 19 (1). Retrieved from https://academicworks. cuny.edu/ulj/vol19/iss1/9.

9   Karl Marx, "Theses On Feuerbach," Theses on Feuerbach, accessed February 27, 2018, https://www.marxists.org/archive/marx/works/1845/theses/theses.htm.

10   Steve Garner, *Whiteness: An Introduction* (London: Routledge, 2007), 3.

11   Sara Ahmed, *Living a Feminist Life* (Durham: Duke University Press, 2017), 14.

The Criminal Legal System, Critical Data and the Possibility of Information Justice

The majority of the chapters in this section are about prisons. Nowhere is white supremacy so pronounced. In a review of recent work on the intersection of queer, trans, and Critical Prison Studies, Elias Walker Vitulli notes that the US prison system is a "central site of US statecraft, social and racial formation, and political control. Critical prison studies scholars have shown that the prison system is particularly enmeshed in white supremacy, helping to produce and ground it."[12] David James Hudson draws connections for us between the myriad and interlocking violences of white supremacy and library work and calls for us to be attuned to the moments wherein our work might, "intersect with the interests and violences of white supremacy." Hudson further suggests that librarianship poses the "imperative that we be first and foremost practical in our library work." We should challenge white supremacy not only in the library but through library work. Prison librarianship illustrates a deep history and a key site in which to do this.

In "Reference Behind Bars: Information Needs, Rights, and Empowerment of Inmates," Danielle Ball and Hannah Lee provide an impassioned argument about "what is required to nourish the souls and minds of individual human beings and citizens" and the profound potential of reference work to provide tools of empowerment. In "Reference by Mail to Incarcerated People" Emily Jacobson tells us about the New York Public Library's long running Reference by Mail program. The questions she outlines remind me of how cool reference work really is—how varied our practices can be—and the extent to which the right to intellectual exploration is a human right.[13] Questions arrive about such varied subjects as Dungeons & Dragons, Emoji's, or legal services; Jacobson outlines the complexity of providing answers to questions by mail and, like each of the prison librarians in this section, notes the strict limits placed on what can be answered and how.

---

12   Elias Walker Vitulli, "Queering the Carceral: Intersecting Queer/Trans Studies and Critical Prison Studies," *GLQ: A Journal of Lesbian and Gay Studies* 19, no. 1 (2013): 111.

13   Recognized, for one, by the United Nations Declaration of Universal Human Rights in Article 19: "Everyone has the right to freedom of opinion and expression; this right includes freedom to hold opinions without interference and to seek, receive and impart information and ideas through any media and regardless of frontiers."

In "2596 Girls School Road: The Indiana Women's Prison Far-Away Reference Desk" Joshua Finnell tells us about the Indiana Women's Prison Higher Education Program Far-Away Reference Desk (organized by Barbara Fister, the well-known and much-loved librarian and writer). In telling the story of this remarkable program, Finnell also grounds us in the history of prison librarianship. He loops in Derrida and Foucault and the practice of "bibliotherapy" and the theory of learned helplessness. In "Dispatches from the Field of Prison Librarianship" Erin Rivero, Marisa Hernandez, Stephanie Osorio, and Vanessa Villarreal remind us that from an international perspective no nation comes close to the genocidal enormity of the American Prison System. The authors ground us in the unprecedented human rights crises of the Prison Industrial Complex in the United States and argue that library spaces are "lifelines to possibility." They go on to offer fascinating profiles of six prison library professionals and one formerly incarcerated person.

In reading about the enormous work that prison libraries and librarians can do (and the enormous constraints on doing it) I found myself thinking again about fissure points. I found myself considering the explosive opportunity (or, perhaps, quiet opportunity) when we really do the work of linking theory (in the sense of exposure to a world of ideas and a life of the mind) to lived experience of injustice. In a recent *New Yorker* article, Larissa MacFarquhar writes about the Underground Scholars Initiative, a group founded by formerly incarcerated individuals, many of whom had meaningful encounters with literature and/or college programs in prison and want to create a "prison-to-school pipeline" and are interested in thinking deeply about larger questions of social justice and racial harmony. The article describes incarcerated students excited by reading *Don Quixote* and *The Grapes of Wrath* AND about the Zapatistas. While the critique of the literature-as-savior narrative/GRIT/inspiration story is duly noted, there is something significant and significantly remarkable about the Underground Scholars. In a group meeting, MacFarquhar describes members deciding that "the incarcerated should not only be objects of study; they should write about themselves."[14] This insight on the part of the Underground Scholars suggests what it means to open up the traditional notions of scholarship. That these encounters might be partnered in, though not

---

14   Larissa MacFarquhar, "Building a Prison-to-School Pipeline," *The New Yorker*, August 17, 2017, accessed February 10, 2018, retrieved from https://www.newyorker.com/magazine/2016/12/12/the-ex-con-scholars-of-berkeley.

mediated, is at the core of a Critical Reference Librarianship rooted in and guided by social justice projects.

In her chapter, "The Case for Critical Data Reference in Public Libraries," Julia Marden makes a convincing argument for the need for a critical data literacy. Marden's work on data connects to the ways in which the prison system has been theorized through the concept of what Michel Foucault terms "biopower," or "the power to make live or let die." For Foucault, the development of the modern prison signifies a shift in how disciplinary power was deployed, an army of technicians became responsible for overseeing the incarcerated body within a complex bureaucratic structure of surveillance and power. Elsewhere Foucault highlights another significant site of biopolitical control: the development of population statistics, "the science of the state" that is "a set of technical knowledge's that describes the reality of the state itself...an apparatus of knowledge, and... an essential dimension in the exercise of power itself."[15] Power and control are baked into the way in which we count, describe and categorize the population through statistics. Marden brings this into relief in her examination of "data inequality" and the role of public reference librarians in providing a "critical" data reference. She critiques the limitations of the Census, explaining that "throughout the history of the Census, the only racial category that hasn't changed is 'White'; everyone else has had to pick from a shifting list of non-White categories that exist to separate, other, and exclude people from the rights and power that come with being counted as American." It's through a critical data literacy, developed in partnership with librarians, that we can navigate the massive biopolitical apparatus of numbers, statistics and datasets, that tell the story of our society and, in many instances, regulate life chances. Here again we see how meaningful it can be to navigate this maze with a librarian. Vulnerable bodies are "reliant on...the same institutions and apparatus that functionalize gender normative and create systematic exclusions."[16] Dean Spade, a lawyer and critical trans activist, may be correct that we "have to carefully consider the limitations of strategies that aim for inclusion into existing economic and political arrangements rather than challenging the terms of those arrangements" but the stakes for political recognition are high in the context

---

15   Michel Foucault, *Security, Territory, and Population: Lectures at the Collège de France, 1977–1978* (New York: Picador, 2009), 274.

16   Jasbir K. Puar, *The Right to Maim Debility, Capacity, Disability* (Durham: Duke University Press, 2017), 35.

of statistical literacy and legibility: it is through these categories of recognition that resources are allocated.[17] In reference work, that one-on-one human connection, that dialog is a powerful tool for navigating nuance and complexity.

In "Hiding in Plain Sight: Reference Archivists as Social Justice Actors" Rachel Dreyer reminds us of how history itself is at stake in the process of an ethical reference practice. Reference is a "kind of social justice workmanship that hides in plain sight." More acutely than anywhere else the archive requires that we ask of ourselves: "Whose voice is heard? Whose voice is left out? What histories are counted and which are foreclosed and erased?" In this way a society's epistemological structure is laid bare. And, as Dreyer's piece makes clear, multiple forces combine to structure the archive; from interlocking policies governing access to who is sitting at the reference desk in the reading room.

Conclusion: Toward a Critical (Affective-Care) Reference Work

The Miami Workers Center's Four Pillars of Social Justice Infrastructure, as relayed by Dean Spade, are: "The Pillar of Policy, The Pillar of Consciousness, the Pillar of Service and the Pillar of Power."[18] How might we, as reference librarians, think along similar dynamic intersectional and coalitional lines to imagine a more engaged kind of research and intellectual mutual aid? Can the reference desk and a critical reference practice be a zone of empowerment even as we are embedded or implicated in the neoliberal industrial complex of higher education and/or the state? The following pieces motion toward an answer to those questions. However, in this closing paragraph, I want to reiterate the need to tie together Critical Reference, social justice and affective care work. I come away from this project more committed than ever to the supposition that we should center affective care work in critical reference. In privileging affective labor over efficiency, and articulating a vision of how library spaces and Critical Reference function, we can dodge the linear productivity mode that undergirds capitalist exchanges. This type of critical reference work can be slow and messy, but is buoyed by the search for ever deeper forms of resistance and

---

17   Dean Spade, *Normal Life: Administrative Violence, Critical Trans Politics, and the Limits of Law*, (Durham: Duke University Press, 2015), 149.

18   Ibid., 180.

mindfulness. In our tiny, local corners, a Critical Reference Librarianship can seek authentic modes of connection and dialogue and strive for social, emotional, and intellectual justice. Reference can be a mode of "radical informal learning" as articulated by Robert Haworth, one that is "[g]eared toward freedom, autonomy, critical reflection, and liberation rather than supporting hierarchical, authoritarian, and economically corrupt institutions and relationships."[19] The pieces you are about to read speak to this in galvanizing ways.

---

19   Robert H. Haworth and John M. Elmore, *Out of the Ruins: The Emergence of Radical Informal Learning Spaces* (Oakland: PM Press, 2017), 7.

Works Cited

Adler, Kate. Radical Purpose: The Critical Reference Dialogue at a Progressive Urban College. *Urban Library Journal* 19 (1). (2013). Retrieved from https://academicworks.cuny.edu/ulj/vol19/iss1/9

Adler, Melissa. *Cruising the Library: Perversities in the Organization of Knowledge.* New York: Fordham University Press, 2017.

Ahmed, Sara. *Living a Feminist Life.* Durham: Duke University Press, 2017.

Elias Walker Vitulli. "Queering the Carceral: Intersecting Queer/Trans Studies and Critical Prison Studies." *GLQ: A Journal of Lesbian and Gay Studies* 19, no. 1 (2013): 111–23.

Drabinski, Emily. "Teaching the Radical Catalog." In Roberto, K. R., and Sanford Berman. *Radical Cataloging: Essays at the Front.* Jefferson: McFarland & Co., 2008.

Foucault, Michel. *Security, Territory, and Population: Lectures at the Collège de France, 1977–1978.* New York: Picador, 2009.

Garner, Steve. *Whiteness: An Introduction.* London: Routledge, 2007.

Haworth, Robert H., and John M. Elmore. *Out of the Ruins: The Emergence of Radical Informal Learning Spaces.* Oakland: PM Press, 2017.

Hudson, David James. "The Whiteness of Practicality." In *Topographies of Whiteness: Mapping Whiteness in Library and Information Studies,* edited by Gina Schlesselman-Tarango, 203-234. Sacramento: Library Juice Press, 2017.

MacFarquhar, Larissa. "Building a Prison-to-School Pipeline." *The New Yorker,* August 17, 2017. Accessed February 10, 2018. https://www.newyorker.com/magazine/2016/12/12/the-ex-con-scholars-of-berkeley.

Marx, Karl. "Theses On Feuerbach." Theses on Feuerbach. Accessed February 27, 2018. https://www.marxists.org/archive/marx/works/1845/theses/theses.htm.

Morrone, Melissa. Introduction to *Informed Agitation: Library and Information Skills in Social Justice Movements and Beyond*, 1–7. Edited by Melissa Morrone. Sacramento: Library Juice Press, 2014.

Puar, Jasbir K. *The Right to Maim: Debility, Capacity, Disability.* Durham: Duke University Press, 2017.

Sloniowski, Lisa. "Affective Labor, Resistance, and the Academic Librarian." *Library Trends* 64, no. 4 (2016): 645–66.

Spade, Dean. *Normal Life: Administrative Violence, Critical Trans Politics, and the Limits of Law.* Durham: Duke University Press, 2015.

2596 Girls School Road: The Indiana Women's Prison Far-Away Reference Desk

Joshua Finnell

Founded in 1873, the Indiana Women's Prison is the first and oldest women's prison in the United States. In 2012, Kelsey Kauffman, a former correctional officer, developed a higher education program at the Indiana Women's Prison. Under the guidance of Kauffman and Jones, students in the college program have recently undertaken a collaborative project to research the prison's history and origin. In 2015, both women wrote in *Perspectives on History*, the magazine of the American Historical Association, about the challenges their students face in conducting archival and historical research. The inability to secure a local university or college affiliate has left many of the students' research questions unanswered. In response, librarian Barbara Fister organized the *Indiana Women's Prison Higher Education Program Far-Away Reference Desk*, a volunteer group of librarians willing to answer reference requests for archival material from the inmates enrolled in the college program. This innovative program seeks to remedy the deficiencies of the prison's library holdings and reference services by crowdsourcing library expertise and collections across the country.

This chapter will contextualize the Indiana Women's Prison Project within the historical trajectory of prison libraries and the psychological framework of Martin Seligman's foundational theory of learned helplessness and underscore how the Indiana Women's Prison Higher Education

Program Far-Away Reference Desk demonstrates the continued need and importance of reference services to marginalized and underserved groups.

A Brief History of Prison Libraries

> "Once again the need to control information in the guise of a 'legitimate penological interest' prevailed against the contemporary ideology—to prepare prisoners for transitioning back to the community—and common sense."
>
> —Brenda Vogel, *The Prison Library Primer*

It is impossible to discuss the history and development of prison libraries in the United States without also discussing the history of prisons in the United States. This brief overview is by no means exhaustive, but serves to provide context for the philosophical and legal development of prison libraries. For a historical overview of incarceration in the United States, I recommend Scott Christianson's 1998 book *With Liberty For Some: 500 Years of Imprisonment in America*. For a comprehensive history of prison libraries, Austin H. MacCormick's foundational book *A Brief History of Libraries in American Correctional Institutions*, and Brenda Vogel's *Down for the Count: A Prison Library Handbook*, give detailed accounts of the policies, organizations, and philosophical approaches that built America's prison library system.

At the outset, it is also helpful to distinguish between a *jail* and a *prison*. Though the terms are often used interchangeably, each institution serves a different function. Whereas a jail is usually run by a city or county and houses individuals awaiting a trial, or a prisoner with a short-term conviction, a prison is operated at the state or federal level and houses inmates found guilty by a court of law and serving long-term convictions.[1] Since prisons house inmates with longer terms of conviction, library services are more common in these institutions.

The first jail constructed in the New World was built in 1570 by Spanish soldiers in St. Augustine, Florida, functioning as a holding cell

---

1   Office of Justice Programs, "Bureau of Justice Statistics (BJS)," *BJS.gov*, last modified September 6, 2016, http://www.bjs.gov/index.cfm?ty=qa&iid=322.

for captured slaves.[2] Over the next century, though no official American legal system existed during the colonial period, jails slowly populated the eastern seaboard, such as Barnstable's Old Gaol in Massachusetts. Needless to say, these primitive jails were temporary enclosures and physical punishment was paramount. It wasn't until after the American Revolution that the nation's first prison systems would be constructed with an eye towards long-term containment over physical punishment.[3] Meanwhile, the eighteenth century would produce the nation's first American subscription library in the form of Benjamin Franklin's Library Company of Philadelphia in 1731.[4] However, it would be another century before these two types of institutions would be linked.

Through most of the eighteenth century, books were a rare commodity in America's prisons, with the exception of bibles and religious literature donated by Christian organizations to help inmates atone for their sins. For example, the Pennsylvania Prison Society, a group largely inspired by Benjamin Rush's *An Enquiry into the Effects of Public Punishments Upon Criminals*, furnished religious texts to the Walnut Street Prison in 1790.[5] Retribution rather than rehabilitation was the ethos of the prison system through much of the eighteenth and nineteenth centuries. A lengthy rumination on eternal suffering, if one did not change his or her ways, was the only form of behavioral modification available to the imprisoned. As Brenda Vogel writes in *The Prison Library Primer*, "For most of its history, the penitentiary has functioned under a consequentialist moral utilitarian ideology. This teleological philosophy operated under the belief that the means will lead to a beneficial end."[6] Though prison libraries were established in the early nineteenth century, it wasn't until the end of the Second Great Awakening in the United States, in 1840, that library

---

2   Scott Christianson, *With Liberty For Some: 500 Years of Imprisonment in America* (Boston, MA: Northeastern Press, 1998), 6.

3   David J. Rothman, *Conscience and Convenience: The Asylum and Its Alternatives in Progressive America* (New York: Aldine Transaction, 2002), 57.

4   "The Library Company of Philadelphia Homepage," *librarycompany.org*, last modified February 15, 2014, http://www.librarycompany.org/.

5   Pennsylvania Prison Society, "Pennsylvania Prison Society Records," *hsp.org*, last modified March 3, 2016, http://hsp.org/sites/default/files/legacy_files/migrated/findingaid-1946prisonsociety.pdf.

6   Brenda Vogel, *The Prison Library Primer: A Program for the Twenty-First Century* (Bethesda: Scarecrow Press, 2009), 2.

services begin to develop in the nation's prisons. Given the lack of education among many inmates, literacy initiatives formed the core early library outreach. Of course, library services were still centered on religious instruction, as chaplains were most likely to serve as the prison's librarians and literacy efforts were focused on reading the Bible.[7]

It was at the state prison in Sing Sing, New York that an early prison reformer, Eliza Farnham, endeavored to modify the behavior of the female inmates not through religious instruction, but through works of popular fiction. A devotee of phrenology, Farnham was interested less in the moral development of the inmates and more in the cerebral organization of the criminal mind. Her early attempts at changing the habits of the inmates through the works of Dickens and travel literature were to be short lived, as her materials were deemed immoral and her tenure as the prison librarian at Sing Sing ended in 1848.[8] However, her efforts laid the foundation for prison libraries to be part of a larger educational, rather than religious, program. Moreover, the prison library itself would begin to symbolize a philosophical shift in the historical prison ethos from retribution to rehabilitation. As a corollary, twenty years later, at the first National Prison Congress in Cincinnati, the American Prison Association was created.[9]

In 1911, almost 200 years after Franklin's subscription library was created, the American Library Association created a Committee on Libraries in Federal Prisons and published the first *Manual for Institution Libraries* four years later.[10] This guidebook would be the first to align the goals of libraries with an ethos of expanding self-improvement through reading and the burgeoning interest of penal institutions to integrate prisoners back into society. One finds the fruits of these initial efforts reflected decades later in the 1942 *Handbook of American Prisons and Reformatories*: "Self-sustained reading encourages sound habits of individual study and thought, because well-established reading habits are likely to continue after release, and because library activities furnish the inmate with a means

7   Price Chenault, "Correctional Institutions Helping the Functionally Illiterate," *ALA Bulletin* 58, no. 9 (1964): 804–9.

8   Vogel, *The Prison Library Primer*, 4.

9   Brenda Vogel, *Down for the Count* (Bethesda: Scarecrow Press, 1995), 5.

10   Rhea Joyce Rubin, *U.S. Prison Library Services and Their Theoretical Bases*, Occasional Papers (Urbana-Champaign: University of Illinois, Graduate School of Library Science, 1973), 4.

of maintaining alertness throughout his sentence and tend to counteract the development of prison stupor."[11] The importance of the prison library to the rehabilitation and reintegration of inmates is now almost intrinsic to the modern prison library mission statement.

However, in addition to basic reading materials, it should also be noted that a prisoner's right to access legal materials in prison, protected by the Fourteenth Amendment of the U.S. Constitution, is a twentieth century phenomenon. Although the 1970 *Gilmore v. Lynch* case, in which inmates sued the California Department of Corrections for access to legal materials, laid the foundation, it was not until the decisive 1977 *Bounds v. Smith* case that prisons were not mandated to provide legal materials through the prison library.[12] The State argued that prisoners, lacking legal knowledge, would not know how to effectively utilize legal materials, rendering access to such materials useless. The court disagreed, but made no ruling as to the quality and quantity of legal materials a prison library must provide. In the 1996 *Lewis v. Casey* ruling, the court made clear that it is a prisoner's responsibility, not the institution's, to demonstrate that a prison's law library is lacking before a claim can be filed.[13]

Sadly, the mere act of reading in prison is still considered a privilege rather than a necessary component of healing and development. Plunging prisons back into a mode of punishment over rehabilitation, the 2006 U.S. Supreme Court, in *Beard v. Banks,* ruled in favor of the state of Pennsylvania's right to deny reading materials to prisoners deemed inveterate.[14] The prevailing opinion underscored that the ruling was consistent with eighteenth century penal philosophy.[15]

These court rulings are important because they limit the types of information prisoners have access to, yet, paradoxically, are based on the as-

---

11   Vogel, *The Prison Library Primer*, 8.

12   Gilmore v. Lynch, 319 F. Supp. 105 (Dist. Court 1970); Bounds v. Smith, 430 US 817 (Supreme Court 1976).

13   Lewis v. Casey, 518 US 343 (Supreme Court 1995).

14   Beard v. Banks, 548 US 521 (Supreme Court 2006).

15   For a comprehensive history of these landmark cases, see Brandon Nichole Wright's chapter, "The Prison Law Library: A Fourteenth Amendment Necessity" in *Perspectives on Libraries as Institutions of Human Rights and Social Justice*, eds. Natalie Greene Taylor, Ursula Gorham, and Paul T. Jaeger, eds. *Perspectives on Libraries as Institutions of Human Rights and Social Justice.* Advances in Librarianship 41. (New York: Emerald Group Publishing Limited. 2016).

sumption that prisoners are fully capable of advocating for their needs, and more importantly, retain the ability, through reading and research, to understand and improve their situations. This belief is grounded in a modern penal philosophy heavily influenced by the rise of the social sciences.[16] An application of the scientific process to society, with an emphasis on the individual, gradually pervaded the twentieth century prison system in the United States. This movement would shift prisons away from a consequentialist moral utilitarian ideology to a belief that, as Brenda Vogel writes, "a multi-focal positivist approach could manage and correct crime and criminals."[17]

Learned Helplessness and Library Research

> "Nature, however, is not always so benign in its arrangement of the contingencies. Not only do we face events that we can control by our actions, but we also face many events about which we can do nothing at all. Such uncontrollable events can significantly debilitate organisms: they produce passivity in the face of trauma, inability to learn that responding is effective, and emotional stress in animals, and possibly depression in man."
>
> —Martin Seligman, *Learned Helplessness*

The mere application of an isolated, positivist approach to rehabilitation often negates the impact of an inmate's experiences, both inside and outside of the prison setting. In *Discipline and Punish: The Birth of the Prison*, Michel Foucault argued that the prison system is a natural component of a "disciplinary society," consisting of schools, hospitals, and militaries that serve to control the body through the regulation of space and time. Through this lens, Foucault rejects the traditional penal dichotomy between rehabilitation and punishment, and argues that prisons are an extension of pre-existing subjection and oppression.[18] Understood in this way, Foucault's work is a structural analysis of power and how it permeates society.

---

16 Johan Heilbron, Lars Magnusson, and Björn Wittrock, eds. *The Rise of the Social Sciences and the Formation of Modernity: Conceptual Change in Context, 1750–1850.* (Boston: Kluwer Academic Publishers, 1998), 154.

17 Vogel, *The Prison Library Primer*, 5.

18 Michel Foucault, *Discipline & Punish: The Birth of the Prison* (New York: Vintage Books, 1995).

In the late 1960s, a young doctoral student in psychology at the University of Pennsylvania was finishing up his research on depression when he stumbled upon conditioning responses in dogs that blatantly contradicted B. F. Skinner's widely held theory of behaviorism. Martin Seligman discovered that dogs repeatedly administered an uncontrollable shock, regardless of good or bad actions, begin to passively accept the pain. Moreover, the dogs did not practice avoidance behavior even when the level of shock was incrementally increased. These findings contradicted Skinner's belief that behavior is determined by its consequences, reward or punishment. Seligman would publish his groundbreaking results under the title, *Learned Helplessness.*[19] In applying this theory to humans, Seligman would eventually incorporate Lyn Yvonne Abramson's work on explanatory styles, how people explain their experiences to themselves.[20] This modification is significant because it helps uncover how empowered people feel about their own lives. Whereas a positive explanatory style attributes negative events in one's life to specific or temporary moments, a negative explanatory style attributes negative events to permanent or global causes. Seligman's theory would usher in the newly minted field of positive psychology, with a wider emphasis on a person's relationships across family, friends, and community.

In the *International Journal of Offender Therapy and Comparative Criminology*, Richard Schill and David Marcus published a study of Seligman's revised theory of learned helplessness within the prison environment.[21] The study interviewed sixty inmates from two prisons in the Texas Department of Criminal Justice system, and grouped them by term of incarceration: thirty inmates were imprisoned for five years or more and thirty were imprisoned for less than year. Schill and Marcus discovered that the longer an inmate had been imprisoned, the more negative his or her attributional style became. In turn, this negative attributional style could lead to isolation and depression. Of course, it should be noted that a prisoner's attributional style can be correlated with several variables, such as

---

19   Martin E. Seligman, "Learned Helplessness," *Annual Review of Medicine* 23, no. 1 (1972): 407–12.

20   Lyn Abramson, Martin E. Seligman, and John D. Teasdale, "Learned Helplessness in Humans: Critique and Reformulation." *Journal of Abnormal Psychology* 87, no. 1 (1978): 49–74.

21   Richard Schill and David K. Marcus, "Incarceration and Learned Helplessness." *International Journal of Offender Therapy and Comparative Criminology* 42, no. 3 (1998): 224–32.

number of outside visitors, and length of term.[22] Curiously, not mentioned in this study was a prisoner's access to books.

Though directed towards a Christian cosmological view, early prison libraries understood the power of books to transform one's "explanatory style." One could argue, that by localizing pain and suffering in original sin, a prison library chaplain hoped to attribute a prisoner's negative actions to a temporary lapse into evil while providing inmates with an eternal, positive attribute as one of God's children. Understood in this way, prison libraries have been engaging in the act of bibliotherapy since the eighteenth century (though the clinical term wouldn't be coined until it was used to treat veterans of World War One, and popularized through the work of William and Karl Menninger).[23] Sara (Sadie) Peterson Delaney, chief librarian of the Veterans' Administration Hospital at Tuskegee Normal and Industrial Institute from 1924 to 1958, was perhaps most successful in using bibliotherapy to help individuals embody familiar experiences and find catharsis through literature.[24] In addition, Eliza Farnham's early attempts to introduce Dickens' novels into the prison library at Sing Sing, with their moralistic tales, perhaps point to her attempt to have prisoners see their own life stories through Oliver Twist.

As a treatment for learned helplessness, cognitive bibliotherapy has proven effective in a prison setting. Pardini et al., in a recent comprehensive study of prison bibliotherapy, conclude that "approximately half of the treated participants achieved clinically significant change."[25] Bibliotherapy is distinctive in that, much like Seligman's theory contradicting Skinner's widely accepted theory of behaviorism, bibliotherapy brings back the importance of subjectivity to a modern penology steeped in objective,

---

22 Lee H. Bukstel and Peter R. Kilmann, "Psychological Effects of Imprisonment on Confined Individuals." *Psychological Bulletin* 88, no. 2 (1980): 469–93; J. D. Wooldredge, "Inmate Experiences and Psychological Well-Being." *Criminal Justice and Behavior* 26, no. 2 (1999): 235–50; Phil Reed, Yousef Alenazi, and Fenella Potterton, "Effect of Time in Prison on Prisoners' Use of Coping Strategies," *International Journal of Prisoner Health* 5, no. 1 (2009): 16–24.

23 Karl Menninger, *Man Against Himself.* (San Diego: Mariner Books, 1956).; Karl Menninger, *The Human Mind, by Karl A. Menninger.* (New York: The Literary Guild of America, 1930).

24 Megan Sweeney, *Reading Is My Window: Books and the Art of Reading in Women's Prisons.* (Chapel Hill: University of North Carolina Press, 2010).

25 Jamie Pardini, et al., "Efficacy and Process of Cognitive Bibliotherapy for the Treatment of Depression in Jail and Prison Inmates." *Psychological Services* 11, no. 2 (2014): 114–52.

numerical output that negates the importance of a prisoner's experience. Evoking the spirit of Foucault, Deborah Dysart-Gale, chair of the Centre for Engineering in Society at Concordia University, writes in defense of bibliotherapy: "Quantification is capable of speaking in an authoritative voice, although it is not always capable of asking useful or even relevant questions."[26]

Of course, asking useful and relevant questions, especially in telling one's life story, requires an examination of the past through both memory and documents. For librarians and historians, the documented past often takes the form of an archive. However, as Jacques Derrida points out in *Archive Fever*, underscoring Foucault's assessment of power, archives are shaped by both social and political forces, determining what can be archived and ultimately remembered.[27] Yet, as products of history themselves, people derive a strong sense of identity by understanding how what came before them shaped their geography, politics, and social interactions. It is this interpretation of a person's past that dictates their explanatory style, in the parlance of Abramson and Seligman.

Prisoner's undertaking archival research, or criminal justice research, face a range of obstacles, from a lack of resources to a rejection of their research as too emotionally charged to be considered objective. In 2014, the journal *Qualitative Inquiry* published a special issue dedicated to "Doing Prison Research Differently." In the introductory essay, Yvonne Jewkes countered the criticism of a prisoner's objectivity, writing: "I believe that our personalities, histories, and emotions penetrate our research in ways that can ultimately enrich our analysis and give life, vividness, and luminosity to our writing."[28] If Foucault is correct in assuming that prison is a mere extension of larger structural powers, and Seligman is correct that repetitive trauma produces a state of learned helplessness, then an inmate's first step towards rehabilitation will ultimately start with their own private, emotional histories.

---

26   Deborah Dysart-Gale, "Lost in Translation: Bibliotherapy and Evidence-Based Medicine," *Journal of Medical Humanities* 29, no. 1 (2007): 41. A comprehensive history of bibliotherapy in prisons can be found in Megan Sweeney's, *Reading is My Window: Books and the Art of Reading in Women's Prisons*.

27   Jacques Derrida, *Archive Fever: A Freudian Impression* (Chicago: University of Chicago Press, 1998).

28   Yvonne Jewkes, "An Introduction to 'Doing Prison Research Differently,'" *Qualitative Inquiry* 20, no. 4 (2014): 387.

For many inmates, the journey towards discovery begins with the personal: their childhood, their family, and often a deep meditation on the antecedents of their convictions. The *Handbook for Writers in Prison,* freely published by the PEN Prison Writing Program, provides inmates with a blueprint of how to transfer the transformative power of storytelling and research into a memoir, a short story, or a poem. Shaka Senghor, a former prisoner who served 19 years incarcerated and founded the Atonement Project, writes in his 2016 memoir: "There's a reason why so many inmates use storytelling as a coping tool. Being in prison and stripped of your freedom is painful and degrading, and each day is a fight to maintain your sanity."[29] Researching and articulating a personal narrative is a necessary component to not only understanding one's place in the world, but also allowing an individual to take control over the interpretation of the past and, ultimately, the future. This is a form of empowerment that is rare in the walls of a prison, as each inmate's' identity is enmeshed within a larger history of the prison-industrial complex. After all, prisoners, stripped of almost all rights, are heavily cataloged and classified: a compilation of cell assignments, conviction records, and demographic information. Yet, underneath those areas of description are personal stories and histories that are rarely articulated or documented.

Indiana Women's Prison Faraway Reference Desk

> "What, it will be asked, has been the result of all this improvement in prison life? We answer: In most cases restored womanhood, to enter again in life able to care for themselves and not a terror or an expense to society."
>
> —*Sarah J. Smith, Superintendent,*
>   *Indiana Reformatory for Women and Girls, 1875*

In the early nineteenth century, men and women were housed in the same prisons. Because men far outnumbered incarcerated women, a separate prison was deemed an unnecessary expense. Moreover, female prisoners at this time were considered beyond redemption and referred to as "fallen" for not living up to Victorian standards of feminine moral virtue. Howev-

---

29 Shara Senghor, *Writing My Wrongs: Life, Death, and Redemption in an American Prison.* (New York: Convergent Books, 2016): 18.

er, between the years of 1840–1860, the rate of female incarceration rapidly increased with the introduction and enforcement of laws that regulated sexual conduct, such as adultery, prostitution, and abortion.[30] Largely as a result of mandatory sentencing and harsher sentencing for drug-related offenses, the rate of incarceration among women remains unabated into the 21st century, with the Vera Institute of Justice reporting that the number of women in prison has risen from 8,000 in 1970 to over 110,000 in 2014.[31] The increased population of female prisoners, and the prevalence of sexual assault and abuse of female inmates, led to the prison reform movement, and the creation of the nation's first women's prisons in the late nineteenth century.[32]

Because many of the early prison reformers were religiously based, some of the first women's prisons in the United States were referred to as reformatories, with an eye toward instilling Christian morals into these "fallen" women. The Indiana Reformatory for Women and Girls (now known as the Indiana Women's Prison, or IWP) was founded in 1873 under this ideology and is often credited as the nation's first women's prison. Sarah J. Smith and Rhoda Coffin, two Quaker women, helped found the prison in Indianapolis in an attempt to save women from the rampant abuse taking place in the state's penal institutions. Today, the Indiana Women's Prison is a medium to maximum security prison located in Indianapolis, housing approximately 611 inmates.[33]

In 2012, in the wake of funding cuts for educational opportunities for prisoners, Kelsey Kauffman, a former correctional officer, helped develop a higher education program at the Indiana Women's Prison. This program is completely staffed by volunteers, and teaches a range of courses. Though not a historian by training, Kaufman took note of the numerous historical documents about the prison at the Indiana State Archives, and

---

30 Cyndi Banks, *Women in Prison: A Reference Handbook*. (Santa Barbara, California: ABC-CLIO, 2003): 3.

31 Timothy Williams, "Number of Women in Jail Has Grown Far Faster Than That of Men, Study Says," *New York Times* August 18 (2016): para. 8.

32 For an overview of the development of Women's Prisons, see Cyndi Banks' *Women in Prison: A Reference Handbook* and Barbara H. Zaitzow and Jim Thomas, eds., *Women in Prison: Gender and Social Control*. (Boulder: Lynne Rienner, 2003).

33 Bruce Lemmon, "Indiana Department of Correction: Offender Population Report," *Justice Reinvestment Advisory Council and State Budget Committee*, last modified May 5, 2016, http://www.in.gov/idoc/2376.htm

thought researching the history of the prison would provide a useful lesson in how to conduct archival research through both primary and secondary sources. However, as the students became engaged in the project, their research uncovered a much darker tale than the "religious savior" narrative through which the prison's history is often presented.

As Michelle Jones, a teaching assistant and inmate at IWP, writes: "As a different picture of our prison began to form, we came to understand that its self-proclaimed successes in reformation would have to be tempered against a dramatic legislative investigation in 1881 into physical abuse of inmates by Superintendent Smith and her staff at the prison. We learned of allegations of waterboarding or 'dunking,' of outright physical abuse, of women stripped naked and put in solitary confinement."[34] What Michelle Jones and other inmates in the course uncovered was the rampant abuse these women faced at the hands of their "reformers." As a corollary, the women in the course began to connect the dots to the larger structural powers that were obscured by this popular history of the prison. Kauffman soon became overwhelmed with reference questions. In a plea to members of the American Historical Association, Kauffman wrote, "I need help tracking down myriad leads on such topics as Sarah Smith's roots in England; the history of the Magdalene laundry in Buffalo, New York; 19th-century sewage systems; and the incidence of female circumcision in the 1870s."[35]

Reading Kauffman's request for help, Barbara Fister, a librarian at Gustavus Adolphus College, organized a group of librarians from across the country in 2016 to form the Indiana Women's Prison Far-Away Reference Desk.[36] The response has been overwhelming, with over fifty librarians at the ready to answer reference questions from students in the course. Utilizing a shared Google Drive, Kaufman relays the student's reference

34 Michelle Jones, "Women's Prison History: The Undiscovered Country," *Perspectives on History: American Historical Association*, last modified February 2016, https://www.historians.org/publications-and-directories/perspectives-on-history/february-2015/womens-prison-history

35 Kelsey Kauffman, "Academia in Prison: The Role of the University in an Era of Mass Incarceration," *Perspectives on History: American Historical Association*, last modified February 2015, https://www.historians.org/publications-and-directories/perspectives-on-history/february-2015/academia-in-prison.

36 Barbara Fister, "Helping Gifted (and Incarcerated) Students Conduct Research—A Volunteer Opportunity." *Library Babel Fish*, last modified May 21, 2016, https://www.insidehighered.com/blogs/library-babel-fish/helping-gifted-and-incarcerated-students-conduct-research-%E2%80%93-volunteer-0.

questions to Barbara, and the librarians start populating the primary and secondary sources. For example, through their own research of early prison records, students in the course discovered that not one woman was incarcerated for any sexual offense. Because this didn't align with the legal history at the time, the students were curious to know where all these women of "ill repute" were imprisoned. They discovered that a parallel reformatory for women had been created at the same time as the Indiana Reformatory for Women and Girls called the House of the Good Shepherd. The first reference question handled by the Far-Away Reference Desk was to locate all information known about the House of the Good Shepherd in every state. Soon, librarians from various institutions created a shared spreadsheet, populated with historical newspaper articles, registries, journal articles, and even letters.

Much like Eliza Farnham's push for prison libraries to provide more than religious texts, Kelsey Kauffmann and her volunteers are pushing prison libraries to be more than a repository of books to ward off boredom. Kauffman writes:

> It was not until we were well into our history project at IWP that I realized that historians and I had been asking the wrong questions about the prison. My students, on the other hand, have consistently asked the right questions—often-cynical, penetrating, exacting ones that not only have exposed new information about the founders of this prison, but have challenged prevailing ideas about where, when, and by whom prisons for women were started and, most importantly, why.[37]

However, finding and asking the right question is a much easier task than fulfilling a research need from an outside source in the IWP, and all prisons. In order to transmit the collected library materials to the inmates in the course, Fister was required to use JPay, a privately held corrections-related-service provider. Founded in 2002 by Ryan Shapiro, JPay has been called the "the Apple of the U.S. Prison System" by *Bloomberg Businessweek*.[38] Handling everything from video visitations to email communica-

---

37   Kauffman, "Academia in Prison: The Role of the University in an Era of Mass Incarceration," para 3.

38   Nick Leiber. "JPay, the Apple of the U.S. Prison System." *Bloomberg Business Week*, last modified September 13, 2012, https://www.bloomberg.com/news/articles/2012-09-13/jpay-the-apple-of-the-u-dot-s-dot-prison-system.

tions, JPay owns and provides a coveted connection to the outside world for over 1 million prisoners in 35 states.[39] However, JPay's business model is built upon charging the end-user: the prisoner. As Barbara Fister soon discovered, technical barriers often impede the best of intentions:

> I have been working a lot with Michelle Jones, who sends me questions using a prison email system (jpay.com) that extracts a lot of money from the incarcerated and those who want to communicate with them. It works, and I'm grateful for it, but the company charges 40 cents per "stamp"–and anything other than a short email costs more than one stamp. You can't attach things like JSTOR articles either. I'm fine paying to do this but for incarcerated people who earn 10–15 cents/hour if they are able to earn at all, it's prohibitive."[40]

For the inmates at IWP, and across the U.S. prison system, the research process is heavily burdened by transaction costs. To satisfy a simple spark of curiosity, an inmate might need to save several months' salary. The paucity of print and electronic collections and personnel resources at prison libraries, coupled with limited outside contact allotted to prisoners, make reference services to prisoners an important act of social justice. Though the Far-Away Reference Desk is an initial attempt to create a fair and just relationship between librarians and inmates, new modes of providing reference services to incarcerated people will need to be explored and tested. The Reference Letters from Prisons initiative, a collaboration between the New York Public Library's Correctional Services Program and Pratt Institute School of Information, is one way for academic and public libraries to leverage their resources at a local level. Replicating this model in cities and states across the country could be an opportunity to build a sustainable network of "far-away reference desks." Noting the challenge her project faces, Fister writes, "I guess I shouldn't be at all surprised that this is difficult to organize–library work is as much about people and social systems as it is about actual information."[41]

In the final essay in the recently published *Perspectives on Libraries as Institutions of Human Rights and Social Justice*, Ursula Gorham, Na-

---

39 ——, "JPay, the Apple of the U.S. Prison System."

40 Barbara Fister, e-mail message to author, March 15, 2017.

41 ——-, e-mail message to author, March 15, 2017

talie Green Taylor, and Paul T. Jaeger conclude: "Information has become the ultimate rights and justice issue in a world defined by the Internet."[42] Sometimes lost in the debate over the necessity of reference services in the age of Google is the variability in quality of both technology and access to information in the U.S. prison system. Often the cost outweighs the speed of a reference interview. With the New York Public Library's Correctional Service Program responding to as many as 60 letters a week from prisoners and the bulk of reference requests at the Law Library of Congress coming from local, municipal, county, state and federal prison facilities, reference services are increasingly in demand.[43] Programs such as the Far-Away Reference Desk are a call for librarians to step outside of institutional silos and uphold the core values of access espoused by the American Library Association that "all information resources that are provided directly or indirectly by the library, regardless of technology, format, or methods of delivery, should be readily, equally, and equitably accessible to all library users."[44] Concluding her essay in *Perspectives on History*, Kauffman muses, "Ironically, prisons today offer an extraordinary opportunity to provide quality higher education to historically marginalized groups of all colors if only we will seize it. So far, we have not."[45] The Far-Away Reference Desk at the Indiana Women's Prison is one attempt at responding to this challenge.

---

42   Natalie Greene Taylor, Ursula Gorham, and Paul T. Jaeger, *Perspectives on Libraries as Institutions of Human Rights and Social Justice*. Advances in Librarianship 41. (New York: Emerald Group Publishing Limited, 2016): 384.

43   Max Kutner, "With No Google, the Incarcerated Wait for the Mail" *Newsweek*, last modified January 1, 2015, http://www.newsweek.com/people-behind-bars-google-answers-arrive-mail-301836.; Margaret Wood, "Prisoner Letters to the Law Library of Congress." *Custodia Legis: Law Librarians of Congress*, last modified April 17, 2013, http://blogs.loc.gov/law/2013/04/prisoner-letters-to-the-law-library-of-congress/.

44   American Library Association, "Access." *Core Values of Librarianship*, last modified July 26, 2006. http://www.ala.org/advocacy/intfreedom/statementspols/corevalues.

45   Kauffman, "Academia in Prison: The Role of the University in an Era of Mass Incarceration," para. 26.

Works Cited

Abramson, Lyn Y., Martin E. Seligman, and John D. Teasdale. "Learned Helplessness in Humans: Critique and Reformulation." *Journal of Abnormal Psychology* 87, no. 1 (1978): 49–74. doi:10.1037/0021-843X.87.1.49.

Adams, Brooke, and Jim Dalrymple Salt Lake Tribune. "Prison Inmates Find Roots By Doing Genealogy Research For Mormons." *The Huffington Post*, 25:31 400AD. http://www.huffingtonpost.com/2014/04/03/utah-prisoners-mormon-genealogy_n_5079776.html.

American Library Association. "Access." *Core Values of Librarianship*. Last modified July 26, 2006. http://www.ala.org/advocacy/intfreedom/statementspols/corevalues.

Banks, Cyndi. *Women in Prison: A Reference Handbook*. Santa Barbara, California: ABC-CLIO, 2003.

Beard v. Banks, 548 US 521 (Supreme Court 2006).

Bounds v. Smith, 430 US 817 (Supreme Court 1976).

Bukstel, Lee H., and Peter R. Kilmann. "Psychological Effects of Imprisonment on Confined Individuals." *Psychological Bulletin* 88, no. 2 (1980): 469–93. doi:10.1037/0033-2909.88.2.469.

Chenault, Price. "Correctional Institutions Helping the Functionally Illiterate." *ALA Bulletin* 58, no. 9 (1964): 804–9.

Christianson, Scott. *With Liberty for Some: 500 Years of Imprisonment in America*. Boston, MA: Northeastern Press, 1998.

Derrida, Jacques. *Archive Fever: A Freudian Impression*. Paperback ed. Religion and Postmodernism. Chicago: University of Chicago Press, 1998.

Dysart-Gale, Deborah. "Lost in Translation: Bibliotherapy and Evidence-Based Medicine." *Journal of Medical Humanities* 29, no. 1 (December 13, 2007): 33–43. doi:10.1007/s10912-007-9050-0.

Fister, Barbara. E-mail message to author, March 15, 2017.

— — —. "Helping Gifted (and Incarcerated) Students Conduct Research—A Volunteer Opportunity." *Library Babel Fish*. Last modified May 21, 2016. https://www.insidehighered.com/blogs/library-babel-fish/helping-gifted-and-incarcerated-students-conduct-research-%E2%80%93-volunteer-0.

Foucault, Michel. *Discipline & Punish: The Birth of the Prison*. Translated by Alan Sheridan. 2nd edition. New York: Vintage Books, 1995.

Gilmore v. Lynch, 319 F. Supp. 105 (Dist. Court 1970).

Heilbron, Magnusson, and Björn Wittrock, eds. *The Rise of the Social Sciences and the Formation of Modernity: Conceptual Change in Context, 1750–1850.* Boston: Kluwer Academic Publishers, 1998.

Jewkes, Yvonne. "An Introduction to 'Doing Prison Research Differently.'" *Qualitative Inquiry* 20, no. 4 (April 1, 2014): 387–91. doi:10.1177/1077800413515828.

Jones, Michelle. "Women's Prison History: The Undiscovered Country." *Perspectives on History: American Historical Association.* Last modified February 2015. https://www.historians.org/publications-and-directories/perspectives-on-history/february-2015/womens-prison-history.

Kauffman, Kelsey. "Academia in Prison: The Role of the University in an Era of Mass Incarceration." *Perspectives on History: American Historical Association.* Last modified February 2015. https://www.historians.org/publications-and-directories/perspectives-on-history/february-2015/academia-in-prison.

Kutner, Max. "With No Google, the Incarcerated Wait for the Mail." *Newsweek.* Last modified January 1, 2015. http://www.newsweek.com/people-behind-bars-google-answers-arrive-mail-301836.

Lemmon, Bruce. "Indiana Department of Correction: Offender Population Report." *Justice Reinvestment Advisory Council and State Budget Committee,* Last modified May 5, 2016. http://www.in.gov/idoc/2376.htm.

Lewis v. Casey, 518 US 343 (Supreme Court 1995).

Leiber, Nick. "JPay, the Apple of the U.S. Prison System." *Bloomberg Business Week.* Last modified September 13, 2012, https://www.bloomberg.com/news/articles/2012-09-13/jpay-the-apple-of-the-u-dot-s-dot-prison-system.

Menninger, Karl. *Man Against Himself.* 1st edition. San Diego: Mariner Books, 1956.

Menninger, Karl Augustus. *The Human Mind, by Karl A. Menninger.* New York: The Literary Guild of America, 1930.

Office of Justice Programs. "Bureau of Justice Statistics (BJS)." Accessed September 6, 2016. http://www.bjs.gov/index.cfm?ty=qa&iid=322.

Pardini, Jamie, Forrest Scogin, Jennifer Schriver, Marla Domino, Dawn Wilson, and Michael LaRocca. "Efficacy and Process of Cognitive Bibliotherapy for the Treatment of Depression in Jail and Prison Inmates." *Psychological Services* 11, no. 2 (May 2014): 141–52. doi:10.1037/a0033378.

PEN Prison Writing Program. *Handbook for Writers in Prison.* New York: Pen American Center, 2006.

Pennsylvania Prison Society. "Pennsylvania Prison Society Records." http://www.hsp. org, last modified March 3, 2016, http://hsp.org/sites/default/files/legacy_files/ migrated/findingaid1946prisonsociety.pdf.

Reed, Phil, Yousef Alenazi, and Fenella Potterton. "Effect of Time in Prison on Prisoners' Use of Coping Strategies." *International Journal of Prisoner Health* 5, no. 1 (March 2009): 16–24. doi:10.1080/17449200802692060.

Rothman, David J. *Conscience and Convenience: The Asylum and Its Alternatives in Progressive America.* New York: Aldine Transaction, 2002.

Rubin, Rhea Joyce. *U.S. Prison Library Services and Their Theoretical Bases.* Occasional Papers. Urbana-Champaign: University of Illinois, Graduate School of Library Science, 1973.

Sampson, Marmaduke B., and Eliza W. Farnham. *Rationale of Crime, and Its Appropriate Treatment; Being a Treatise on Criminal Jurisprudence Considered in Relation to Cerebral Organization. … From the Second London Edition, with Notes and Illustrations by E.W. Farnham.* New York, 1846.

Schill, Richard A., and David K. Marcus. "Incarceration and Learned Helplessness." *International Journal of Offender Therapy and Comparative Criminology* 42, no. 3 (September 1, 1998): 224–32. doi:10.1177/0306624X9804200304.

Seligman, Martin E. "Learned Helplessness." *Annual Review of Medicine* 23, no. 1 (1972): 407–12. doi:10.1146/annurev.me.23.020172.002203.

Senghor, Shara. *Writing My Wrongs: Life, Death, and Redemption in an American Prison.* Convergent Books, 2016.

Sweeney, Megan. *Reading Is My Window: Books and the Art of Reading in Women's Prisons.* Chapel Hill: University of North Carolina Press, 2010.

Taylor, Natalia Greene, Gorham, Ursula, and Jaeger, Paul T., eds. *Perspectives on Libraries as Institutions of Human Rights and Social Justice.* Advances in Librarianship 41. New York: Emerald Group Publishing Limited, 2016. http://www.emeraldinsight. com/doi/book/10.1108/S0065-2830201641.

"The Library Company of Philadelphia Homepage." Accessed September 2, 2016. http://www.librarycompany.org/.

Vogel, Brenda. *Down for the Count: A Prison Library Handbook.* Bethesda: Scarecrow Press, 1995.

———. *The Prison Library Primer: A Program for the Twenty-First Century.* Bethesda: Scarecrow Press, 2009.

Williams, Timothy. "Number of Women in Jail Has Grown Far Faster Than That of Men, Study Says." *The New York Times*, August 18, 2016. http://www.nytimes. com/2016/08/18/us/number-of-women-in-jail-has-grown-far-faster-than-that-of-men-study-says.html.

Wood, Margaret. "Prisoner Letters to the Law Library of Congress." *Custodia Legis: Law Librarians of Congress.* Last modified, April 17, 2013. http://blogs.loc.gov/ law/2013/04/prisoner-letters-to-the-law-library-of-congress/.

Wooldredge, J. D. "Inmate Experiences and Psychological Well-Being." *Criminal Justice and Behavior* 26, no. 2 (June 1, 1999): 235–50. doi:10.1177/0093854899026002005.

Zaitzow, Barbara H., and Jim Thomas, eds. *Women in Prison: Gender and Social Control.* Boulder: Lynne Rienner, 2003.

Reference Behind Bars: Information Needs, Rights, and Empowerment of Inmates

Danielle Ball and Hannah Lee

Introduction

Societies function according to rules that govern the behavior and actions of people. The explicit rules are codified into laws, while the implicit rules derive from a less explicitly defined social contract. Although laws create a system of justice and punishment, society is not governed entirely by written legislation. Those considered "dangerous" by society and separated within correctional institutions are easily reduced to mere numbers needing basic human needs of food and shelter necessary for survival.

Human life, if it is to have full dignity, requires more. Because inmates completely depend upon a correctional facility for the basics of human life, it is unlikely that institutions will provide beyond what is legally required of them. Prison libraries are a prime example of the gulf between what may be required legally and what is required to nourish the souls and minds of individual human beings and citizens. We assert that those whom society chooses to incarcerate maintain their right to information and intellectual pursuits. Prison librarians attempt to provide inmates with access to information but face a difficult task. Confronted with what is legally afforded to inmates and the institutionalization of incarceration, as information providers librarians are torn between their duties to inmates and their duties to society as information gatekeepers. Unlike other librarians (e.g., public librarians or academic librarians), prison librarians face a unique challenge in preventing access to certain information while attempting to keep the general populace safe from any assumed dangers.

This chapter addresses how reference in prison libraries provides a critical service by empowering inmates during their incarceration. We begin with a brief examination of social contract theory and how it provides a valuable framework for a discussion on the rights and empowerment of inmates. Then, we provide background information on applicable statutes and standards that apply to a discussion on prison libraries in California. Using the experiences of one prison librarian and her reference services in a California prison as an example, we demonstrate how to enable prisoners to be a part of their information seeking process.

By demonstrating how reference can be a tool of empowerment for inmates, the primary goal of this chapter is to generate discussion on the need for more (and better) reference services to the prison community. Another goal is to discuss the ethical dilemma prison librarians face when attempting to balance: 1) the need and want for information, 2) the information restrictions of the prison system itself, and 3) the duties of librarians to their patrons.

Social Contract Theory

A social contract is the implicit agreement of those in society to behave and adhere to rules that govern it. There are numerous, exhaustive debates on the "right" interpretation of the social contract, from Lockean natural rights of man to Hobbesian authoritative government, or even further back, to Greco-Roman conceptions of citizenship.[1] What all of these philosophies have in common is the understanding that: 1) there is an inherent relationship between citizens and their government, and 2) there are rights that citizens should have. If a citizen commits a crime or otherwise violates the laws enforced and created by the government, then a citizen forfeits some of their rights. The debate arises when attempting to de-

---

1   See John Locke, *Two Treatises of Government and A Letter Concerning Toleration* (New Haven: Yale University Press, 2003); Thomas Hobbes, *Leviathan* (New York: Cambridge University Press, 1968); Derek Heater, *A Brief History of Citizenship* (New York: New York University Press, 2004).

termine what kind and level of authority governments have over citizens as well as the specific rights of citizens in society.

In the United States, the Declaration of Independence marked the dissolution of a social contract American colonists had with the British monarchy. In it, Thomas Jefferson wrote that people have the inalienable right to "Life, Liberty, and the pursuit of Happiness."[2] To secure these inalienable rights, the people give their consent to be governed by the government. However, the power of the government is not unlimited. The Constitution of the United States starts with the words, "We the people…" to establish the will of the then-budding American citizens against monarchical rule.[3] The Articles along with the Bill of Rights provides the guidelines for the governing of the United States. It follows that in the United States, citizens have inalienable rights, and to protect those rights, power is given to the government to create rules, laws, and order, thereby creating a social contract.

The core aspect of the social contract that this chapter focuses on is that when a social contract is broken, it does not mean that *all* of a person's inalienable rights are removed. Incarceration should not equate to stripping people of their needs and rights. While there are many issues with the current prison system that require attention, this chapter operates under the assumption that inmates should be afforded the right to information. As librarians, we believe we must not pass judgment on our patrons; libraries should serve their communities regardless of whom those communities comprise. For inmates who have severely limited access to resources, the services of prison libraries and librarians are critical.

Background on Prison Libraries

Discussions of prison libraries have traditionally focused on access to legal material which provides inmates the resources to attack their convictions or file civil rights complaints. In *Bounds v. Smith* (1977), the United States Supreme Court established a definitive right of meaningful access to the courts for prison inmates. The ruling stipulated that prisons must "assist inmates in the preparation and filing of meaningful legal papers by providing prisoners with adequate law libraries or adequate assistance from

---

2   Thomas Jefferson, The Declaration of Independence (1776).

3   U.S. Constitution, Preamble.

persons trained in the law."[4] Before this decision, the courts were reluctant to interfere with prison regulations that impeded inmates from accessing the courts.[5] After the *Bounds* decision, the majority of states began creating law libraries onsite at their prisons to comply with the courts and avoid inmate lawsuits.

The Court revisited the issue in *Lewis v. Casey* (1996) when a class of inmates in Arizona claimed that the law libraries in the state correctional system were so inadequate as to deny them their constitutional rights. Here, the Court found that while inmates have a constitutional right to access the courts, they did not have "an abstract, freestanding right to a law library or legal assistance."[6] Furthermore, *Lewis* required that inmates must demonstrate that they have been injured and unable to pursue a viable legal claim due to the failings of the law libraries.[7] This resulted in the significant downsizing of prison law library collections across the country. Fortunately, law libraries in prison have not completely vanished. States have adopted the more affordable and space-saving option of delivering legal material via electronic databases accessible to inmates.[8]

In California, the effect of the *Lewis* decision was not as negatively impactful as they were in other states. Instead, California had been guided by *Gilmore v. Lynch*, which was initially brought by San Quentin State Prison inmates in 1966 in regards to legal books and access to the courts. *Gilmore* resulted in a 1972 order "requiring that all California prisons maintain a specified list of legal research material in their libraries."[9] California later adopted regulations which mandated that "all inmates, regardless of their classification or housing status, shall be entitled to physical law library ac-

---

4   Bounds v. Smith, 430 U.S. 817 (1977).

5   O. James Werner, "Law Libraries for Correctional Facilities," *Library Trends* 26 (Summer 1977): 71.

6   Lewis v. Casey, 518 U.S. 343 (1996).

7   Ibid.

8   Jonathan Abel, "Ineffective Assistance of Library: the Failings and the Future of Prison Law Libraries," *The Georgetown Law Journal* 101, no. 5 (2013): 1173, https://georgetownlawjournal.org/articles/122/ineffective-assistance-of-library/pdf.

9   "Gilmore Injunction Over Prison Libraries Terminated After 38 Years," last modified December 15, 2010, https://www.prisonlegalnews.org/news/2010/dec/15/california-gilmore-injunction-over-prison-libraries-terminated-after-38-years/.

cess that is sufficient to provide meaningful access to the courts."[10] These regulations, being codified into law and enforceable by the state courts, have resulted in a standardized legal library collection across thirty-four California prisons and a termination of the *Gilmore v. Lynch* court order.

The ability of inmates to have access to the courts through legal literature in a meaningful way, however "meaningful" is described by the courts, cannot be overstated as a fundamental, constitutional right. However, mandates to purchase costly legal materials have often hindered the development of non-legal reference material and other general library collections. As Supreme Court Justice Thurgood Marshall wrote in the decision for a class action lawsuit regarding mail censorship in California prisons:

> When the prison gates slam behind an inmate, he does not lose his human quality; his mind does not become closed to ideas; his intellect does not cease to feed on a free and open interchange of opinions; his yearning for self-respect does not end; nor is his quest for self-realization concluded. If anything, the needs for identity and self-respect are more compelling in the dehumanizing prison environment.[11]

Prison inmates have a range of interests and information needs which extend beyond the legal realm. The response of prisons in meeting these information needs has reflected social values over time. Prior to and throughout the nineteenth century, for example, information provided to inmates in the library largely consisted of Christian religious material meant to evangelize inmates.[12] By the twentieth century, the rehabilitative and educational value of library services to inmates began to be recognized. Austin MacCormick, a celebrated criminologist, prison reformer, and champion of correctional education, wrote in 1931 that "if one could choose only one program of education in a penal institution, he would do well to choose an adequate library."[13] Recent correctional trends have focused on

---

10 California, *California Code of Regulations.* Title 15, Division 3, Chapter 1 (Sacramento: California Office of State Printing, 2016), 86.

11 Procunier v. Martinez, 416 U.S. 396 (1974).

12 Barratt Wilkins, "The Correctional Facility Library: History and Standards," *Library Trends* 26 (Summer 1977): 120.

13 Austin MacCormick, *The Education of Adult Prisoners: a Survey and a Program* (New York: National Society of Penal Information, 1931), 150.

the reduction of recidivism and assisting inmates in the successful reentry into society.[14]

Advocating for literacy in the last several decades, the American Library Association (ALA) and the American Correctional Association (ACA) have collaborated to develop standards for prison libraries, which emphasize "building collections according to the needs and interests of the prison population."[15] Prison systems seeking accreditation by the ACA are required to incorporate these standards for library programs, which include a selection of current reference materials. For example, the California Department of Corrections and Rehabilitation (CDCR) sets out in its department manual that:

> Library materials shall be selected and provided to meet the needs and interests of the entire inmate population. Materials provided shall encompass the American Correctional Association's and the American Library Association's recommended standards and shall be augmented by reference materials necessary to meet the needs of the facility.[16]

The standards recognize the need for reference collections stocked with reference sources, as well as material for literacy, educational support, and "life survival skills."[17] Unfortunately, these standards have not been updated since 1992, despite ALA statements strongly advocating for the intellectual freedom of inmates. As a result, prison librarians are left with departmental policies that mandate a bare-minimum collection that often fails to meet the information needs of their patrons. To provide successful reference services, prison librarians must pursue the development of robust collections through meager budgets, grants, and donations. However, first, they must understand the information needs of the population they serve.

---

14   Wilkins, "The Correctional Facility Library," 121.

15   Vibeke Lehmann, "Challenges and Accomplishments in U.S. Prison Libraries," *Library Trends* 59, no. 3 (2011): 493.

16   California, *Department Operations Manual* (Sacramento: California Department of Corrections and Rehabilitation, 2016), 815.

17   Ibid.

Information Needs of Inmates

Incarcerated individuals are often confronted with new information needs stemming from their legal situation or current environment. For example, inmates may for the first time need or desire to understand their legal rights. However, Chatman theorized that inmates hold a "small world" mentality wherein inmates sharing a social reality will avoid or trivialize information that comes from the outside world.[18] The very institution of incarceration creates not only physical barriers to information seeking behaviors but mental ones as well.

Chatman also maintained that inmates would "cross information boundaries" as long as the information sought was perceived as critical and relevant or if the uncertainty of living within the shared social reality is perceived as no longer functioning.[19] The existence of programs such as New York Public Library's (NYPL) Correctional Services Program demonstrates that inmates are crossing information boundaries and seeking assistance from libraries to meet their information needs, even when a single reference interview spans weeks. What information, then, is of importance to inmates that they seek out reference services?

To answer this question, Drabinski and Rabina reviewed letters from inmates sent to NYPL's Correctional Services Program and found inmates' information requests could be categorized into three main areas: re-entry, self-help, and reference. Specifically, the inquiries related to reentry and self-help information (56%) included career information, social services, educational opportunities, and information about rights for incarcerated people.[20] Forty-six percent of the requests were categorized as general reference requests and were much more varied. Examples included requests for song lyrics, medical information, baseball statistics, and publisher catalogs, among others.[21] Overall, inmates using the service were found to have

---

18   Elfreda A. Chatman, "A Theory of Life in the Round," *Journal of the American Society for Information Science* 50, no. 3 (1999): 214.

19   Ibid, 214.

20   Emily Drabinski and Debbie Rabina, "Reference Services to Incarcerated People, Part I: Themes Emerging from Answering Questions from Prisons and Jails," *Reference and User Services Association* 55, no. 1 (2015): 46.

21   Ibid, 47.

diverse information needs that reflected the "myriad reasons humans seek out information over the course of a lifetime."[22]

This summary echoes Burt's assertion four decades earlier that "inmates of correctional facilities have a wide range of information needs," and that within the prison library, the most important service is for "the information needs of inmates be met."[23] Reference material of particular interest may also include that which includes information on successful parole. For example, inmate demand for re-entry materials with geographical information on housing, food assistance, and other parolee services have been documented for many decades.[24] Inmates do not, as the prior legislation implied, only need access to literature related to the conditions surrounding their incarceration.

How it Works: Reference in Practice

While recommendations on the development of reference collections can be found in the professional literature provided by ALA and other sources, the actual process of delivering reference services in prison libraries has not been adequately addressed. This gap in knowledge sharing is no doubt exacerbated by the reality that no two prisons operate exactly alike, even within the same state systems. Budgets, levels of censorship, and inmates' physical access to the library can vary considerably between institutions, especially considering the differences between the security levels of prisons.

The following is a description of what reference looks like in one California prison from the perspective of one of the authors:

Reference at my prison library can be described as a three-tier system. The first tier involves reference transactions between the library's trained inmate workers and the library patrons. These transactions take place at both the legal reference desk and the general reference desk and may include utilizing the electronic library catalog to search for appropriate reference material. Ongoing training of inmate library workers on how to use various print resources, how to conduct reference interviews and provide

---

22   Ibid, 46.

23   Lesta N. Burt, "Information Needs of Inmates," *Library Trends* 26 (Summer 1977): 35–6.

24   See Burt, "Information Needs," 35; Jeff Mellow and James M. Dickinson, "The Role of Prerelease Handbooks for Prisoner Reentry," *Federal Probation* 70, no. 1 (2006): 70–6.

excellent customer service, and how to search the catalog effectively are essential in providing a quality level of service in the first tier of reference. Hiring inmate workers who are inquisitive and tend towards helping their peers is inarguably more imperative than hiring those inmates with formal education and training in library services.

When inmate library workers are unsuccessful at assisting patrons in meeting their information needs, the second-tier of reference services involves a referral to the librarian—me. Professional library staff can lead patrons to existing resources in the collection that have not been previously identified, or they may assist them in utilizing identified materials more productively. It should be noted that the transition from the first tier to the second tier of reference services is by no means formal nor is it necessary for an inmate to first seek help from an inmate library worker before me. Librarians at our facility have an "open door" policy when engaged in the staff office and can just as often be found on the library floor interacting with the library patrons, engaged in what has been described as roving reference. There exist many reasons an inmate may prefer seeking reference service from either the inmate library workers or a librarian, particularly when researching sensitive topics, such as medical diagnoses.

For the second-tier of reference services to be successful, I need to be extremely familiar with the library's collection and with traditional print resources. Whereas many public and academic libraries trend toward a reduced print collection in favor of electronic resources, prison libraries remain dependent on authoritative print materials, such as directories, dictionaries, thesauri, encyclopedias, almanacs, and gazetteers. Librarians who have been trained during the digital age and find themselves working in prison libraries should be willing and able to learn how to successfully use what may be considered old-fashioned resources. Collection development, then, is also paramount in delivering first and second-tier reference services, as "selection of materials cannot be separated from information needs."[25] Great care is taken to acquire material that is geared toward the interest and needs of the inmate population and not toward any person's impression of what inmates ought to be reading. Maintaining a suggestion box in the library and creating an inmate library advisory committee are two helpful strategies which I have employed to help make collection development decisions.

---

25   Burt, "Information Needs," 34.

Here it should also be noted that an effort needs to be made when providing legal reference to avoid giving legal advice. Not only is it illegal for non-attorneys to provide this type of assistance, but a prison librarian could also greatly lead an inmate astray and open him- or herself- to litigation and other negative consequences. Prison librarians must abstain from explaining legal options to inmates or sharing their interpretation of laws and statutes in the course of the reference transaction. It is prudent to become familiar with the legal reference collection and know when to refer an inmate to particular resources without giving legal advice. For prison libraries with an electronic legal database, such as what is available in my prison, librarians can teach inmates how to perform effective searches using keywords or case citations. Also, creating a library environment that is conducive to group collaboration is helpful as inmates are lawfully allowed to assist each other in the preparation of legal documents.[26]

The third tier of reference services is used when the library patron's information needs cannot be met using the library collection with the assistance of inmate library workers or the librarian. It involves the librarian obtaining information on the patron's behalf using resources that the inmate population does not have access to, namely, the Internet. Drabinski and Rabina rightly point out that without Internet access and robust library collections, many information needs of inmates go unanswered.[27] Therefore, this method of obtaining information can certainly assist librarians in meeting the information needs of the library patrons; yet, its use opens up many practical problems.

Inmates have an unbridled curiosity about the Internet, which unfortunately must be tempered by library staff; the demand for Internet searches far outweighs the capability of staff due to staffing shortages and time constraints. Perhaps more importantly, prison safety and security can be compromised when librarians disseminate Internet-sourced information which has not first been vetted by institutional administrators. Librarians who use the Internet as a resource for inmates need to have common sense and discretion, safeguards against inmate manipulation, and a strong knowledge of the rules and regulations regarding inmate access to certain types of information. How then can librarians safely provide this level of service?

---

26   Johnson v. Avery, 393 U.S. 483 (1969).

27   Drabinski and Rabina, "Reference Services to Incarcerated People," 42.

At my facility, librarians have developed an in-house reference request form for inmates to complete should they need information from the Internet. For the reasons listed above, the scope of Internet searches is very limited; this would be clearly indicated on a paper request form. The form is completed by inmates and delivered to the librarian for review. Once reviewed, the librarian will decline or approve the search, delivering an answer to the inmate within a few days. This provides a time frame to locate the information, as the librarian cannot always drop other duties to spend time searching the Internet. It also allows the librarian to research if the requested information is allowed per the rules and regulations of the institution. One negative aspect of this process is that the inmate is more removed from the discovery of information, which is often an important component of reference services. On the other hand, it provides information to inmates who cannot locate it anywhere else; in this respect, it is an important and worthwhile service. However, this process of being an information gatekeeper comes with many ethical concerns, further discussed in a subsequent section.

Empowerment Through Reference

Because inmates are limited in their ability to physically and mentally engage outside of their immediate surroundings, information found in libraries and through reference by librarians plays a critical role in inmates' process of empowering themselves. The concept of empowerment varies within and across disciplines, discussed within both an individual and a larger societal context. Empowerment within this discussion is simply a process by which people, who are typically oppressed in some way, can gain some control over their lives. Specifically, Lord and Hutchison define empowerment as "processes whereby individuals achieve increasing control of various aspects of their lives and participate in the community with dignity."[28]

Prison inmates have little autonomy. Decision-making opportunities, power over their living circumstances, and ability to seek information are overwhelmingly limited. They often develop a strong sense of dependency by relying on correctional staff to determine every aspect of their

---

28 John Lord and Peggy Hutchison, "The Process of Empowerment: Implications for Theory and Practice," *Canadian Journal of Community Mental Health* 12, no. 1 (1993): 9.

lives, including what they eat, what they wear, the types of medical treatments they receive, and the educational, vocational, or self-help programs in which they participate. The transfer from street to institution is experienced as dehumanizing, marked by inmates receiving their state prison number and officially becoming "'Property of the State.'"[29] The effects of institutionalization are such that inmates often "find themselves struggling with decision-making dilemmas and too much choice, the experience of surveillance and control having disempowered and de-skilled them."[30]

While inmates are held in the correctional facility, the prison library represents an opportunity for prisoners to "consent to be governed."[31] This consent allows prisoners to participate in pro-social institutions (within the larger institution) and activities to begin their process of empowerment. At my facility, we view reference services as a powerful tool for inmates to use in empowering themselves. They can define their information needs and, with assistance from library staff, develop the skills to solve them using the resources available in the library. We propose that inmates "understand their own needs far better than anyone else and as a result should have the power both to define and act upon them."[32] The reference desk (whether a literal space or not) provides the mechanism for inmates to take that action. Whereas many public and academic libraries are now seeking to automate the delivery of information, the limitations of the prison library require a reliance on human-to-human interactions via the traditional reference interview. Inmates benefit from the resulting discourse, by not only learning traditional information seeking processes (which has been lost in a rush towards digital literacy) but also gaining a sense of personal empowerment by uncovering the value of information.[33]

Lord and Hutchison found that individuals felt that services which were "personalized, responsive, interactive, and providing a degree of

---

29   Barbara H. Zaitzow, "Empowerment Not Entrapment: Providing Opportunities for Incarcerated Women to Move Beyond 'Doing Time,'" *Justice Policy Journal* 3, no. 1 (2006): 7, http://www.cjcj.org/uploads/cjcj/documents/empowerment_not.pdf

30   Ibid, 16.

31   Judith Jordet, "Part I: The Prison Library as Pro-Social Institution," *Corrections. com*, April 11, 2011, accessed January 21, 2017, www.corrections.com/news/article/27732-the-prison-library-as-pro-social-institution.

32   Lord and Hutchison, "The Process of Empowerment," 8.

33   Tibro Koltay, Sonja Spiranec, and Laszlo Z. Karvalics, *Research 2.0 and the Future of Information Literacy* (New York: Elsevier, 2016).

self-reliance and consumer control" to be more helpful in the empowerment process than those services which were "bureaucratic, congregating, and controlling."[34] Reference services at our prison library are kept as informal as possible, a departure from the usual formal methods of requesting correctional staff assistance. For example, reference requests are typically answered in-person and at the time of need, and when it is necessary to submit a written request for information, it is submitted on an in-house form rather than an official departmental form, as described previously.

The value of the library reference service comes from the inmate investing their own time, with the assistance of library staff, to find the information they are seeking. Rather than delivering an automatic answer to inmates, we encourage self-reliance by pointing inmates to appropriate resources and allowing them to struggle at times through the material. Relying on themselves rather than on external resources (i.e. library staff) fosters the prisoner's self-efficacy and "confidence in their ability to take the initiative in changing their lives."[35] At the same time, we desire that the inmate has a successful reference experience, which typically implies they find the information they seek. Such information is important as it increases inmates' knowledge which will enable them to develop themselves during incarceration and beyond. Thus, the actual process of reference and the information gained through reference both play a role in empowerment.

While reference in the library seeks to empower individual patrons, the potential for group empowerment exists here as well. Reference provides inmates with information which leads to an "awareness and ability to see the world and their place in it," including their relation to others around them.[36] Awareness of one another and identification with each other enables inmates to build an "internal community," exemplified by peer-to-peer education groups and inmate-led governance.[37] Information is important because it forms the basis of organizing and implementing these internal communities. Thus, library reference provides an avenue to transition from group awareness to group action. Whether empowering the individual patron or collective group, however, prison librarians en-

---

34 Lord and Hutchison, "The Process of Empowerment," 15.

35 Ibid, 19.

36 Dustin Cantrell, "Correctional Education as Democratic Citizenship Education," *The Journal of Correctional Education* 63, no. 2 (2012): 33.

37 Ibid, 32.

counter prison regulations which aim to limit the information accessible to inmates. Therefore, library reference services involve a balance between upholding inmates' legal and intellectual rights and complying with the objectives of prison authorities.

Balancing Rights and Realities

Prison librarians face a conflict when core professional values, such as privacy and confidentiality, are not recognized within a prison setting. Consider the process of researching Internet material for inmates: by requiring inmates to place their request in writing, there is a potential for privacy and confidentiality issues to arise in the future as library staff is required to retain documentation of written inmate requests for a given number of years. Furthermore, by placing the request under review and scrutiny (unlike non-prison libraries), it creates the appearance that the librarian is making a judgment of whether or not the inmate's request is a legitimate information need. In reality, the librarian needs this review time to ensure its completion would not violate department policies.

The above example is but one instance of the tension prison librarians experience while attempting to uphold their ethics within the correctional environment. Censorship becomes a common practice that prison librarians must employ despite the profession's advocacy for intellectual freedom. Security is the priority in all areas of the prison, including the library, and sometimes seemingly benign information can be detrimental to the safety of staff and inmates alike. While ALA asserts that only material presenting "an actual compelling and imminent risk to safety and security should be restricted," this proclamation is infrequently realized in the real-life setting of prison.[38] Prison authorities with regressive opinions on inmate rights may exploit the safety-first mandate to justify unreasonable restrictions placed on inmate access to information.[39]

Intellectual freedom issues have long been complicated in the correctional environment. Traditionally, prison regulations allowed prison authorities to censor almost anything they desired without inventions by the

---

38 American Library Association, "Prisoner's Right to Read: An Interpretation of the Library Bill of Rights," *Newsletter on Intellectual Freedom* 59, no. 5 (2010): 193.

39 Brenda Vogel, *The Prison Library Primer: A Program for the Twenty-first Century* (Lanham, MD: Scarecrow Press, 2009), 42–3.

courts. In *Procunier v. Martinez* (1974), however, the U.S. Supreme Court ruled that California prison mail regulations were overly broad and often served to merely "eliminate unflattering or unwelcome opinions" from the perspective of prison officials.[40] The court articulated a standard in which prison regulations must act to further the "legitimate governmental interest in prison security and order, or prisoner rehabilitation," and must "be no greater than necessary or essential" to protect those government interests.[41]

Despite the gains made by *Procunier*, the courts have become increasingly deferential to prison authorities over the last few decades. *Turner v. Safley* (1987) perhaps had the most impact, setting the current standard allowing prison authorities to curtail prisoners' constitutional rights with regulations "reasonably related to legitimate penological concerns."[42] The term "legitimate penological interest" is vague and broad, giving prison officials a wider latitude to restrict access to certain types of information.

Prison librarians widely report restrictions of materials that are considered a threat to institutional security.[43] Most recognize the need to restrict materials with content "that would aid in escape," contain "instructions on making explosives, weapons, or alcohol," or are "promoting hatred or violence against certain groups."[44] Unfortunately, censorship is a reality of the correctional environment which prison librarians should not expect to escape. Library reference should not be used as a method of circumventing the regulations which limit inmate access to information.

Rather than censure or formal reprimand by providing information that is banned to inmates, prison librarians should consider advocacy and collaboration with correctional authorities to design collection development and reference policies that both serve inmates and align with the prison's regulations. This may often come down to choosing one's battles. By recognizing the need to limit some types of information, prison librarians can focus their efforts to advocate for other material that might frequently be challenged, such as nudity in art books, novels with erotic scenes, or medical texts with anatomical drawings. These types of content do not

---

40   Procunier v. Martinez, 416 U.S. 396 (1974).

41   Ibid.

42   Turner v. Safley, 482 U.S. 78 (1987).

43   Sandra Annette Greenway, Library Services Behind Bars, *Bookmobile and Outreach Services* 10, no. 4 (2007): 53.

44   Ibid.

pose a threat to institutional safety and security, yet may frequently be viewed as obscene using strict interpretations of prison regulations.

Clark and MacCreaigh described that "honoring the spirit of ALA's highest ideals while following the correctional facility's rules... [is] an interesting and daily challenge that demands common sense, diplomacy, patience, and not a little give-and-take."[45] Although Clark and MacCreaigh may understate how taxing this "daily challenge" can be for prison librarians, the essence of their words is clear: more needs to be done to balance the restrictions of a correctional facility with the duty that librarians have to serve its community. It is simply not enough to adhere to the letter of strict rules and regulations inherent in prisons but to advocate outside of the prison bars to better serve a severely underserved community. Librarians continue to struggle through these issues and refine our process to ensure quality reference services to a community in dire need of the services librarians can provide.

Conclusion

Library reference within a prison provides one of the few opportunities for inmates to seek information empowerment. While the availability of librarians and collections exists to meet mandates required by the law, inmates have as much of a right to information as another member of society. The materials and reference services provided by prison librarians give inmates the opportunity to find some measure of empowerment stripped from them.

Inmates are individuals with an innate curiosity that extends beyond the mandate of legal literature; they need information that only a prison library can provide during their incarceration. Physical confinement must not equate to mental confinement. Inmates should be allowed to find some measure of autonomy through the reference interview and information seeking. This process encourages inmates, removed from the benefits other members of society possess, to develop critical skills that would otherwise be left fallow. However, for this process to happen with any degree of success, the library profession must advocate more strongly to serve a com-

---

45 Sheila Clark and Erica MacCreaigh, *Library Services to the Incarcerated: Applying the Public Library Model in Correctional Facility Libraries* (Westport, CT: Libraries Unlimited, 2006), 15.

munity often overlooked and dismissed by society. Just as their patrons are marginalized, prison librarians experience the stigma of serving those who are incarcerated. The profession must be proactive in bringing the important work of prison librarians to light. Furthermore, rather than simply declaring that inmates have a right to read and access information, the library profession must actively collaborate with prison authorities to ensure library ethics and values can penetrate the prison walls. For individual librarians, awareness can be transitioned to action with the consideration of working as a prison librarian, serving an information-starved community in desperate need of the traditional reference services found in libraries.

Works Cited

Abel, Jonathan. "Ineffective Assistance of Library: The Failings and the Future of Prison Law Libraries." *The Georgetown Law Journal* 101, no. 5 (2013): 1171–1215. https://georgetownlawjournal.org/articles/122/ineffective-assistance-of-library/pdf.

American Library Association. "Prisoner's Right to Read: An Interpretation of the Library Bill of Rights." *Newsletter on Intellectual Freedom* 59, no. 5 (2010): 19293.

Burt, Lesta N. "Information Needs of Inmates." *Library Trends* 26 (Summer 1977): 27–38.

California. *California Code of Regulations. Title 15, Division 3, Chapter 1.* Sacramento: California Office of State Printing, 2016.

California. *Department Operations Manual.* Sacramento: California Department of Corrections and Rehabilitation, 2016.

Cantrell, Dustin. "Correctional Education as Democratic Citizenship Education." *The Journal of Correctional Education* 63, no. 2 (2012): 27–36.

Chatman, Elfreda A. "A Theory of Life in the Round." *Journal of the American Society for Information Science* 50, no. 3 (1999): 207–17.

Clark, Sheila and Erica MacCreaigh. *Library Services to the Incarcerated: Applying the Public Library Model in Correctional Facility Libraries.* Westport, CT: Libraries Unlimited, 2006.

Drabinski, Emily and Debbie Rabina. "Reference Services to Incarcerated People, Part I: Themes Emerging from Answering Questions from Prisons and Jails." *Reference and User Services Association* 55, no. 1 (2015): 42–8.

Greenway, Sandra Annette. "Library Services Behind Bars." *Bookmobile and Outreach Services* 10, no. 4 (2007), 43–64.

Heater, Derek. *A Brief History of Citizenship.* New York: New York University Press, 2004.

Hobbes, Thomas. *Leviathan.* New York: Cambridge University Press, 1968.

Jordet, Judith. "Part I: The Prison Library as Pro-Social Institution." *Corrections.com*, April 11, 2011. Accessed January 21, 2017. http://www.corrections.com/news/article/27732-the-prison-library-as-pro-social-institution.

Koltay, Tibro, Sonja Spiranec, and Laszlo Z. Karvalics. *Research 2.0 and the Future of Information Literacy.* New York: Elsevier, 2016.

Lehmann, Vibeke. "Challenges and Accomplishments in U.S. Prison Libraries." *Library Trends* 59, no. 3 (Winter 2011): 490–508.

Locke, John, and Ian Shapiro. *Two Treatises of Government: And a Letter Concerning Toleration.* New Haven: Yale University Press, 2003.

Lord, John and Peggy Hutchison. "The Process of Empowerment: Implications for Theory and Practice." *Canadian Journal of Community Mental Health* 12, no. 1 (1993): 5–22.

MacCormick, Austin. *The Education of Adult Prisoners: a Survey and a Program.* New York: National Society of Penal Information, 1931.

Mellow, Jeff and James M. Dickinson. "The Role of Prerelease Handbooks for Prisoner Reentry." *Federal Probation* 70, no. 1 (2006): 70–6.

Vogel, Brenda. *The Prison Library Primer: A Program for the Twenty-first Century.* Lanham, MD: Scarecrow Press, 2009.

Werner, O. James. "Law Libraries for Correctional Facilities." *Library Trends* 26 (Summer 1977): 71–96.

Wilkins, Barratt. "The Correctional Facility Library: History and Standards." *Library Trends* 26 (Summer 1977): 119–23.

Zaitzow, Barbara H. "Empowerment Not Entrapment: Providing Opportunities for Incarcerated Women to Move Beyond 'Doing Time.'" *Justice Policy Journal* 3, no. 1 (Spring 2006): 1–24. http://www.cjcj.org/uploads/cjcj/documents/empowerment_not.pdf.

Reference by Mail to Incarcerated People

Emily Jacobson

Since the early 1980s, New York Public Library (NYPL) has operated a reference by mail program for people who are incarcerated. Men and women who are incarcerated in New York State and across the country send NYPL's Correctional Services department questions and research requests. Library staff and volunteers compile the requested information and send it back to each writer. Jails and prisons are notorious information deserts, most of which completely lack access to research materials, Internet, or current events. If there are facility libraries, they may be nearly impossible to access,[1] and the collections may be badly outdated.[2] Curious people cannot just access whatever book or topic they happen to be interested in, a point that our patrons make to us regularly.

Incarcerated people write to NYPL's Correctional Services program asking every conceivable research question, ranging from basic, ready-reference questions to those that are more in-depth. Straightforward requests—for song lyrics, addresses, reentry resources, and career questions—can be answered quickly by NYPL staff using Google. Those that are more ob-

---

1 Correctional Association of New York. "Prison Visiting Project." New York: Correctional Association of New York. Accessed April, 2017.

2 Delaney, Ruth, Ram Subramanian, and Fred Patrick. "Making the Grade Developing Quality Postsecondary Education Programs in Prison." *Vera Institute.* 2016.

scure—the history of dreadlocks, a biological explanation of laughter, the inner workings of the parking meter industry, or how to prepare for a move overseas—require considerably more attention. The people responding have to familiarize themselves with each topic before they can make choices about what research to include.

It can be easy to wish for a reference interview, where the librarian could ask clarifying questions in order to narrow down what the patron is looking for. An open-ended question, or one that starts with "tell me absolutely everything about creating an emoji" begs for a follow up question from the librarian doing the research. Does the writer want the history or a technical guide? If someone asks something that is unclear, it is up to the responder to make their best guess as to what the writer was looking for. Luckily, people write back often to share their feedback. Writers point out to us clarifications where responders were wrong, or to say that something in the research they received sparked a new line of thought. Writers also share essays they have been working on, which incorporate their research. Mail is a slow form of communication, and sending a letter through a prison's busy mailroom (and then through the library's busy mailroom) leads to a very drawn out exchange. The process of finding the sought-after information takes time.

Without a face-to-face reference interview, responders must take their best guess and make succinct choices about which resources to include and how to gauge letters for context clues about the writer's comprehension. For example, large handwriting could indicate low vision. Additionally, in New York State, all incarcerated people have an identification number, the first two digits indicating the year they entered prison. This number can be used to gauge how much background knowledge they have on a subject. If a writer asks about how eBay works, and they have been incarcerated since 1985, it is likely they want an overview of the company and not necessarily a deep dive into the coding behind the site.

Because an exchange takes place over several months, it is important for NYPL responders to explain their research thoroughly. Each response reminds the writer what they were looking for, and describes how a search was conducted. Sometimes, a person's query is unanswerable, but we would like to show where we looked. This also can give the writer an idea of how we interpreted their request. Since letters are distributed between NYPL staff and volunteers, it is unlikely that a writer will get in touch with the same responder over several exchanges. If a responder went off in a completely different direction, the writer can ask their question again in a different way to steer us back.

One of the most common requests we receive is for *Connections*, an annual guidebook that NYPL produces, which lists over 500 reentry resources in New York City.[3] NYPL sends it to prisons in New York State, libraries in New York City, and social service organizations. We also send free copies to individuals who write and request it. Writers often ask for reentry resources from other cities as well. Every year, when the Correctional Services team edits and updates this guide, we look at the letters we receive, to see if we can incorporate the most frequently asked questions into the book. Not only does this serve an information need, it also cuts down on NYPL having to research the same question again and again.

The NYPL Correctional Services Department

The reentry and reference services are only a small part of NYPL's Correctional Services department. The bulk of our time is spent providing library services on Rikers Island at city jails. Each month between 1,000–1,300 people take part in our circulating book service. We offer family programming, where incarcerated parents participate in early literacy workshops, then record a favorite picture book for their children. In the past year we have started teaching ESOL classes, opened the first permanent library space on Rikers Island (as opposed to mobile book carts), and launched a video visitation program so families can connect with their loved ones over a Skype-like connection, rather than go through the complicated process of a physical visit. We conduct library orientations at state prisons, familiarizing men who are nearing release with public library services. We run a book club in federal prison, as well. In short, we are incredibly busy. NYPL's first Correctional Services Librarian, Steve Likosky, started many of our foundational services. Our libraries on Rikers Island, *Connections,* and answering letters have been steadily growing for over 30 years.

We view answering letters as a core part of our department. The exchanges we make with our writers are professional and respectful. The staff and volunteers who answer letters always treat reference questions with equal validity, whether someone is looking for the characteristics of a Gemini and Aquarius match, or if they are asking how to finance their ed-

---

3   New York Public Library, *Connections: a Guide for Formerly Incarcerated People in New York City.* New York City: The New York Public Library, Astor, Lenox and Tilden Foundations, 2017.

ucation. In turn, patrons ask their questions and follow up with respect as well. Again, since mail is such a slow process, extra patience on our behalf and our patron's behalf goes a long way.

NYPL Correctional Services staff reads each of the letters before they are distributed to a team of volunteers, students, and staff who answer them. Any letter that is inappropriate is discarded. However, discarding a letter outright is rare. With each response we include a copy of rules for using the service, so that participants are aware of the extent of the service. The rules are mostly disclaimers about what we cannot send. NYPL can't provide legal advice, we can't get in touch with anyone on the writer's behalf, and we can't send adult materials, information about how to make weapons, or information about illegal drugs. We do not send information on what is considered contraband by prisons. In Kansas, our patrons are not allowed to send rules for role-playing games, such as Dungeons & Dragons. In Delaware, we have a group of writers who always request increasingly complex rules to Dungeons & Dragons every month, and this, seemingly, is not a violation. We will do referrals for many things that we can't provide, or are outside our scope, or are beyond our staff power. We will refer writers to other organizations that have books to prison programs, provide pro bono legal research, or provide reentry resources for specific areas.

NYPL has also set up a parameter that people can only write to the program twice a month. This is a severe limitation, especially if one imagines using Google this infrequently. However, we limit the number of letters we accept per person, per month, in order to manage the flow of mail. Otherwise, the program would be overwhelmed by too many requests. Of course, one letter does not mean a writer has only asked one question. Letters come stuffed full of questions, asked in every format, from very formal inquiries to quick half-completed phrases. In general, even with the best efforts, responses lag at least two months behind.

To help us manage this workload, NYPL is deeply indebted to our volunteers, whose dedication and enthusiasm keeps the quality of research very high. The Correctional Services team is small, and there isn't one staff person who is dedicated to answering the mail full time. It is easy to quickly compile addresses of banks in Allentown, Pennsylvania, between trips to Rikers Island for library service. It is much harder to find several hours to look for a transcript from an obscure late-night radio show or to explain the significance of numerology in different cultures. Volunteers receive scans of letters weekly, do their research remotely, and email their responses back.

Collaborating with MSLIS Classes

We find many volunteers at Pratt Institute, where NYPL has an ongoing collaboration. Correctional Services works with two introductory reference classes each semester. Students are assigned three letters per semester. They gain experiential reference skills, as opposed to many introductory reference classes that offer experience by hunting for "Easter eggs"—obscure facts in hard to find places. The classes receive letters every week, scanned and sent via email to the professors. Names and contact information are blocked out to protect the writer's privacy, and a number identifies each piece of correspondence. If a writer's personal information is relevant to answering their request (they need information on resources specific to a place or they want to find articles about themselves), we will include it. Students send their answers to the professor for review within a week, the average turnaround time for face-to-face reference work. The professor will either ask for edits, or email the answer back to NYPL. We will review the letters one more time, plug in the names and addresses, and mail them. Copies of the letters with the writer's name and location are not saved, and all original correspondence is shredded. Even though we do not save the letters, we have compiled a Google site with frequently requested resources, so it is easier to pull information that our patrons often want. This includes: reentry resources for places outside of New York City, organizations that provide pro bono legal help, or how to write a business plan.

An important aspect of this work is information organization. In MSLIS programs, there is a heavy emphasis on how digital content is presented, and on user experience. Even though snail mail is analog, the way that information is laid out on paper is an important part of responding. If someone has asked a dozen questions months ago, smashing them into a lengthy word document is not helpful. We ask all our responders to give a lot of thought to the physical layout of letters, providing adequate spacing between queries, page numbers, formatting pictures, and taking out useless hyperlinks. This ends up being time consuming—copying and pasting a Wikipedia article, then wrestling with it to "look nice" is an unexpectedly tedious task.

We try to send the classes the most challenging questions. For easier, more ready- reference questions, we have an independent team of volunteers. Occasionally, we host answer-a-thons. Groups of librarians, or volunteers who love to research, get together for several hours to answer letters. It is always enjoyable to research in a group, to discuss challenging questions and learn new things. Also, it is a good way to introduce a lot of people to the idea of answering letters from people in prison.

Although the logistics of this program can be seen as complicated (there is a lot of detail-oriented work, keeping track of every letter, making sure the responses match up with the right answer), having a large number of future librarians help out with this project hopefully normalizes information seeking from an often-ignored group of people. Writers trust this service with very private, personal, disparate details. Someone who wants information on fighting for custody of a child also can want pictures to trace in the same letter. Their expectation that they will be treated like people and not inmates is significant. We hope this creates awareness among librarians that this is an important population to serve, both during incarceration and after, when they become patrons at a public library branch.

This program has never been formally advertised, and yet the library receives letters from all over the country, averaging about 40 per week. This number has grown steadily over time, especially since NYPL began working with Pratt. Although individuals cannot write to the library more frequently than twice a month, the library often gets letters from people who say they heard about us from their peers, and are curious if the service actually "works," and so our patron base grows.

NYPL Correctional Services does not track patron feedback in any formal way, other than receiving thank you letters or suggestions. We never track participants once they are released, either. Although we have no data on how our patrons use this information, it is well documented that education in prison reduces recidivism rates significantly.[4] While the library does not *only* educate people, access to information certainly provides a way for incarcerated people to pursue their own knowledge. The professors we work with at Pratt, Debbie Rabina and Emily Drabinski, insightfully posit that "[i]n the face of dramatically reduced employment options, incarcerated people may turn to entrepreneurship and self-employment as their best available option."[5] Our hope is that having private questions validated can help people gain confidence in seeking information in the future, and that they will continue going to the public library to do so.

---

4 Lois M. Davis, Robert Bozick, Jennifer L. Steele, Jessica Saunders and Jeremy N. V. Miles, *Evaluating the Effectiveness of Correctional Education: A Meta-Analysis of Programs That Provide Education to Incarcerated Adults,* (Santa Monica: RAND Corporation, 2013), 57.

5 Emily Drabinski and Debbie Rabina, "Reference Services to Incarcerated People, Part I," *Reference & User Services Quarterly* 55, no. 1 (2015): 47.

Conclusion

In *Locked Down, Locked Out*, Maya Schenwar writes how correspondence with people who are incarcerated actually can promote safety, quoting Rev. Jason Lydon from the advocacy group Black & Pink:

> Receiving letters during mail call can serve as a function that resembles the other definition of "mail:" a protective shield against potential violence. As noted earlier, it alerts guards that you've got contacts and advocates on the outside, so you're less likely to be mistreated. Such "mail" is also useful when it comes to prisoners potentially harming themselves. … Having a reminder that you're cared for and not forgotten—and part of a larger thing—can help you deal with the mental and emotional struggle that is the reality of being locked up.[6]

Unfortunately, our work is often done in a vacuum. NYPL would be interested in hearing what other library systems do to help their incarcerated patrons, or share how we've shaped our reference by mail program. More librarians working with incarcerated people would be beneficial. Patrons would get their questions answered faster, and it would be ideal for librarians to share resources across systems. NYPL is aware of only one other system, San Francisco Public Library's recently-launched reference by mail program, which is doing this work. There is an endless information void that could be addressed. To ignore it is to assume that some people's information needs are greater than others, and this is not the ideology of public libraries.

Sixty-two percent of the inmate population in New York State has less than two years to their earliest release dates.[7] This means it is very uncommon for people to be incarcerated for life. To prepare people for coming back to a community is a benefit for the individual, their family, and their entire community. To withhold or cut people off from information is not only a disservice but also an unjust and malicious act. To keep someone willfully ignorant imposes a level of punishment that is unnecessary.

---

6 Maya Schenwar, *Locked Down, Locked Out: Why Prison Doesn't Work and How We Can Do Better.* (Oakland: Berrett-Koehler Publishers, 2014), 112.

7 Ibid., 22.

People are entitled to access to information[8] and the right to improve their lives. As gatekeepers, librarians should keep the door to information access as open as possible. The more knowledge and resources people have at their disposal, the better choices they can make.

While Correctional Services does not present specifically as social justice-oriented, the effect of delivering information where there is a deliberate lack is a progressive act. Prison emphasizes a lack of agency and choice. To pursue knowledge, entertainment, and skills is a powerful choice for someone who is in a system that is designed to narrow their world. This program brings awareness to how public library services can extend beyond the walls of a branch to reach its patrons in different ways. Patrons are free to pursue knowledge and follow their own curiosity, even if they cannot inhabit physically inhabit a library space.

---

8   American Library Association Council. "Intellectual Freedom Manual." ALA.com, last modified 2010.

Works Cited

American Library Association Council. "Intellectual Freedom Manual." Last modified 2010. http://www.ala.org/advocacy/intfreedom/iftoolkits/ifmanual/intellectual.

Correctional Association of New York. "Prison Visiting Project." New York: Correctional Association of New York. Accessed April, 2017. http://www.correctional association.org/pp/prison-visit-2004-present.

Davis, Lois M., Robert Bozick, Jennifer L. Steele, Jessica Saunders and Jeremy N. V. Miles. "Evaluating the Effectiveness of Correctional Education: A Meta-Analysis of Programs That Provide Education to Incarcerated Adults." Santa Monica: RAND Corporation, 2013. http://www.rand.org/pubs/research_reports/RR266.html.

Delaney, Ruth, Ram Subramanian, and Fred Patrick. "Making the Grade: Developing Quality Postsecondary Education Programs in Prison." *Vera Institute.* 2016. https://storage.googleapis.com/vera-web-assets/downloads/Publications/making-the-grade-postsecondary-education-programs-in-prison/legacy_downloads/making-the-grade-postsecondary-education-programs-in-prison.pdf

Drabinski, Emily, and Debbie Rabina. "Reference Services to Incarcerated People, Part I." *Reference & User Services Quarterly* 55, no. 1 (2015): 42–8.

Drake, Deborah. *Prisons, Punishment* and the Pursuit of Security. New York: Palgrave Macmillan, 2014.

Kutner, Max. "With No Google, the Incarcerated Wait for the Mail. *Newsweek,* January 25, 2015. http://www.newsweek.com/people-behind-bars-google-answers-arrive-mail-301836.

New York Public Library. *Connections: a Guide for Formerly Incarcerated People in New York City.* New York City: The New York Public Library, Astor, Lenox and Tilden Foundations, 2017. https://www.nypl.org/corrections.

New York State Department of Corrections and Community Supervision. *Under Custody Report: Profiles of Under Custody Population.* Albany: New York State Department of Corrections and Community Supervision, 2016. http://www.doccs.ny.gov/Research/Reports/2016/UnderCustody_Report_2016.pdf.

Schenwar, Maya. *Locked Down, Locked Out: Why Prison Doesn't Work and How We Can Do Better.* Oakland: Berrett-Koehler Publishers, 2014.

Dispatches from the Field of Prison Librarianship

Erin Rivero, Marisa Hernandez, Stephanie Osorio, and Vanessa Villarreal

Five by Nine

Brooks Hatlen, the elderly incarcerated librarian of *The Shawshank Redemption*, is approved for parole after fifty years of incarceration.[1] Just before leaving Shawshank State Penitentiary, Hatlen releases his pet bird, Jake, through the bars of the prison library window. In Stephen King's original novella version, Shawshank prisoners later discover the released bird in the prison yard, dead.[2] Outside prison walls, Hatlen struggles to make sense of life, waking from nightmares and day dreaming of committing crime as a way to return to the prison that raised him. Not long thereafter, he hangs himself from the ceiling joist of his halfway house. "That's institutionalized," nods Ellis 'Red' Redding, the go-to prisoner at Shawshank who arranges deliveries of goods and contraband from the outside. "They send you here for life. That's exactly what they take. The part that

---

1   *The Shawshank Redemption*, directed by Frank Darabont (1994; Burbank: Warner Bros., 2012), Amazon video.

2   Stephen King, "Hope Springs Eternal: Rita Hayworth and Shawshank Redemption," in *Different Seasons* (New York: Scribner, 1982), 3–113.

counts anyway."[3] Avion Rose, incarcerated at Maryland's Jessup Correctional Institution, echoes Red in his poem, *Jailbird*:

> Now I understand the
> Experience
> Of why the caged bird
> refused to sing
> Why he remained unhappy
> and unproductive
> In everything between
> scenes of an
> Unjustice system that
> never taught
> Him how to use his wings[4]

From the vantage of Rose's five by nine foot cell, "time draws out like a blade," and the silence is deafening.[5] Forty-five years earlier, incarcerated people at New York's Attica Prison broke the silence. The 1971 uprising included demands for law library materials and newspapers.[6] In 1977, the United States Supreme Court ruled that prisons must have libraries. The Bounds v. Smith decision mandated prison employees provide adequate law libraries or an individual with legal knowledge to assist incarcerated people in legal preparation and filing. This was a milestone for social justice in US prisons, carving out equal opportunity to exercise civil, political, and human rights. Today, prison libraries can be a space of social justice for incarcerated people by ensuring access to resources, encouraging human development, and helping people find a new way forward.

Donald Trump's 2016 presidential victory reverberated on Death Row at San Quentin State Prison, whose October 2016 mock election re-

---

3　*The Shawshank Redemption*, Darabont, Amazon video.

4　Avion Rose, "Jailbird," Inside Prison Podcast, last modified May 2, 2016, http://insideprisonpodcast.strikingly.com/#jailbird.

5　King, "Hope Springs Eternal," 5.

6　Heather Thompson, *Blood in the Water: The Attica Prison Uprising of 1971 and its Legacy* (New York: Pantheon Books, 2016); and PBS (Public Broadcasting Service), "Attica Inmate Demands, 1971," *American Experience*, last modified August 23, 2006, http://www.pbs.org/wgbh/amex/eyesontheprize/sources/ps_attica.html.

sults favored Hillary Clinton.[7] "Believed to be the most comprehensive survey on condemned men's opinions—on any topic—ever done," the San Quentin mock election conducted in partnership with the University of California at Berkeley was a model for social justice-oriented prison library programming.[8] Academic institutions are but one partnership with prison libraries, working jointly to elevate the rights of incarcerated people through opportunity to exercise their voices.

As global markets plunged in response to Trump's election, private prison stock soared.[9] CoreCivic, formerly Corrections Corporation of America (CCA), saw a 58 percent rise as the largest private prison corporation in the US.[10] The rise was unsurprising, given that Trump's Super PAC received $150,000 from GEO Group, the nation's second largest private prison contractor, and Trump expressed confidence in the efficacy of prison privatization during his campaign.[11] His confidence is shared by others in the international community. Prison privatization has become a global trend across eleven countries in five continents.[12] In opposition to this growing movement, Senator Bernie Sanders and Congressman Raul Grijalva co-authored the Justice Is Not For Sale Act in 2014.[13] At its core, this legislation aimed to ban private prison contracts, citing high rates of violence in private prisons and the perverse profit incentives of private prison corporations.[14] Indeed, the CEO of CoreCivic (formerly CCA), Damon Hininger, earned $3.4 mil-

---

7   Juan Haines, "Mock Election Draws Huge Turnout," *San Quentin News*, October 20, 2016, http://sanquentinnews.com/mock-election-draws-huge-turnout.

8   Ibid.

9   Roque Planas, "Private Prison Stocks Surge After Donald Trump Victory," *The Huffington Post*, November 11, 2016, http://www.huffingtonpost.com/entry/ private-prison-stocks-trump_us_582336c5e4b0e80b02ce3287.

10   Ibid.

11   Nadia Prupis, "Wall Street and Private Prison 'Licking Their Lips' Over Trump Presidency," *Common Dreams*, November 17, 2016, http://www.commondreams.org/ news/2016/11/17/wall-street-and-private-prisons-licking-their-lips-over-trump-presidency.

12   Cody Mason, "International Growth Trends in Prison Privatization," *The Sentencing Project*, August 2013, http://sentencingproject.org/wp-content/uploads/2015/12/ International-Growth-Trends-in-Prison-Privatization.pdf.

13   Bernard Sanders and Raul M. Grijalva, "Justice is not for Sale," Congress, 2014, http://www.sanders.senate.gov/download/summary-of-justice-is-not-for-sale-?inline=file.

14   Ibid.

lion in 2015 alone; meanwhile, privatized prisons have a higher rate of assault on staff and between prisoners compared with public prisons of similar size and security.[15] An undercover recording in a private prison captured the following statement from a new cadet-training officer: "The only thing that's important to us is that we go home at the end of the day. Period. So if them fools want to cut each other, well, happy cutting."[16]

While private prisons blur the line between business enterprise and correctional service, racial disparity complicates incarceration further. In the US, people of color are disproportionately incarcerated.[17] US Immigration and Customs Enforcement has a mandate to detain a daily quota of 34,000 people.[18] This figure may double, according to a Trump administration memo to the Department of Homeland Security recommending an increase to 80,000 detainees per day.[19] Private prisons could stand to benefit by meeting this projected demand for facility expansion.[20] Additionally, in all but two states, a felony results in permanent loss of voting rights, making mass incarceration a modern civil rights issue for 5.58 million Americans.[21] While the US represents 5% of the world's popula-

---

15   Shaun Bauer, "My Four Months as a Private Prison Guard," *Mother Jones*, July/August 2016, http://www.motherjones.com/politics/2016/06/cca-private-prisons-corrections-corporation-inmates-investigation-bauer; and James Austin and Garry Coventry, "Emerging Issues on Privatized Prisons," U.S. Department of Justice, 2001, https://www.ncjrs.gov/pdffiles1/bja/181249.pdf.

16   Ibid.

17   NAACP, "Criminal Justice Fact Sheet," accessed November 3, 2016, http://www.naacp.org/criminal-justice-fact-sheet.

18   Sanders and Grijalva, "Justice is Not for Sale Act," 2.

19   Brian Bennett, "Not Just 'Bad Hombres': Trump is Targeting Up to 8 Million People for Deportation," *The Los Angeles Times,* February 4, 2017, http://www.latimes.com/politics/la-na-pol-trump-deportations-20170204-story.html.

20   Hanna Kozlowska, "Private Prisons are Already Experiencing a Boon Under Trump-and Critics want to Know Why," *Quartz,* April 3, 2017, https://qz.com/948509/trump-turnaround-on-private-prisons-raises-questions-on-donors-from-senators-chris-van-hollen-and-cory-booker.

21   California Elections Code, "California Elections Code Section 2211c," Elections Code, n.d., http://www.leginfo.ca.gov/cgi-bin/displaycode?section=elec&group=02001-03000&file=2200-2213; Jessica Sarhan, "2016 Election: America's Prison Voters," *Al Jazeera*, October 1, 2016, http://wwbiblw.aljazeera.com/indepth/features/2016/09/2016-election-america-prison-voters-160906085936094.html; and Michelle Alexander, *The New Jim Crow: Mass Incarceration in the Age of Colorblindness* (New York: The New Press, 2012).

tion, US correctional facilities hold 25% of the world's prison population.[22] Scandinavian prisons, for comparison, are small and well staffed with relatively low incarceration rates compared to other international prison environments.[23] More comparable to the US, market-focused nations such as Australia and New Zealand still boast relatively lower incarceration rates.[24] From an international lens, there are simply no nations in the world that come close to approximating the US in terms of the sheer size and business implications of mass incarceration. These realities underscore the need for spaces where people undergoing incarceration can dwell in possibility, overriding the "hidden assumptions of peril that give us the world we see."[25]

These spaces are prison libraries. As one ideal example, prison libraries in Norway, Sweden, and Denmark are known as "normal zones" designed to imitate life on the outside.[26] Similarly, the International Federation of Library Associations and Institutions (IFLA) confirms the value of prison libraries as lifelines to the outside world, providing normalcy and ownership in learning, and encouraging constructive use of time.[27] More than a legal information outlet, the prison library offers space for growth and articulating the human voice—hope, in a place where despair otherwise seeps into walls and veins.

---

22   NAACP, "Criminal Justice Fact Sheet," accessed November 3, 2016,
      http://www.naacp.org/criminal-justice-fact-sheet.

23   Hilde Kristin Ljodal and Erlend Ra, "Prison Libraries the Scandinavian way: An
      Overview of the Development and Operation of Prison Library Services," *Library
      Trends* 59, no. 3, (2011), 475.

24   Emanuele Ferragina and Martin Seeleib-Kaiser, "Welfare Regime Debate: Past, Present,
      Futures?" *Policy & Politics* 39, no. 4, (2011), 601–02; Australian Bureau of Statistics,
      "4517.0–Prisoners in Australia, 2016," Accessed April 23, 2017, http://www.abs.gov.au/
      ausstats/abs@.nsf/mf/4517.0; Department of Corrections and Statistics New Zealand,
      "New Zealand's Prison Population," accessed April 24, 2017, http://www.stats.govt.nz/
      browse_for_stats/snapshots-of-nz/yearbook/society/crime/corrections.aspx; and World
      Prison Brief, "New Zealand," accessed April, 24, 2017, http://www.prisonstudies.org/
      country/new-zealand.

25   Benjamin Zander and Rosamund Zander, *The Art of Possibility: Transforming
      Professional and Personal Life*, (New York: Penguin Books, 2000), 162.

26   Ibid, 473.

27   Vibeke Lehmann and Joanne Locke, "Guidelines for Library Services to Prisoners: 3rd
      Edition," International Federation of Library Associations and Institutions (2005), 6–7,
      http://www.ifla.org/publications/ifla-professional-reports-92.

Yet the prison library is not a panacea, nor can it shoulder the entirety of rehabilitation. The success of correctional service depends upon the conscious decision to evolve—an opportunity that can be ignored or undermined by either inmate or librarian, let alone other stakeholders. Moreover, prison life is grim and has the power to eclipse the prison library's potential. Johnny Cash captured this despair in his album notes for *Folsom Prison Blues*, recorded live at Folsom State Prison in 1968:

> The culture of a thousand years is shattered with the clanging of the cell door behind you … You sit on your cold, steel mattressless bunk and watch a cockroach crawl out from under the filthy commode, and you don't kill it. You envy the roach as you watch it crawl out under the cell door … You'd like to say that you are waiting for something, but nothing ever happens. There is nothing to look forward to.[28]

In contrast, as Zander and Zander put it, "we can open a window on a world where all is sound, our creative powers are formidable, and unseen threads connect us all."[29] Certainly this window can come from visitors, care packages, or concert programming rather than the prison library. Still, prison librarians are a prisoner's figurative point of reference to the rest of the world, a physical embodiment of a window to the outside. An incarcerated person with the opportunity to read, discover, write, regret, and restitute for their choices is indeed one with the ability to offer something positive to society despite conviction for an indelible crime.[30] Such possibility holds the inherent power to defeat despair, though this is neither inevitable nor absolute.

Along these lines, formerly incarcerated Dennis Gaddy is a social justice success story. In prison, Dennis leveraged learning opportunities to prepare for life upon reentry. After nearly six years of incarceration, he developed the Community Success Initiative, a nonprofit helping former-

---

28   Johnny Cash, *At Folsom Prison,* Album, Columbia Records, CS 9639, 1968.

29   Benjamin Zander and Rosamund Zander, *The Art of Possibility: Transforming Professional and Personal Life* (New York: Penguin Books, 2000), 162.

30   Jeffrey Toobin, "The Legacy of Lynching, on Death Row," *The New Yorker,* August 22, 2016, http://www.newyorker.com/magazine/2016/08/22/ bryan-stevenson-and-the-legacy-of-lynching.

ly incarcerated people transition back into society after prison.[31] Kipen emphasizes the significance of libraries, noting that "all the research out there… points toward reading enjoyment as the surest predictor of health, wealth and good citizenship."[32] A prisoner exhibiting good citizenship while incarcerated is a future good citizen upon release. "The vast majority of men that I encounter in here do eventually return to their communities and neighborhoods," notes Ervin Bell, librarian of Saginaw Correctional Facility in Michigan—"it is in the best interest of us all to assist them in successfully transitioning back to their friends and families."[33] Ervin reveals the end game: beyond the five by nine foot cell, prison libraries facilitate social reintegration of some of society's most discounted individuals. As human beings humbled and moved by the power of education and information access, prisoners, prison library professionals, and their community partners are redefining social justice.

The following profiles are based on author interviews conducted with one formerly incarcerated person and six prison library professionals in California, Michigan, and New York. The primary challenge of the interview process was the geographically dispersed nature of the interviewers and interviewees. To meet this challenge, the authors conducted all but one interview remotely. Interview techniques included email correspondence, a question and answer Google Doc template, and Zencastr's web-based audio recording platform. Oral interviews were recorded and transcribed. The authors crafted and presented a uniform set of questions to each prison library professional, and a unique set of questions for the formerly incarcerated adult. Question content surrounded reference librarianship experiences in correctional services, and the authors asked additional follow-up questions during oral interviews. The authors developed a consent form and obtained permission for usage of interview content. The authors also gave each interviewee the opportunity to review and revise usage of their commentary. In the following profiles, the authors paraphrased, synthesized, and occasionally edited interview content for clarity. In sum, these interviews reveal the

---

31 "Community Success Initiative," *G. Smith Reynolds Foundation,* February 6, 2014, http://www.zsr.org/articles/community-success-initiative.

32 David Kipen, "How to Weather the Trump Administration: Head to the Library," *Los Angeles Times,* November 10, 2016, http://www.latimes.com/books/jacketcopy/la-ca-jc-kipen-essay-20161110-story.html.

33 Ervin Bell (Saginaw Correctional Facility, Librarian) in discussion with Erin Rivero, October 24, 2016.

unique array of challenges and opportunities faced by correctional services library professionals seeking to uphold social justice. These are their stories.

Profiles in Social Justice

A Day in the Life

Brian Richardson spent his incarceration at Sheridan Correctional Center in Illinois, serving 22 months for four felonies. Sheridan's law library struggled to meet IFLA's standards for correctional institutions.[34] Brian recalls that the law library was only open occasionally.[35] Lacking personnel to handle legal questions, the law library was often closed or unable to assist, including a time when Brian needed help writing an affidavit. Moreover, wait times exacerbated the lack of law library time; it took up to two weeks per visit for Brian to gain access to the law library.[36] This is consistent with the observations of investigative journalist Shaun Bauer, who observed a lack of law library time and resources for incarcerated people.[37] Moreover, outdated resources and unreliable materials like "Xerox copies and just old books" made the library collection obsolete.[38] Brian's experience reveals the jarring inattention to IFLA's standards for services and management of prison libraries.[39]

Thankfully not every prison library is a picture of inaccessibility—just as every public library is different, so, too, is every prison library. From virtual visitations to hand-written book pocket inserts, prison libraries exhibit a wide variety of characteristics and strategies for best practice in light of challenges and limitations unique to prison library settings. At Rikers Island Correctional Center in New York, for example, daily librarian time is absorbed by the preparation of materials and resource guides, and re-

---

34 Brian Richardson (formerly incarcerated individual) in discussion with Vanessa Villarreal, September 26, 2016.

35 Brian Richardson (formerly incarcerated individual), September 26, 2016.

36 Ibid.

37 Bauer, "My Four Months," chapter 2.

38 Brian Richardson (formerly incarcerated individual), September 26, 2016.

39 Lehmann and Locke, "Guidelines for Library Services to Prisoners," 12.

mote handling of reference requests.[40] Correctional services libraries bring answers and items to the island during scheduled visits, which can be canceled for various security reasons, making it difficult to provide consistent service.[41] This is in contrast with Michigan's Saginaw Correctional Facility, where the prison library is on site, is staffed seven days a week from 6:30 am to 9:00 pm, and rarely closes for holidays. Access includes the use of a digital law library database for legal research.[42] Ervin, librarian at Saginaw, oversees library usage for incarcerated people in pre-arranged, one-hour segments, or 'callouts.' In 2014, the law and general library received a total of 28,279 visits. Prisoners borrowed a total of 10,314 fiction and non-fiction books from a collection of approximately 19,000 titles.[43]

Although there is no catalog at Rikers due to the high frequency of lost or missing materials, NYPL staff know their prison library collections "very, very well," reaching 800–1300 people per month.[44] "Think broadly about what correctional service librarianship is," encourages Emily Jacobson, Correctional Services Librarian for NYPL.[45] "Besides actually going into facilities and handing out books, there's a lot of other outreach that can be done from branches, around reentry, and around supporting families of people who are incarcerated." Accordingly, a great deal of Emily's time is spent maintaining an extensive resource document called *Connections*, a directory of services and resources for reentry updated annually.[46] NYPL staff also run an early childhood literacy program for incarcerated parents, a video visitation project to bring together families separated by prison, a book discussion group for federal incarcerated people, and library

---

40 Emily Jacobson (New York Public Library, Correctional Services Librarian) in discussion with Erin Rivero, November 3, 2016.

41 Ibid.

42 Ervin Bell (Saginaw Correctional Facility, Librarian), October 24, 2016.

43 Ibid.

44 Emily Jacobson (New York Public Library, Correctional Services Librarian), November 3, 2016.

45 Ibid.

46 Ibid; also see "Connections 2016: A Guide for Formerly Incarcerated People in New York City," *The New York Public Library*, 2016, https://www.nypl.org/sites/default/files/Connections%202016.pdf.

orientations for those approaching release.[47] Their virtual visitation project, TeleStory, is a collaboration between NYPL, Brooklyn Public Library, and the Queens Library—a national model for prison library service.[48]

George Carter is Senior Librarian Supervisor at Patton State Hospital, a medical correctional facility in California.[49] People who are incarcerated at Patton are patients. George notes the emotional burden of reference duties for patients, including providing a sympathetic ear, engaging in conversation, and sometimes even playing a game of chess.[50] "I am not here to pass judgment," writes George. "I am here to assist as best I can with the resources I have. I do think it is unfair when people refer to the patients of this hospital as inmates or as criminally insane… These patients are human, they are sick and they need help. I am here to play a small part in their recovery."[51]

Jameson Rohrer is Senior Librarian near the California-Mexico border at Centinela State Prison, where over 60% of the incarcerated population is Hispanic.[52] One of Jameson's three incarcerated clerks is bilingual, serving monolingual Spanish-speaking prisoners.[53] Incarcerated people at Centinela may access a standalone computer with LexisNexis, updated on a quarterly basis.[54] When Jameson began at Centinela, the collection held approximately 500 titles; it now holds 4,000, thanks to Jameson's community partnerships and collection development efforts.[55]

---

47   Ibid.

48   Nicholas Higgins, "TeleStory: Library Based Video Visitation for Children of Incarcerated Parents," *Knight Foundation*, April 22, 2016, https://www.newschallenge. org/challenge/how-might-libraries-serve-21st-century-information-needs/winning/ library-to-jail-video-visitation-connecting-children-to-incarcerated-parents.

49   George Carter (Patton State Hospital, Senior Librarian) in discussion with Marisa Hernandez, November 8, 2016.

50   Ibid.

51   Ibid.

52   Jameson Rohrer (Centinela State Prison, Senior Librarian) in discussion with Erin Rivero, Marisa Hernandez, and Vanessa Villarreal, September 25, 2016.

53   Ibid.

54   Ibid.

55   Ibid.

Valerie Schultz, a Library Technical Assistant, handles day-to-day operations of a men's state prison library, where she ensures access to the twelve-step program, outside associations like the Innocence Project, and enrichment activities like a weekly writers group and quarterly newsletter.[56] As with all prison libraries in the US, Valerie's library collection bans materials deemed "detrimental to the security, good order, or discipline of the institution or if it might facilitate criminal activity," according to the Federal Bureau of Prisons.[57] Ervin, Saginaw librarian, points to similar restrictions on information access. Prison libraries generally exclude books depicting escape ideas, maps, or weapon building, as well as anything with staples or hardback binding.[58] Additionally, Michigan policy and the federal Prison Rape Elimination Act prevent Ervin from adding anything to the collection depicting sexual acts between men.[59]

In the 1974 Procunier v. Martinez decision, Supreme Court Justice Thurgood Marshall argued that incarcerated people must not lose their humanity; accordingly, the American Library Association (ALA) is committed to preserving intellectual freedom for all those incarcerated.[60] Still, while opposed to censorship, the ALA understands that correctional facilities operate within the bounds of federal, state, and local court decisions.[61] For example, banned books at the Centinela State Prison library fill a 22-page list maintained by the California Department of Corrections.[62] Despite these limits, collections tend to feature popular science fiction, fantasy, and westerns, as well as bilingual books, resources address-

---

56 Valerie Schultz (Library Technical Assistant), in discussion with Erin Rivero, October 10, 2016.

57 Valerie Schultz (Library Technical Assistant), October 10, 2016; and "Censorship and Banned Book Lists in Correctional Facilities," *National Institute of Corrections,* November 4, 2014, http://nicic.gov/ topics/5192-censorship-and-banned-book-lists-in-correctional-facilities.

58 Ervin Bell (Saginaw Correctional Facility, Librarian), October 24, 2016.

59 Ibid.

60 1. *Procunier v. Martinez,* 416 U.S. 396 (1974); Association of Specialized and Cooperative Library Agencies, *Library Standards for Adult Correctional Institutions* (Chicago: American Library Association, 1992); and Association of Specialized and Cooperative Library Agencies, *Library Standards for Juvenile Correctional Facilities* (Chicago: American Library Association, 1999).

61 Ibid.

62 Jameson Rohrer (Centinela State Prison, Senior Librarian), September 25, 2016.

ing mental health and second language needs, wide-ranging reading levels, and a minimal number of materials could resonate with or be representative of LGBTQI audiences.[63]

Unique Challenges

In addition to security issues and collection constraints, technology limits pose a unique challenge. "Librarians have a huge information need to fill," writes Emily, as most incarcerated populations have no Internet access.[64] Legal research software available to incarcerated people can also pose a challenge in terms of "teaching inmates who've been incarcerated for decades how to use the computers," notes Valerie.[65] Although reference librarians in public libraries undertake similar information literacy efforts, the prison environment restricts Internet usage for self-help in gaining computer skills, or acquiring and practicing on personal equipment outside of the prison library. Additionally, Internet usage can be limited for staff, causing delayed answers to reference requests. George, for example, takes research requests and fulfills them later, unable to roam with his phone to provide instant information.[66] Furthermore, he cannot use free Internet solutions to troubleshoot lack of legal software available to his patients.[67]

For Jameson at Centinela, another related challenge is operating without a law library background.[68] Often, a prison librarian must simply respond with whatever available resource best meets an incarcerated person's needs, helping to answer any given question as best as possible, without having the benefit of extensive legal training or a paralegal coworker to

---

63 Ibid.; Ervin Bell (Saginaw Correctional Facility, Librarian), October 24, 2016; Emily Jacobson (New York Public Library, Correctional Services Librarian), November 3, 2016; Valerie Schultz (Library Technical Assistant), October 10, 2016; and George Carter (Patton State Hospital, Senior Librarian), November 8, 2016.

64 Emily Jacobson (New York Public Library, Correctional Services Librarian), November 3, 2016.

65 Valerie Schultz (Library Technical Assistant), October 10, 2016.

66 George Carter (Patton State Hospital, Senior Librarian), November 8, 2016.

67 Ibid.

68 Jameson Rohrer (Centinela State Prison, Senior Librarian), September 25, 2016.

offer guidance.[69] In the midst of this, prison librarians serve "certain prisoners who are very manipulative and demanding," necessitating strict adherence to department policy and maintenance of a highly structured environment.[70] "Do not do anything for one prisoner that you would not or could not do for all prisoners," cautions Ervin—"you may have empathy but not sympathy for those you work with every day."[71] Boundaries and consistency in service are essential for maintaining personal safety in a prison library environment. Also, in light of serving populations with learning disabilities or emotional distress, prison librarians thrive on leadership communication and emotional intelligence. To help confront these challenges, Ervin, Emily, and Valerie all cite the importance of maintaining a librarian network through email, staying connected to exchange ideas.[72] "The learning curve was steep," recalls Ervin.[73] Still, the community of librarianship proves supportive, and despite the challenges of providing reference service in a prison, Ervin concludes, "working here has had a profound impact on my life."[74]

Uncommon Heroes

The prison library is a sanctuary. For those incarcerated, "it is a place to forget for a moment that you're incarcerated," and gain "a sense of peace and quiet and space, which is in short supply otherwise."[75] For this reason, the prison library is "unlike any other room in the facility"—and "figuratively speaking, an avenue of escape."[76] Although some prison libraries are not housed on site, as is the case of Riker's prison library services, the act of choosing books offers respite for incarcerated people "in a space where there

---

69   Ibid.

70   Ervin Bell (Saginaw Correctional Facility, Librarian), October 2016.

71   Ibid.

72   Ervin Bell (Saginaw Correctional Facility, Librarian), October 2016; Emily Jacobson (New York Public Library, Correctional Services Librarian), November 3, 2016; and Valerie Schultz (Library Technical Assistant), October 10, 2016.

73   Ervin Bell (Saginaw Correctional Facility, Librarian), October 2016.

74   Ibid.

75   Valerie Schultz (Library Technical Assistant), October 10, 2016.

76   Ervin Bell (Saginaw Correctional Facility, Librarian), October 24, 2016.

is often very little personal choice."[77] Thus, the prison librarian helps incarcerated people obtain information, navigate conviction appeals, satisfy curiosity on a subject, or simply lose themselves in the freedom of literature.[78]

Prison library staff are not only role models for those they serve—they are raising consciousness about incarcerated populations within their communities. "I try to bring awareness to the community about the work we do at Saginaw," notes Ervin, who maintains relationships with local schools, community groups, and public libraries, which results in generous book donations and Saginaw's interlibrary loan program.[79] In this sense, prison librarianship has evolved over time, becoming more visible, notes Emily.[80] "We're doing work to make our programs robust and sustainable," she adds, seeking support from New York's Department of Corrections.[81] Despite losing books amongst incarcerated populations, she adds, "we'd much rather that the books are out and being read, rather than sitting on our shelves untouched!"[82] Ervin echoes this sentiment: "I've been accused, threatened, lied to and stolen from," he explains, "but none of it has embittered me."[83] At Saginaw in Michigan, Ervin facilitates a program bringing youth offenders on field trips to the prison library where he discusses programs and services offered to them by him as well as by the local public library.[84] Emily notes a similar public library orientation program for incarcerated people in New York preparing to reenter society.[85] In many instances, these interactions with prison librarians and orientations with the public library are the first positive library experience for an incarcerated individual; such moments have the potential to change lives. Ervin put it best:

77   Emily Jacobson (New York Public Library, Correctional Services Librarian), November 3, 2016.

78   Ervin Bell (Saginaw Correctional Facility, Librarian), October 24, 2016.

79   Ibid.

80   Emily Jacobson (New York Public Library, Correctional Services Librarian), November 3, 2016.

81   Ibid.

82   Ibid.

83   Ervin Bell (Saginaw Correctional Facility, Librarian), October 24, 2016.

84   Ibid.

85   Emily Jacobson (New York Public Library, Correctional Services Librarian), November 3, 2016.

Many of the prisoners who use our library come from inner-city environments where life was tough and opportunities were few. Commonly they've dropped out of school, have limited employment histories, and have had frequent encounters with the law from an early age... Still, some of the most intelligent and talented people that I've ever met in my life were wearing a prison uniform. What many of them have lacked, however, is opportunity. They were living the only life they knew how to live and this turned out tragically for both them and their victims. The key to changing these men, and society in the process... is to expose them to a different way of thinking and thereby a different way of living. We need to show them new options that might lead to a far different future... By using the tools and resources that the library has I try to open their eyes and minds to new possibilities. I want them to dream of, and aspire towards, a new and better life. If they can accomplish this we all win.[86]

"You can make a difference," Valerie adds, "and perhaps prevent future crime from happening. We have a saying: Today's prisoner is tomorrow's neighbor. So rehabilitation is a worthy goal."[87] Valerie, like her prison librarian peers, strives to treat prisoners as human beings.[88] "If not now, when?" adds George, another advocate for seeing the humanity in his patients.[89] "This position allows me an avenue for doing good work for people who need someone to show up for them."[90]

Partners in Justice and Prison Reference

Literacy for Incarcerated Teens

Bounds v. Smith, mandating law libraries or legal assistance for incarcerated people, does not apply to juveniles; over 250,000 incarcerated youth do

---

86   Ibid.

87   Valerie Schultz (Library Technical Assistant), October 16, 2016.

88   Ibid.

89   George Carter (Patton State Hospital, Senior Librarian), November 8, 2016.

90   Ibid.

not access prison libraries.[91] In response to this gap in service, New York-based Literacy for Incarcerated Teens (LIT) addresses inadequacies in juvenile library resources. Their primary mission is to end illiteracy among incarcerated teens, inspiring reading with author visits, drama and writing clubs at Rikers, and a magazine subscription for the School Program for Incarcerated Youth at the Nassau County Correctional Center on Long Island.[92] Finally, LIT works with school libraries supporting incarcerated youth by providing books at three times the rate of state funding.[93] They are merely one example of successful partners in prison reference, empowering young incarcerated populations.

REFORMA: Children in Crisis Project

Since 2014, over 100,000 children have entered the United States illegally, many of whom are held in detention centers for 72 hours upon entry.[94] After this initial processing, detained children are placed in group homes or shelters.[95] Although these facilities have libraries, they are underdeveloped and exhibit signs of underutilization.[96] REFORMA, a division of the American Library Association, promotes library and information services to Spanish-speaking communities—their Children in Crisis (CIC) project responds to these library shortcomings.

Established in 2014, CIC's task force consists of bilingual and bicultural librarians who can communicate with Spanish-speaking detain-

---

91 Marybeth Zeman, "Literacy For Incarcerated Teens," *Public Libraries Online*, August 23, 2016, http://publiclibrariesonline.org/2016/08/literacy-for-incarcerated-teens.

92 Ibid.

93 Ibid.

94 U.S. Immigration and Customs Enforcement, "Performance-Based National Detention Standards 2011," (U.S. Immigration and Customs Enforcement, Washington, DC, 2011), 401, https://www.ice.gov/doclib/detention-standards/2011/pbnds2011.pdf; Barack Obama, "Letter from the President—Efforts to Address the Humanitarian Situation in the Rio Grande Valley Areas of Our Nation's Southwest Border," *The White House,* June 30, 2014, https://www.whitehouse.gov/the-press-office/2014/06/30/letter-president-efforts-address-humanitarian-situation-rio-grande-valle.

95 Ibid.

96 "REFORMA Children In Crisis Project," *REFORMA*, accessed on October 1, 2016, http://refugeechildren.wixsite.com/refugee-children.

ees.[97] The CIC initiative asks for Spanish language book donations, with the mission to provide detained children appropriate materials, story time, and the latest information on library resources available in the US.[98] REFORMA maintains guidelines for acceptance of materials and a list of recommended donations.[99] Additionally, the project accepts monetary donations, which support the purchase of current material so as to avoid donations of dated or discarded books.[100] Preferred material includes illustration-focused literature accessible to those with limited or emergent literacy, such as graphic novels, picture books, and ALA/REFORMA Pura Belpré award-winning children's titles.[101] Since 2014, REFORMA has delivered hundreds of such books.[102] REFORMA also developed a free toolkit aimed at improving the immigrant and refugee experience at detention center libraries.[103] The second phase of the project aims to send children released from detention facilities with a backpack containing art supplies and a book.[104]

Moved by photographs of detained children reminiscent of his own children, Ramirez began working with the initiative in 2014.[105] He observed that REFORMA's San Diego chapter, LIBROS, has relationships with Tijuana librarians helping refugee children and those in lower socio-economic status. Ramirez notes that prior to July 2014, US Customs and Border Protection was not allowed to accept book donations; thus REFORMA's CIC project has made a significant impact on government

---

97   Hannah Hehrlich, "Spotlight on: REFORMA's Children in Crisis Project," *Lee & Low Books* (blog), July 24, 2015, http://blog.leeandlow.com/2015/07/24/spotlight-on-reformas-children-in-crisis-project.

98   Ibid.

99   REFORMA Recommended Book List," *REFORMA,* accessed on March 10, 2017, http://refugeechildren.wixsite.com/refugee-children/reforma-recommended-book-list.

100   Ibid.

101   Ibid.

102   Ibid.

103   "Toolkit for Librarians," *REFORMA,* accessed on October 2, 2016, http://www.ibby.org/fileadmin/user_upload/Toolkit_for_Librarians__REFORMA_Feb_2016.pdf.

104   Ibid.; and Hehrlich, "REFORMA Children in Crisis Project," 2016.

105   Sylvia Aguiñaga, and Ricardo Ramirez, "The REFORMA Children in Crisis Project: A Personal Account," *ALSC Blog,* February 6, 2016, http://www.alsc.ala.org/blog/2016/02/the-reforma-children-in-crisis-project-a-personal-account.

standards as well as the lives of detained children.[106] Furthermore, Mexican and American librarians continue building partnerships to support detention center libraries. The *Seguimos Creando* (Continue Believing) conference, sponsored by LIBROS, celebrated its fifth year in 2016 by holding its bilingual workshop sessions across borders in both San Diego and Tijuana libraries.[107] Together, these institutions and initiatives are exemplary partnerships across borders, improving libraries and empowerment for incarcerated children without a voice. Both REFORMA's CIC project and the *Seguimos Creando* conference can build on their vision by reporting out on measurable outcomes surrounding their efforts.[108]

Academic and Public Partners

Rashema Melson is a Georgetown University scholar enrolled in a class called the Prison Reform Project.[109] As a student, she partners with maximum-security prisoners from Maryland's Jessup Correctional Institution, many of whom have been incarcerated since adolescence.[110] Growing up as one of 1.36 million American homeless students, Rashema managed to escape her brother's prison destiny, despite the murder of her drug-dealing father, and attending ten schools with "no sense of home."[111] Rashema found books—and while reading R. L. Stein's *Goosebumps* series, she made a conscious choice not to be constrained by her circumstances.[112] Today she gives back, leading prison programming to encourage human expression, like *Jailbird,* by Avion Rose.[113]

---

106   Ibid.

107   "Seguimos Creando Enlaces," *Seguimos Creando Enlaces,* accessed on October 28, 2016, http://www.creandoenlaces.org/content/seguimos-creando-enlaces.

108   Authors sought but were unable to find outcome reports for these REFORMA initiatives.

109   Dan Zak, "In This Class, Prisoners and Georgetown Students Grapple with Difficult Lessons," *The Washington Post Magazine,* September 8, 2016, https://www.washingtonpost.com/lifestyle/magazine/in-this-class-prisoners-and-georgetown-students-grapple-with-difficult-lessons/2016/09/07/268644f8-fcfa-11e5-9140-e61d062438bb_story.html.

110   Ibid.

111   Ibid.

112   Ibid.

113   Ibid.

Incarcerated young adults cite feelings of exclusion from school, making public libraries a prime support network for at-risk youth.[114] With this in mind, Elizabeth Tanner, Teen Services Coordinator for the County of Los Angeles Public Library, helped design the Los Padrinos Juvenile Hall Library, a collaboration between three Los Angeles County agencies.[115] Los Padrinos creates a seamless transition to public libraries after incarceration through parallels in physical design and services. Elizabeth explains:

> The minute [teens] enter Los Padrinos, they are assigned a card, and when they leave, it's part of their exit packet… We are hoping that as a result of this library… they'll feel comfortable going to our libraries wherever they live.[116]

Thus, public librarians empower at-risk youth to kite their hopes, dreams, and ideas through a prison-to-public library transition. Academic partners support human development through people who have successfully avoided prison yards, earning the right to be heard. Together, academic and public partners in prison reference librarianship weave a story of "relational social justice"—the intersection of education and human relationships, bending a kink in the prison pipeline and edging a dam against recidivism.[117] Through materials, programming, and space for human interaction without judgment, these partnerships facilitate successful prisoner rehabilitation and reentry. Such initiatives are a direct contribution to public safety, encouraging a life of books over crime.

---

114   Sara Hyde, "We Need to Talk About Prisons," *TEDxExerter,* June 9, 2015, https://youtu.be/cJbpiCQRFco.

115   Abby Sewell, "'I Want to Cry. I'm In Book Heaven.' How One Reading Advocate Hopes to Change the Lives of Juvenile Hall Detainees Through a Library," *Los Angeles Times,* September 26, 2016, http://www.latimes.com/local/lanow/la-me-ln-juvenile-hall-library-20160926-snap-story.html; and Elizabeth Tanner (County of Los Angeles Public Library, Teen Services Coordinator) in discussion with Marisa Hernandez, September 29, 2016.

116   Elizabeth Tanner (County of Los Angeles Public Library, Teen Services Coordinator), September 29, 2016.

117   Hyde, "We Need to Talk About Prisons," 2015.

Prison Libraries in Popular Culture: Myths and Reality

Prison library depictions in film and television are a mix of accuracy and exaggeration. In season two of *Orange is the New Black*, an incarcerated woman's request for *50 Shades of Grey* is denied because of its sexual content, though the library collection includes sexually explicit *Outlander*.[118] Similarly, in season three of *Orange*, prisoners pass around a copy of an erotic story by Suzanne 'Crazy Eyes' until the administration confiscates it.[119] Theoretically, prisoner stories could circulate as an underground source of fiction—and while prison library collections do ban books of explicit sexual content, other titles and genres persist despite their questionable suitability for a prison population. For instance, *The Count of Monte Cristo* is popular at Centinela's prison library, despite its subject matter; featured in *The Shawshank Redemption*, "it's about a prison break," notes Andy the librarian—"file that under educational," replies Red.[120] Additionally, the library collection at Centinela includes the *The Art of War*, one of the most popular prison library books featured in HBO's *The Night Of*, set at Rikers.[121] "They are constantly checked out," Jameson adds, referring to his library's two copies of *The Art of War*.[122]

Fictional Shawshank librarian Andy Dufresne stretches a $500 annual budget, after soliciting funds from the state for years.[123] Similarly, Jameson and Ervin stretch resources, seeking donations and forging partnerships with the local community.[124] Like Hatlen from Shawshank,

---

118   Joe Hardenbrook, "Why the Hell Would I Want to Leave the
       Library–The Library on 'Orange is the New Black," *Mr. Library
       Dude*, June 14, 2014, https://mrlibrarydude.wordpress.com/2014/06/14/
       why-the-hell-would-i-want-to-leave-the-library-the-library-on-orange-is-the-new-black.

119   Jonathan Dornbush, "Orange is the New Black Season 3 Book Plot Line,"
       Entertainment Weekly, June 24, 2015, http://www.ew.com/article/2015/06/24/
       orange-new-black-season-3-books-fan-fiction.

120   Ibid.; Jameson Rohrer (Centinela State Prison, Senior Librarian), September 25, 2016;
       and *The Shawshank Redemption*, Darabont, Amazon video.

121   Jameson Rohrer (Centinela State Prison, Senior Librarian), September 25, 2016.

122   Ibid.

123   *The Shawshank Redemption*, Darabont, Amazon video; and *The Shawshank
       Redemption*, King, 1982.

124   Jameson Rohrer (Centinela State Prison, Senior Librarian), September 25, 2016; and
       Ervin Bell (Saginaw Correctional Facility, Librarian), October 24, 2016.

NYPL librarians still push a book cart through Rikers.[125] There are no atlases, however, like the one Red uses to pinpoint Andy's escape route, nor any prisoners helping staff complete their tax filings. Still, incarcerated people do help one another—"the barter system is king in prison," notes Valerie.[126] Prisoners "help each other with court filings, fixing radios, making greeting cards… all sorts of 'services.'"[127] This is depicted in *Within the Law*, the first film representation of a female prison librarian.[128] As an incarcerated librarian, the main character guides a fellow prisoner towards law books as a means of pursuing justice.[129] While today's prison librarians are degreed, incarcerated clerks continue to work and support one another as a vital part of the library.

In season three of *Orange is the New Black*, the prison library gets bedbugs, and most of the books are burned.[130] In fact, bedbug infestation has caused real-life library collection devastation in Tulsa, Oklahoma among other locations.[131] In another fictional depiction approximating reality, season two of *The Wire* features a murder in the library.[132] In reality, extreme violence against prison librarians has not yet resulted in murder, though two instances came close.[133] In a Wisconsin prison in 2014,

125   Emily Jacobson (New York Public Library, Correctional Services Librarian), November 3, 2016.

126   Valerie Schultz (Library Technical Assistant), October 16, 2016.

127   Ibid.

128   *Within the Law,* directed by Gustav Machaty (1938; Beverly Hills: Metro-Goldwyn-Mayer, November 12, 2011), YouTube video.

129   Jennifer Snoek-Brown, "Within the Law," *Reel Librarians*, March 5, 2013, https://reel-librarians.com/2013/03/05/within-the-law.

130   *Orange is the New Black*, "Bedbugs and Beyond," directed by Constantine Makris, written by Jenji Kohan and Jim Danger Gray (June 11, 2015), Netflix.

131   Dee Duren, "Bed Bug Discovery Closes Tulsa Central Library," *News on 6*, July 17, 2012, http://www.newson6.com/story/19045845/tulsa-central-library-closed; and Catherine Saint Louis, "A Dark and Itchy Night," *The New York Times,* December 5, 2012, http://www.nytimes.com/2012/12/06/garden/bedbugs-hitch-a-ride-on-library-books.html.

132   *The Wire*, "All Prologue," directed by Steve Shill, written by David Simon, Joy Kecken, and Rafael Alvarez (July 6, 2003), Home Box Office.

133   Annoyed Librarian, "Braver Librarians Than Me," *Library Journal,* May 18, 2015, http://lj.libraryjournal.com/blogs/annoyedlibrarian/2015/05/18/braver-librarians-than-me.

a prisoner attacked the librarian, beating and stabbing her with a pair of dull scissors.[134] The librarian survived but did not return to the job.[135] In a Maine prison in 2008, a prisoner tied, threatened, and assaulted the prison librarian and a fellow prisoner for seven hours.[136] Using typewriter wire and a makeshift ice pick, the attacking prisoner bound and threatened to stab the librarian if she did not help him to access pornographic sites, MySpace, and the season finale of *Tila Tequila*.[137] The librarian complied and was unharmed, but the attacker cut the hostage prisoner's face from ear to mouth with a razor blade.[138]

Aside from such instances of extreme violence in recent history, prison libraries are generally safe spaces—especially given a prisoner's incentive for good behavior in exchange for library privileges. Over the years, Ervin has observed instances of violence or illicit behavior around the library, such as prisoners concealing drugs or razor blades in books, outsiders attempting to smuggle items in books for prisoners, or violence in the hallway outside the library.[139] Ervin has never been assaulted by prisoners, but he has been threatened after denying requested materials.[140] Valerie concurs that prisoners and outsiders are creative at sneaking in contraband, although all donations are screened.[141] Like Ervin, Valerie has pushed the alarm to stop fights, writing up troublemakers and banning them from the library.[142] Jameson only experienced one instance of violence in the two years he has worked at Centinela.[143] "Film and TV rely on lots of violence and drama, and there is little drama in everyday prison life," Val-

---

134   Ibid.

135   Ibid.

136   Annoyed Librarian, 2015.

137   Ibid.

138   Heather Steeves, "Prison Librarian Testifies on Attack in Case Against Inmate," *Bangor Daily News*, January 30, 2011, http://bangordailynews.com/2010/08/10/news/prison-librarian-testifies-on-attack-in-case-against-inmate.

139   Ervin Bell (Saginaw Correctional Facility, Librarian), October 24 2016.

140   Ibid.

141   Valerie Schultz (Library Technical Assistant), October 16, 2016.

142   Ibid.

143   Jameson Rohrer (Centinela State Prison, Senior Librarian), September 25, 2016.

erie notes.[144] "Most inmates just want to do their time and keep their heads down," just as *Orange is the New Black* depicts Poussey working peacefully in the prison library.[145] Such portrayals reinforce the prison library as a sanctuary for incarcerated people—an image that can help eliminate the temptation of violence, instead elevating prison libraries as safe spaces and incubators of social justice.[146]

The Way Forward

From 1980 to 2008 the US prison population quadrupled, peaking at 2.3 million in 2014, representing a quarter of the world's total prison population.[147] Of these 2.3 million people, nearly half are African American, incarcerated at roughly six times the rate of whites.[148] Today's changing political atmosphere reveals a trend toward prison privatization, feeding the prison industrial complex and reinforcing the need for courageous correctional services librarianship. Now, more than ever, prison librarians must facilitate human development and rehabilitation, fighting the status quo with the dual forces of education and information access. Such efforts represent social justice—upholding opportunities to exercise civil, political, and human rights through access to resources and creative use of the human voice. The social justice-oriented reference work of correctional services library professionals forges a way forward for people who are incarcerated.

Real-life parallels exist between prison libraries and their media portrayal, illuminated through the lens of correctional services librarians across the nation. These uncommon heroes, together with nonprofit and public agency partners, are both a window to the outside world and a pillar of advocacy for human and civil rights. They exemplify best practice and serve as models of local and international partnerships, improving library services to incarcerated populations of all ages. "All of human history

---

144 Valerie Schultz (Library Technical Assistant), October 16, 2016.

145 Ibid.

146 Ibid.; and *Orange is the New Black*, "(Don't) Say Anything," directed by Andrew McCarthy, written by Jim Danger Gray (June 17, 2016), Netflix.

147 NAACP, "Criminal Justice Fact Sheet;" and World Prison Brief, "United States of America," http://www.prisonstudies.org/country/united-states-america.

148 Ibid.

hinges on small decisions that, had they gone the other way, things could be radically different," notes George of Patton State Hospital in California.[149] Ultimately, prison reference librarians withhold judgment and uphold knowledge, providing a sanctuary and positive direction for some of the most marginalized members of society.

Prison librarians are not bystanders, but first responders and social activists, providing gateways to societal integration and a richer human existence. It is not a battle for the weak of heart—prison libraries in the US face a number of unique challenges. With a legal mandate to provide law materials, prison library staff maintain an even keel amidst strained resources and overcrowded conditions.[150] While navigating legal precedent, guidelines, and security constraints, prison libraries are propelled forward by human beings committed to empowering incarcerated people through social justice-oriented reference work. It is a collective effort to facilitate successful reentry and meaningful contribution to society, forged by those who dwell in possibility, upholding an invincible dedication to human decency.

---

149   George Carter (Patton State Hospital, Senior Librarian), November 8, 2016.

150   Boston Woodard, "Overcrowded Population Strains Library Resources," *San Quentin News* (San Quentin, CA), January 8, 2013, http://sanquentinnews.com/overcrowded-population-strains-library-resources.

Works Cited

Alexander, Michelle. *The New Jim Crow: Mass Incarceration in the Age of Colorblindness.* New York: The New Press, 2012.

Alloway, Tracy, and Lily Katz. "Private Prison Stocks are Surging After Trump's Win." *Bloomberg News.* November 9, 2016. http://www.bloomberg.com/news/articles/2016-11-09/private-prison-stocks-are-surging-after-trump-s-win.

Annoyed Librarian. "Braver Librarians Than Me." *Library Journal.* May 18, 2015. http://lj.libraryjournal.com/blogs/annoyedlibrarian/2015/05/18/braver-librarians-than-me.

Association of Specialized and Cooperative Library Agencies. *Library Standards for Adult Correctional Institutions.* Chicago: American Library Association, 1992.

Association of Specialized and Cooperative Library Agencies. *Library Standards for Juvenile Correctional Institutions.* Chicago: American Library Association, 1999.

Austin, James, and Garry Coventry. "Emerging Issues on Privatized Prisons." U.S. Department of Justice. 2001. https://www.ncjrs.gov/pdffiles1/bja/181249.pdf.

Australian Bureau of Statistics. "4517.0–Prisoners in Australia, 2016." August 12, 2016. http://www.abs.gov.au/ausstats/abs@.nsf/mf/4517.0.

Bauer, Shaun. "My Four Months as a Private Prison Guard." *Mother Jones.* July/August 2016. http://www.motherjones.com/politics/2016/06/cca-private-prisons-corrections-corporation-inmates-investigation-bauer.

Bennett, Brian. "Not Just 'Bad Hombres': Trump is Targeting Up to 8 Million People for Deportation." *The Los Angeles Times.* February 4, 2017. http://www.latimes.com/politics/la-na-pol-trump-deportations-20170204-story.html.

Branco, Jorge. "Townsville Youth Prison Riot: 20 Prisoners Face Charges Over Night-Long Turmoil." *Brisbane Times.* November 11, 2016. http://www.brisbanetimes.com.au/queensland/townsville-youth-prison-riot-20-prisoners-face-charges-over-nightlong-turmoil-20161111-gsnblw.html.

California Elections Code. "California Elections Code Section 2211c." Accessed October 26, 2016. http://www.leginfo.ca.gov/cgi-bin/displaycode?section=elec&group=02001-03000&file=2200-2213.

Cash, Johnny. *At Folsom Prison.* Album. Columbia Records. 1968.

"Censorship and Banned Book Lists in Correctional Facilities." *National Institute of Corrections.* November 4, 2014. http://nicic.gov/topics/5192-censorship-and-banned-book-lists-in-correctional-facilities.

"Community Success Initiative." *G. Smith Reynolds Foundation*, February 6, 2014. http://www.zsr.org/articles/community-success-initiative.

"Connections 2016: A Guide for Formerly Incarcerated People in New York City." *The New York Public Library*. Accessed November 3, 2016. https://www.nypl.org/sites/default/files/Connections%202016.pdf.

Dornbush, Jonathan. "Orange is the New Black Season 3 Book Plot Line." *Entertainment Weekly*. June 24, 2015. http://www.ew.com/article/2015/06/24/orange-new-black-season-3-books-fan-fiction.

Duren, Dee. "Bed Bug Discovery Closes Tulsa Central Library." *News on 6*. July 17, 2012. http://www.newson6.com/story/19045845/tulsa-central-library-closed.

Ferragina, Emanuele, and Martin Seeleib-Kaiser. "Welfare Regime Debate: Past, Present, Futures?" *Policy & Politics* 39, no. 4 (2011): 601–2.

Haines, Juan. "Mock Election Draws Huge Turnout." *San Quentin News*. October 20, 2016. http://sanquentinnews.com/mock-election-draws-huge-turnout.

Hardenbrook, Joe. "Why the Hell Would I Want to Leave the Library–The Library on Orange is the New Black." *Mr. Library Dude*. June 14, 2014. https://mrlibrarydude.wordpress.com/2014/06/14/why-the-hell-would-i-want-to-leave-the-library-the-library-on-orange-is-the-new-black.

Higgins, Nicholas. "TeleStory: Library Based Video Visitation for Children of Incarcerated Parents." *Knight Foundation*. Last updated April 22, 2016. https://www.newschallenge.org/challenge/how-might-libraries-serve-21st-century-information-needs/winning/library-to-jail-video-visitation-connecting-children-to-incarcerated-parents.

Hyde, Sara. "We Need to Talk About Prisons." *TEDxExerter*. June 9, 2015. https://youtu.be/cJbpiCQRFco.

King, Stephen. "Hope Springs Eternal: Rita Hayworth and Shawshank Redemption." In *Different Seasons*, 3–113. New York: Scribner, 1982.

Kipen, David. "How to Weather the Trump Administration: Head to the Library." *Los Angeles Times*. November 10, 2016. http://www.latimes.com/books/jacketcopy/la-ca-jc-kipen-essay-20161110-story.html.

Kozlowska, Hanna. "Private Prisons are Already Experiencing a Boon Under Trump—and Critics want to Know Why." *Quartz*. April 3, 2017. https://qz.com/948509/trump-turnaround-on-private-prisons-raises-questions-on-donors-from-senators-chris-van-hollen-and-cory-booker/.

Lehmann, Vibeke, and Joanne Locke. "Guidelines for Library Services to Prisoners: 3rd Edition." *International Federation of Library Associations and Institutions*. 2005, 6–7. http://www.ifla.org/publications/ifla-professional-reports-92.

Ljodal, Hilde, and Erlend Ra. 2011. "Prison Libraries the Scandinavian Way: An Overview of the Development and Operation of Prison Library Services." *Library Trends* 59, no. 3 (2011): 473–89. doi 10.4403/jlis.it-10082.

Mason, Cody. "International Growth Trends in Prison Privatization." *The Sentencing Project*. August 2013. http://sentencingproject.org/wp-content/uploads/2015/12/International-Growth-Trends-in-Prison-Privatization.pdf.

NAACP. "Criminal Justice Fact Sheet." Accessed November 3, 2016. http://www.naacp.org/criminal-justice-fact-sheet.

"New Zealand's Prison Population." Department of Corrections and Statistics New Zealand. Accessed April 24, 2017. http://www.stats.govt.nz/browse_for_stats/snapshots-of-nz/yearbook/society/crime/corrections.aspx.

Obama, Barack. "Letter from the President—Efforts to Address the Humanitarian Situation in the Rio Grande Valley Areas of Our Nation's Southwest Border." *The White House*. June 30, 2014. https://www.whitehouse.gov/the-press-office/2014/06/30/letter-president-efforts-address-humanitarian-situation-rio-grande-valle.

Orange is the New Black. "(Don't) Say Anything." Directed by Andrew McCarthy. Written by Jim Danger Gray. June 17, 2016. Netflix.

Orange is the New Black. "Bedbugs and Beyond." Directed by Constantine Makris. Written by Jenji Kohan and Jim Danger Gray. June 11, 2015. Netflix.

PBS (Public Broadcasting Service). "Attica Inmate Demands, 1971." *American Experience*. Last modified August 23, 2006. http://www.pbs.org/wgbh/amex/eyesontheprize/sources/ps_attica.html.

Planas, Roque. "Private Prison Stocks Surge After Donald Trump Victory." *The Huffington Post*. November 11, 2016. http://www.huffingtonpost.com/entry/private-prison-stocks-trump_us_582336c5e4b0e80b02ce3287.

Procunier v. Martinez, 416 U.S. 396 (1974).

Prupis, Nadia. "Wall Street and Private Prison 'Licking Their Lips' Over Trump Presidency." *Common Dreams*. November 17, 2016. http://www.commondreams.org/news/2016/11/17/wall-street-and-private-prisons-licking-their-lips-over-trump-presidency.

"REFORMA Children In Crisis Project." *REFORMA*. Accessed on October 1, 2016. http://refugeechildren.wixsite.com/refugee-children.

Rose, Avion. "Jailbird." Inside Prison Podcast. Last modified May 2, 2016. http://insideprisonpodcast.strikingly.com/#jailbird.

Rosenberg, Eli, Jennifer Medina, and John Eligon. "Protesters Take Anti-Trump Message to His Doorstep, and Plan Next Steps." November 12, 2016. *The New York Times.* http://www.nytimes.com/2016/11/13/us/trump-protest-rallies.html?_r=0.

Saint Louis, Catherine. "A Dark and Itchy Night." *The New York Times.* December 5, 2012. http://www.nytimes.com/2012/12/06/garden/bedbugs-hitch-a-ride-on-library-books.html.

Sanders, Bernard and Raul M. Grijalva. "Justice Is Not For Sale Act." Last modified 2014. http://www.sanders.senate.gov/download/summary-of-justice-is-not-for-sale-?inline=file.

Sarhan, Jessica. "2016 Election: America's Prison Voters." *Al Jazeera.* October 1, 2016. http://wwbiblw.aljazeera.com/indepth/features/2016/09/2016-election-america-prison-voters-160906085936094.html.

"Seguimos Creando Enlaces." *Seguimos Creando Enlaces.* Accessed on October 28, 2016. http://www.creandoenlaces.org/content/seguimos-creando-enlaces.

Sewell, Abby. "'I Want to Cry. I'm In Book Heaven.' How One Reading Advocate Hopes to Change the Lives of Juvenile Hall Detainees Through a Library." *Los Angeles Times.* September 26, 2016. http://www.latimes.com/local/lanow/la-me-ln-juvenile-hall-library-20160926-snap-story.html.

The Shawshank Redemption. Directed by Frank Darabont. 1994. Burbank: Warner Bros., 2012. Amazon video.

Snoek-Brown, Jennifer. "Within the Law." *Reel Librarians.* March 5, 2013. https://reel-librarians.com/2013/03/05/within-the-law.

Steeves, Heather. "Prison Librarian Testifies on Attack in Case Against Inmate." *Bangor Daily News.* January 30, 2011. http://bangordailynews.com/2010/08/10/news/prison-librarian-testifies-on-attack-in-case-against-inmate.

Thompson, Heather. *Blood in the Water: The Attica Prison Uprising of 1971 and its Legacy.* New York: Pantheon Books, 2016.

Toobin, Jeffrey. "The Legacy of Lynching, on Death Row." *The New Yorker.* August 22, 2016. http://www.newyorker.com/magazine/2016/08/22/bryan-stevenson-and-the-legacy-of-lynching.

"Toolkit for Librarians." *REFORMA.* Accessed on October 2, 2016. http://www.ibby.org/fileadmin/user_upload/Toolkit_for_Librarians__REFORMA_Feb_2016.pdf.

U.S. Immigration and Customs Enforcement. "Performance-Based National Detention Standards 2011." U.S. Immigration and Customs Enforcement, Washington, DC., 2011, https://www.ice.gov/doclib/detention-standards/2011/pbnds2011.pdf.

The Wire. "All Prologue." Directed by Steve Shill. Written by David Simon, Joy Kecken, and Rafael Alvarez. July 6, 2003. Home Box Office.

Within the Law. Directed by Gustav Machaty. 1938. United States: Metro-Goldwyn-Mayer (MGM). YouTube video.

Woodard, Boston. "Overcrowded Population Strains Library Resources." *San Quentin News.* January 8, 2013. http://sanquentinnews.com/overcrowded-population-strains-library-resources.

World Prison Brief. "United States of America." Accessed November 3, 2016. http://www.prisonstudies.org/country/united-states-america.

Zak, Dan. "In This Class, Prisoners and Georgetown Students Grapple with Difficult Lessons." *The Washington Post Magazine.* September 8, 2016. https://www.washingtonpost.com/lifestyle/magazine/in-this-class-prisoners-and-georgetown-students-grapple-with-difficult-lessons/2016/09/07/268644f8-fcfa-11e5-9140-e61d062438bb_story.html.

Zander, Benjamin and Rosamund Stone Zander. *The Art of Possibility: Transforming Professional and Personal Life.* New York: Penguin Books, 2000.

Zeman, Marybeth. "Literacy For Incarcerated Teens." *Public Libraries Online.* August 23, 2016. http://publiclibrariesonline.org/2016/08/literacy-for-incarcerated-teens.

The Case for Critical Data Reference in Public Libraries

Julia Marden

"We're living in a time of unprecedented levels of data collection," writes Mimi Onuoha at the beginning of her Missing Datasets project.[1] Her art installation depicts the datasets that those in power choose not to collect. A white filing cabinet is filled with empty folders: "Native American voting statistics (historical)" and "People excluded from housing due to criminal records."[2] We are not counting the most marginalized in our society. Onuoha's Missing Datasets project[3] is meant to track the datasets that those in power have yet to collect. "It wasn't until quite recently," she writes, "thanks to initiatives like D. Brian Burghart's "Fatal Encounters" website and *The Guardian*'s The Counted campaign, that we as a public started to have an idea of the number of civilians killed during interactions with legal enforcement agencies. Prior to their work, that was a missing dataset."[4]

---

1   Mimi Onuoha,"Missing Datasets," Nov. 15, 2015,
    http://mimionuoha.com/thoughts/2015/11/15/missing-datasets.

2   Ibid.

3   Mimi Onuoha, "Missing Datasets,." *GitHub*,
    https://github.com/MimiOnuoha/missing-datasets.

4   Onuoha, "Missing Datasets."

Daniel Castro at the Center for Data Innovation calls this the "data divide—the social and economic inequalities that may result from a lack of collection or use of data about an individual or community."[5] I'd go one step further and call it data inequity, or what danah boyd and Kate Crawford refer to as "a new kind of digital divide: the Big Data Rich and the Big Data Poor."[6] In the era of Big Data, data scientists across many fields and disciplines access vast networks of data to trace patterns and make connections about our individual lives and communities.[7] Much of that networked big data is given freely by the public in exchange for access to websites like Facebook and Google, use of smartphones, GPS, and other engagement with digital spaces and technology. Access to data and computational tools for analysis have expanded the definitions of who can analyze data and how we create knowledge from data.[8] Those that can access and analyze data have great power in how that data is collected, used, and applied to decisions that affect our world.[9]

If we, the public, are contributing so much to the data that is shaping our lives, it is imperative that public libraries do everything they can to help and encourage patrons to access, analyze, and contribute to the body of knowledge being created with this data.

Public libraries have the opportunity to change this landscape and create a more inclusive climate for the public to engage with data. In this chapter I will explore the reasons why public reference and instruction librarians should provide Critical Data Reference Services to patrons as a means of making this happen.

Public Libraries and Open Data

Why does it matter that more of the public feel like they have roles to play and the skills to engage with data and data analysis? It turns out that the

---

5 Daniel Castro, "The Rise of Data Poverty in America," *Center for Data Innovation*, September 10, 2014, https://www.datainnovation.org/2014/09/the-rise-of-data-poverty-in-america/.

6 danah boyd and Kate Crawford, "Six Provocations for Big Data," (paper presented at A Decade in Internet Time: Symposium on the Dynamics of the Internet and Society, Oxford, England, September 21, 2011), 13.

7 boyd and Crawford, "Six Provocations.".

8 Ibid.

9 Ibid.

more people who can participate in data collection and analysis, the better the outcomes for research and policy.

Data quality issues plague researchers across many fields-data scientists often say that "80% of data analysis is spent on the process of cleaning and preparing."[10] Chattanooga Public Library found that engaging the public with new datasets on the City's open data portal helped improve data quality.[11] In 2013, Chattanooga Public Library partnered with the City of Chattanooga to launch an open data portal with a $50,000 grant from the Knight Foundation.[12] The library became the host for the municipal government's datasets, working to make them more accessible both to city employees and members of the public. Today, Tim Moreland works out of the Mayor's Office in collaboration with Melinda Harris, based out of Chattanooga Public Library. The Open Data Portal has a message board where people can request specific datasets. When someone posts, Moreland responds with a link to an appropriate dataset or government website with the appropriate information or works with Harris to make that dataset available.

Harris believes strongly in the library's role in this open data partnership. Her previous role was as a data analyst within the Chattanooga Police Department, but she finds a purpose in being based within the library system. People trust the library to be a neutral provider of quality data, and they trust librarians to help them find that data. "As a citizen, if you're looking for information about the city, the library and your librarian is your ultimate search engine."[13]

However, they learned they need to do extra work to make sure the public is aware that these resources are available. "We open a dataset and there's crickets. We have to be more actively engaged about pushing to social media and doing special events around datasets."[14]

In order to engage the public, the open data team has been doing outreach events to neighborhood leaders, local universities, and associations. They are also considering offering open data workshops to educate

10   Hadley Wickham, "Tidy Data," *Journal of Statistical Software* 59, no. 10 (2014): 1.

11   Moreland, interview.

12   Chattanooga Public Library, "Kicking off the Knight Foundation Open Data Project in Chattanooga."

13   Harris, interview.

14   Moreland, interview.

the public on how to use the data that is now freely available: "One thing we do find is that for 99% of people, just having access to data on the open data portal is not usable. So, they need additional training and support to be able to use it."[15] But when the public does engage with the city's open data, everybody wins. "The community helps crowdsource the quality control of the data," says Moreland. When they released a dataset from the local fire department, it was members of the public who identified the need to add a field for station locations and to provide a data dictionary so anyone could interpret internal department codes.[16]

Engaging members of the public can also improve research outcomes. When predominantly white researchers collect data in communities that are low income, minority, or otherwise typically underrepresented in research communities, they struggle to build trust and it is difficult for them to collect high quality data.[17] Making strides to include more people in the data research process *can illuminate problems previously ignored and lead to change.*

In 2011, a group of Asian American actors, frustrated with the lack of roles and representation on Broadway, came together as the Asian American Performers Action Coalition (AAPAC) to conduct a data analysis. While the industry had collected copious data about Broadway shows, audiences, and finances, they had never looked at the race or ethnicity of Broadway performers. AAPAC found that White performers were cast in 80% of Broadway roles between 2008 and 2015. By tracking this "missing" data, the group was able to start a conversation in the industry and share evidence beyond anecdotal or personal experience. For actor and lead researcher Pun Bandhu, the project was valuable: "Our main goal was to open up equal access opportunities and for now, it seems like it's moving in that direction."[18]

In Boston, where the public library is directly involved with the city's open data portal, a group of Boston citizens recently built a data visualiza-

---

15 Ibid.

16 Ibid.

17 Wrenetha Julion and Deborah Gross, "Recruiting Families of Color from the Inner City: Insights from the Recruiters," *Nursing Outlook* 48, no. 5 (2000): 230–37.

18 Mimi Onuoha, "Broadway Won't Document Its Race Problem, so a Group of Actors Quietly Gathered the Data Themselves," *Quartz*, December 4, 2016, https://qz.com/842610/broadways-race-problem-is-unmasked-by-data-but-the-theater-industry-is-still-stuck-in-neutral/.

tion tool they named "Who Owns What"[19] to explore the web of property ownership across the city. Using open data from the public portal, this tool helps people explore whether there are renter and landlord classes in Boston and what other relationships affect housing affordability across the city.

Libraries that choose to face the challenge of data inequity stand to benefit greatly as they assume a role in providing critical data reference services. Academic data librarian Celia Emmelhainz imagined the role of a data librarian in the public sector:

> Data librarians could help patrons access public data, and even teach some of the skills that would allow people to make better use of these new resources. Given the cachet of "big data" in popular culture, publicizing the existence of "data librarians" could reinforce the relevance of public librarians as guides in the internet age.[20]

Chattanooga and Boston Public Libraries both received substantial grants from the Knight Foundation to pursue open data initiatives with their cities.[21] Partnering with municipal government in order to offer comprehensive data services is one way for libraries to define their role in twenty-first century information environments and ultimately better serve the public.

Critical Data Reference Services

As public libraries begin to engage with open data, how can we as reference librarians engage our patrons to make use of this new resource?

Kristin Partlo, a data librarian at Carleton College, describes the roles of data librarians in academic libraries: they help "bridg[e] systems of meaning and act as translators"[22] and "socializ[e] new researchers into the

---

19   W.O.W. Boston, "W.O.W.Boston Overview," *Medium*, May 15, 2017,
     https://medium.com/@wowbos/intro-to-w-o-w-boston-ca3708cbf55c.

20   Emmelhainz, "Data Librarians in Public Libraries," *Public Libraries Online*, May 18, 2015,
     http://publiclibrariesonline.org/2015/05/data-librarians-in-public-libraries/.

21   "Open Data to Open Knowledge,"
     https://www.boston.gov/innovation-and-technology/open-data-open-knowledge.

22   Kristin Partlo, "From Data to Creation of Meaning Part II: Data Librarian as
     Translator," *IASSIST Quarterly* 38 (2014): 13.

community of scholarship" through *pedagogical data reference interviews.*[23] Partlo argues that reference is a practice that can help undergraduate patrons build the research skills they need to acculturate into their chosen academic discipline. She emphasizes the need to "seek language that spans the practices of social science, sciences, humanities, and performing arts," creating an inclusive environment for data users from diverse disciplinary backgrounds, and listen for the language and context of their patrons' questions so that they can empathize with and meet their patron's information needs.[24]

This translation and teaching work makes data reference unique; librarians must stretch outside of traditional subject matter expertise because of data's potential to be reused in so many different applications beyond the original scholar's intent. While new data users may not anticipate the amount of work they will need to put into their data in order to answer their research questions, they have "equally legitimate motivations for looking for data."[25] With a thorough reference interview, both the librarian and patron can stretch their research skills so that the patron can incorporate data into their own scholarship.

Partlo's approach to data reference can be extended to the public library, where members of the public may be exploring open data portals relevant to their community or grappling with societal level research and data analysis—the kind that drives policy and business decisions that affect all our lives. In order to acculturate the public into the academic and civil circles that collected and released this data, I propose we need to provide the following to our patrons:

- *Data Literacy*: There are many definitions for data literacy, but I am aligning data literacy with information literacy, or the skills needed to find data, use data, and contribute to the conversation. In a public library setting, a reference librarian might assist a patron in effectively searching an open data portal, finding relevant statistics or a downloading a dataset, and then assisting a patron to access tools needed to analyze, visualize, or cite that data.

---

23 Kristin Partlo, "The Pedagogical Data Reference Interview," *IASSIST Quarterly* 33/34, no. 4 (December 2009): 6.

24 Partlo, "From Data to Creation of Meaning."

25 Partlo, "The Pedagogical Data Reference Interview," 8.

- *Critical Skills*: Arguably this is a part of data literacy, but it can be challenging for reference librarians to help their patrons acquire these skills, and they deserve extra attention. Critical skills refers to the ability to critique data as a cultural artifact, created or collected by authors with inherent biases and limitations.

- *Identity*: As Harris and Moreland found in Chattanooga, many people will not seek out open data on their own. We need to empower patrons to recognize that they have the right and the ability to contribute to a conversation previously dominated by researchers and institutions.

Data Literacy

As reference librarians, we are skilled at helping our patrons acquire digital research skills; we routinely show patrons how to conduct effective searches or navigate databases. Some libraries are beginning to expand their reference and instruction services to teach patrons to access and search their local open data portals. I have taught open data workshops at Brooklyn Public Library, as have representatives from the NYC Mayor's Office of Data Analytics. The Carnegie Library of Pittsburgh has partnered with the Western Pennsylvania Regional Data Center (WPRDC) to offer Data 101 workshops to their patrons.[26] As we start to provide instructional programming for our patrons, we must also provide opportunities for patrons to build critical evaluation skills, and the belief that open data is personally relevant to their search for knowledge.

Critical Skills

In a discussion of where data literacy fits in relation to information, statistical, and science literacy, Calzada Prado and Angel Marzal write about the essential component of "critical thinking, which draws from mathematical and statistical aptitudes, general knowledge and the values of the persons concerned."[27] With advances in computing and machine learning, it might feel like none of us have a grasp as to how data is being used. We hear terms

---

26   "Fulfilling the Promise of Open Data through Data Literacy Training." *Microsoft New York* (blog), August 1, 2017. https://blogs.microsoft.com/newyork/2017/08/01/fulfilling-the-promise-of-open-data-through-data-literacy-training/.

27   Javier Calzada Prado and Miguel Ángel Marzal, "Incorporating Data Literacy into Information Literacy Programs: Core Competencies and Contents," *Libri* 63, no. 2 (2013).

like "data science" and "algorithm" thrown about as though they are completely new, but the same principles that underpin scientific discovery still apply. As librarians, we have the ability to demystify these concepts and skills and make them accessible to the public by putting them in context. Even if a patron is not seeking to become an expert programmer or statistician, they still have the right to understand the process by which statisticians, programmers, and data scientists are creating knowledge with data and using it to influence decisions.

In reaction to news that EPA Administrator Scott Pruitt was disputing climate change science, Emily Graslie, an employee of Chicago's Field Museum tweeted, "Science illiteracy isn't misunderstanding data- we have [science] illiteracy when [people] don't understand the process itself."[28] What Graslie is talking about here is the fundamental process of creating knowledge, from forming a hypothesis to collecting data to analyzing and interpreting results. As librarians, we can reinforce the scientific method with patrons as we help them to navigate open data sources and understand their provenance.

We may think of data as a static set of numbers collected impartially, but data is collected by humans, using different methods and approaches, much like any other source of information, and it is incumbent on librarians to present datasets through that lens. The scientific community has rigorously evaluated climate change data.[29] Other datasets like the U.S. Census have been systematically collected, but have known biases and inaccuracies.

As a librarian, I regularly answer questions about the U.S. Census, but I struggle with how to introduce the limitations of the Census into reference interactions. Border Crossers, a non-profit that trains educators on how to dismantle racism and injustice in their communities, incorporates this critical data literacy into their workshops.[30] They draw direct connections between the race and ethnicity data we get from the Census and our country's structuralized racism. Throughout the history of the Census, the

---

28   Emily Graslie, "Emily Graslie on Twitter: 'Science Illiteracy Isn't Misunderstanding Data- We Have Sci Illiteracy When Ppl Don't Understand the Process Itself," *Twitter,* https://twitter.com/Ehmee/status/872796740906254336.

29   Michael Shermer, "Why Climate Skeptics Are Wrong," Scientific American, November 26, 2017, https://doi.org/10.1038/scientificamerican1215-81.

30   Border Crossers, (presentation, ScriptEd Mid-Year Training New York, NY January 28, 2017).

only racial category that has not changed is White; everyone else has had to pick from a shifting list of non-White categories that exist to separate, other, and exclude people from the rights and power that come with being counted as American.[31] The Census is also limited when it comes to describing other important aspects of our identity. In 2017, the Census Bureau made news for dropping questions from the 2020 Census that would have counted LGBTQ Americans for the first time in history.[32]

As librarians, we can do better at helping our patrons to grapple with the ways in which bias and prejudice can affect the quality and use of data that we typically don't question. As Teneya Gethers, a public librarian, puts it, "When the voices of some are silenced, when their stories, struggles, and victories are erased from society's record, what value do we place on their existence?"[33]

And for those Americans who have always known the limitations of such data, who have long been aware that the Census, for example, doesn't reflect their lived experiences, how can librarians create space for them to enter the conversation?

Identity

We can start by helping our patrons to see themselves as capable data analysts. Many organizations in New York City are working with the public to meet their data information needs, particularly those who are themselves marginalized and underrepresented both in data careers and in the datasets. The following case studies come from a research institute, a public school system, and a civic technology non-profit. None of them consider themselves librarians, but I believe their work speaks directly to our work as reference librarians, and how we can build a data identity for our patrons.

31 Ibid.

32 Fernandes, Praveen. "Opinion | The Census Won't Collect L.G.B.T. Data. That's a Problem." *The New York Times*, May 10, 2017, sec. Opinion. https://www.nytimes.com/2017/05/10/opinion/the-census-wont-collect-lgbt-data-thats-a-problem.html.

33 Teneya Gethers, "Knowledge My Public Library Kept Secret: The Urgent Need for Culturally-Responsive Library Services," in *Informed Agitation: Library and Information Skills in Social Justice Movements and Beyond*, edited by Melissa Morrone (Sacramento: Library Juice Press, 2013).

Vera Institute

At the Vera Institute, an organization dedicated to reforming the American justice system, researchers seek to address the power imbalance inherent in conducting research on justice-involved youth. Ryan Shanahan, Director of Research, conducts collaborative research projects with incarcerated youth and others directly involved with the justice system. Participants are included in data collection and form hypotheses about the data's meaning. This approach to collaborative research and data analysis is just one example of participatory action research, a practice which seeks to build equity in knowledge creation. Participatory action research is typically conducted in the public, and has a natural affinity for public libraries, as places where research teams can meet, collect data, and collaborate in the interpretation and communication of results.

During research projects, Shanahan and her team calculate summary statistics and create visualizations of the data to share with all research participants. Together, participants can examine the visualizations and hypothesize what they mean and how they could be applied to reform efforts. In order to engage incarcerated youth and prison staff with this research, Shanahan's team confronts their own power and privilege. Shanahan looks for institutional researchers who can "teach without being condescending, create an environment for co-teaching and co-learning, and be self-reflective and willing to change based on what they hear from the research community."[34] These research qualities echo the values of a critical reference librarian committed to exposing the power dynamics inherent in the pursuit of information. Shanahan finds this approach not only more inclusive, but more effective in creating change: "All our research leads to action, it leads to reform."[35] Her team builds the trust of stakeholders throughout the research process, including prison staff, and court appointees, ensuring a higher quality of data collection and more likelihood that prisons will enact reforms based on the research.

Computer Science For All (CS4All)

Francisco Cervantes is a Director of Computer Science Education at CS4ALL, a public-private partnership of the New York City Department of Education tasked with providing every student a meaningful, high-qual-

---

34   Shanahan, interview.

35   Ibid.

ity computer science education by 2025. Cervantes developed a lesson plan to teach high school students how algorithms affect sentencing and assessment in criminal courts. Describing how his unit came together, he says: "Along the way, I've also done a little bit of studying as to how kids join gangs... Part of that is identity... If the goal is to increase student interest in the field, then you have to do some change of identity. We're asking kids to join a community of people. But these folks are not gang members, they're scientists."[36] Cervantes' lesson engages students who typically don't see themselves as having power in the system and encourages them to find another identity as a scientist or analyst, someone who can collect and find meaning in data. With the power to understand how data informs algorithms and how algorithms influence policy, they become analysts with the power to critique and potentially change the justice system itself.[37]

Using the worksheet, students can break down a risk-assessment algorithm used to determine whether someone who is involved in the justice system is a high or low risk for committing a crime in the future, and consider how data is being collected and how it's being used. Students identify the company that developed the algorithm and accompanying software,[38] and examine how proxies for race create a bias that unfairly targets people of color. Cervantes works to demystify what an algorithm is and how it works to influence people's experiences with the courts. Public libraries can adapt Cervantes' approaches to deconstructing complicated concepts in data analysis and giving information seekers the tools to critique both the interpretation of data and its application.

BetaNYC

BetaNYC, an NYC-based civic technology nonprofit, began teaching open data workshops several years ago, and is constantly seeking ways to improve their pedagogy. In 2016, it partnered with the NYC Department of Parks and Recreation to help launch a new open data set, the 2015 Street Tree Census. Collected largely by volunteers, this dataset offered the most accurate count of the trees lining New York City's streets in history. In order to engage the public with this new data, they held a one-day hackathon and open data workshop, creating space for New Yorkers of all back-

---

36   Cervantes, interview.

37   Ibid.

38   Kirchner, "Machine Bias."

grounds and abilities to discover what could be learned from this data. I joined them for this event, leading a full-day workshop for new data users to learn to explore and analyze the Street Tree dataset. Meanwhile, groups worked together to explore how this data might help local neighborhood advocacy groups, organizations working to mitigate the effects of global warming, and NYC Parks maintenance.

BetaNYC builds their open data curricula around datasets rather than data skills; they endeavor to help people relate to the data in a personal way. "Data analysis is about storytelling," says Executive Director Noel Hidalgo.[39] Recently, BetaNYC developed a card game that New Yorkers can use to explore data stories within the 311 dataset before they dive into the technical skills needed to extract and analyze the data.[40] 311 is the City's customer service line, capturing complaints on everything from noisy neighbors to a building's heat or hot water. Nearly every New Yorker can find a story in the data that in some way relates to their experience as part of the city. BetaNYC's goal is to help their students craft questions and structure data analyses with the data, and empower users to feel that they have a right and ability to access and use the dataset.[41] Similar to the ways in which reference librarians help their patrons shape research questions, BetaNYC helps data enthusiasts figure out which questions they can ask of the data, and helps them build the skills they need to seek out answers.

Conclusion

We are not the only profession struggling with how to engage the public in open data resources; researchers, educators, and civic technologists are all working to bring more people into an emerging community of data users. With our professional commitment to information literacy, accessibility, and empowerment, reference librarians have crucial experience and expertise to bring to these efforts.

Margaret Janz, a data librarian at the University of Pennsylvania, has noted the value of librarians in the Data Refuge project, a cross-sector initiative to preserve academic and government data. She writes about her

---

39   Hidalgo, interview.

40   Hidalgo, "@betanyc's 1st #opendata Card Game on @nyc311 Data."

41   Hidalgo, interview.

experience joining this collaboration: "One of the lessons we've learned in working on the Data Refuge project is that librarians aren't the only people who have, for years, been discussing how to solve the problems associated with so much of our most important governmental information only available digitally and online."[42] But, she argues, librarians are essential to the collaboration, with their cross-sector knowledge and translation abilities: "Would people other than librarians be able to build this network?"

As reference librarians, we have the opportunity to expand the data network past professional sectors and into the realm of the public. As a society, we need broader involvement, particularly from marginalized and underrepresented people, to improve our data quality, ask better questions of the data, and create better research findings and policy decisions. And our patrons deserve parity when it comes to deciding how their data gets collected, used, and interpreted. By adopting some of the pedagogical role of academic data librarians, and the practices of organizations already trying to engage the public with open data, public libraries can meet the data needs of their patrons and communities-at-large.

"One of the most traditional roles of librarians…helping users meet their information needs, and answering questions—is indeed highly politicized and powerful, even if is not generally perceived as such."[43]

---

42 Janz, "Communication across Communities: Why Isn't This Working?" *Libraries+ Network*, May 5, 2017, https://libraries.network/blog/2017/5/5/communication-across-communities.

43 Maura Seale, "Information Literacy Standards and the Politics of Knowledge Production: Using User-Generated Content to Incorporate Critical Pedagogy," in *Critical Library Instruction: Theories and Methods*, edited by Maria T. Accardi, Emily Drabinski, and Alana Kumbier (Duluth: Library Juice Press, 2009).

Works Cited

Border Crossers. Presentation at the ScriptEd Mid-Year Training, New York, NY, January 28, 2017.

boyd, danah, and Kate Crawford. "Six Provocations for Big Data." In *A Decade in Internet Time: Symposium on the Dynamics of the Internet and Society*, vol. 21. Oxford: Oxford Internet Institute, 2011. doi:10.2139/ssrn.1926431.

Calzada Prado, Javier, and Miguel Ángel Marzal. "Incorporating Data Literacy into Information Literacy Programs: Core Competencies and Contents." *Libri* 63, no. 2 (2013): 123–34.

Castro, Daniel. "The Rise of Data Poverty in America." *Center for Data Innovation*, September 10, 2014. Retrieved from https://www.datainnovation.org/2014/09/the-rise-of-data-poverty-in-america/.

Chattanooga Public Library. "Kicking off the Knight Foundation Open Data Project in Chattanooga." Accessed August 4, 2017. http://chattlibrary.org/content/kicking-knight-foundation-open-data-project-chattanooga.

Emmelhainz, Celia. "Data Librarians in Public Libraries" *Public Libraries Online*, May 18, 2015. Retrieved from http://publiclibrariesonline.org/2015/05/data-librarians-in-public-libraries/.

Fernandes, Praveen. "Opinion: The Census Won't Collect L.G.B.T. Data. That's a Problem." *The New York Times*, May 10, 2017, sec. Opinion. https://www.nytimes.com/2017/05/10/opinion/the-census-wont-collect-lgbt-data-thats-a-problem.html.

Francisco Cervantes (Director of Computer Science Education, CS4All), interviewed by Julia Marden, May 1, 2017, Brooklyn, NY, transcript, personal archive, Brooklyn, NY.

"Fulfilling the Promise of Open Data through Data Literacy Training." *Microsoft New York* (blog), August 1, 2017. https://blogs.microsoft.com/newyork/2017/08/01/fulfilling-the-promise-of-open-data-through-data-literacy-training/.

Gethers, Teneya. "Knowledge My Public Library Kept Secret: The Urgent Need for Culturally-Responsive Library Services." In *Informed Agitation: Library and Information Skills in Social Justice Movements and Beyond*, edited by Melissa Morrone. Sacramento: Library Juice Press, 2013.

Graslie, Emily. "Science Illiteracy Isn't Misunderstanding Data- We Have Sci Illiteracy When Ppl Don't Understand the Process Itself. https://Www.Washingtonpost.Com/News/Capital-Weather-Gang/Wp/2017/06/07/Epas-Scott-Pruitt-Wants-to-Set-up-Opposing-Teams-to-Debate-Climate-Change-Science/ …." Tweet. @Ehmee, June 7, 2017. https://twitter.com/Ehmee/status/872796740906254336.

Hidalgo, Noel. "@betanyc's 1st #opendata Card Game on @nyc311 Data." Accessed August 4, 2017. https://www.instagram.com/p/BWvRQ8ugC7ZiBDgYeURimwYI Odg5u1vtR5Qptw0/?taken-by=n0neck_.

Noel Hidalgo (Director, BetaNYC), interviewed by Julia Marden, May 12, 2017, Brooklyn, NY, transcript, personal archive, Brooklyn, NY.

Horrigan, John B. "Digital Readiness Gaps." *Pew Research Center: Internet, Science & Tech*, September 20, 2016. Retrieved from http://www.pewinternet.org/2016/09/20/ digital-readiness-gaps/.

Janz, Margaret. "Communication across Communities: Why Isn't This Working?" *Libraries+ Network*, May 5, 2017. Retrieved from https://libraries.network/ blog/2017/5/5/communication-across-communities.

Julion, Wrenetha, and Deborah Gross. "Recruiting Families of Color from the Inner City: Insights from the Recruiters." *Nursing Outlook* 48 (2000): 230–37.

Tim Moreland and Melinda Harris (Chattanooga Open Data Portal), interviewed by Julia Marden, May 3, 2017, phone, transcript, personal archive, Brooklyn, NY.

Onuoha, Mimi. "Broadway Won't Document Its Race Problem, so a Group of Actors Quietly Gathered the Data Themselves." *Quartz*, December 4, 2016. Retrieved from https://qz.com/842610/broadways-race-problem-is-unmasked-by-data-but-the-theater-industry-is-still-stuck-in-neutral/.

— — —. "Missing Datasets." Mimi Onuoha. Accessed November 24, 2017. http://mimionuoha.com/thoughts/2015/11/15/missing-datasets.

— — —. *The Library of Missing Datasets*, December 2016.

— — —. "Missing Datasets." *GitHub, n.d.* https://github.com/MimiOnuoha/missing-datasets.

"Open Data to Open Knowledge." *Boston.Gov, n.d.* Retrieved from https://www.boston. gov/innovation-and-technology/open-data-open-knowledge.

"Open Data to Open Knowledge Project Moving to New Data Platform." *Boston.Gov*, November 4, 2016. Retrieved from https://www.boston.gov/news/open-data-open-knowledge-project-moving-new-data-platform.

Partlo, Kristin. "The Pedagogical Data Reference Interview." *IASSIST Quarterly* 33/34, no. 4 (December 2009): 6–10.

———"From Data to Creation of Meaning Part II: Data Librarian as Translator." *IASSIST Quarterly* 38 (2014): 12–15.

Ryan Shanahan (Research Director, Vera Institute, interviewed by Julia Marden, May 15, 2017, New York, NY, transcript, personal archive, Brooklyn, NY.

Seale, Maura. "Information Literacy Standards and the Politics of Knowledge Production: Using User-Generated Content to Incorporate Critical Pedagogy." In *Critical Library Instruction: Theories and Methods*, edited by Maria T. Accardi, Emily Drabinski, and Alana Kumbier. Duluth: Library Juice Press, 2009.

Shermer, Michael, and Michael Shermer. "Why Climate Skeptics Are Wrong." *Scientific American*. Accessed November 26, 2017. https://doi.org/10.1038/scientificamerican1215-81.

Wickham, Hadley. "Tidy Data." *Journal of Statistical Software* 59, no. 10 (2014): 1–23. Retrieved from http://vita.had.co.nz/papers/tidy-data.pdf.

W.O.W. Boston. "W.O.W.Boston Overview." Medium, May 15, 2017. Retrieved from https://medium.com/@wowbos/intro-to-w-o-w-boston-ca3708cbf55c.

Hiding in Plain Sight: Reference Archivists as Social Justice Actors

Rachael Dreyer

Archival Reference Work Is Social Justice Work

Much of the archival profession focuses attention on archives as a site of social justice engagement. The bulk of the discussion centers on collecting, appraisal, donor relations, and diversifying the archival record through systemic change. While access and use is addressed, it often assumes a peripheral position in the literature. Use is acknowledged as a necessary component of archival value and social change, but an explicit view of how reference and access services are provided has not emerged from the discussion in the way that other common archival practices have. There are several possible explanations for this, but it is not because reference archivists are uninvolved in social justice work. Perhaps more than any other specialization in the archival profession, reference is naturally imbued with social justice work. Providing reference services that align with best practices, reference archives inherently serve the social justice aims of increasing access to archival collections. The work itself, rather than activism conducted apart from the core duties of the job, constitutes social justice action. Or, to put it a different way, this is "archival practice as a form of social, cultural and political activism."[1] Reference work takes place out in the open. It's the kind of social justice workmanship that hides in plain

---

1 Andrew Flinn and Ben Alexander, "'Humanizing an Inevitability [sic] Political Craft': Introduction to the Special Issue on Archiving Activism and Activist Archiving," *Archival Science* 15, no. 4 (2015): 332.

sight—we may take it for granted. We should not. Reference archivists utilize and mobilize archival power structures in order to level the playing field and disperse the power of the archives and the information held therein, and for this reason, archival reference work is the work of social justice.

While "we acknowledge that much of the relationship between archives and social justice remains implicit and unstated,"[2] it is worth unpacking some of the assumptions surrounding the connections between social justice and reference service because they haven't been specifically addressed in the archival field. Archival reference maps well to a social justice framework, as it is through archival reference that information which has historically been siloed and inaccessible is made available to anyone. Indeed, as Wendy Duff and her colleagues explain, "social justice concerns the distribution of power and wealth in society,"[3] and in the archival environment, we work towards the (re-)distribution of power through information. Thus, if we articulated social justice objectives in the practice of archival reference work, we would focus on these: 1) to treat each reference encounter with the utmost importance; 2) to provide services that meet the researcher's needs (even if that means scaling up the service level); 3) to guarantee equal access, and 4) to allow each researcher agency in their own research.

Such tenets of reference service have particular resonance in the archival and special collections environment, in which the research interaction is so heavily mediated by archivists. In order to see any physical item, a researcher must locate the desired material using descriptive tools created by archivists, using local practices which vary from institution to institution, and they must ask for it to be retrieved. As a result, incorporating the four objectives outlined above into the reference encounter allows public service archivists to provide an ethical and just level of access to primary source collections. To underscore this, the Society of American Archivists' code of ethics[4] establishes both access and use as one of the main goals of any archival institution, activities facilitated and supported by public service archivists.

---

2   Wendy M. Duff, Andrew Flinn, Karen Emily Suurtamm, and David A. Wallace, "Social Justice Impact of Archives: A Preliminary Investigation," *Archival Science* 13, no. 4 (2013): 318.

3   Duff, Flinn, Suurtamm, and Wallace, "Social Justice Impact of Archives," 321.

4   "Archivists promote and provide the widest possible accessibility of materials, consistent with any mandatory access restrictions, such as public statute, donor contract, business/institutional privacy, or personal privacy. Although access may be limited in some instances, archivists seek to promote open access and use when possible. Access to records is essential in personal, academic, business, and government settings, and use of records should be both welcomed and actively promoted." From the "SAA Core Values Statement and Code of Ethics," Society of American Archivists, http://www2.archivists.org/statements/saa-core-values-statement-and-code-of-ethics, accessed 12 September 2016.

At archival service points, reference archivists make materials available, and through this access, these records develop value. Indeed, "[a]rchives create potential societal value through the process of identifying and preserving documentation, but unless records are accessible and used for evidence, accountability, or research there is no true benefit to society. Reference and access services provide the essential link between records and people."[5] Collections have no intrinsic value unless they are used. By facilitating access, we provide researchers of all skill and expertise levels with proxy access to the power structures that created these records, and through the records, we supply researchers with the tools with which these power structures can be dismantled and deconstructed. Use equals value; this applies to the diary hidden away, recorded by a famous historical figure, which might possess intrinsic monetary value. Nevertheless, it is essentially worthless if it cannot be used for educational or research purposes. This holds equally true for the archived stream of tweets documenting the actions of a protest march; it has no monetary value, but it can be an invaluable source of documentary evidence if it is accessible to end users. Therefore, we need to include reference work in our approach to social justice and archival work because it is through access and use that researchers construct a narrative that challenges existing power centers. We must ensure that our public service delivery model for archives is one that continues to make our collections more accessible, diverse, inclusive, and representative of the many voices in a community.[6]

Promoting Social Justice through the Archival Research Experience

In order to promote a more just society, reference archivists need to engage, educate, and empower researchers to access archival materials. When we

---

5 Randall Jimerson, *Archives Power: Memory, Accountability, and Social Justice* (Chicago: Society of American Archivists, 2009): 314.

6 One of the most public aspects of social justice work and archives is the drive for community collecting initiatives and archives. As Michelle Caswell explains, community archives "are archives for the people, by the people, that eliminate the traditional middlemen of the archivist and university or government repository. In these institutions, decisions about what materials to collect, how to describe those materials, and who should have access to them are made by community members, generally all or most of whom are not professionally trained archivists." (Michelle Caswell, "South Asian American Struggles Against Racism: Community Archives in a Post 9/11 World," eds. Anna Reading and Tamar Katriel, *Cultural Memories of Nonviolent Struggles: Powerful Times* [New York: Palgrave Macmillan, 2015], 194).

foster authentic and direct access to collections, we become research partners working together with our patrons. We relinquish our status as "experts," and as a result, our researchers gain the independent research skills
needed to critically engage with the authoritative systems that created the
archival record. As research partners, "there is the responsibility to be hospitable... to 'the other'—the other ways of knowing and of doing, the ways
outside a society's mainstream... and to engage it with a willingness to
have one's own ways of knowing and doing changed in the process."[7] This
is a good model for the reference interaction, too, as so often we learn from
our researchers as they engage with our holdings. Researchers have different approaches to the material that may allow us to see the records, as well
as an avenue of inquiry, in a completely new light. This changes our individual way of knowing, and expands it, and is one way to incorporate social justice into the ways we provide reference service.

To systemically integrate a social justice practice into our professional reference services, we need to recognize that due to barriers and inequalities created by race, class, (dis)ability, citizenship status etc., not all
our users navigate the archival environment with ease. To increase ease of
access for new users, how might we apply and interpret institutional policies in a way that would be fair, if not always equal? For example, providing a patron greater staff assistance in order to experience the archives on
the same level as a more experienced researcher, even if it means less time
for the latter. In this case, providing both researchers with the same access, requires that we spend unequal amounts of time with them as a form
of distributive justice. The balance might be difficult to achieve, but if we
look at the issue as one of equal access, we are limiting access to inexperi-
enced researchers by only giving equal time, attention, and instruction to
both. This "fair but unequal" approach means interrogating our supposed
neutrality[8] in order to expand access in a socially just way. As Randall Jimerson posits, "archival ethics of justice may require providing 'unequal services' to individuals who do not know how to conduct archival research or
to read sources against the grain to uncover the truth, particularly when
victims seek to redress past injustices."[9]

---

7   Verne S. Harris, *Archives and Justice: A South African Perspective*
     (Chicago: Society of American Archivists, 2007), 261.

8   Howard Zinn, "Secrecy, Archives, and the Public Interest,"
     The Midwestern Archivist 2 no. 2 (1977): 20.

9   Randall Jimerson, *Archives Power*, 318.

Reference archivists conduct impromptu archival literacy instruction in our reading rooms daily—these primary source research skills provide the essential foundation for a positive and productive research experience. By making it easier for new researchers to access our collections by providing them with the framework of archival literacy, we bring social justice into archival reference work. Educating researchers about the ways in which our collections are organized and accessed will enable them to find the information they seek. We need to enable them to direct the course of their research, making sure that they are aware of the sources available. For example, our navigational tools are not intuitive. To help expedite a researcher's visit, we might identify boxes that fit within the scope of their research question. Yet, in doing so, we may inadvertently redirect and limit the course of the individual's research. What needs to happen, instead, is engaged instruction in the ways that researchers can access our collections. As reference archivists, we can offer suggestions regarding which primary source collections contain the necessary information, but we must remain mindful that our suggestions should not impede the researcher's own search strategy.

If outreach efforts are successful, then more first-time researchers will visit archival repositories and encounter the research process. Any staff member working the reference desk, in any environment, provides the first link from the researcher to the information: one person has the power to impact a researcher's entire experience. First impressions do matter, and they should not be ones that elicit perceptions of gate-keeping or of deliberately restricting access. A new researcher may feel bewildered when confronted with the rules and policies of an archival repository; most prohibit food, beverages, gum, ink pens, book bags, and briefcases. Libraries have become more permissive in policies pertaining to food, so while archival repositories often look like libraries, it can be confusing for researchers to be asked to leave certain items in lockers, or to throw out a $6 coffee. This is a necessary precaution for the integrity of the collections, but to many researchers, it seems unwelcoming and even aggressive, and illustrates why some may feel rebuffed by the time they begin their research. Sometimes, they turn away altogether.

A periodic review of our policies will ensure that we enforce them in the most inviting and welcoming way possible. In our public spaces, we have the opportunity to engage new researchers in teachable moments to explain the outcomes of conscientious handling practices. By providing an educational experience at public service points, not just a research experience, we demonstrate the value of unique and rare materials and the researcher's role in preserving them for future use. A search of archives and special collections' webpages consistently returns a list of what to expect upon arrival at the repository, but it is most often a list of behaviors and items that are or are not acceptable in reading rooms. Some institutions are increasingly moving towards a more interactive and educational model of posting rules and prohibitions, using videos[10] and online tutorials to explain the reasons for what appear to be draconian regulations. If we see positive results from our outreach efforts to communities that are underrepresented in our holdings, as well as in our researcher demographics, we need to first demonstrate that we are in fact accessible to all, and we welcome researchers of all experience levels. This is essential if we are to fulfill our social justice mission through opening the archival information silo.

In considering reference interactions of the future, we tend to think that they will take place in the online ecosystem. Located in closed stacks that do not support the ability to browse, archives' collections have not always been as accessible as mass digitization projects now make them. In the past, researchers needed to work in quiet reading rooms, meaning that only those with the time and financial resources were able to peruse original documents and first editions. Now, many repositories strive to ensure that primary source documents are digitized and made accessible through collaborative digital collections portals. While this is a positive move towards ensuring wider and more inclusive access for archival materials, it takes for granted that users are comfortable navigating often clunky digital collections' websites, or are interested in accessing the available content arranged around a particular topic. Although we need to remain mindful of the barriers to access posed by the digital divide, we also need to ensure that the collections we provide digitally are collections with relevance to our end users. Even in our increasingly technology-dependent society, many are without reliable internet access, email addresses, or basic digital literacy skills. Social justice requires that we balance equal service for individuals on both sides of the digital divide. As research work takes place outside the Reading Room, it becomes more independent and increasingly dispersed through digitization projects, though we continue to need archival professionals who are willing to connect with and instruct researchers of all levels of expertise in the use of the unintuitive and anachronistic navigational tools used by archivists for both analog and digital materials.

---

10   An example is a video titled "Kislak Center for Special Collections: Registration, Rules, and Requesting Material," University of Pennsylvania Libraries, https://youtu.be/BlZwyChKH78, accessed 14 April 2017.

Representation Matters: Diverse Collections, Diverse Researchers

We can also provide access to community collecting projects, and to place these alongside more traditional collections to validate them as equally valuable sources of information. Community collecting work can take place in the reading room or during a reference interview; necessary acquisition and deed of gift signatures can be obtained, and researchers (each a potential collection donor) can see how their donation contributes to the vibrancy of intellectual inquiry. But first, we need to look at our reference spaces as the archival core where individuals from underrepresented communities have a voice, purpose, and a contributing role. A large percentage of the work being done at the intersection of social justice and archival work addresses the need to collect materials from communities, to get their histories into the archives.[11] Much less attention has been directed to the need to get individuals from communities into the archives, but it is an effective way to demystify what archivists do, as well as to invite and welcome the history from those communities into the archives.

Community archives, created, arranged, and described by members of communities that are under-represented in the archives are valuable and essential to ensure that the many voices in society are represented and preserved. However, some communities may not have the time or resources to preserve their own history. Under-represented and under-documented communities need to know that their histories are welcome alongside the "archival canon" of white male voices; collaborative collecting initiatives that bring together the communities' knowledge and the archival expertise of an institution can result in the long-term preservation of a community's unique history. While institutional collecting of under-documented communities' records may open the door to critiques, it is one option for preserving and making accessible the histories that have been missing from the archival record. Communities deserve to maintain control of their own history. At the same time, lodging it in the care of a well-resourced public institution so that it stands as a counterpoint to dominant narratives is also a sustainable way to share a community's story. Indeed,

---

11   Archivists frequently feel the dual pressures of wanting communities to remain in control and possession of their own history, and the possibility that the historical records could be rendered inaccessible due to a change of resources or leadership. Archivists who work primarily with acquisitions never want to appropriate a community or organization's history; instead there is a genuine desire to make the records accessible, regardless of whether that occurs at an archival repository or a grass-roots archive.

one of the most compelling arguments for developing collecting partnerships between underrepresented communities and institutions is the constant question, "where am I in this?" Many of the students whom we serve come to our reading rooms hoping to find material in our collections that can help them to incorporate their personal histories into research papers. Students of color face challenges that their white counterparts do not because as a profession, legacy collecting practices have created a body of collections which skews white and male.

Restricted Collections' Implication for Social Justice in the Reading Room

A firmly entrenched and decidedly unwelcoming barrier to access, and therefore the larger goals of social justice, are the restrictions on collections. Waldo Gifford Leland, whose efforts provided much of the impetus for the founding of the National Archives, admitted in 1912 that restrictions were "undoubtedly convenient from the administrative point of view, but [they are] artificial and needlessly [hamper] or [make] quite impossible many lines of investigation."[12] In many ways, we have yet to move away from these arbitrary restrictions: in many cases, donors are permitted to dictate the terms and length of restrictions. Hilary Jenkinson's prioritization of an archivist's responsibilities reminds us, in part, of the dramatic shift of archivists' understanding of how to best serve our communities and our collections. "The Archivist, then, is the servant of his Archives first and afterwards of the student Public. It follows that when, but not before, he has done all that is necessary by his Archives his duty is to devote himself to publication in the interests of Research workers."[13] This clearly illustrates that in the early days of professional archival practice, the emphasis was on service to the records as a primary concern. Nearly 100 years later, the profession's ethical statements denote a clear shift towards privileging access and use; while we must maintain the integrity of the collections, it would be a failure of archival (as well as social) justice if records were to be acquired, arranged, and described without any plan for them to be made accessible.

---

12   Waldo Gifford Leland, "The National Archives: A Programme," *The American Historical Review* 18, no. 1 (1912): 27.

13   Hilary Jenkinson, *A Manual of Archive Administration Including the Problems of War Archives and Archive Making* (Oxford: Clarendon Press, 1922), 107.

Restrictions maintain the siloed status of archival information; they protect the creator of the records, and therefore, are a representation of the power and authority that created the records originally. Yet restrictions can also be used to protect the privacy of individuals represented in the records who may not have control over their recorded information. Open records sometimes have the potential to lead to the persecution or arrest of vulnerable populations. In my own experience, faculty members frequently include student assignments among their own papers with a transfer to the archives, and union records' membership rolls include names and addresses of members. We must remain mindful of the right to privacy, and if individuals' information ends up in the archives without their consent, we need to consider how best to handle these collections that respects those privacy rights. We have ethical obligations to protect "legitimate privacy and confidentiality rights of individuals."[14] But in general practice, if restrictions limit use to the extent that collections are rendered inaccessible, we have disregarded some of the most central guiding principles of archival practice. As professionals who work directly with researchers, reference archivists should advocate with acquisitions staff for a reduction in restrictions during communications and negotiations with donors, unless restrictions concern a legitimate privacy risk. Not only do excessive restrictions limit access in direct conflict with the "access = value" equation, but they can be difficult to enforce. For instance, collections under restriction may be accessed unintentionally or held back from the researcher if descriptive information is unclear, or if portions of the collection are restricted while others are not. There might be set time limits for restrictions, such as twenty years from the date the document was created, but boxes of archival records could contain folders that contain a mix of restricted and open records. If restrictions are uneven within a collection, it creates confusion for both researcher and archivist and impedes access because most archivists are risk-averse: if there is uncertainty over a question of restrictions, archivists tend to limit access to the material rather than open it for research. It is always possible to make it available once the open status is confirmed, rather than to ask a researcher to forget the contents of a still-restricted folder they mistakenly received.

We must make sure that the collections we are accepting into our holdings are restricted only if necessary; unnecessary restrictions undermine records' enduring archival value. As restrictions typically are assigned when new collections are acquired and organized physically and intellectu-

---

14 Jimerson, *Archives Power*, 314.

ally, reference archivists must often abide by the repository's decision on restrictions. Experienced researchers are aware of the ways in which restrictions can be circumvented, such as Freedom of Information Act requests or special petitions to the governing bodies of an institution. We can help our researchers to navigate the system of restrictions, but if we offer this service to one researcher, we must be able to offer it for all. If we don't have the time or resources to offer the same level of service to everyone, then we need to ensure that we adjust our access policies accordingly. Again, if researchers encounter restrictions in the course of their engagement with the materials, we can further the educational experience by communicating why materials are restricted, e.g. per donor specifications, institutional policy, or an overabundance of personally identifying information. We can then offer alternative collections or sources if the initial collection is restricted, though that is not always a perfect substitute for the information that is inaccessible due to its restricted status.

A more liberal, access-conscious policy would encourage the implementation of use agreements, rather than restricting access outright. For example, a collection might be rife with personally identifying information, including names, addresses, social security numbers, and personality profiles. Often, in these cases, collections are closed for access for 70 years after the date of one's death, but this can difficult to confirm. Or, perhaps the collection's donor promised confidentiality to subjects in an oral history project included in the gift of their personal papers. Or, perhaps the archival institution has inherited a collection full of black lung lawsuits, but there is no agreement from the donor on file. Instead of forbidding a researcher from accessing the collection in its entirety, instead, reference archivists could consider a well-defined use agreement. In this agreement, researchers would acknowledge the existence of sensitive and/or personal information and would agree not to share or cite that information except in anonymized aggregate. This satisfies the obligation to collection donors, but it also better meets the needs of researchers and allows wider and more inclusive access to archival information—one of the central ways that archival reference work incorporates the goals of social justice action.

Concluding Thoughts: An Appeal

The need to interweave social justice goals in our archival reference work is all the more vital when we work with those most in need of access to archival collections, but who are often the least experienced. Individuals may need access to the collections to produce documentation or proof to secure insurance coverage, pension benefits, or to fight for legal recognition or reparation. These researchers are often unfamiliar with archives' jargon-y approach to providing research service: finding aid, accretion, restrictions, deed of gift, donor agreement, offsite storage, and registration. These terms have lost their distinct meanings; they've grown fuzzy around the edges through overuse. We no longer think about what they might mean when someone initially encounters them.

My institution recently met a researcher who had traveled from out of state to use our collections. We received the initial request to access a restricted collection; per our standard policy, we had sent the permission form used by the curator to grant access to the collection, per the donor's stipulation in the memorandum of understanding. We were waiting on the return of the permission form and had not heard back from the researcher until ten days later when they appeared in our reading room. The researcher was frustrated because they believed we had not responded to their initial request. I quickly produced a hard copy of the permission form, delivered it to the curator, and received immediate approval. We couldn't grant immediate access to the collection because it was stored offsite. The researcher was upset, and understandably so. I promised to request the boxes from our offsite storage location and indicated that the boxes would arrive the next afternoon. The patron's face fell—they were flying out of an airport four hours away the next morning. The request was simple: to track down employment records to prove that pension benefits had been vested after a certain number of service years. The collection in question doesn't often contain individual records of that sort, but we offered to review the boxes the patron had requested. In the end, we apologized and offered what assistance we could, but the patron was essentially turned away empty-handed. This interaction has led to many sleepless nights since, turning over the question of how to do better for this patron and how to handle similar situations. How do we change our approach to communication with patrons about our collections and their research needs? How can we ensure that we're reaching everyone who wants or needs access to the collections? These are ongoing questions, surely, and as our collections and services evolve to fit the increasingly digital environment in which we live and work, new questions will surface. However, as basic best practice of the archival reference model, we must continue to promote equal access, we must ensure that the language we use with researchers is inclusive and welcoming, and if we fall short, we must work to do better. As Randall

Jimerson asserts, "Society can and must embrace archives for all."[15] I truly believe in the transformative power of archives to contribute to progressive social justice change—but in order for that to occur, archival records need to be *used*. Indeed, archives have historically promoted equality of access, as "[t]he end of all archival effort is to preserve valuable records and make them available for use… [The archivist] provides access to records under conditions that will satisfy both government officials and the general public and makes records equally available to both."[16] Specifically as reference archivists, we must also work for equality of representation within the content of our holdings, for equality of access among new user communities, for greater transparency in our approach to restrictions and limits on access, and for reference policies and practices that utilize distributive justice when allocating reference resources for archival literacy education. Instead of hiding in plain sight, reference archivists must use their public-facing roles to advocate for researchers' access to collections and to educate both peers and the public about the foundational role they serve in archives' social justice work.

15 Jimerson, *Archives Power*, 278.

16 T.R. Schellenberg, *Modern Archives: Principles and Techniques* (Chicago: University of Chicago Press, 1956): 224.

Works Cited

Alexander, Ben and Andrew Flinn. "'Humanizing an Inevitability [sic] Political Craft': Introduction to the Special Issue on Archiving Activism and Activist Archiving." *Archival Science* (2015): 329–35.

Caswell, Michelle. "South Asian American Struggles Against Racism: Community Archives in a Post 9/11 World." In *Cultural Memories of Nonviolent Struggles: Powerful Times*, ed. Anna Reading and Tamar Katriel, 188–204. New York: Palgrave Macmillan, 2015.

Harris, Verne S. *Archives and Justice: A South African Perspective*. Chicago: Society of American Archivists, 2007.

Jenkinson, Hilary. *A Manual of Archive Administration Including the Problems of War Archives and Archive Making*. Oxford: Clarendon Press, 1922.

Jimerson, Randall. *Archives Power: Memory, Accountability, and Social Justice*. Chicago: Society of American Archivists, 2009.

Leland, Waldo Gifford. "The National Archives: A Programme." *The American Historical Review* 18, no. 1 (1912): 1–28.

Schellenberg, T. R. *Modern Archives: Principles and Techniques*. Chicago: University of Chicago Press, 1956.

Society of American Archivists. *SAA Core Values Statement and Code of Ethics*. Accessed September 12, 2016. http://www2.archivists.org/statements/saa-core-values-statement-and-code-of-ethics.

University of Pennsylvania Libraries. "Kislak Center for Special Collections: Registration, Rules, and Requesting Material." *YouTube*. Accessed April 14, 2017. https://youtu.be/BlZwyChKH78.

Duff, Wendy M., Andrew Flinn, Karen Emily Suurtamm, and David A. Wallace. "Social Justice Impact of Archives: A Preliminary Investigation." *Archival Science* 13, no. 4 (2013): 317–48.

Zinn, Howard. "Secrecy, Archives, and the Public Interest." *The Midwestern Archivist* (1977): 14–26.

Beyond Efficient Answers with a Smile: Seeking Critical Reference Praxis

Eamon Tewell

Like reference work, praxis relies on continual reciprocity and exchange; a dialogue. In praxis, the non-exclusive categories of theory, practice, and reflection overlap, intermingle, and mutually inform one another to result in critical action and contributing to a better understanding of the world and how it might be changed. Praxis is iterative and ongoing, and can be defined as the "process of applying theory through practice to develop more informed theory and practice, specifically as it relates to social change."[1] It is a component vital to identifying and interrupting the structures of domination and privilege we exist within, structures which are positioned as natural through hegemony. As David James Hudson observes, it is necessary that we problematize the strict delineations between theory, practice, and praxis itself, considering that "theory is material, theory is action, theory is practice," and to ignore the materiality of scholarship is to misapprehend it and the lived experiences it entails.[2] Hudson further argues that

---

1   John J. Doherty, "Towards Self-Reflection in Librarianship: What is Praxis?" *Progressive Librarian* 26 (Winter 2005/2006): 11.

2   David James Hudson, "The Whiteness of Practicality," in *Topographies of Whiteness: Mapping Whiteness in Library and Information Science*, ed. Gina Schlesselman-Tarango (Sacramento: Library Juice Press, 2017), 226.

"critical work is always a practice of translation," dependent on the various environments we inhabit.[3] Each chapter in this section delves into different conceptual frames and inspirations, offering new insights and acts of translation for informing reference work and successfully blurring the arbitrary lines that separate theory, practice, and reflection.

Much of the scholarly discussion concerning reference has focused upon whether library users take advantage of reference services. A great deal of hand-wringing has taken place over a decline in the number of "transactions" recorded in libraries across the United States, and when reference is not lamented as a waste of librarians' time or criticized for being cost-ineffective, it has in various accounts been subjected to transformation, met with dismissal, or sentenced to death. At best, different models of reference are considered, as though the answer to meaningful reference work lies simply in finding the "correct" model to be applied.

What so much of this existing discussion has failed to account for, and what the authors in this section accomplish so fully, is an examination of the reference worker's role, as laborer, interlocutor, and contributor to an ongoing reference dialogue occurring within libraries that often repeats itself, accumulates over time, and, sometimes, opens up unforeseen possibilities for librarians and patrons alike. A focus on the relational dynamics between reference worker and patron is particularly useful considering the identity of the library user is often constructed in ways that "[do] not necessarily liberate the user from the constraints of the system, and for both librarians and users, there is no easy way out of the web of discursive power."[4] The library is a place with unique potential, but it acts to reproduce systems of domination in ways similar to any other institution. The sooner we realize there is no existing outside of these systems, the better.

Critical self-reflection upon our work and the relational nature of reference is crucial in ensuring it reflects both the needs of patrons and our social justice goals as library workers. As Freeda Brook, Dave Ellenwood, and Althea Eannace Lazzaro note, within reference work "communication is always imbued with power dynamics, which are shaped by racialized identity and cultural practices. Library staff, however, are typically not

---

3   Ibid, 227.

4   Kimmo Tuominen, "User-Centered Discourse: An Analysis of the Subject Positions of the User and the Librarian," *The Library Quarterly* 67, no. 4 (1997): 367.

asked to be cognizant of these dynamics."[5] Recent work such as Brook et al.'s as well as new collections have already begun to take up these efforts, most notably *The Feminist Reference Desk: Concepts, Critiques, and Conversations*.[6] The specific ways that patriarchy, heteronormativity, racism, and ableism function and are reproduced among various sites of library work are increasingly being described and made visible. Rose L. Chou and Annie Pho, for example, describe the experiences of women of color librarians with the reference desk as a focal point, while April Hathcock and Stephanie Sendaula show how racial microaggressions are directed at librarians of color at the reference desk.[7] Considering two recent titles that examine race and gender in libraries, *Pushing the Margins: Women of Color and Intersectionality in LIS* and *Topographies of Whiteness: Mapping Whiteness in Library and Information Science*, it is clear that the "pink-collar immaterial labor" of librarianship is continuing to be interrogated along with interlocking systems of oppression.[8] As Fobazi Ettarh writes regarding librarianship and intersectionality, "When librarianship is viewed through a single-axis that is reflective of the dominant culture, certain values, such as individualism and assertiveness color the advice and practices deemed acceptable."[9] It is only through apprehending these multiple axes that hegemony can be challenged.

---

5   Freeda Brook, Dave Ellenwood, and Althea Eannace Lazzaro, "In Pursuit of Antiracist Social Justice: Denaturalizing Whiteness in the Academic Library," *Library Trends* 64, no. 2 (2015): 269.

6   Maria Accardi, ed., *The Feminist Reference Desk: Concepts, Critiques, and Conversations* (Sacramento: Library Juice Press, 2017).

7   Rose L. Chou and Annie Pho, "Intersectionality at the Reference Desk: Lived Experiences of Women of Color Librarians," in *The Feminist Reference Desk: Concepts, Critiques, and Conversations*, ed. Maria T. Accardi (Sacramento: Library Juice Press, 2017), 225–252; April M. Hathcock and Stephanie Sendaula, "Mapping Whiteness at the Reference Desk," in *Topographies of Whiteness: Mapping Whiteness in Library and Information Science*, ed. Gina Schlesselman-Tarango (Sacramento: Library Juice Press, 2017), 247–56.

8   Rose L. Chou and Annie Pho, eds., *Pushing the Margins: Women of Color and Intersectionality in LIS* (Sacramento: Library Juice Press, 2018); Gina Schlesselman-Tarango, ed., *Topographies of Whiteness: Mapping Whiteness in Library and Information Science* (Sacramento: Library Juice Press, 2017); Lisa Sloniowski, "Affective Labor, Resistance, and the Academic Librarian," *Library Trends* 64, no. 4 (2016): 645.

9   Fobazi Ettarh, "Making a New Table: Intersectional Librarianship," *In the Library with the Lead Pipe* (2014).

The university I work at, which is made up predominantly of students of color, has seen increased activism in the wake of the 2016 U.S. Presidential Election. Students are responding to the hateful rhetoric and policies of the current administration by organizing in and outside of the university, participating in rallies, conducting panels, and petitioning to have the university recognized as a sanctuary campus. This growth in political organizing is heartening to see at a school not particularly known for its activism. The reference desk has been one place for these students to drop off flyers, update librarians on their organizing efforts, and ask about possibilities for sponsorship of their events. Reference, of course, has always been well-suited to this type of informational exchange. What has changed in the last few months is an increased solidarity with student activists, working to shape the university and their world. As a public place that encourages impromptu conversations and helps us maintain the enthusiasm that is so important to creating change, I am glad our reference desk allows us to connect with students and discuss not just immediate needs, but our greater hopes and goals moving forward.

The most valuable aspects of reference may be creating friction in the teflon tunnel of the neoliberal university and world at large, as Patti Ryan and Lisa Sloniowski phrase it.[10] Reference is a space where we are less likely to assess or be assessed, and where relating with other people and exercising compassion is key. As we are demanded to demonstrate our value and prove our contributions, perhaps the most useful thing reference workers can do is embrace the fleeting and unexpected nature of reference. Let's use our positions in reference to foster solidarity with our patrons and create meaningful connections. Most significantly of all, let's use our time and energy to give attention to and care for others, in a time when care is an uncommon, essential, and radical act.

---

10   Patti Ryan and Lisa Sloniowski, "The Public Academic Library: Friction in the Teflon Tunnel," in *Information Literacy and Social Justice: Radical Professional Praxis*, ed. Shana Higgins and Lua Gregory (Sacramento, CA: Library Juice Press, 2013), 275–96.

Works Cited

Accardi, Maria, ed. *The Feminist Reference Desk: Concepts, Critiques, and Conversations.* Sacramento: Library Juice Press, 2017.

Brook, Freeda, Dave Ellenwood, and Althea Eannace Lazzaro. "In Pursuit of Antiracist Social Justice: Denaturalizing Whiteness in the Academic Library." *Library Trends* 64, no. 2 (2015): 246–84. Retrieved from http://hdl.handle.net/1773/34983.

Chou, Rose L., and Annie Pho, eds. *Pushing the Margins: Women of Color and Intersectionality in LIS.* Sacramento: Library Juice Press, 2018.

Doherty, John J. "Towards Self-Reflection in Librarianship: What is Praxis?" *Progressive Librarian* 26 (Winter 2005/2006): 11–17. Retrieved from http://www.progressivelibrariansguild.org/PL/PL26/011.pdf.

Ettarh, Fobazi. "Making a New Table: Intersectional Librarianship." *In the Library with the Lead Pipe* (2014). Retrieved from http://www.inthelibrarywiththeleadpipe.org/2014/making-a-new-table-intersectional-librarianship-3/.

Hathcock, April M., and Stephanie Sendaula. "Mapping Whiteness at the Reference Desk." In *Topographies of Whiteness: Mapping Whiteness in Library and Information Science*, edited by Gina Schlesselman-Tarango, 247–56. Sacramento: Library Juice Press, 2017. Retrieved from http://hdl.handle.net/2451/40072.

Hudson, David James. "The Whiteness of Practicality." In *Topographies of Whiteness: Mapping Whiteness in Library and Information Science*, edited by Gina Schlesselman-Tarango, 203–34. Sacramento: Library Juice Press, 2017. Retrieved from http://hdl.handle.net/10214/11619.

Ryan, Patti, and Lisa Sloniowski. "The Public Academic Library: Friction in the Teflon Tunnel." In *Information Literacy and Social Justice: Radical Professional Praxis*, edited by Shana Higgins and Lua Gregory, 275–96. Sacramento: Library Juice Press, 2013. Retrieved from http://hdl.handle.net/10315/26285.

Schlesselman-Tarango, Gina, ed. *Topographies of Whiteness: Mapping Whiteness in Library and Information Science.* Sacramento: Library Juice Press, 2017.

Sloniowski, Lisa. "Affective Labor, Resistance, and the Academic Librarian." *Library Trends* 64, no. 4 (2016): 645–66. http://dx.doi.org/10.1353/lib.2016.0013

Tuominen, Kimmo. "User-Centered Discourse: An Analysis of the Subject Positions of the User and the Librarian." *The Library Quarterly* 67, no. 4 (1997): 350–71. Retrieved from http://www.jstor.org/stable/40039589.

From Interpersonal to Intersubjective: Relational theory and mutuality in reference

Veronica I. Arellano-Douglas

At the core of reference lies a relationship. It is the coming together—however brief—of two individuals who each possess unique experiences, emotions, and needs with the intent of sharing knowledge. Yet contemporary characterizations of reference range from consumerist (*reference transactions),* to neutral and objective (*reference interactions*), to those that imply some kind of interpersonal connection but retain an inherent power differential (*reference interviews or consultations*). In this chapter, I propose a model of reference informed by Relational-Cultural Theory and the concept of *intersubjective mutuality,* which can be used to foster an empathetic, feminist, and egalitarian practice of reference work. With this approach to reference, the subjectivity—or unique personhood—of the librarian and that of the library patron is in conversation, which creates the kind of growth and learning opportunities unique to libraries.

Reference Librarianship Through a Relational Lens

Since Samuel Green's 1876 essay on *Personal Relations Between Librarians and Readers*, reference librarianship has existed within a relational context. By its very definition it is the kind of work that cannot be done alone, but rather necessitates the personal interactions between librarian and patron that Green heavily promoted.[1] His emphasis on creating a hospitable, home-like library atmosphere relied heavily on the affective labor of (primarily women) librarians, who were responsible for cultivating meaningful interpersonal relationships with patrons.[2] Although comfort, respect, and a "democratic spirit" were central to these relationships, they still retained an air of hierarchy, with librarians acting as guardians of culture and knowledge for the masses.[3] In 1915 W. W. Bishop refined the definition of the reference librarian as one who offers service "in aid of some sort of study."[4] It is a subtle shift, but one with strong implications for librarian-patron relationships. With this underpinning of study as focus, the primary relationship is between the patron and her information need, with the librarian acting as intermediary. The interpersonal framework then consists of the librarian, the patron, and the inquiry, which has become the primary driver of interaction and the foundation for librarian-patron relationships in the 20th century.[5]

It is a strange relationship in which the two human actors are not the most important subjects. Yet this unequal triad is the model of reference work that seems to have "stuck." The first of edition of William Katz's classic reference textbook, *Introduction to Reference Work*, stressed the invisibility of the reference librarian, who should "vanish" in the face of a patron's need, stripping librarians of any importance or authority.[6] Modern conceptions of reference librarianship emphasize "information consultations in which library staff recommend, interpret, evaluate, and/or use information resources to help others to meet particular information needs," creating relationships in which information is central, and librarians act more like information conduits than valued partners.[7]

---

1 Samuel Green, "Personal Relations Between Librarians and Readers," *Library Journal* 1, no. 2–3 (1876): 74–81.

2 Lisa Sloniowski, "Affective Labor, Resistance, and the Academic Librarian," *Library Trends* 64, no. 4 (Spring 2016): 659.

3 Green, "Personal Relations Between Librarians and Readers," 80–81.

4 Marcella D. Genz, "Working the Reference Desk," *Library Trends* 46, no. 3 (1998): 510–11.

5 Bernard Vavrek, "The Nature of Reference Librarianship," *RQ* 13, no. 3 (1974): 214.

6 Genz, "Working the Reference Desk," 518.

7 Reference and User Services Association, "Definitions of Reference," *Reference & User Services Association (RUSA)*, 2008, http://www.ala.org/rusa/guidelines/definitionsreference; Genz, "Working the Reference Desk," 518.

Although the *Professional Competencies for Reference and User Services Librarians* advocate for treating "the user [patron] as a collaborator and partner in the information seeking process," the emphasis is still on collaboration as a means of facilitating the information transaction or coming to an answer, rather than on the collaborative relationship itself.[8] A need to assert oneself in the face of this subordinate status may be the impetus for the creation of the librarian-as-information-expert identity, which, not surprisingly, arose in the information proliferation of the later decades of the 20th century.[9] The advent of difficult to use online library databases likely added fuel to this fire, as patrons were unable to access needed information from clunky interfaces and awkward algorithms without the help of the skilled and educated reference librarian.[10] The arrival of semantic searching, full-text online archives, and perpetual internet access has done much to undermine librarians' claims to expertise— anyone, at any time, can find *something*—bringing into question once again the status of the reference librarian within the librarian-patron relationship. This is the root of existing tensions in reference librarianship: the constant need for the reference librarian to redefine her relational role to library patrons.

The reference interview is an attempt to clarify this relationship by giving librarians and patrons well-defined relational roles. The librarian is responsible for putting the patron at ease, discovering her *true* information need, and guiding her to needed information.[11] The patron is in need of information, and more importantly, assistance in uncovering and understanding what exactly it is that she really wants to know.[12] Finding desired information is still the primary driver of this relationship, but there is a strong emphasis on the interpersonal interactions that take place

8   Reference and User Services Association, "Professional Competencies for Reference and User Services Librarians," *Reference & User Services Association (RUSA)*, 2003, http://www.ala.org/rusa/resources/guidelines/professional.

9   Emily Drabinski, "Toward a Kairos of Library Instruction," *The Journal of Academic Librarianship* 40, no. 5 (September 2014): 480–85.

10   Genz, "Working the Reference Desk," 518.

11   Kay Ann Cassell and Uma Hiremath, *Reference and Information Services in the 21st Century: An Introduction*, 2nd edition (London: Facet Publishing, 2009), 15.

12   Catherine Sheldrick Ross, Kirsti Nilsen, and Marie L. Radford, *Conducting the Reference Interview: A How-To-Do-It Manual for Librarians*, 2nd edition (New York: Neal-Schuman Publishers, 2009), 5–7.

along the way. Marie Radford's research on interpersonal communication in academic library reference work and Constance Mellon's identification of library anxiety inform the contemporary practice of reference interviews, and by extension, the librarian-patron relationship.[13] Librarians are encouraged to put students at ease by being unobtrusive but friendly, smiling and making eye contact but at the same time remaining matter-of-fact, and conducting themselves in generally pleasant ways.[14] This is a big piece of the construction of the library as "an extension of the domestic sphere."[15] A highly feminized labor force of librarians is not only expected to be warm and welcoming, but to make it appear incidental, thereby erasing all of the work that goes into this service provider facade. It is a practice that places all of the relational burden—or work of sustaining the relationship—on the reference librarian, who must perform the role of the approachable, interested, non-judgemental, always neutral, *professional* information guide. For at the same time that librarians must set a pleasant affective tone in their work, they must still maintain an image of professionalism, which is often based on white, masculine constructions of work that value autonomy and authority.[16] It is an exhausting, imbalanced dance that leaves librarians prone to "provider pessimism," the feeling that the help and assistance they have to give is not quite good enough.[17]

---

13 Marie L. Radford, *The Reference Encounter : Interpersonal Communication in the Academic Library*, ACRL Publications in Librarianship: No. 52 (Chicago : Association of College and Research Libraries, 1999); Constance A. Mellon, "Library Anxiety: A Grounded Theory and Its Development," *College and Research Libraries* 47, no. 2 (March 1, 1986): 160–65.

14 Ross, Nilsen, and Radford, *Conducting the Reference Interview*, 39–59.

15 Sloniowski, "Affective Labor," 646.

16 Joyce K. Fletcher, "Relational Practice: A Feminist Reconstruction of Work," in *The Handbook of Women, Psychology, and the Law*, ed. by Andrea Barnes (Hoboken, NJ: John Wiley & Sons, 2005), 84–85.

17 Kathy Butler and Jason Byrd, "Research Consultation Assessment: Perceptions of Students and Librarians," *Journal of Academic Librarianship* 42, no. 1 (January 2016): 83–86; Derek Hansen, Margeaux Johnson, Elizabeth Norton, and Anne McDonough, "Virtual Provider Pessimism: Analysing Instant Messaging Reference Encounters with the Pair Perception Comparison Method," *Information Research* 14, no. 1 (2009).

Attempts at subverting this all-give and no-take librarian-patron relationship have been made by Holberg[18] and Cavanagh,[19] who advocate for a relational approach to reference that promotes shared learning and communities of practice between librarians and patrons. These conceptions of reference differ from their predecessors in their emphasis on the reference relationship as a one-to-one *learning relationship* rather than a service. This emphasis on *reference-as-learning* is the first step towards a reciprocal librarian-patron relationship within the context of reference work. Learning is an interrelational act that includes not just an exchange of knowledge, but a mingling of perspectives and emotions. There is an affective component to the educational experience, which is as much about recognition of self as it is about content delivery.[20] Teachers and students are whole people and bring with them a set of existing knowledge and life experiences to any educational situation.[21] This perspective on learning has gained traction within the librarian teaching and learning community, whose members have embraced a critical pedagogical approach that positions librarians and students as co-learners working toward creating new, shared knowledge based on existing experience.[22] It is unclear why this strongly egalitarian relational approach to library instruction has not made its way into the recent literature of reference work. Perhaps there still exists some disconnect between the idea of reference as a service and learning in the library. But what else is reference work really, but a one-to-one learning relationship? This idea is the much needed foundation for an application of Relational-Cultural Theory.

---

18 John E. Holberg, "Relational Reference: A Challenge to the Reference Fortress," In *An Introduction to Reference Services in Academic Libraries*, ed. by Elizabeth Connor, Haworth Series in Introductory Information Science Textbooks (New York, NY: Haworth Information Press, 2006), 39–47.

19 Mary F. Cavanagh, "Interpreting Reference Work with Contemporary Practice Theory," *Journal of Documentation* 69, no. 2 (2013): 214–42.

20 Mark Murphy and Tony Brown, "Learning as Relational: Intersubjectivity and Pedagogy in Higher Education," *International Journal of Lifelong Education* 31, no. 5 (October 2012): 651.

21 Maria T. Accardi, *Feminist Pedagogy for Library Instruction* (Sacramento, CA: Library Juice Press, 2013), 44.

22 Maria T. Accardi, Emily Drabinski, and Alana Kumbier, *Critical Library Instruction: Theories and Methods* (Duluth, MN: Library Juice Press, 2010).

Relational-Cultural Theory

Psychologist Jean Baker Miller's 1976 classic book, *Toward a New Psychology of Women*, acknowledged and valued the strengths of women typically overlooked in traditional models of psychology. As founding director of the Stone Center for Developmental Services and Study at Wellesley College, Miller worked with colleagues Alexandra Kaplan, Judith V. Jordan, Irene P. Stiver, and Janet L. Surrey to move away from what they saw as the harmful effects on women of traditional therapy models. These models were based on a Western, patriarchal model of human development that emphasized the masculine, autonomous self as the human ideal.

Psychological theory, like any other cultural institution, reflects the larger Western patriarchal culture in the unexamined assumption that the white, middle class, heterosexual 'paradigm' man defines not just his own reality but human reality. Thus without a critique of patriarchal bias in existing approaches to 'human development' the experience of the 'paradigm man' will be reified as 'truth' while that of others will be distorted for not conforming to patriarchal dictates.[23]

Previous models of development failed to account for women's lived experiences, being based largely on studies of white men, and therefore pathologized women as both overly-dependent and deficient in their need for connection and relationships with others.[24] In their writings throughout the 1980s and 1990s, the Stone Center scholars proposed a theory of human psychology that stressed the "interactive self," also known as the "being-in-relation" or "self-in-relation" to others.[25] This sense of self was not to be confused with dependency, but rather an alternative means of viewing development in which human growth occurs not through separation, but through emotional connection. People "grow in, through, and towards relationship."[26] We are constantly negotiating our reality and iden-

---

23 Judith V. Jordan, Alexandra G. Kaplan, Jean Baker Miller, Irene P. Stiver, and Janet L. Surrey, *Women's Growth in Connection: Writings from the Stone Center* (New York: Guilford Press, 1991), 7.

24 Sharon Freedberg, *Relational Theory for Social Work Practice : A Feminist Perspective* (New York : Routledge, 2009), 22.

25 Freedberg, *Relational Theory for Social Work Practice*, 22; Jean Baker Miller, "The Development of Women's Sense of Self," in *Women's Growth in Connection: Writings from the Stone Center* (New York: Guilford Press, 1991), 21.

26 Freedberg, *Relational Theory for Social Work Practice*, 26.

tity through the context of important relationships, therefore, "to feel more related to another person means to feel one's self enhanced, not threatened."[27] Drawing on the work of Nancy Chodorow, Carol Gilligan, Mary Field Belenky, and Adrienne Rich, the Stone Center scholars expanded on their ideas of relational development to include the importance of culture in identity and selfhood, noting that a person's socio-cultural context shapes both their worldview and their experience of/with power in the world.[28] Thus a Relational Theory grew to encompass the intersections of race, ethnicity, sexual orientation, socioeconomic status, and gender to become a Relational-Cultural Theory. This response to the dominant white, male narrative of psychological development merged a feminist critique of therapy with a new way of looking at how all people—not just women— benefit from relationships throughout the lifespan. This is important to keep in mind as we examine learning within reference work as a relational activity, and the librarian-patron interaction as both a personal and educational relationship.

The Importance of Empathy

In dismissing the primacy of autonomy and self-reliance, Stone Center scholar Judith Jordan focused on the process of relational activity as one revolving around empathy. Expanding on Heinz Kohut's work on empathy as the "human echo," Jordan asserted that "without empathy, there is no intimacy, no real attainment of an appreciation of the paradox of separateness within connection."[29] This paradox is what makes empathy and empathic relationships so complex and essential to human growth. Contrary to the belief that empathy is a "primitive mode of functioning," Jordan defined it as a complex cognitive and emotional state.[30] To express empathy requires a well-differentiated sense of self as well as an awareness of and appreciation for another's subjectivity. It is the process of opening your-

27   Miller, "The Development of Women's Sense of Self," 15, 52.

28   Freedberg, *Relational Theory for Social Work Practice*, 64; Jordan et al., *Women's Growth in Connection*, 7.

29   Judith V. Jordan, "Empathy and Self Boundaries," in *Women's Growth in Connection: Writings from the Stone Center* (New York: Guilford Press, 1991), 69.

30   Ibid., 80.

self to the emotions and experiences of others, while sharing your own, all the while differentiating and identifying sameness between the two. Empathy is not "regressive merging." You do not assume another's emotional state. Rather, you gain a greater understanding of yourself and the other person in your relationship through this process of openness, sharing, and vulnerability.[31]

In "helping" professions such as psychology, social work, and education, empathy is critical to engaging with clients and students. It validates and reaffirms their sense of self and provides a safe space for them to be honest and authentic.[32] A Relational-Cultural perspective on empathy encourages the helper to be vulnerable and express deep concern and emotional connection, rather than remaining neutral in the face of the emotions of their client or student.[33] Feminist theorist and educator bell hooks embodies this spirit of empathy as a dynamic, reciprocal process, when she encourages faculty to take the same risks they ask of their students: to be open, vulnerable, and willing to change.[34] This is where Relational-Cultural Theory and Feminist Pedagogical Theory express significant overlap. The ethic of care espoused by Feminist Pedagogy encourages teachers to take into account the affective dimension of learning, see their students as whole people, and honor their voice and experience while sharing their own perspective and emotions as a person.[35] In a therapeutic context, Relational-Cultural Theory stresses affective resonance, which moves slightly beyond emotional reciprocity to feeling deeply with the client, "showing her that she has moved you… and vice versa." The client would be given the same recognition and care, as well as an open door to express the same to the therapist.[36]

The key to empathy, and what differentiates it from a friendly interpersonal interaction, is deep emotional attunement and genuine understanding. It is an act of mutual recognition that is affirming and intersub-

---

31 Ibid., 69, 73.

32 Freedberg, *Relational Theory for Social Work Practice*, 63.

33 Ibid., 53–4.

34 bell hooks, *Teaching to Transgress: Education as the Practice of Freedom* (New York: Routledge, 1994), 21.

35 Accardi, *Feminist Pedagogy*, 44.

36 Freedberg, *Relational Theory for Social Work Practice*, 63.

jective—recognizing the subjectivities or unique personhood of others.[37] A contemporary definition of empathy includes some of the same elements that you would find in any characterization of good reference work or interpersonal skills, such as "active listening, positive regard, and understanding."[38] But unlike the reference interview or good customer service, empathy is not *performative*. It is an expression of genuine interest and concern, and, when applied to reference work, requires a willingness to engage in the affective component of learning, assimilate the patron's emotions and experiences into your own, and reflect on the overlap and difference between the two.[39]

Bringing It All Together: Intersubjective Mutuality

Jordan's conception of empathy in relationships relies heavily on a dynamic, oscillating relationship of care. In healthy, growth-oriented relationships, empathy and concern flow both ways, deepening interpersonal understanding and connection and creating "a sense of self as a part of a larger relational unit."[40] This is the concept of *intersubjective mutuality,* or growth through empathy exchange. It is characterized by each person's:

- interest in and awareness of the other as a unique, whole person;
- emotional attunement through empathy;
- vulnerability through selected self-disclosure;
- acknowledgement, but not imposition of personal needs;
- commitment to enhancing the growth of the other; and
- openness to change through the relationship.[41]

---

37 Ibid., 55.

38 Ibid., 53; Reference and User Services Association, "Guidelines for Behavioral Performance of Reference and Information Service Providers," *Reference & User Services Association (RUSA),* May 28, 2013, http://www.ala.org/rusa/resources/guidelines/guidelinesbehavioral.

39 Jordan, "Empathy and Self Boundaries," 74.

40 Judith V. Jordan, "The Meaning of Mutuality," in *Women's Growth in Connection: Writings from the Stone Center* (New York: Guilford Press, 1991), 82.

41 Jordan, "The Meaning of Mutuality," 82–83.

It is a departure from the work of earlier psychologists who often based the importance of empathy on its ability to meet one person's needs and ultimately steer them towards autonomy.[42] With intersubjective mutuality the process and exchange of empathy is what's important. This continuous exchange provides people with the opportunity for deeper understanding of one another, as well as self-reflection and new self-definition.[43] Different aspects of ourselves are expressed in our different relationships. You as a sibling, parent, daughter, colleague, and librarian are still *you*, but the aspects of you that are most pronounced may vary depending on the relational context. Similarly, a new relationship may reveal a part of yourself previously unknown and thus help grow your sense of self. Intersubjective mutuality is the antithesis of the domination/subordination relationship, which relies heavily on disconnection and inequality. Within this power dynamic a sense of safety and validation cannot exist. Self-disclosure then decreases, as does any hope of growth through sharing. Thus an egalitarian or near-egalitarian relationship is required for growth and development.[44]

Intersubjective mutuality additionally relies on *relational authenticity*, which encourages helping professionals to shed the pretense of neutral, objective authority in favor of *selectively* sharing feelings, experiences, and imperfections.[45] I stress the word *selectively* as a concession to critics of Relational-Cultural Theory in practice, who in many ways express misgivings similar to those made by critics of Feminist Pedagogical Theory. As feminized professions, there is a common acceptance in helping fields like social work, librarianship, and teaching, that boundaries are a good thing. Boundaries protect the helper and allow her to maintain a certain sense of authority and power in a world where her position might be undervalued or deprofessionalized.[46] But Relational-Cultural Theory in practice does not smash all boundaries. It is emphasis on constantly negotiating a person's sense of self and other's subjectivity positions the helper to create her own boundaries *in collaboration with* the client, student, or patron, who does the same in turn. These boundaries become the meeting

---

42   Ibid., 85.

43   Ibid., 89.

44   Ibid., 93; Freedberg, *Relational Theory for Social Work Practice*, 43.

45   Freedberg, *Relational Theory for Social Work Practice*, 43.

46   Ibid., 46–47; Accardi, *Feminist Pedagogy for Library Instruction*, 47–49.

points where the two individuals experience interdependence, growth and empowerment through their relationship.[47]

Intersubjective mutuality has been adopted in feminist reconstructions of social work practice and more recently in attempts to subvert the neoliberal practices of contemporary academic institutions.[48] The incorporation of the psychosocial and emotional aspects of teaching and learning into higher education is considered a coup within colleges and universities where efficiency and productivity reign. Bringing intersubjective mutuality into education provides the opportunity for deeper learning and connection between teacher and student and sets a foundation for meaningful critical pedagogy.[49] However, there is always the risk that, as Eisenhower and Smith write, this kind of "counterhegemonic work" can ultimately support "the bureaucratic structures of the university," and the points-of-view and attitudes we are actively trying to change.[50] It is worth keeping this in mind as we explore a relational model of reference work that seeks to incorporate this kind of work.

Within the context of reference work, intersubjective mutuality has the power to transform librarian-patron interactions into moments of "connected learning."[51] Librarian and patron take the perspective, emotion, and knowledge (*subjectivity*) of the other, connect it to their own, and through that process together create new knowledge and ways of knowing.[52] It is a powerful way to foster personal, emotional, and intellectual growth that stands in contrast to the practice of reference as the interaction between a librarian-expert and a patron-neophyte. We are co-learners rather than authorities. The patron can be honest without fear of judgement, and recognized and validated as a whole person. The librarian is under no

---

47   Jordan, "The Meaning of Mutuality," 82.

48   Freedberg, *Relational Theory for Social Work Practice*; Murphy and Brown, "Learning as Relational."

49   Murphy and Brown, "Learning as Relational."

50   Cathy Eisenhower and Dolsy Smith, "The Library as 'Stuck Place': Critical Pedagogy in the Corporate University," in *Critical Library Instruction: Theories and Methods*, ed. by Maria T. Accardi, Emily Drabinski and Alana Kumbier (Duluth, MN: Library Juice Press, 2010), 314.

51   Janet L. Surrey, "Relationship and Empowerment," in *Women's Growth in Connection: Writings from the Stone Center* (New York: Guilford Press, 1991), 167.

52   Ibid., 171.

pressure to perform the role of all-knowing-researcher, but rather, can be her authentic self. This Relational-Cultural approach frees us from striving towards creating the information literate *independent* researcher. Instead, it thrives on and encourages the relationships forged through research, and empowers librarian and patron to recreate these meaningful relationships in their work, education, and personal lives. It is the relationship differentiation that previously formalized conceptions of the reference librarian—as host, guardian, guide, expert, consultant—strived but failed to achieve. Those roles, with their clearly defined and impervious boundaries, were harmful to both the librarian's sense of self and the quality of the librarian-patron relationship. They constructed a model of reference librarianship that was, at best, difficult to achieve in practice, and at worst, contrary to the intuitive sense librarians had that reference was a deeply human relationship. Through a practice of intersubjective mutuality, the librarian is free to define her own librarian-identity within the context of her relationship with the patron and the patron can do the same.

Intersubjective Mutuality Meets the Reference Appointment: Letty's Case

The following example illustrates what a Relational-Cultural practice based on empathy, authenticity, and intersubjective mutuality might look like in reference work. I share the following story, of my interaction with a student I will call Letty, because it is one I think is relatable within the context of academic librarianship, but can also be extrapolated and applied in the context of other libraries. Letty, a third year student at my small liberal arts college, emailed me during the last week of classes of the fall semester with a request for help on a research paper. She was investigating sustainability in agricultural practices in Latin America and needed help finding "sources." We arranged a time to meet in person the next morning to discuss her topic and explore potential information resources.

As an early-career librarian, my approach to an upcoming appointment with a student would have mirrored much of the traditional reference practices I learned in library school. I would have done several searches in different databases and catalogs related to Letty's research topic, noted preferred keywords and applicable subject headings, created a handout with recommended resources, and perhaps even printed out a few relevant articles. My focus would have been on the transfer of content, rather than on the interaction with Letty, a result of a need to be seen as the expert-librarian I thought I'd been hired to be. At our meeting I would have presented this information to Letty and described it to her in detail; conducted a reference interview as my due diligence; and asked her a few questions to make sure I had met her information need. I would be warm, friendly, and non-judgemental, but detached. It was, after all, Letty's responsibility to do the work of research herself now that I had provided my expertise.

But this appointment did not take place in my first year as an academic librarian, and the actual meeting progressed quite differently. In an attempt to focus on Letty, and our—however brief—relationship, I didn't "prep" for this appointment. When Letty arrived I thanked her for meeting me in my office, noting that she had to walk across campus to get here. I asked her how her day was going, and although she replied with the usual "fine" Letty was visibly exhausted and agitated. I offered that I and many of my colleagues were struggling to make it through the last bit of the semester, which seemed to set her at ease a bit. I then asked her to share her research idea with me, which she proceeded to do, answering any clarifying questions I had. When I asked if she had started her research on this topic, and whether she had brought any of what she had found with her, I noticed her facial expression taking on a pained look. She averted her eyes, hunched over, and admitted to not having started her research even though the paper was due in two days. Noting her embarrassment, I found myself recalling a similar experience of shame in college (one of many). I had waited until the last minute to write a paper that had to incorporate at least one "academic article" and had no idea what that meant. Approaching a librarian at my university library had felt mortifying, both because of my self-imposed time constraint and because of my lack of familiarity with something that I felt should have been basic knowledge. This personal experience informed how I proceeded interacting with Letty.

I assured her that not having started her research was fine, and that we all make choices to concentrate on different tasks based on what we have going on in our lives. I shared that I too had waited until the last minute to write papers in college. I shared the above story with her and went so far as to admit that I did not really have a reason for putting off the work other than that I had thought it would be easy to do. I also admitted to occasionally continuing this last-minute work process during stressful moments at work and home. The moment of sharing opened up the conversation for Letty. She looked up and proceeded to share the various stressors and demands on her time at the moment. Letty was in the midst of planning for a study abroad trip, studying for two other challenging exams, and dealing with some conflicts in her friendships. This agricultural paper had simply fallen by the wayside. I tried my best to validate her feelings by expressing similar feelings of being "stretched too thin" at work and home, and characterized our meeting as a chance for her to tackle this looming research paper and eliminate one of her stressors.

This exchange was in no way focused on the research paper, on finding information, or identifying resources. What it did was establish a relationship with this student, making us both more open to sharing, listening, and learning from one another. Letty and I proceeded to explore different information resources together over course of the next 30 minutes. I acknowledged that aspects of her topic were challenging to research, and allowed her to see my failed searches and misguided attempts at discovery. She expressed relief that she was not the only one who approached searching as a trial-and-error process, and offered helpful suggestions based on her experience with the topic and her own disciplinary knowledge. In the end we were able to identify a few different avenues for a research focus and locate several helpful information sources, but the takeaways from the meeting were more than the articles and books Letty obtained. She expressed disappointment in not spending more time on a topic that was clearly interesting to her-she had aspirations of interning on an organic farm-focused on community supported agriculture-and found the idea of research in the future less scary and more about exploring personally meaningful topics and ideas.

My interaction with Letty reinforced the idea that students are whole people who have a variety of demands on their time and attention. My role in that relationship was not about providing Letty with information or linking her to resources; it was about practicing the process of research. Given my dearth of subject knowledge in her area of interest, I learned far more about environmental issues surrounding Bolivian agricultural practices than she did, and was completely open to not being the expert in the room.

I ran into Letty at my local farmer's market the following fall, working the stand for an excellent organic farm. She recognized and thanked me for being so helpful with her research project the previous year. I don't know that I helped Letty find any information that she would not have found on her own, given enough time and energy. The way I think I helped was by creating a learning environment in which her feelings and decisions were valued. It made us both more open to sharing information and engaging in an honest exchange of knowledge and sentiment. I practiced respecting her needs and wants while constantly being aware of my own desire to learn, model process, and demystify research. It was an empowering and recharging experience due in large part to this modified approach to reference work that incorporated empathy, authenticity, and intersubjective mutuality.

Conclusion

I recognize that not all reference work has the potential for mutuality and intersubjective exchange. There is likely not a high degree of empathetic connection inherent in directing a patron to the staplers, nor is there much time to get to know someone when they're clearly in a rush to find a book and dash. The scenario I described with Letty was, in some respects, the ideal situation for this kind of relationship-building. Letty was open, engaged, and receptive to the experience, and the two of us had the time and inclination to learn from one another. I valued her subject expertise and she appreciated my research experience in return. This made it much easier for me to be my authentic self and dispense with any kind of authority-performance that would likely have contributed to her alienation during our meeting. Developing this foundation for empathy and intersubjective exchange would have been much more difficult—if not impossible—with a patron who was disinterested or condescending, and understandably so. Intersubjective mutuality is not meant to position librarians as emotional doormats to hostility. It is meant to foster an egalitarian relationship, which, in some cases, involves empowering the patron and in other cases may require the librarian to position herself on equal footing with someone who views librarianship as a servile, rather than service profession.[53] This perceived or actual power differential is most pronounced when patrons are faculty, or, in the case of women and women of color in particular, when the patron is consciously or unconsciously exhibiting sexist or racist biases. Intersubjective mutuality is based on, among other things, mutual care and respect, and when that is not present, or is not possible, it is not the responsibility of the librarian to defer to disrespect to foster care. What I do propose is being *open* to moments of intersubjectivity in our reference work.

---

53   Roxanne Shirazi, "Reproducing the Academy: Librarians and the Question of Service in the Digital Humanities," *Roxanne Shirazi,* July 15, 2014, https://roxanneshirazi.com/2014/07/15/reproducing-the-academy-librarians-and-the-question-of-service-in-the-digital-humanities/.

By explicitly adopting Relational-Cultural Theory in reference librarianship we are also bringing the affective labor inherent in our work front and center, where it can be appropriately valued. This is a good step towards what Roma Harris describes as a "(re)commitment to [library] service based on a female rather than a male model."[54] Librarianship suffers from its feminization in a world where women's work is undervalued.[55] Rather than continue to provide the kind of affective shadow labor that is expected and exploited in our feminized profession, explicitly framing reference work within a intersubjective context serves to emphasize the importance of relationships, empathy, and mutuality as critical to human and educational development.[56] This practice has the potential to empower patrons who might otherwise feel alienated, disenfranchised, or simply not heard within the context of their college education or life. There is power in recognition and strength in validation, and intersubjective mutuality encompasses both in the spirit of growth and change.

By focusing solely on information exchange or finding the right answers to questions we limit opportunities to connect to our library patrons on a human level. In forcing ourselves to smile, look friendly, and perform concern we distance ourselves from our authentic sense of self, an aspect of emotional labor that's been proven to lead to burnout.[57] Viewing our work as reference librarians as a relationship with our patrons opens the possibility to growth in our professional lives and personal fulfillment. It also serves as a means of empowering patrons by bringing their personal selves into an educational or research context and valuing their emotions and previous experiences. Relational-Cultural Theory has the capacity to bring authentic relationships, empathy, and intersubjectivity to learning and a create a feminist egalitarian practice of reference librarianship.

---

54   Roma Harris, *Librarianship: The Erosion of a Woman's Profession* (NJ: Ablex Publishing, 1992), 164.

55   Roma Harris, *Librarianship*, 10–16.

56   Shirazi, "Reproducing the Academy;" Sloniowski, "Affective Labor," 654–55.

57   Megan Browndorf, "What Am I Doing and Why Am I Here? Meaning, the Moment, and Combating Burnout" (presentation, LOEX Annual Conference, Pittsburgh, PA, May 6–7, 2016).

Works Cited

Accardi, Maria T. *Feminist Pedagogy for Library Instruction*. Sacramento, CA: Library Juice Press, 2013.

Accardi, Maria T., Emily Drabinski, and Alana Kumbier. *Critical Library Instruction: Theories and Methods*. Duluth, MN: Library Juice Press, 2010.

Browndorf, Megan. "What Am I Doing and Why Am I Here? Meaning, the Moment, and Combating Burnout." Presentation at the LOEX Annual Conference, Pittsburgh, PA, May 6–7, 2016.

Butler, Kathy, and Jason Byrd. "Research Consultation Assessment: Perceptions of Students and Librarians." *Journal of Academic Librarianship* 42, no. 1 (January 2016): 83–86. doi:10.1016/j.acalib.2015.10.011.

Cassell, Kay Ann, and Uma Hiremath. *Reference and Information Services in the 21st Century: An Introduction*. 2nd edition. London: Facet Publishing, 2009.

Cavanagh, Mary F. "Interpreting Reference Work with Contemporary Practice Theory." *Journal of Documentation* 69, no. 2 (2013): 214–42. doi:10.1108/00220411311300057.

Drabinski, Emily. "Toward a Kairos of Library Instruction." *The Journal of Academic Librarianship* 40, no. 5 (September 2014): 480–85. doi:10.1016/j.acalib.2014.06.002.

Eisenhower, Cathy and Dolsy Smith. "The Library as 'Stuck Place': Critical Pedagogy in the Corporate University," in *Critical Library Instruction: Theories and Methods*, edited. by Maria T. Accardi, Emily Drabinski and Alana Kumbier, 305–17. Duluth, MN: Library Juice Press, 2010.

Fletcher, Joyce K. "Relational Practice: A Feminist Reconstruction of Work." In *The Handbook of Women, Psychology, and the Law*, edited by Andrea Barnes, 79–123. Hoboken, NJ: John Wiley & Sons, 2005.

Freedberg, Sharon. *Relational Theory for Social Work Practice : A Feminist Perspective*. New York : Routledge, 2009.

Genz, Marcella D. "Working the Reference Desk." *Library Trends* 46, no. 3 (1998): 505–25.

Green, Samuel. "Personal Relations Between Librarians and Readers." *Library Journal* 1, no. 2–3 (1876): 74–81.

Hansen, Derek, Margeaux Johnson, Elizabeth Norton, and Anne McDonough. "Virtual Provider Pessimism: Analysing Instant Messaging Reference Encounters with the Pair Perception Comparison Method." *Information Research* 14, no. 1 (2009). http://www.informationr.net/ir/14-4/paper416.html.

Harris, Roma. *Librarianship: The Erosion of a Woman's Profession.* NJ: Ablex Publishing, 1992.

Holberg, John E. "Relational Reference: A Challenge to the Reference Fortress." In *An Introduction to Reference Services in Academic Libraries*, edited by Elizabeth Connor. Haworth Series in Introductory Information Science Textbooks. New York, NY: Haworth Information Press, 2006.

hooks, bell. *Teaching to Transgress: Education as the Practice of Freedom.* New York: Routledge, 1994.

Jordan, Judith V. "Empathy and Self Boundaries." In *Women's Growth in Connection: Writings from the Stone Center.* New York: Guilford Press, 1991.

———. "The Meaning of Mutuality." In *Women's Growth in Connection: Writings from the Stone Center.* New York: Guilford Press, 1991.

Jordan, Judith V., Alexandra G. Kaplan, Jean Baker Miller, Irene P. Stiver, and Janet L. Surrey. *Women's Growth in Connection: Writings from the Stone Center.* New York: Guilford Press, 1991.

Mellon, Constance A. "Library Anxiety: A Grounded Theory and Its Development." *College and Research Libraries* 47, no. 2 (March 1, 1986): 160–65.

Miller, Jean Baker. "The Development of Women's Sense of Self." In *Women's Growth in Connection: Writings from the Stone Center.* New York: Guilford Press, 1991.

Murphy, Mark, and Tony Brown. "Learning as Relational: Intersubjectivity and Pedagogy in Higher Education." *International Journal of Lifelong Education* 31, no. 5 (October 9, 2012): 643–54. doi:10.1080/02601370.2012.700648.

Radford, Marie L. *The Reference Encounter : Interpersonal Communication in the Academic Library.* ACRL Publications in Librarianship: No. 52. Chicago : Association of College and Research Libraries, 1999.

Reference and User Services Association. "Definitions of Reference." *Reference & User Services Association (RUSA)*, 2008. http://www.ala.org/rusa/guidelines/definitionsreference.

Reference and User Services Association. "Guidelines for Behavioral Performance of Reference and Information Service Providers." *Reference & User Services Association (RUSA)*, May 28, 2013. http://www.ala.org/rusa/resources/guidelines/guidelinesbehavioral.

Reference and User Services Association. "Professional Competencies for Reference and User Services Librarians." *Reference & User Services Association (RUSA)*, 2003. http://www.ala.org/rusa/resources/guidelines/professional.

Ross, Catherine Sheldrick, Kirsti Nilsen, and Marie L. Radford. *Conducting the Reference Interview: A How-To-Do-It Manual for Librarians.* 2nd edition. New York: Neal-Schuman Publishers, 2009.

Shirazi, Roxanne. "Reproducing the Academy: Librarians and the Question of Service in the Digital Humanities." *Roxanne Shirazi.* July 15, 2014. https://roxanneshirazi. com/2014/07/15/reproducing-the-academy-librarians-and-the-question-of-service-in-the-digital-humanities/.

Sloniowski, Lisa. "Affective Labor, Resistance, and the Academic Librarian." *Library Trends* 64, no. 4 (Spring 2016): 645–64.

Surrey, Janet L. "Relationship and Empowerment." In *Women's Growth in Connection: Writings from the Stone Center.* New York: Guilford Press, 1991.

Vavrek, Bernard. "The Nature of Reference Librarianship." *RQ* 13, no. 3 (1974): 213–17.

Social Justice, Sentipensante Pedagogy, and Collaboration: The Role of Research Consultations in Developing Critical Communities

Carrie Forbes and Jennifer Bowers

All education, including co-curricular learning experiences between students and librarians, must take into account the academic growth of the student. Education that focuses only on "academic" learning neglects to prepare students for a complex future with never-ending, ever more difficult social, political, and cultural challenges. *Sentipensante* pedagogy, developed by Laura I. Rendón, offers a transformative vision of education that emphasizes the complementary relationship between the *sentir* of intuition and the *pensar* of intellect and scholarship: between teaching and learning, between formal knowledge and wisdom, and between Western and non-Western ways of knowing.[1] This holistic methodology provides a structure that librarians can employ in reference consultations, one-on-one meetings between researchers and librarians, to address the needs of the whole-person, thereby balancing the external academic realm and the internal personal realm. In tandem with this teaching philosophy, the social work and education literature proposes complementary strategies

---

1   Laura I. Rendón, *Sentipensante (Sensing/Thinking) Pedagogy: Educating for Wholeness, Social Justice and Liberation* (Sterling, VA: Stylus Publishing, LLC, 2012), 1.

for how librarians can help students interrogate the hegemonic nature of knowledge valued by the academy in order to further the goals of social justice.[2] Using sentipensante pedagogy, along with best practices from education and social work, librarians can transform reference services from a privileged, hierarchical interaction into a collaborative research consultation model that empowers students to take ownership of their learning not only to enhance their academic and personal lives, but also to enact change for the greater good of society.

This chapter will define the theories and methodologies of sentipensante pedagogy as well as the critical literacy and research approaches taught in social work and education. Through a discussion of both theory and praxis, the authors will illuminate how research consultations in academic libraries can be reimagined to address not only the intellectual needs of students, but also their social, emotional, and spiritual growth. In order to transform our pedagogy to a more holistic practice, librarians need to understand that the intellectual, social, emotional, and spiritual are not separate and distinct, but are intertwined, interdependent, and mutually influential. By actively acknowledging this integration, librarians can move beyond the traditional approach to reference that focuses solely on students' intellectual development and become participants in the greater educational effort to build emerging *critical communities*.[3] When employing pedagogies to address specific social-emotional competencies and ethical dispositions, librarians provide an essential foundation for critical understanding and life-long learning. Holistic, sentipensante research consultations engender compassion, collaboration, and reflective engagement with critical information literacy and ultimately foster the development of a critical community of learners for social justice research and action.

As White, heterosexual, cisgendered, able-bodied women with more than two decades of experience providing reference and instructional services in academic libraries, we acknowledge that we approach this work

---

2   Wendy Cumming-Potvin, "Social Justice, Pedagogy and Multiliteracies: Developing Communities of Practice for Teacher Education," *Australian Journal of Teacher Education* 34, no. 3 (2009): 82–99; and Shawn A. Ginwright and Julio Cammarota, "Teaching Social Justice Research to Undergraduate Students in Puerto Rico: Using Personal Experiences to Inform Research," *Equity and Excellence in Education* 48, no. 2 (2015): 162–77.

3   Silvia Cristina Bettez, "Building Critical Communities Amid the Uncertainty of Social Justice Pedagogy in the Graduate Classroom," *Review of Education, Pedagogy, and Cultural Studies* 33, no. 1 (2011): 76–106.

from a place of privilege. When we meet with researchers (both students and faculty), we endeavor to redefine our role from a sentipensante pedagogical perspective. Our intention with this chapter is to offer librarians and other educators suggestions about how Rendón's model may be applied to reconceptualize power dynamics between librarians and researchers during research consultations. Such methods, in order to be effective, require on-going practices for fostering critical communities, which will, of course, include missteps and opportunities for collaborative learning. We encourage all readers of this chapter to begin this challenging yet transformative work to the best of their ability.

Sentipensante Pedagogy

Throughout the chapter, we refer to social justice as the goal of sentipensante research consultations and draw from Hackman's conceptualization of social justice education as "an examination of systems of power and oppression combined with a prolonged emphasis on social change and student agency in and outside of the classroom."[4] Reference consultations are an important element of the co-curriculum and can serve as a bridge between formal classroom learning and more personal, informal ways of knowing. In order to advocate for social justice, educators, including librarians, need a well-defined theory of pedagogy based on the union of the heart and mind. Employing findings from a study that involved interviews with sixteen two- and four-year college faculty in diverse disciplines, Rendón defines sentipensante (sensing/thinking) pedagogy as a way to unite and privilege both the poetry and rationality of teaching. Sentipensante pedagogy involves learning with heart and mind, connecting and engaging teachers and students, attending to individual needs while fostering relationships among students and teachers, privileging multicultural epistemologies (including attention to non-Western structures of knowledge), joining action with theory and measuring student outcomes, while fostering the sense that learning never stops and that the journey of learning is more important than a grade or test score.[5]

---

4   Heather W. Hackman, "Five Essential Components for Social Justice Education," *Equity & Excellence in Education* 38, no. 2 (2005), 104.

5   Rendón, *Sentipensante*.

Through sentipensante pedagogy, Rendón ultimately presents a new vision for higher education. She argues that modern models are limited by their neglect of holistic pedagogy. Her intent is clear: "The purpose of this book is to assist in guiding the transformation of teaching and learning in higher education so that it is unitive in nature... I seek to shatter the belief system that has worked against wholeness, multiculturalism, and social justice."[6] Her work examines the shortcomings of traditional education and presents a framework for her new vision of holistic education. Rendón sees the current model of education in America as rooted in the model of industrialization: schools are factories with the desired product of functional workers. This core problem is why a sentipensante pedagogy is necessary. In her critique of mainstream education, she analyzes seven "agreements" and offers seven alternative "agreements" from her vision of sentipensante pedagogy. For her, sentipensante is a "model, guided by a nondual epistemology and ontology, [that] is based on integration and consonance, representing the union of sensing and thinking processes and the balance between inner and outer knowing."[7] She describes the seven original agreements as: 1) the agreement to privilege intellectual/rational knowing; 2) the agreement of separation; 3) the agreement of competition; 4) the agreement of perfection; 5) the agreement of monoculturalism 6) the agreement to privilege outer work; and 7) the agreement to avoid self-examination.[8]

After scrutinizing each of the present agreements carefully, she offers a new construction, which forms the basis of sentipensante pedagogy: 1) the agreement to work with diverse ways of knowing in the classroom; 2) the agreement to embrace connectedness, collaboration, and transdisciplinarity; 3) the agreement to engage diverse learning strategies (i.e., competitive and collaborative learning, and individual-based and community-based learning) in the classroom; 4) the agreement to be open and flexible about being grounded in knowing and not knowing; 5) the agreement of multiculturalism and respect for diverse cultures; 6) the agreement to balance our personal and professional lives with work, rest, and replenishment; and 7) the agreement to take time for self-reflexivity.[9] Using the

---

6   Ibid., 1.

7   Ibid., 42.

8   Ibid., 26.

9   Ibid., 26–49.

seven agreements as the foundation, this chapter will elucidate how librarians can incorporate these ideas into research consultations through best practices found in education and social work.

Why Education and Social Work?

Examining the social justice literature in education and social work illuminates consistent themes that echo and reinforce Rendón's sentipensante pedagogical approach. Throughout, traditional power dynamics are questioned and reimagined in order to facilitate collaborative relationships, in which participants are equally engaged and responsible for learning. Central to this process, individuals are called upon to critically reflect on their social identities, including biases, assumptions, and positionalities, so that they can challenge dominant power structures and narratives and cultivate a deeper understanding of themselves and others. Just as Rendón calls for integrating the intuitive as well as intellectual components into learning, social justice practices as expressed in social work and education recognize the necessity of holistic engagement. These ideas encourage librarians to reevaluate current practices in reference services, which typically are modeled on and perpetuate traditional paradigms that often tend to emphasize intellectual development and position the librarian as expert.[10] Critiquing specifically the racialized nature of reference, Freeda Brook, Dave Ellenwood, and Althea Eannace Lazzaro suggest adopting a critical pedagogy based on a "reciprocal, dialogic process" in which "librarians and patrons would share and be affected by each other's knowledge, care, and actions."[11] Research consultations in particular, in which librarians and students work together on research projects over an extended time, offer an ideal opportunity for cultivating these dialogical relationships, thereby transforming reference services to align more closely with social justice values and practices.

---

10   John J. Doherty, "Reference Interview or Reference Dialogue?" *Internet Reference Services Quarterly* 11, no. 3 (2006): 97–109; and Mark Stover, "The Reference Librarian as Non-Expert: A Postmodern Approach to Expertise," *The Reference Librarian* 42, no. 87/88 (2004): 273–300.

11   Freeda Brook, Dave Ellenwood and Althea Eannace Lazzaro, "In Pursuit of Antiracist Social Justice: Denaturalizing Whiteness in the Academic Library," *Library Trends* 64, no. 2 (2015): 274–75.

In a world of increasing technological change and cultural diversity, alternative ways of defining and doing literacy through social justice work should be viewed as essential for empowering students for academic, economic, and personal success.[12] By integrating the concepts of literacy pedagogy and social justice research from education and social work within a framework of sentipensante pedagogy, this chapter aims to extend knowledge about the teaching and learning of information literacy and promote discussion about needed changes in reference services. In current Western educational climates touting 'back to basics' literacy and increased academic performance, discussions which promote deep reflection about teaching literacy for a socially just world are imperative.[13]

Research Consultations as Communities of Practice

Research consultations have been described in the library science literature as in-depth, one-on-one instructional sessions that expand the services offered at a desk.[14] Much of the literature has noted that research consultations are ideal for graduate students and faculty researchers who need advanced research training. While many libraries now offer consultations for researchers engaged in any stage of the research process, consultations with a librarian are still largely marketed as an opportunity to meet with an "expert."[15] Much of the application of sentipensante pedagogy has been aimed at the classroom environment, but this chapter will show that critical pedagogies can have just as large an impact in one-on-one teaching encounters, such as research consultations. Sentipensante pedagogy embraces a personalized approach to teaching, which may be more effectively utilized in re-

12   Colin Lankshear and Michele Knobel, *New Literacies: Everyday Practices and Social Learning* (Maidenhead, UK: Open University Press, 2011); and Henry A. Giroux, "Literacy, Pedagogy, and the Politics of Difference," *College Literature* 19, no. 1 (1992): 1–11.

13   Michael W. Apple, *Official Knowledge: Democratic Education in a Conservative Age* (New York: Routledge, 2014).

14   Deborah Lee, "Research Consultations: Enhancing Library Research Skills," *The Reference Librarian* 41, no. 85 (2004): 169–80.

15   Crystal D. Gale and Betty S. Evans, "Face-to-Face: The Implementation and Analysis of a Research Consultation Service," *College & Undergraduate Libraries* 14, no. 3 (2007): 85–101.

search consultations where the librarian and researcher define the content together, rather than one-shot information literacy sessions where the librarian may have a prescribed curriculum to follow.[16] In addition, the consultation model described in this chapter is underpinned by sociocultural theory, which reflects the view that learning is constructed and negotiated actively through social experiences.[17] Supporters of a socio-cultural perspective of literacy argue that a close relationship exists between cognitive skills, cultural technology, and societal institutions through which understandings and practices are developed.[18] The individual is studied systematically within the social environment, with literacy defined as a social and historical construction that evolves dynamically. Being literate implies more than superficial contacts with print, but an understanding of how to manipulate words and concepts through complex daily social interactions in an accepted manner through cultural apprenticeship.[19] One-on-one dialogues between researchers and librarians provide an opportunity to engage with the complexity and nuance of information literacy beyond the boundaries of the formal curriculum and classroom space.

Jean Lave and Etienne Wenger's theory of situated learning and the metaphor of communities of practice have emerged in the field of education over the past decade as helpful for understanding literacy from a socio-cultural perspective.[20] With roots in Vygtosky's social emphasis on learning, this work is particularly pertinent for investigating how students develop understandings through interaction in complex communities of practice to become professionals. A community of practice is defined as a

---

16 James Elmborg, "Libraries in the Contact Zone: On the Creation of Educational Space," *Reference & User Services Quarterly* 46, no. 1 (2006): 56–64.

17 Lev Vygotsky, *Thought and Language*, trans. by Eugenia Hanfmann and Gertrude Vakar (Cambridge, MA: Massachusetts Institute of Technology, 1986).

18 Alan Luke, "The Social Construction of Literacy in the Classroom," in *Literacy Learning and Teaching: Language as Social Practice in the Primary School*, ed. Len Unsworth (South Melbourne: Macmillan Education Australia, 1993), 3–53; and Karen T. Dooley, "Multiliteracies and Pedagogies of New Learning for Students of English as an Additional Language," in *Multiliteracies and Diversity in Education: New Pedagogies for Expanding Landscapes*, ed. Annah Healy (South Melbourne, Australia: Oxford University Press, 2008), 102–25.

19 Barbara Rogoff, *Apprenticeship in Thinking: Cognitive Development in Social Context* (New York: Oxford University Press, 1990).

20 Jean Lave and Etienne Wenger, *Situated Learning: Legitimate Peripheral Participation* (New York: Cambridge University Press, 1999).

group of people with several characteristics, such as: sharing a concern or passion about a topic, deepening knowledge and expertise in the area by interacting on an ongoing basis, mutually negotiating actions, introducing newcomers into the community, and acquiring knowledge about how to ask for help during learning.[21] Acquiring knowledge within a community of practice is viewed as the newcomer gradually moving from peripheral to full participation. Wenger also describes communities of practice as ubiquitous, across work, home, and leisure settings.[22] Silvia Cristina Bettez further defines such communities as supportive networks both within and beyond the classroom for fostering critically aware students and for countering the solitary and emotionally taxing nature of the academic experience.[23] At their core, critical communities recognize students as partners in learning, emphasize critical thinking and collective engagement, encourage self-reflection and compassion, and acknowledge the integration and importance of intellect and emotion.[24]

Information literacy development, like all literacies, requires interaction between people and the involvement of people with texts produced by others, making information literacy events intersubjective in character. Sohair F. Wastaway, Charles W. Uth, and Christopher Stewart contend that, "The social nature of information seeking means that essentially all information seeking can be seen as collaborative at some level."[25] If one views the authors of texts and creators of information as part and parcel of the literacy event, then the individual is never truly working in isolation.

The idea that information literacy needs community is a complex view that extends beyond the individual learner and further requires that librarians understand the interrelation between community members and their processes related to information. Before students can make assumptions about how to contribute to communities of learning, they need to define and navigate the social, political, and cultural characteristics of that

---

21   Etienne Wenger, *Communities of Practice: Learning, Meaning and Identity* (Cambridge, England: Cambridge University Press, 1998).

22   Ibid.

23   Bettez, "Building Critical Communities."

24   Ibid., 96.

25   Sohair F. Wastaway, Charles W. Uth, and Christopher Stewart, "Learning Communities: An Investigative Study into Their Impact on Library Services," *Science & Technology Libraries* 24, no. 3–4 (2004): 341.

community. There are two trends on the horizon that suggest directions for dealing with communities and information literacy, while also extending librarians' pedagogical practices and research agendas. One direction for understanding communities, advocated by Annemaree Lloyd, encourages an ethnographic, "outside observer" position as a vantage point to recognize the information needs and literacies of specific groups.[26] James Elmborg's work on critical information literacy suggests another approach, whereby the librarian takes an activist stance within a community of learners.[27]

Lloyd's research, based on observation and research into the practice of firefighters, concluded that "understanding information literacy in a workplace context requires recognition that information and knowledge are socially produced and distributed, and that access to it can be effected by social relationships."[28] Lloyd's "workplace information literacy" is comprised of a constellation of skills, practices, and processes that depend on relations with experts who afford and mediate the process and thereby enhance the information practices of the novice.[29] While situating information literacy development in the realm of landscapes and other natural environments may encourage a deterministic view of information literacy development, Lloyd's aim in using these metaphors is to suggest a big-picture perspective on how information literacy "shows itself" in the activities of the community. Learning outcomes and opportunities for instruction can then be developed to help enhance information literacy learning by focusing on current practice.

In "Critical Information Literacy: Implications for Instructional Practice," Elmborg argues for a more complicated model of information literacy development that speaks to the social and political concerns of critical literacy theorists Paulo Friere, Henry Giroux, and others. As opposed to the focus on individuals as learners and performers, Elmborg's critical information literacy recognizes how the production, distribution, and uses of information are sociopolitical processes that require and encourage community involvement. Elmborg contends that "people produce, read,

---

26 Annemaree Lloyd, "Information Literacy Landscapes: An Emerging Picture," *Journal of Documentation* 62 (2006): 570–83.

27 James Elmborg, "Critical Information Literacy: Implications for Instructional Practice," *Journal of Academic Librarianship* 32 (2006): 192–99.

28 Lloyd, "Information Literacy Landscapes," 576.

29 Ibid.

and interpret texts in communities, not in isolation. Communities reach consensus about interpretation, sometimes easily and sometimes contentiously. Literacy cannot be described, therefore, in broad terms as a set of universal skills and abstract processes. Rather, literacy is in constant flux and embedded in cultural situations, each situation nuanced and different from others."[30] Critical literacy, here blended with information literacy, encourages librarians to take an activist stance within learning communities (e.g. research consultations), as members and as educators.

Employing the Seven Agreements in Research Consultations

In deconstructing the tenets of mainstream education, Rendón takes issue with the academy's privileging of intellectual, objective, and rational knowing, which, she argues, neglects and marginalizes ways of inner knowing, such as "deep wisdom, wonder, sense of the sacred, intuition, and emotions."[31] Rather than favor one type of knowing at the expense of other ways, Rendón calls for a multifaceted understanding of human intelligence. The academic library, as central to the higher education enterprise, naturally supports and mirrors our institutional goals in developing students' intellectual abilities. For reference librarians in particular, who often teach instruction sessions and who view reference interactions as another learning opportunity, the components of information literacy guide our efforts to cultivate critical thinking in our students. But this emphasis on the intellect does not necessarily preclude adopting a critical pedagogical approach to research consultations. In fact, critical thinking, as a key component to social justice, can be directly employed in our work with students to get them to question notions of research neutrality, to look more closely for potential biases in sources, and to examine whose perspectives and voices are given preference or excluded in the academic literature and, ultimately, in the evidence they use to support their projects. Adapting strategies similar to those advocated by Nicole Nicotera and N. Eugene Walls to "focus students' critical thinking skills on issues of position, power, and status within

---

30   Elmborg, "Critical Information Literacy," 195.

31   Rendón, *Sentipensante*, 27.

the context of consuming social science research,"[32] librarians can encourage students to evaluate research through a socially aware and critical lens.

The following sections will review Rendón's seven agreements for sentipensante pedagogy in more detail to show how they can serve as a guiding framework for employing social justice pedagogy into research consultations to contribute to the development of critical communities in both the formal curriculum and co-curriculum. Although the same approach could be used within different reference models more generally, the extended time allowed in research consultations, as well as the opportunity to develop collaborative relationships with students, make consultations a more conducive environment for applying these ideas.

Agreement 1: Recognize diverse ways of knowing

The student population in higher education is increasingly diverse in terms of socio-economic background, sexual orientation, gender, ethnicity, and ability. Such diversity requires new approaches to teaching that might help students to manage the complexities of an ever changing and pluralistic world.[33] Deanna Kuhn and Wadiya Udell suggest the goal of higher education should be to help students to deal with these complexities by teaching the tools of wisdom, which include critical thinking.[34] An important aspect of critical thinking is that students are able to reflect on and evaluate evidence and make informed decisions in their professional work. Thus, it is important that a focus on thinking processes, not just the curriculum content, be included in higher education to help students deal with ill-defined problems in complex settings. Kuhn and Udell argue that students' beliefs about the nature of knowing and knowledge, known as epistemological beliefs, are the basis on which critical thinking can be promoted.[35]

---

32   Nicole Nicotera and N. Eugene Walls, "Challenging Perceptions of Academic Research as Bias Free: Promoting a Social Justice Framework in Social Work Research Methods," *Journal of Teaching in Social Work* 30, no. 3 (2010): 346.

33   Henry A. Giroux, *Border Crossings: Cultural Workers and the Politics of Education*, (New York: Routledge, 1992).

34   Deanna Kuhn and Wadiya Udell, "The Path to Wisdom," *Educational Psychologist* 36, no. 4 (2001): 261–64.

35   Ibid.

So how might we acknowledge and incorporate a broader spectrum of knowing into research consultations? Reimagining research consultations in this way might comprise three different approaches: 1) thinking about the types of research or evidence that we help students find and evaluate: valuing but also looking beyond standard academic sources and incorporating studies that employ a range of research methodologies, when possible; 2) engaging students' affective, as well as cognitive abilities, when collaborating with them throughout the research process; and 3) considering how intuition and emotional connection impact the interaction between librarian and student. Academic reference librarians are accustomed to helping students find scholarly and authoritative sources for their research projects and class assignments. Depending on the requirements set by faculty, this usually means guiding students toward peer-reviewed journal articles, books published by university and academic presses, and reports, statistics, and other materials created by recognized authorities. Although this is certainly a generalization, nevertheless, it still fairly accurately reflects what we do and teach. These sources typically represent White, Western European, English-language, print-based, and hegemonic narratives and ways of knowing. As Marisa Elena Duarte and Miranda Belarde Lewis pointedly describe the situation, "From the perspective of the systemically oppressed, library catalogs read like a great mirror of the modern Western consciousness, post-Conquest, post-Settlement, and through the rise of industrialization, 1898-beyond."[36] Even though we are constrained by project and information need requirements, when appropriate, we can consider introducing other types of sources and ways of knowing into our consultations that would include a more diverse range of views, values, and perspectives. For example, we could draw on indigenous methods, such as oral histories and storytelling, use alternative newspapers published by communities of color and underrepresented groups in addition to mainstream sources, and incorporate non-textual resources such as photographs, videos, and artifacts.

The research consultation should ultimately be a learning experience, in which we work together with students to illuminate the research process, typically with some goal or outcome, in mind. To foster critical information literacy, it is crucial that we approach consultations in a holistic manner. As Karun Kishor Karki emphasizes, "My identity is tied into my

---

36   Marisa Elena Duarte and Miranda Belarde-Lewis, "Imagining: Creating Spaces for Indigenous Ontologies," *Cataloging and Classification Quarterly* 53, no. 5–6 (2015): 683.

research interest. What I want to know, whom I want to know, and how I want to know are all interconnected."[37] Critical thinking and emotional engagement are intertwined and necessary for comprehending the foundational elements of information literacy—formulating questions (not only what to ask but why it matters), understanding that scholarship is an ongoing discussion with many viewpoints, and information is a commodity that is often produced and controlled by majority cultures.[38] Indeed, Miriam Matteson specifically recommends integrating emotional and cognitive awareness with teaching information literacy content, based on the findings of her research into the role of emotional intelligence, dispositional affect, motivation, and coping skills on information literacy scores. She argues that "Even the most thoughtfully created IL content, delivered with the most dynamic teaching methods, seamlessly integrated into a core curriculum, may not ultimately result in successful learning if students' cognitive, emotional, and social characteristics have not been considered."[39]

As outlined above, reference librarians typically focus on the intellectual aspects of knowledge acquisition, but we can do more to foster students' emotional learning by recognizing students' lived experiences and current emotional state and how these impact their learning. In her study of academic reference librarians' perspectives on their work, Amy VanScoy found that intuition and empathy were important and integral components to, what she terms, a "fully engaged practice."[40] The librarians described using their affective abilities in reference interactions, referring to words such as *receptive, empathy*, and *instinct*, in order "to understand a specific need, gauge their success, identify opportunities, and keep abreast of what is going on in their user communities."[41] Since librarians may al-

---

37   Karun Kishor Karki, "Walking the Complexities Between Two Worlds: A Personal Story of Epistemological Tensions in Knowledge Production," *Qualitative Social Work* 15, no. 5–6 (2016): 629.

38   Association of College and Research Libraries, "Framework for Information Literacy for Higher Education," last modified January 11, 2016, accessed December 4, 2016, http://www.ala.org/acrl/standards/ilframework.

39   Miriam L. Matteson, "The Whole Student: Cognition, Emotion, and Information Literacy," *College and Research Libraries* 75, no. 6 (2014): 862.

40   Amy VanScoy, "Fully Engaged Practice and Emotional Connection: Aspects of the Practitioner Perspective of Reference and Information Service," *Library and Information Science Research* 35 no. 4 (2013): 274.

41   Ibid.

ready be doing this unconsciously, we can bring more attention to the emotional components of our work and recognize that these factors are equally at play for our students. Developing affective abilities is an ongoing process for many librarians that should be cultivated through training and professional development opportunities.

Agreement 2: Embrace connectedness, collaboration, and transdisciplinarity

In discussing her integrative approach to pedagogy, Rendón emphasizes connectedness at multiple levels, including increasing collaboration between students and teachers as well as drawing connections between academic disciplines (transdisciplinary). Both of these concepts apply to research consultations between students and librarians and we can again draw on the literature in education and social work for concrete examples.

Social work and education examine the dynamic between student and teacher as well as the relationship between researcher and subject. In a classroom setting, teaching students to interrogate the positionality of researcher and subject was central to the work of Nicotera and Walls in their University of Denver social work course, "Disrupting Power and Privilege in Research and Practice."[42] In the course, students were asked to read a selected research article, look for evidence of dominance and subordination, and discuss how "values, power, and amplified or silenced voices impact the construction of practice knowledge."[43] The power dynamic of researcher and subject is further problematized when considering the past role of some scientific research in oppressing marginalized or minority groups, thereby creating a legacy of historical trauma and mistrust.[44] Social justice

---

42   Nicotera and Walls, "Challenging Perceptions," 334–50.

43   Nicole Nicotera and Hye-Kyung Kang, "Beyond Diversity Courses: Strategies for Integrating Critical Consciousness Across Social Work Curriculum," *Journal of Teaching in Social Work* 29, no. 2 (2009): 200.

44   Zuleka Henderson, Lucinda A. Acquaye-Doyle, Shayna Waites and Tyriesa Howard, "Putting Principles into Practice: Addressing Historical Trauma, Mistrust, and Apprehension in Research Methods Courses," *Journal of Social Work Education* 52, no. 1 (2016): 69–78; Ransford Danso, "An Integrated Framework of Critical Cultural Competence and Anti-Oppressive Practice for Social Justice Social Work Research," *Qualitative Social Work* 14, no. 4 (2015): 579–80; and Ron Strier, "Anti-Oppressive Research in Social Work: A Preliminary Definition," *British Journal of Social Work* 37, no. 5 (2007): 861.

research and evaluating research from a justice perspective both emphasize the importance of the researcher and participant relationship, which can either (intentionally or unintentionally) uphold or deconstruct potentially oppressive, hegemonic power structures.

To develop anti-oppressive alternatives to dominant research power relationships, Justin Rogers proposes that social work researchers pursue meaningful collaboration with participants, which could range from active involvement in research design, data analysis and dissemination of findings, to user-led research and the use of empowering research methodologies.[45] Acknowledging the role of participants in creating knowledge produced by anti-oppressive research, Strier calls for researchers to "reduce the exclusionary barriers to genuine participation and to provide participants with a sense of real control over the research process.[46] These strategies are consistent with a critical, social justice pedagogy that recognizes the dialogic nature of student-teacher relationships, in which "Asking questions and listening… moves us toward preserving the autonomy of the learner and focuses our attention on cultivating the conditions where students actively participate in the construction of knowledge."[47] Whether expressed in the classroom, research setting, or research consultation, social justice approaches "view the creation of knowledge as a collective process that is shared between the researcher and community members."[48] Within research consultations, librarians can look for opportunities to co-construct knowledge with students, rather than always assuming the role of information expert.

In addition to shared connections with students, Rendón also urges social justice educators to help students see the broader connections between disciplines. Henry Giroux refers to disciplines as structures that teachers need to "escape" in order to have the "possibility of creating new languages and social practices that connect rather than separate education and cultural work from everyday life"[49] He sees the division of knowledge and learn-

---

45 Justin Rogers, "Anti-Oppressive Social Work Research: Reflections on Power in the Creation of Knowledge," *Social Work Education* 31, no. 7 (2012): 866–79.

46 Strier, "Anti-Oppressive Research in Social Work," 862.

47 Tracy Davis and Laura M. Harrison, Advancing Social Justice: Tools, Pedagogies, and Strategies to Transform Your Campus (San Francisco, CA: Jossey-Bass, 2013): 97.

48 Ginwright and Cammarota, "Teaching Social Justice Research," 165.

49 Giroux, *Border Crossings*, 242.

ing into disciplines as a form of "ghettoization," wherein each group is made poorer by its lack of association with other groups. Disciplines stand in the way of the public spaces that are crucial to critical pedagogy.[50] Giroux's critical pedagogy rests upon a commitment to public spaces for learning, where diverse forms of knowledge can be exchanged and developed; where students and teachers engage critically with those knowledges, and with one another; and through which genuine democratic ideals can be pursued. Disciplines are regarded as antithetical to these aims, because they are considered closed, elitist, and perpetuate conservative forms of relationships and types of knowledge. Thus, critical pedagogy in this sense seeks instead to escape disciplinary boundaries and build interdisciplinary spaces in which such public and political realms can exist and prosper. While academic librarians must still work within the boundaries of the disciplines, research consultations, particularly in public spaces such as libraries, offer a setting where librarians can model for students the connections between disciplines by sharing resources and search strategies from multiple perspectives as well as connecting students with others in different disciplines doing similar work.

Agreement 3: Engage diverse learning strategies

Rendón proposes that teaching and learning contexts can become places that attend to the education of the whole person. In so doing, teaching and learning activities connect to the outer world of action, service, and intellectual pursuits with the inner world of reflection, emotion, and self-awareness. One kind of learning is not privileged over others. Rather, multiple intelligences are seen as connected and integral to the education of the whole person. The theory of multiple intelligences was developed by Howard Gardner in the early 1980s. According to Gardner, individuals possess eight or more relatively autonomous intelligences that they use to create expressions of knowledge (research papers, posters etc.) and solve problems.[51] The eight intelligences identified by Gardner are linguistic, logical-mathematical, spatial, musical, bodily-kinesthetic, naturalistic, interpersonal, and intrapersonal.

---

50   Henry A. Giroux and Susan G. Searls, *Take Back Higher Education* (New York: Palgrave, 2004).

51   Howard Gardner, *Frames of Mind: The Theory of Multiple Intelligences* (New York: Basic Books, 2011).

Educators from a diverse range of higher education institutions have embraced the theory with tremendous enthusiasm. Nevertheless, it is important to bear in mind that multiple intelligences theory offers neither an established curriculum nor an educational goal for either students or educators to pursue. Rather, the theory is an idea about the concept of intelligence. Thousands of different teachers, schools, and researchers have applied it to education in many different ways. Some schools have utilized the vocabulary of multiple intelligences among their faculty to discuss the strengths and weaknesses of students. Other educators have explicitly sought to develop curricula and lesson plans that allow students to draw upon several different intelligences.

While much of the library literature talks about multiple intelligences in terms of learning styles, Trina J. Magi and Patricia E. Mardeusz note in their article on research consultations that librarians need to deepen their skills in active listening and providing affective support.[52] Librarians can use reference interviewing skills and active listening techniques to better understand the meaning behind students' words. They can ask clarifying questions, and our conversations with students can enable us to assess the ways in which students need support or affirmation, or the ways in which students may be confused and struggling. Librarians are then able to adjust their consultation technique for the student, taking into account personality, level of research knowledge, and complexity of the assignment, as well as social, emotional, and spiritual needs. Much of the library science literature notes that librarians can play a key role in providing students with reassurance, encouragement, and confidence-building, serving as "cheerleaders" or "coaches" and working to lower the psychological and emotional barriers that many student researchers face. One method of integrating both emotional and social learning with intellect during a consultation is presented by Corinne Laverty and Elizabeth A. Lee in their book chapter. The authors describe the use of dialogic mapping during research consultations to encourage student self-reflection about their topic and also to help alleviate research anxieties.[53] Using research consulta-

---

52　Trina J. Magi and Patricia E. Mardeusz, "Why Some Students Continue to Value Individual, Face-To-Face Research Consultations in a Technology-Rich World," *College & Research Libraries* 74, no. 6 (2013): 605–18.

53　Corinne Laverty and Elizabeth A. Lee, "Dialogic Mapping: Evolving Reference into an Instructional Support for Graduate Research," in *Rethinking Reference for Academic Libraries: Innovative Developments and Future Trends*, eds. Carrie Forbes and Jennifer Bowers (Lanham: MD: Rowman & Littlefield, 2014), 135–52.

tions as a chance to build a relationship between a student and librarian can go a long way in helping further develop a critical community of support, encouragement, and even challenge for both students and librarians.

Agreement 4: Be grounded in knowing and not knowing

Rendón counters the agreement that, as professionals, we should strive for perfection and present ourselves as experts. She calls instead on teachers and students to be open to the generative possibilities of not knowing. Drawing on the work of Andrew Cohen, she suggests that expertise, when manifest as overconfidence, is limiting and that operating as seekers who value the process of coming to know enables us to liberate, rather than confine our learning. To emphasize this perspective, she writes, "true learning results from a deep and continuous surrender to the unknown."[54] These ideas resonate with those expounded in social work education and research in terms of challenging the traditional power dynamic of expert and novice, teacher and student, and researcher and participant, that is often played out in academic institutional settings, including the library. In many research paradigms, the researcher is cast as the expert and consequently assumes an asymmetrical position of power and privilege.[55] Social justice social work research, participant action research, and other social justice-oriented methodologies aim to change this power imbalance by creating a more equal and collaborative relationship between the researcher and the participants, positioning them as co-learners. "Power is shared as much as possible between the researcher and the community and each is considered to have different but equivalent wisdom, knowledge, and experience."[56] Shawn A. Ginright and Julio Cammarota describe this partnership as key to social justice research, accomplished by building alliances with community members in order to collaboratively develop research questions, topics, and methods.[57] Adital Ben-Ari and Guy Enosh, however,

---

54   Rendón, *Sentipensante Pedagogy*, 40.

55   Rogers, "Anti-Oppressive Social Work Research:" 867; and Adital Ben-Ari and Guy Enosh, "Power Relations and Reciprocity: Dialectics of Knowledge Construction," *Qualitative Health Research* 23, no. 3 (2012): 422–29.

56   Danso, "An Integrated Framework," 576.

57   Ginwright and Cammarota, "Teaching Social Justice Research," 172.

argue that power differentials will likely always exist, with both researcher and participant exerting power at different stages in the research, and that viewing this relationship as based on indirect reciprocity enables each to benefit from bringing "different forms of expert knowledge to the exchange."[58] Rather than positioning ourselves as the knowledge gatekeeper, we can embrace (and recognize the advantages of) shared knowledge, freeing us and the students with whom we work in a research consultation with the burden of needing to know everything.

Reference librarians are very familiar with, and the library science literature also validates, the anxiety experienced by students about conducting library research.[59] This anxiety is often based on the fear of *not knowing*, "not knowing where to find things in the library, not knowing what to do in the library, and not knowing how to conduct library searches."[60] When we meet with students, we can begin with assessing their confidence in the research process and then build on their confidence level, wherever it may be, by acknowledging and validating their expertise and experiences as equally important components of the consultation. This is not to relinquish our professional role but rather to acknowledge the student's knowledge and demonstrate, through an open and reflective process of asking questions, sharing opinions, cross-checking, and working together, that the learning process is a shared journey.

At the same time, librarians need to be comfortable with and transparent about our knowledge gaps. Although there are some studies about academic librarian anxiety, these focus primarily on anxiety related to classroom instruction or center on frustration, rather than *not knowing*.[61] As Anne Powers learned from her survey, "There is a specific aspect of 'anxiety'

---

58   Ben-Ari and Enosh, "Power Relations and Reciprocity," 427.

59   Heather Carlile, "The Implications of Library Anxiety for Academic Reference Services: A Review of the Literature," *Australian Academic and Research Libraries* 38, no. 2 (2007): 129–47; Constance A. Mellon, "Library Anxiety: A Grounded Theory and Its Development," *College and Research Libraries* 76, no. 3 (2015): 276–82; and Steve Black, "Psychosocial Reasons Why Patrons Avoid Seeking Help from Librarians: A Literature Review," *The Reference Librarian* 57, no. 1 (2016): 35–56.

60   Carlile, "The Implications of Library Anxiety," 134.

61   Kaetrena D. Davis, "The Academic Librarian as Instructor: A Study of Teacher Anxiety," *College and Undergraduate Libraries* 14, no. 2 (2007): 77–101; and Anne Powers, "'Librarian's Anxiety'? How Community College Librarians Feel About Their Reference Desk Service," *Community and Junior College Libraries* 16, no. 1 (2010): 54–70.

among community college reference and instruction librarians which manifests itself, not in the fear of interpersonal interaction with patrons or doubt of their professional ability to deliver services, but in frustration at being stymied in performing what they believe are their true responsibilities," in this case, being able to fulfill their teaching role in reference services.[62]

To embrace not knowing requires a combination of working collaboratively with students and also being comfortable with failure—failure to always be the expert and to always have a successful, empowering research consultation. In other words, we need to accept occasional failure, or an inability to help the student to the degree we would wish, and transform these situations into learning opportunities.[63] As a possible model, we could take inspiration from the FAILURE:LAB which sees the creative and empowering possibilities in failure, seeking "to eliminate the fear of failure and to encourage intelligent risk taking."[64] Recognizing that knowledge acquisition is an ongoing and shared activity, librarians can embrace and make the most of uncertainty, in all its various forms, throughout the research process.

Agreement 5: Show respect for diverse cultures and multiculturalism

Higher education, Rendón argues, continues to support a monocultural framework that privileges Western knowledge while simultaneously admitting a more diverse student body.[65] Her agreement to embrace multiple perspectives challenges the assumed superiority and placement of Western ways of knowing and this subsequent disconnect between education as practiced in the academy and the real, lived experiences of our students. The social work literature provides some ideas for how we might center and empower marginalized communities through developing cultural competence and championing diverse perspectives.

---

62   Powers, "'Librarian's Anxiety,'" 68.

63   VanScoy, "Fully Engaged Practice and Emotional Connection," 275.

64   *FAILURE:LAB*, 2016, accessed December 5, 2016, http://failure-lab.com.

65   Rendón, *Sentipensante Pedagogy*, 44.

Social work educators and practitioners consciously strive to develop critical and culturally aware practices.[66] To prepare students to work with diverse clients and to understand the impact of oppression and privilege, multiculturalism is integrated throughout the social work curriculum.[67] Ransford Danso argues for the necessity of cultural competence in anti-oppressive research practices as well. Defining cultural competence as "the awareness, knowledge, and skills social workers need to develop in order to deliver culturally appropriate services,"[68] he takes this idea further, using critical cultural competence to prompt social workers "to engage in high-level action-oriented, change-inducing analyses of culture- and diversity-related phenomena."[69] Cultural competence is tied directly to social justice outcomes. Based on his work teaching indigenous studies and anti-racism social work courses in Australia, David Hollinsworth emphasizes the importance of critical reflection in cross-cultural encounters, so that social workers initiate a process of moving from "casting cultural differences as 'other' or alterity to an unexamined and normative 'whiteness' to recognition of our intercultural world where all identities are formed and work within interpenetrating and inter-referential social and cultural domains."[70] He recommends eliciting and listening to clients' life stories as a strategy that illuminates "what is salient to them including their negotiation of diverse cultural identities while avoiding culturalism and deterministic interpretations."[71] Librarians also recognize the importance of developing cultural competence in order to be effective professionals

---

66 Laura S. Abrams and Jené A. Moio, "Critical Race Theory and the Cultural Competence Dilemma in Social Work Education," *Journal of Social Work Education* 45, no. 2 (2009): 245–61; Kesha Blunt, "Social Work Education: Achieving Transformative Learning Through a Cultural Competence Model of Transformative Education," *Journal of Teaching in Social Work* 27, no. 3–4 (2007): 93–104; and Jayshree S. Jani, Phillip Osteen and Stacy Shipe, "Cultural Competence and Social Work Education: Moving Toward Assessment of Practice Behaviors," *Journal of Social Work Education* 52, no. 3 (2016): 311–24.

67 Nicotera and Walls, "Challenging Perceptions of Academic Research," 334.

68 Danso, "An Integrated Framework," 574.

69 Ibid.

70 David Hollinsworth, "Forget Cultural Competence; Ask for an Autobiography," *Social Work Education* 32, no. 8 (2013): 1054.

71 Ibid., 1056.

in the current environment.[72] Patricia Montiel Overall presents a framework for cultural competence within cognitive, interpersonal, and environmental domains that could be adopted by library and information science professionals. Specifically, she recommends cultivating competence through cultural self-awareness, building cultural knowledge and appreciation, developing an ethic of caring through personal and cultural interaction, reflecting on values, and considering the impact of environmental factors, such as barriers to library use, language, the information environment, and the library space.[73]

To put Rendón's agreement and the tenets of multiculturalism and cultural competence into practice during research consultations, librarians can employ many of the ideas already put forth in this chapter, including diversifying the range of sources to which we direct students, recognizing more inclusive ways of knowing, cultivating empathy, emphasizing a dialogic reciprocal relationship, and validating our students' diverse identities, backgrounds, abilities, and range of experiences. In addition, we could also follow or adapt the guidelines suggested by Brook, Ellenwood, and Lazzaro to shift reference services toward an antiracist practice: revise service guidelines to ensure that library staff "learn about, consider, and act upon the historical context and power dynamics that shape racialized communication and racialized lives;" provide ongoing training and professional development in order to build library staff's "knowledge of their own cultural backgrounds and assumptions, the racial and ethnic diversity of the campus community, and the history of oppression, power, and privilege experienced by various groups;" work to understand and minimize the impact of racial microaggressions; and use "problem-posing methods of critical pedagogy… to draw out patrons' struggles against oppression and to help build strong and lasting solidarities with patrons."[74] Research consultations practiced in this manner and with this foundation, by culturally

---

72   Fiona Blackburn, "'Cultural Competence is for Everyone': Cultural Competence in the United States Library and Information Sector. Is It Relevant to Australian Libraries?" *Australian Academic and Research Libraries* 46, no. 3 (2015): 176–93; Patricia Montiel Overall, "Cultural Competence: A Conceptual Framework for Library and Information Science Professionals," *Library Quarterly* 79, no. 2 (2009): 175–204; and Nicole A. Cooke, Miriam E. Sweeney, and Safiya Umoja Noble, "Social Justice as Topic and Tool: An Attempt to Transform an LIS Curriculum and Culture," *Library Quarterly: Information, Community, Policy* 86, no. 1 (2016): 107–24.

73   Overall, "Cultural Competence," 175–204.

74   Brook, Ellenwood and Lazzaro, "In Pursuit of Antiracist Social Justice," 276.

knowledgeable and sensitive librarians, would create more responsive and socially just interactions for our students and advance the goal of building supportive and inclusive campus communities.

Agreement 6: Balance our personal and professional lives

Rendón acknowledges that the work of social justice and incorporating holistic pedagogies into teaching can be difficult and emotionally taxing work. While she urges educators to care deeply for their students, she notes that teachers cannot take care of students without first taking care of themselves. It may at times be necessary to create some balance between our personal and professional lives to ensure that we don't get burned out. Feminist educators writing about the ethic of care have called attention to this same issue and offer some advice.

Among these scholar-educators, Joan Tronto's work is unique in that she has developed the political ethics of care as a theoretical framework, and more latterly, as a framework for democratic care. She sees care as both a practice and a disposition—as an activity through which we maintain and repair our world so that we can flourish.[75] Particularly, since her early work in the 1990s, Tronto has concentrated on the notion of "privileged irresponsibility." In considering the power that racism confers on a majority group, she coined this phrase to refer to the ways in which the majority group fails to acknowledge the exercise of power, thus maintaining their taken-for-granted positions of privilege. In her later work, she views democracy as a system where caring responsibilities are allocated to some social groups (e.g. women, immigrants), while it allows others (e.g. men, majority groups) to "simultaneously rely on and disavow" the work of these groups, or in Tronto's terms to exercise privileged irresponsibility.[76]

This view of democracy and care helps educators critique the narrow moral and political frame that underlies conventional divisions of labor including teaching itself and traditional caring roles. Most importantly, Tronto's political ethics of care enables critical educators to be cognizant of and consequently to delve into the difficult emotional knowledge arising from

---

75 Joan Tronto, *Moral Boundaries: A Political Argument for an Ethic of Care* (New York: Routledge, 1993).

76 Joan Tronto, *Caring Democracy: Markets, Equality, and Justice* (New York: New York University Press, 2013).

practices of privileged irresponsibility within or beyond the context of education—for example, feelings of moral indignation when caregivers are treated unjustly or inhumanely, or emotions of guilt and shame when care-receivers realize that they have been engaging in privileged irresponsibility.

Caregiving work that women and other less advantaged groups of people are engaged in frequently goes unnoticed, and is consistently undervalued or devalued in terms of material rewards and status. Women are still the majority in traditionally gendered and care-based careers such as teaching, librarianship, nursing, and domestic care work and service and continue to carry the load of care in domestic and community contexts. In higher education and in schools in many contexts, women, particularly those who occupy marginal positions (such as poor, non-citizen, Black women), engage in devalued practices, while men tend to dominate in management and/or research positions.[77]

Caregivers, such as teachers and others involved in hands-on caregiving processes can be so focused on others that they do not pay enough attention to making sure that their own needs are supported. For example, in higher education, women are most often engaged with meeting students' needs while men get to the important business of publishing.[78] As Tronto reminds us, it is essential to be self-reflexive about our own needs for care and ensure that the self not be subsumed in the caring relationship.[79] Tony Monchinski also comments that, "to fail to care for oneself impairs one's capacity to function as a fully responsible moral agent."[80] Importantly, being self-reflexive about our own needs for care is a deeply emotional process that highlights the entanglement between reflection, emotion, and care of the self.

Tronto's politics of care also view care as an ongoing social, political, and emotional practice. In other words, care is not just a disposition, as some authors have referred to it, but is a laborious activity which is crucial for human life and involves several aspects including thought, emotion, action, and work.[81] Seeing care as a social, political, and emotional practice means also

---

77   Ibid.

78   Sarah Winslow, "Gender Inequality and Time Allocations Among Academic Faculty," *Gender and Society* 24, no. 6 (2010): 769–93.

79   Tronto, *Moral Boundaries.*

80   Tony Monchinski, *Education in Hope: Critical Pedagogies and the Ethics of Care* (New York: Peter Lang, 2010), 98.

81   Tronto, *Caring Democracy.*

that, as a practice, it is constituted within a specific context and therefore it cannot be simply viewed as a particular gender's or race's responsibility to be carried out. This understanding of care is relevant to writings in critical pedagogy that highlight how some caring practices may be superficial and sentimental, if they do not challenge inequalities. Therefore, Tronto's political ethics of care is particularly valuable for those educators who want to interrogate the intersections among power, emotion, and praxis in society and education.[82]

Finally, this definition sees care as a general activity that includes collective care, rather than a dyadic one existing between two people. Tronto observes that caring very rarely happens only between a single caregiver and a receiver, but is more complex, even in the space of the family, where usually multiple people are caring for each other.[83] In the context of education, Tronto's broader definition of care provides a perspective that sees value in collaborative teaching and learning practices.[84] This understanding of care is important for critical education because it acknowledges both the relational and political aspects of caring responsibilities. For example, the idea of the political ethics of care implies not seeing the educator as expert but engaging with many and different sources of authority in epistemic communities that are defined by shared meanings of the world—meanings that challenge hegemonic views on care. Recognizing care for students as operating on multiple levels allows librarians to create more balance in their lives; they can let go of some of the guilt knowing that they alone are not responsible for "saving" a failing student. Librarians can also take heart that their feelings of being undervalued and unappreciated are not unwarranted, but part of a larger political environment that must be challenged in order to fully value service-oriented work.

Agreement 7: Take time for self-reflexivity

Central to each learning endeavor is the need for students and teachers to understand how their identities and lived experiences shape their fluid positions of privilege and marginalization which in turn impacts their abili-

---

82   Ibid.

83   Ibid.

84   Ibid.

ty to empathize with and understand the experience of others.[85] Critically examining their own positionality, biases, and practices ensures that social justice goals and anti-oppressive practices remain at the forefront for practitioners and students alike. Christine Morley outlines several strategies for integrating reflective practice into the social work curriculum, based on her work with undergraduate students. She connects critical reflection to transformative learning, an outcome of students questioning dominant ideologies and assumptions, being open to new ideas, and "challenging dominant power relations and structures in a bottom up process, and operationalizing progressive social change strategies at the interpersonal level."[86] Likewise, Hollinsworth connects critical awareness with a "learning and teaching approach that recognizes where each of us has come from, what we value and why, and how these impact on our openness or resistance to acknowledging others' perspectives and the partiality of our own."[87] Critical reflexivity is an ongoing and essential process that originates with a critical awareness of the self but moves outward to question the dominant roles and structures that maintain privilege and power in society. Danso suggests that in the context of anti-oppressive research, this can take the form of researchers and participants engaging in "constructive *confessional dialogue* in which they openly acknowledge and work through their cultural biases and assumptions to propel the research to successful completion."[88]

Regardless of the setting, critical reflexivity can be challenging and destabilizing (as it is meant to be), requiring the need to recognize and support the emotional as well as cognitive aspects of this work.[89] Jan Fook and Gurid Aga Askeland highlight the importance of personal and emotional experiences to critical reflection and transformative learning, but also point out how this is counter to the traditional academic emphasis on rational and intellectual thought. "The role of personal and emotional ex-

---

85   Carolyn Campbell, "The Search for Congruency: Developing Strategies for Anti-Oppressive Social Work Pedagogy," *Canadian Social Work Review/ Revue Canadienne de Service Social* 19, no. 1 (2002): 32.

86   Christine Morley, "Teaching Critical Practice: Resisting Structural Domination through Critical Reflection," *Social Work Education* 27, no. 4 (2008): 418.

87   Hollinsworth, "Forget Cultural Competence," 1054.

88   Danso, "An Integrated Framework," 576–77.

89   Andrew Hart and Jane Montague, "'The Constant State of Becoming': Power, Identity, and Discomfort on the Anti-Oppressive Learning Journey," *Journal of Psychological Issues in Organizational Culture* 5, no. 4 (2015): 43.

perience is therefore as important in framing knowledge, as are cognitive abilities and behaviours, since the whole person is the research instrument. This means that personal and emotional experiences are crucial as food for learning and change in critical reflection. Yet to draw on personal experiences in order to gain general knowledge is not traditionally acknowledged as scientifically acceptable. Further, it is not recognised that what new knowledge we are able to take into possession depends on our personal experiences, opinions, values, and emotions."[90] In order for scholars and students to practice critical reflection, there needs to be a significant shift in the academy, so that the emotional component to learning is equally valued. Rendón also grounds her agreement about self-reflexivity in the necessity of examining our positionalities and how they impact our interactions with students in the classroom, which could equally be applied in the library. Taking time for critical reflection, she reasons, is just as important as action for transformation to occur at the personal and institutional level. She writes, the "work of transformation is not only about changing what is 'out there'; it is about transforming what is 'in here,' our own internal views and assumptions."[91] Heidi L. M. Jacobs also calls for reflective practice in the library profession, specifically as relevant for information literacy instruction, stating, "If we are going to address the issues of librarians' roles within educational endeavors systemically, we, as a discipline, need to foster reflective, critical habits of mind regarding pedagogical praxis within ourselves, our libraries, and our campuses."[92] For reference librarians this means not only examining our own positions, biases, and backgrounds (and how they impact what we do) but also how we teach students during a research consultation.

A reflective process is one that can be, quite literally, modeled for the student by thinking out loud and reciprocated by talking through the process together. In this manner, the student can understand how we approach a research challenge—starting with what we know about disciplinary and subject areas, databases, potential resources, search and evaluation strategies, and so forth. By talking aloud about the process and getting feedback from the student, we also become more conscious of the practices that we

---

90 Jan Fook and Gurid Aga Askeland, "Challenges of Critical Reflection: 'Nothing Ventured, Nothing Gained,'" *Social Work Education* 26, no. 5 (2007): 527.

91 Rendón, *Sentipensante Pedagogy*, 48.

92 Heidi L. M. Jacobs, "Information Literacy and Reflective Pedagogical Praxis," *The Journal of Academic Librarianship* 34, no. 3 (2008): 256.

follow, perhaps without being fully aware of our decisions. When we involve students in our thought processes during a research consultation and invite them to ask questions like, How? Why? Why not?, and What about?, we can view the research process from new and fresh perspectives, truly making the experience a more collaborative one.

Conclusion

In her seven agreements, Rendón provides direction for how we can implement and integrate social justice into our daily work. Moreover, the social work and education fields, with their deep commitment to social justice, also offer models for transformative change. Research-based pedagogies, such as sentipensante, should only provide a framework for teachers and librarians, not a definitive structure. The ideas presented in this chapter are suggestions, not prescriptive guidelines. Socially just pedagogies require well-educated librarians who know the research literature, but mediate it through a careful reading of the demands and specificities of their students, classes, and locale. Indeed, as Jan McArthur makes a case for tailoring the broad ideals of critical pedagogy to each specific context, we can also think of sentipensante pedagogy as "*a way of approaching*" how to enact positive change in the classroom or in our reference interactions.[93]

Trust in librarians should also be a feature of socially just reference and research services. A professional development orientation in which academic librarians focus on various aspects of sentipensante pedagogy (based on their levels of experience) in collaboration with faculty only works within a dynamic of trust and flexibility. Furthermore, librarians cannot work towards social justice goals in isolation. In order to affect change, we need not only to transform our reference services, but also to think about how we are part of the larger academic community. Change will be most effective when we reach out and engage with other educators interested in promoting social justice work on campus. Building connections, exchanging ideas, supporting our students and each other—these are some of the ways that we can create empowering critical communities. For as Bettez emphasizes, "Community in this sense is both a process and a goal."[94]

---

93 Jan McArthur, "Achieving Social Justice Within and Through Higher Education: The Challenge for Critical Pedagogy," *Teaching in Higher Education* 15, no. 5 (2010): 501.

94 Bettez, "Building Critical Communities," 80.

In a world in which inequalities are growing, and in which higher education administrators seem to disregard explicit social justice policies, we stress the need for librarians to actively engage in larger social justice teaching discussions happening on their campuses as a necessary complement to the sorts of progressive pedagogies considered in this chapter. Of course, neoliberal educational policy agendas and discourses make such politics an almost Sisyphean struggle today.[95] According to Michael W. Apple, socially just pedagogies alone cannot challenge extremist politics and discourses and their very real material effects. We need to work politically and in research and theoretical terms towards more socially just reference services as part of a larger coalition in higher education. Sentipensante pedagogy is one step in this process of creating more just and holistic research consultations and reference practices. The important message here is that change begins with us, at the individual level, but only through connections with others are we able to set positive transformation in motion.

---

95   Michael W. Apple, "The Shock of the Real: Critical Pedagogies and Rightist Reconstructions," in *Revolutionary Pedagogies: Cultural Politics, Education, and the Discourse of Theory*, ed. Peter Pericles Trifonas (New York: Routledge, 2000), 225–50.

Works Cited

Abrams, Laura S. and Jené A. Moio. "Critical Race Theory and the Cultural Competence Dilemma in Social Work Education." *Journal of Social Work Education* 45, no. 2 (2009): 245–61.

Apple, Michael W. "The Shock of the Real: Critical Pedagogies and Rightist Reconstructions." In *Revolutionary Pedagogies: Cultural Politics, Instituting Education, and the Discourse of Theory*, edited by Peter Pericles Trifonas, 225–50. New York: Routledge, 2000.

———. *Official Knowledge: Democratic Education in a Conservative Age*. New York: Routledge, 2014.

Association of College and Research Libraries. "Framework for Information Literacy for Higher Education." Last modified January 11, 2016, accessed December 4, 2016. http://www.ala.org/acrl/standards/ilframework.

Ben-Ari, Adital and Guy Enosh. "Power Relations and Reciprocity: Dialectics of Knowledge Construction." *Qualitative Health Research* 23, no. 3 (2012): 422–29.

Bettez, Silvia Cristina. "Building Critical Communities Amid the Uncertainty of Social Justice Pedagogy in the Graduate Classroom." *Review of Education, Pedagogy, and Cultural Studies* 33, no. 1 (2011): 76–106.

Black, Steve. "Psychosocial Reasons Why Patrons Avoid Seeking Help from Librarians: A Literature Review." *The Reference Librarian* 57, no. 1 (2016): 35–56.

Blackburn, Fiona. "'Cultural Competence is for Everyone': Cultural Competence in the United States Library and Information Sector. Is It Relevant to Australian Libraries?" *Australian Academic and Research Libraries* 46, no. 3 (2015): 176–93.

Blunt, Kesha. "Social Work Education: Achieving Transformative Learning Through a Cultural Competence Model of Transformative Education." *Journal of Teaching in Social Work* 27, no. 3–4 (2007): 93–104.

Brook, Freeda, Dave Ellenwood, and Althea Eannace Lazzaro. "In Pursuit of Antiracist Social Justice: Denaturalizing Whiteness in the Academic Library." *Library Trends* 64, no. 2 (2015): 246–84.

Campbell, Carolyn. "The Search for Congruency: Developing Strategies for Anti-Oppressive Social Work Pedagogy." *Canadian Social Work Review/ Revue Canadienne de Service Social* 19, no. 1 (2002): 25–42.

Carlile, Heather. "The Implications of Library Anxiety for Academic Reference Services: A Review of the Literature." *Australian Academic and Research Libraries* 38, no. 2 (2007): 129–47.

Cooke, Nicole A., Miriam E. Sweeney, and Safiya Umoja Noble. "Social Justice as Topic and Tool: An Attempt to Transform an LIS Curriculum and Culture." *Library Quarterly: Information, Community, Policy* 86, no. 1 (2016): 107–24.

Cumming-Potvin, Wendy. "Social Justice, Pedagogy and Multiliteracies: Developing Communities of Practice for Teacher Education." *Australian Journal of Teacher Education* 34, no. 3 (2009): 82–99.

Danso, Ransford. "An Integrated Framework of Critical Cultural Competence and Anti-Oppressive Practice for Social Justice Social Work Research." *Qualitative Social Work* 14, no. 4 (2015): 572–88.

Davis, Kaetrena D. "The Academic Librarian as Instructor: A Study of Teacher Anxiety." *College and Undergraduate Libraries* 14, no. 2 (2007): 77–101.

Davis, Tracy and Laura M. Harrison. *Advancing Social Justice: Tools, Pedagogies, and Strategies to Transform Your Campus.* San Francisco, CA: Jossey-Bass, 2013.

Doherty, John J. "Reference Interview or Reference Dialogue?" *Internet Reference Services Quarterly* 11, no. 3 (2006): 97–109.

Dooley, Karen T. "Multiliteracies and Pedagogies of New Learning for Students of English as an Additional Language." In *Multiliteracies and Diversity in Education: New Pedagogies for Expanding Landscapes,* edited by Annah Healy, 102–25. South Melbourne, Australia: Oxford University Press, 2008.

Duarte, Marisa Elena and Miranda Belarde-Lewis. "Imagining: Creating Spaces for Indigenous Ontologies." *Cataloging and Classification Quarterly* 53, no. 5–6 (2015): 677–702.

Elmborg, James. "Critical Information Literacy: Implications for Instructional Practice." *Journal of Academic Librarianship* 32 (2006): 192–99.

———. "Libraries in the Contact Zone: On the Creation of Educational Space." *Reference & User Services Quarterly* 46, no. 1 (2006): 56–64.

FAILURE:LAB, 2016. Accessed December 5, 2016. http://failure-lab.com.

Fook, Jan and Gurid Aga Askeland. "Challenges of Critical Reflection: 'Nothing Ventured, Nothing Gained.'" *Social Work Education* 26, no. 5 (2007): 520–33.

Gale, Crystal D. and Betty S. Evans. "Face-to-Face: The Implementation and Analysis of a Research Consultation Service." *College & Undergraduate Libraries* 14, no. 3 (2007): 85–101.

Gardner, Howard. *Frames of Mind: The Theory of Multiple Intelligences.* New York: Basic Books, 2011.

Ginwright, Shawn A. and Julio Cammarota. "Teaching Social Justice Research to Undergraduate Students in Puerto Rico: Using Personal Experiences to Inform Research." *Equity and Excellence in Education* 48, no. 2 (2015): 162–77.

Giroux, Henry A. *Border Crossings: Cultural Workers and the Politics of Education.* New York: Routledge, 1992.

— — —. "Literacy, Pedagogy, and the Politics of Difference." *College Literature* 19, no. 1 (1992): 1–11.

Giroux, Henry A. and Susan G. Searls. *Take Back Higher Education.* New York: Palgrave, 2004.

Hackman, Heather W. "Five Essential Components for Social Justice Education." *Equity & Excellence in Education* 38, no. 2 (2005): 103–09.

Hart, Andrew and Jane Montague. "'The Constant State of Becoming': Power, Identity, and Discomfort on the Anti-Oppressive Learning Journey." *Journal of Psychological Issues in Organizational Culture* 5, no. 4 (2015): 39–52.

Henderson, Zuleka, Lucinda A. Acquaye-Doyle, Shayna Waites, and Tyriesa Howard. "Putting Principles into Practice: Addressing Historical Trauma, Mistrust, and Apprehension in Research Methods Courses." *Journal of Social Work Education* 52, no. 1 (2016): 69–78.

Hollinsworth, David. "Forget Cultural Competence; Ask for an Autobiography." *Social Work Education* 32, no. 8 (2013): 1048–60.

Jacobs, Heidi L. M. "Information Literacy and Reflective Pedagogical Praxis." *The Journal of Academic Librarianship* 34, no. 3 (2008): 256–62.

Jani, Jayshree S., Phillip Osteen, and Stacy Shipe. "Cultural Competence and Social Work Education: Moving Toward Assessment of Practice Behaviors." *Journal of Social Work Education* 52, no. 3 (2016): 311–24.

Karki, Karun Kishor. "Walking the Complexities Between Two Worlds: A Personal Story of Epistemological Tensions in Knowledge Production." *Qualitative Social Work* 15, no. 5–6 (2016): 628–39.

Kuhn, Deanna and Wadiya Udell. "The Path to Wisdom." *Educational Psychologist* 36, no. 4 (2001): 261–64.

Lankshear, Colin and Michele Knobel. *New Literacies: Everyday Practices and Social Learning.* Maidenhead, UK: Open University Press, 2011.

Lave, Jean and Etienne Wenger. *Situated Learning: Legitimate Peripheral Participation.* New York: Cambridge University Press, 1999.

Laverty, Corinne and Elizabeth A. Lee. "Dialogic Mapping: Evolving Reference into an Instructional Support for Graduate Research." In *Rethinking Reference for Academic Libraries: Innovative Developments and Future Trends*, edited by Carrie Forbes and Jennifer Bowers, 135–52. Lanham: MD: Rowman & Littlefield, 2014.

Lee, Deborah. "Research Consultations: Enhancing Library Research Skills." *The Reference Librarian* 41, no. 85 (2004): 169–80.

Lloyd, Annemaree. "Information Literacy Landscapes: An Emerging Picture." *Journal of Documentation* 62 (2006): 570–83.

Longres, John F. and Edward Scanlon. "Social Justice and the Research Curriculum." *Journal of Social Work Education* 37, no. 3 (2001): 447–63.

Luke, Alan. "The Social Construction of Literacy in the Classroom." In *Literacy Learning and Teaching: Language as Social Practice in the Primary School*, edited by Len Unsworth, 3–53. South Melbourne: Macmillan Education Australia, 1993.

Magi, Trina J. and Patricia E. Mardeusz. "Why Some Students Continue to Value Individual, Face-To-Face Research Consultations in a Technology-Rich World." *College & Research Libraries* 74, no. 6 (2013): 605–18.

Matteson, Miriam L. "The Whole Student: Cognition, Emotion, and Information Literacy." *College and Research Libraries* 75, no. 6 (2014): 862–77.

McArthur, Jan. "Achieving Social Justice Within and Through Higher Education: The Challenge for Critical Pedagogy." *Teaching in Higher Education* 15, no. 5 (2010): 493–504.

Mellon, Constance A. "Library Anxiety: A Grounded Theory and Its Development." *College and Research Libraries* 76, no. 3 (2015): 276–82.

Monchinski, Tony. *Education in Hope: Critical Pedagogies and the Ethics of Care.* New York: Peter Lang, 2010.

Morley, Christine. "Teaching Critical Practice: Resisting Structural Domination through Critical Reflection." *Social Work Education* 27, no. 4 (2008): 407–21.

Nicotera, Nicole and Hye-Kyung Kang. "Beyond Diversity Courses: Strategies for Integrating Critical Consciousness Across Social Work Curriculum." *Journal of Teaching in Social Work* 29, no. 2 (2009): 188–203.

Nicotera, Nicole and N. Eugene Walls. "Challenging Perceptions of Academic Research as Bias Free: Promoting a Social Justice Framework in Social Work Research Methods." *Journal of Teaching in Social Work* 30, no. 3 (2010): 334–50.

Overall, Patricia Montiel. "Cultural Competence: A Conceptual Framework for Library and Information Science Professionals." *Library Quarterly* 79, no. 2 (2009): 175–204.

Powers, Anne. "'Librarian's Anxiety'? How Community College Librarians Feel About Their Reference Desk Service." *Community and Junior College Libraries* 16, no. 1 (2010): 54–70.

Rendón, Laura I. *Sentipensante (Sensing/Thinking) Pedagogy: Educating for Wholeness, Social Justice and Liberation*. Sterling, VA: Stylus Publishing, LLC, 2012.

Rogers, Justin. "Anti-Oppressive Social Work Research: Reflections on Power in the Creation of Knowledge." *Social Work Education* 31, no. 7 (2012): 866–79.

Rogoff, Barbara. *Apprenticeship in Thinking: Cognitive Development in Social Context*. New York: Oxford University Press, 1990.

Stover, Mark. "The Reference Librarian as Non-Expert: A Postmodern Approach to Expertise." *The Reference Librarian* 42, no. 87/88 (2004): 273–300.

Strier, Ron. "Anti-Oppressive Research in Social Work: A Preliminary Definition." *British Journal of Social Work* 37, no. 5 (2007): 857–71.

Tronto, Joan. *Caring Democracy: Markets, Equality, and Justice*. New York: New York University Press, 2013.

— — —. *Moral Boundaries: A Political Argument for an Ethic of Care*. New York: Routledge, 1993.

VanScoy, Amy. "Fully Engaged Practice and Emotional Connection: Aspects of the Practitioner Perspective of Reference and Information Service." *Library and Information Science Research* 35 no. 4 (2013): 272–78.

Vincent, Neil J. "Exploring the Integration of Social Justice into Social Work Research Curricula." *Journal of Social Work Education* 48, no. 2 (2012): 205–22.

Vygotsky, Lev. *Thought and Language*. Translated by Eugenia Hanfmann and Gertrude Vakar. Cambridge, MA: Massachusetts Institute of Technology, 1986.

Wastaway, Sohair F., Charles W. Uth, and Christopher Stewart. "Learning Communities: An Investigative Study into Their Impact on Library Services." *Science & Technology Libraries* 24, no. 3–4 (2004): 327–74.

Wenger, Etienne. *Communities of Practice: Learning, Meaning and Identity*. Cambridge, England: Cambridge University Press, 1998.

Winslow, Sarah. "Gender Inequality and Time Allocations Among Academic Faculty." *Gender and Society* 24, no. 6 (2010): 769–93.

A Blueprint on Self-Exploration to Justice: Introduction to "Referencing Audre Lorde" & "Lesbian Librarianship for All"

Shawn(ta) Smith-Cruz

Praxis operates as a blueprint. This mapping, if we allow it, has the potential to merge our professional selves with our societal selves, humanizing our work, allowing for an evolution toward justice. Reference service reminds us that, like in any map, users of library service require a source key to navigate from their place of knowledge to a new space where information lives. My approach to social justice problematizes the profession by challenging the librarian to focus inwardly to a space concentrated with identity and self-exploration.

To galvanize justice, the librarian may impose her or himself into the reference interaction as an element of praxis. This requires a deconstruction of the imposed body and layers of societal implications. If the physical presentation of clothing, gender, race, age, perceived ability combined with the voice, movement, and pacing is explored, the reference interaction is then ripe for questions. How long have I been speaking vs. listening? Will it matter if I am sitting or standing? When does my positioning matter? Am I being received as a peer, servant, or an authority, and why? In the following two chapters, I use my own self-exploration to exemplify how social justice may be applied to reference. Each chapter reconciles my lesbian of color identity with my reference practice, but also invites the reader to use his or her own identity by first using mine. The map to de-construct oneself offers a sampling of an outside perspective as navigation. In other words, *you be the lesbian librarian.* To start, we will reference one.

Audre Lorde resides in a canon outside of the queer or African American diaspora, yet her professional identity as a librarian has historically been under acknowledged. In "Referencing Audre Lorde," I present Lorde as an example for applying lesbianism to librarianship. Unlike most close readings of Lorde which deconstruct her poetry or prose, this chapter combines her writings with unpublished archival material, specifically audio recordings of her facilitation practice at a black lesbian conference. This analysis of Lorde, identity coupled with practice, unveils a formula for us as librarians to implicate her actions as reflective of librarianship and thereby applicable to our daily work.

Just as reference librarianship is an iconic depiction of library work, it is important for me to present an iconic description of lesbians while staying on task to supply applicable praxis for all librarians. If we can reference Audre Lorde in our methodologies for teaching and serving the public (and I believe we can), then with that single act, I attest that all librarians can be lesbian librarians, leading us on the path toward justice. "Lesbian Librarianship for All" is written as a manifesto focused on the two L-words and their diminishing relevance amongst their own communities, lesbians amongst queers and librarians amongst faculty. This chapter allows us to exercise a shift in perspective at best, or at the very least, a rearticulation. Both are attributes in praxis toward justice.

Referencing Audre Lorde

Shawn(ta) Smith-Cruz

Lorde: a refugee librarian who sought asylum in writing. This close reading and textual analysis of canonical texts, speeches, and archived audio recordings of Audre Lorde embraces Lorde's many identities, including her identity as a librarian who chose to depart from the library as a means of survival.[1] As reference librarians, we should study Lorde's example. It is our duty as reference librarians today to learn from Lorde's choice to act in a space where silence can be transformed into language and action. If we are able to acknowledge these limitations and opportunities in our own service and institutional structures, we may move toward a realm of reference librarianship and justice.

Aside from the work-in-progress research by librarian Dr. Ethelene Whitmire, there is no comprehensive publication on Audre Lorde's life as a librarian.[2] Until Whitmire's use of unpublished archival evidence is unveiled, what is currently available on Lorde as a librarian are brief autobiographical sketches from interviews or secondary-sourced chronologies.

---

1   This is in direct contrast to other close readings of Lorde which view Lorde's poetry, teachings, fiction, or speeches as post-nationalist, lesbian-feminist, or non-essentialist.

2   Ethelene Whitmire, "The Audre Lorde Was a Librarian Project: Audre Lorde, Black Lesbian Feminist Mother Poet Warrior, Was a Librarian," *The Audre Lorde Was a Librarian Project*, April 9, 2013, http://theaudrelordelibrarianproject.blogspot.com/2013/04/audre-lorde-black-lesbian-feminist.html.

We learn that it was Lorde's intention to become a librarian as a way to effect social change. This was coupled with her experience as a young adult
coming of age in libraries—where she experienced from both books and
the physical library a sense of joy.[3] Her first position at a library was as a
young adult librarian at the Mount Vernon, New York Public Library in
1960. She then completed her Masters in Library Science from Columbia
University in 1961. By 1968, Lorde served as Head Librarian at the private
Town School in New York City. The good feeling that the library provided would eventually prove to be "not enough" for Lorde.[4] She published
her first volume of poetry in 1968 and also taught her first writing course
from a National Endowment for the Arts grant at Tougaloo College, Mississippi. This transition led her to become a lecturer at City College of the
City University of New York, a simultaneous shift with her introduction to
Frances Clayton, whom she would spend almost two decades as life partner. Upon leaving librarianship, Lorde moved toward identifying her life
as a lesbian/poet/revolutionary.

What then, can we learn from Lorde's transition from librarian to
lesbian/poet/revolutionary? What if anything, did Lorde carry with her
from her librarian training to the world of poetry, teaching, and community leadership? And how do we *reference Audre Lorde* and her work in our
own library reference practice?

Refugee Librarian

As a United States-born, West-Indian-identified activist, Lorde's identification with nation and state was deeply rooted in her Black radical feminism
and teachings of unification. In describing Lorde's diasporic relationships
to Grenada, her ancestral home-country, Black lesbian scholar Dr. Alexis
Pauline Gumbs supplies Lorde's analysis of military engagement amongst
Black soldiers: "Lorde tells us … we are related through racist systems that
we do not control, and we can create solidarity only if we acknowledge our

---

3   Nina Winter, "Audre Lorde," in *Conversations with Audre Lorde*, ed. Audre Lorde and
    Joan Wylie Hall (Jackson: University Press of Mississippi, 2004), 11.

4   Audre Lorde and Adrienne Rich, "An Interview with Audre Lorde," *Signs* 6,
    no. 4 (1981): 722.

different relationships to power."⁵ The institutional affiliation of the library with the State was likely antithetical to Lorde's revolutionary transitions and identifications. Scholar Cheryl Higashida identifies Lorde's connections to a multi-layered nationalism, which she coins as a "cultural nationalism." Higashida posits,

> Lorde's post-invasion prose and poetry that she most explicitly and consistently explores [is] a nationalist internationalism positing that African Americans are morally and politically bound to support Third World and indigenous struggles for national sovereignty and that anti-colonial struggles illuminate and impact African Americans' situation in the United States as an oppressed people.⁶

These international and diasporic layers of nationalism, coupled with second-wave Black feminism are highly referenced in Lorde's text "Grenada Revisited," which Higashida views as a "beginning of a new leg of Lorde's political development."⁷ Higashida explains, "Lorde fully elaborates her nationalist internationalism in 'Grenada Revisited' which counters U.S. state discourses… In doing so, she foregrounds the impact of independence and (neo)colonialism."⁸

For Lorde, teaching was "a survival technique."⁹ The sense of joy that was once attributed to the library was "no longer enough" for Lorde, prompting her to move into a realm of social justice.¹⁰ An exit from an administrative and non-faculty position in Library and Information Science to a field suited for revolutionary action (one which could be argued was made possible by the autonomy granted to a college lecturer, poet, and scholar with faculty status) is indicative of a political need to exit from the role of administering tasks

---

5   Alexis Pauline Gumbs, "'But We Are Not the Same': Generating a Critical Poetics of Diaspora," in *Audre Lorde's Transnational Legacies*, eds. Sabine Broeck and Stella Bolaki (Boston: University of Massachusetts Press, 2015), 169.

6   Cheryl Higashida, "Audre Lorde Revisited: Nationalism and Second-Wave Black Feminism," in *Black Internationalist Feminism: Women Writers of the Black Left, 1945–1995* (Urbana: University of Illinois Press, 2011), 137.

7   Ibid., 137.

8   Ibid., 141.

9   Lorde and Rich, "An Interview with Audre Lorde," 719.

10   Ibid., 722.

for the nation-state. This comparison of library to state is congruous with Stephen E. Bales's application of French Marxist Louis Althusser's concept of the "Ideological State Apparatus" (ISA), where he provides a Marxist analysis of academic libraries in the western world as educational and religious ISAs. "These early library temples helped to maintain the political/economic *status quo,* illustrating the seemingly perpetual connection between religion, politics, and money."[11] Lorde's intention to move outside of, or at the very least to no longer perpetuate oppressive systems, led her to a natural progression outside of the library. Her relationship to power and its practical application, it is argued here, did not however remove her applications of reference service or learned librarianship from her continued teaching and writing practice.

War in the realm of the unicorn

Swaziland-born artist Nandipha Mntambo creates sculpture of the female body and identity in relation to her creation of half-woman and half-bull figures. In her use of the bull, Mntambo articulates "a fascination with 'the in-between space and how it leads to understanding the world in a more global way."[12] Creating visual representations of space that reside between "the binaries of attraction/repulsion, male/female, animal/human, myth/reality, black/white, Africa/Europe," Mntambo's use of her own body and her mother's body to construct these mythological forms suggest that "… the politics of representing *other people* is complex and can create strange friction" (italics mine).[13] If compared to Mntambo's bull-creatures, Lorde's metaphorical creatures in her collection of poetry, *Black Unicorn,* urge the reader in a "Litany for Survival" to speak in a world where silence is expected and encouraged. Lorde writes: "and when we speak we are afraid/ our words will not be heard/ nor welcomed/ but when we are silent/ we are still afraid/ So it is better to speak/ remembering/ we were never meant to survive."[14]

---

11   Stephen E. Bales, "The Academic Library as Crypto-Temple: A Marxian Analysis," in *Class and Librarianship: Essays at the Intersection of Information, Labor and Capital,* eds. Erik Sean Estep and Nathaniel F. Enright (Sacramento, CA: Library Juice Press, 2016), 8.

12   Seattle Art Museum, Fowler Museum at UCLA, and Brooklyn Museum, *Disguise: Masks and Global African Art,* 2015, 34.

13   Ibid.

14   Audre Lorde, "A Litany for Survival," in *The Black Unicorn: Poems* (New York: Norton, 1978), 31–32.

As with her teaching, Lorde's unicorn responds to a need for survival. Like Mntambo's bull, Lorde repels the friction created by normative binaries and instead measures the "we" inside of a unifying in-between space. In these definitions, "we" are all in-between. If one considers their many self-identifying qualities, there is likely a piece of ourselves that has been pushed to silence, that resides between the binaries, that is authentically our body or that of our mother. Separation from *other people*, any group outside of our own parallelisms, is the first step to understanding self-determination, to then understand how we are similarly "related" to the "systems that we do not control."[15]

Lorde's identification with lesbian feminist, and at times separatist, frameworks can inform reference work and service. In-between spaces create strange friction at the reference desk, for example, a space that holds two or more co-existing bodies negotiating boundaries and hierarchical roles, which will contextualize the exchange of information at bay.[16] Friction is further exacerbated if and when the representations of the bodies which occupy the reference desk already hold societally inequitable positions. Using Lorde's response to a need for survival, or perhaps her decision to leave librarianship for teaching, we are reminded of the stark power relationship between librarian and user. Further, if we consider the library an ISA, and if it is from the State that we, those of us who champion social justice, all fight to survive, the library will not shield us from social death.

Whiteness Studies in Library and Information Science defines societal inequity as a collective truth. According to librarians of the online journal, *In the Library with the Lead Pipe,* librarian nina de jesus suggests that through a lens of whiteness, "libraries very much participate in a larger imperial project that justifies war."[17] In the case where a patron and a librarian

---

15   Gumbs, "'But We Are Not the Same': Generating a Critical Poetics of Diaspora," 169. A reiteration of the quote on noting the relationships between black soldiers from different nations.

16   Shawn(ta) D. Smith, "Patricia's Child, Patrick's Penis & the Sex of Reference: A Lesbian Librarian's Log of Perverse Patronage," in *Out behind the Desk: Workplace Issues for LGBTQ Librarians,* ed. Tracy Marie Nectoux, Series on Gender and Sexuality in Librarianship, no. 1 (Duluth, MN: Library Juice Press, 2011). In this essay, I articulate a personal example of an exchange at the reference desk, where the librarian may be victim of sexual harassment as a result of the implied and actual sexual orientations of the librarian and patron.

17   nina de jesus, "Locating the Library in Institutional Oppression," *In the Library with the Lead Pipe,* September 24, 2014, http://www.inthelibrarywiththeleadpipe.org/2014/locating-the-library-in-institutional-oppression.

are of differing if not contrasting races, genders, ages, sexual orientations, or religions, whiteness is active during the reference interaction. As librarian April Hathcock writes, "the normativity of whiteness works insidiously, invisibly, to create binary categorizations of people as either acceptable to whiteness and therefore normal or different and therefore other."[18] Despite this binary recognition of whiteness, the solution can only exist outside of the realm of the State, which could mean a solution only exists outside of the library space. In the realm of the bull and the unicorn, where "we" exist in an in-between space, where we were never meant to survive, where the library is an apparatus upholding the regime of the nation-state, regardless of the identities of either individual, once any two bodies meet the friction persists, and without a doubt the two bodies are at war.

In 1977, Lorde spoke on a panel at the Modern Language Association in Chicago and subsequently published this talk as "The Transformation of Silence into Language and Action" in *Sinister Wisdom, A Lesbian Literary and Art Journal* in 1978. One of her most canonical speeches, Lorde reveals her confrontation with death as a result of preparing for an unexpected need for breast surgery. In addition, she notes that this battle for survival led her to recall life's regrets, which she found, were her silences. "Death," she says, "is the final silence."[19] Lorde's meditation on silence can be synonymous with the iconic caricature of the "shh-ing librarian." In the library, our immobilization from the very act of silence and silencing feeds tools of whiteness. Lorde teaches us that despite an inescapability of whiteness, "it is not difference that immobilizes us, but silence."[20]

Survival amidst silence

By the 1980s, Lorde was a frequent public speaker, leading international discussions on language, poetry, and social change. One speech in particular was an address to the Black feminist community of the Women's Center of Medgar Evers College at the City University of New York. Her

---

18 April Hathcock, "White Librarianship in Blackface: Diversity Initiatives in LIS," *In the Library with the Lead Pipe*, October 7, 2015, http://www.inthelibrarywiththeleadpipe. org/2015/lis-diversity/.

19 Audre Lorde, "The Transformation of Silence into Language and Action," in *Sister Outsider: Essays and Speeches* (Trumansburg, NY: Crossing Press, 1984), 40.

20 Lorde, "The Transformation of Silence into Language and Action."

speech, "I Am Your Sister: Black Women Organizing Across Sexualities" was later published as a pamphlet as a part of the Freedom Organizing Pamphlet Series of the Kitchen Table: Women of Color Press. Of the many points made in this speech, a pivotal lesson comes at the very start.

> Black women are not one great vat of homogenized chocolate milk. We have many different faces, and we do not have to become each other in order to work together. It is not easy for me to speak here with you as a Black Lesbian feminist, recognizing that some of the ways in which I identify myself make it difficult for you to hear me. But meeting across difference always requires mutual stretching, and until you can hear me as a Black Lesbian feminist, our strengths will not be truly available to each other as Black women.[21]

In the above quote, Lorde assumes a formulation of agency for both parties. "Mutual stretching" is required "across difference." In order for two entities to truly meet each other difference must be penetrated, intersected. Meeting across difference is synonymous to enacting the line connecting two binaries—channeling that in-between space is required to share strengths. This is a radical formula to apply to reference service, which assumes a hierarchical position on behalf of the library (State) and the patronage. In the remainder of the chapter, an in-depth look of this formula, outlined as a three-step process, will further explain how we may reference Lorde in our future applications of reference service with an aim to employ social justice in our work.

In Lorde's concept of sisterhood and embracing difference, a student does not need to know the library as the librarian does in order to navigate the space. Similarly, the librarian does not need to know more about the patron than is provided by the patron on his or her own terms. "Because I feel it is urgent that we do not waste each other's resources, that we recognize each sister on her own terms so that we may better work together toward our mutual survival."[22] Among any differing groups, whether it be Black-lesbian-feminist/Black-non-lesbian-feminist (as it was in the "I Am Your Sister Speech") or librarian/patron (as it is here), it is in the in-between space which is required to assure mutual survival. For Lorde, this formula of survival could be stated in three parts: 1) Acknowledgement of

---

21 Audre Lorde, "I Am Your Sister: Black Women Organizing Across Sexualities," in *A Burst of Light: Essays* (Ithaca, NY: Firebrand Books, 1988), 19.

22 Ibid., 20.

difference, 2) mutual stretching (to hear past the silences), and, 3) resource sharing to ultimately receive each other on her own terms.

This three-step process is cyclical. Meeting someone on her own terms, step three, means an acknowledgement of difference, step one. Lorde aims to clarify by stating: "I do not want you to ignore my identity, nor do I want you to make it an insurmountable barrier between our sharing of strengths."[23] A Black lesbian poet and contemporary of Lorde, Pat Parker, makes a similar claim in her well-known poem, "For the white person who wants to know how to be my friend." In the first verse, Parker writes, "The first thing you do is to forget that I'm Black./ Second, you must never forget that I'm Black."[24]

Archival material of Lorde

A summary of Audre Lorde's special collection of materials (special because these are the materials that she chose to donate) can be found on a curated WordPress site of selected archival special collections held at the Lesbian Herstory Archives (LHA). The description of her collection states:

> Audre Lorde (1934–1992) was a poet, activist, and influential feminist thinker. This collection consists primarily of drafts, manuscripts, and corrected proofs of her writings, including *Zami: A New Spelling of My Name* and *The Black Unicorn*. Lesbian Herstory Archives also has a large collection of digitized Audre Lorde tapes. Holdings include a recording of Audre Lorde's famous "The Master's Tools Will Never Dismantle the Master's House" speech from the Second Sex Conference at NYU in 1979. Please note that some of Audre Lorde's collection is stored offsite. If you are a researcher interested in her collection, you are advised to contact Lesbian Herstory Archives in advance of your visit. [2.085 linear ft.][25]

---

23   Ibid.

24   Pat Parker, *The Complete Works of Pat Parker*, ed. Julie R. Enszer, First edition, Sapphic Classics 102 (Brookville, NY: A Midsummer Nights Press; Dover, FL: Sinister Wisdom, Inc., 2016), 76.

25   Lesbian Herstory Archives, "1979–1983," *Special Collections: A Guide to Lesbian Herstory Archives' Special Collections*, July 24, 2012, https://herstoryspecialcollections.wordpress.com/1979-1983/.

Lorde's special collection, numbered 8323, as the twenty-third collection processed in 1983, includes additional references to photographs, audio recordings, video recordings, books of poetry, and ephemeral materials housed in other parts of the collection. Her audio recordings were digitized as a result of a project and collaborative relationship with a local library school who subsequently donated digital audio recordings back to LHA and created an Omeka site hosted on their servers to share Lorde's voice.[26]

Of the many recordings, three sides of tape represent the facilitation of the *Committee for the Visibility of the Other Black Woman* event held in New York City in 1980. Lorde's facilitation style in a room of lesbians was very "librarian," by enacting the theories of the three-part formula outlined above. As if listening to a bibliographic instruction session, with community self-determination rather than databases as its source material, this archival evidence illustrates Lorde's process of placing herself at the center, while simultaneously exhibiting the expectation from others to do the same. To adequately reference Audre Lorde as a conduit for library reference work, her voice, or in this case, transcript excerpts, will lead to a better understanding of her praxis.

Audre Lorde constructing an In-between space

The *Committee for the Visibility of the Other Black Woman* held an event to commemorate and introduce the community of women in New York City to the first national Black Lesbian Conference, set to occur on October 17–19 1980 in San Francisco. Livinia Pinscin, a member of the Committee, and board member of the first third-world-women (lesbian of color) lesbian organization in the country, *Salsa Soul Sisters*, introduced the event by naming Audre Lorde as a "surprise facilitator" followed by cheers from the

---

26   Shawn(ta) D. Smith-Cruz, "Tape-by-Tape : Digital Practices and Cataloging Rituals at the Lesbian Herstory Archives," in *Queers Online: LGBT Digital Practices in Libraries, Archives, and Museums*, ed. Rachel Wexelbaum (Sacramento, CA: Litwin Books, 2015), 85–110. More on this relationship and digitization process can be found in this book chapter. In "Tape-By-Tape," I describe Maxine Wolfe, an LHA coordinator who spearheaded and negotiated the project and who mailed Audre Lorde's family copies of the recordings before they went live onto the website. I recall the voicemail left on the LHA answering machine by Elizabeth Lorde Rollins, Lorde's daughter, who was overcome with generosity at the sound of her mother's voice emitting from the newly digitized recordings inside the surprise package. Her emotional output can be reimagined by a listening to these remarkable recordings currently available online.

women in the room. Lorde begins her facilitation by interrupting herself: "When Livinia spoke of the Black Lesbian community, she said very rightly so that we were a very diverse (can you hear me in the back?—a little louder, okay well why don't I stand up)." This act of self-interruption, in order to ensure a cohesive room was followed by a change in her own positioning—she subsequently stood up so that she could be heard. This move of her own body not only allowed for her own voice to be audible, but immediately changed the dynamics of the room, which had up until that point, focused on a hierarchy of speaker, and audience. Lorde did not address the room, she worked *with* the room to engage in mutual stretching.

Once Lorde stands, she goes on to speak for two minutes, all of which is excerpted here by my transcription:

> I think it's very true that we are a very diverse group. And this diversity should be not a reason for necessarily conflict, but it should be a source of our strength. However, I think we need to remember that as black lesbians we nonetheless have grown up in what is a very abnormal situation. Which is this society, that tells us to begin with, the fact that we are black women, meaning that we are cyphers, the fact that we are black women-identified-women, black lesbians, make us even less so. Okay? But it is not diversity, it is not *difference* which is the source of conflict, but our inability to recognize those differences, our inability to recognize each other and our differences, and to work together. As I said a few nights ago, we have been schooled within this place to believe that "comfortable sameness" is the answer to all of our problems, but that same "comfortable sameness" that we want to relax into inevitably becomes another name for death. So at the same time as we recognize our differences, they are not reasons to separate us, they are reasons to bring us together. They are a kind of wonder, a kind of cross-pollination that we could all enjoy, that we can all deal with, that really can fuel our movements for change. And I think we need to keep that in mind both when we listen to our speakers, and when we begin to deal within ourselves what are the pieces within each one of us, right, that harkens to something we are not familiar with; what are the pieces within ourselves that we

can use and expand, out of contact with someone or something, that is very different from ourselves.[27]

A close reading of Lorde's opening facilitative remarks mirror ideas promoted in her writings and speeches. She continues to reiterate that difference and self-recognition are tools toward unification and survival. Lorde defines collective truths: diversity, societal burdens, and a false sense of community through sameness as another name for death. If, however, we apply the survival formula, then Lorde enacts acknowledgement, mutual stretching, and resource sharing. 1) Acknowledgement of difference is expressed plainly by defining diversity as a collective truth. 2) Mutual stretching (to hear past the silences) is enacted by the call to notice the "comfortable sameness," to then push past this comfort to hear beyond what is recognizable. Finally, Lorde shows the room how to participate in 3) resource sharing to ultimately receive each other on ones own terms, to reach inside ourselves—activated by "contact with someone or something, that is very different from ourselves."

Conclusion

Lorde's teachings and philosophies may be applied to library service only if we understand the library as a structure that supports a maladjusted and inequitable State. Reference librarians' roles as individual bodies, interacting with other individual bodies, during one-on-one reference interactions, or in large classroom instructions, are ripe with the opportunities to come into "contact with someone or something, that is very different from ourselves." Acknowledgement of these differences, mutually stretching, and then sharing our resources on our own terms is a challenging yet possible move toward survival.

To those reading this book, or happening upon this book chapter, this formula for referencing Lorde may seem redundant to current practice, however, it should not be assumed that librarians harbor tools for interaction that include acknowledgement, mutual stretching and resource

---

27   Audre Lorde, *Conflicts in the Black Lesbian Community, Brooklyn NY, Organized by the Committee on the Visibility of the Other Black Woman (Tape 2 of 3)* (Committee for the Visibility of the Other Black Woman), accessed April 12, 2017, http://herstories.prattinfoschool.nyc/omeka/document/SPW1163. Transcribed from digitized online version, omitting any additional voices for the purposes of this chapter.

sharing. Policies are being adopted slowly, such as the ACRL *Framework*[28] which calls for increased engagement in student interaction during instruction and derives its conceptual analyses from "metaliteracy with special focus on metacognition, or critical self-reflection, as crucial to becoming more self-directed in that rapidly changing [information] ecosystem."[29] The six frames of the ACRL *Framework* as a result, are directly related to Lorde's three-part-formula. The first frame, Authority is Constructed, for example, contains a disposition for learners to "develop awareness of the importance of assessing content with a skeptical stance and with a self-awareness of their own biases and worldview."[30]

A distinction from Lorde and the frames, however, is highlighted in Lorde's focus on collective truths of difference within the State, which acts as an apparatus from which we all seek to survive. Compared to the first frame, where individual bodies are named as "learners," "experts," and "authorities," Lorde's work teaches us (think back to the land of the unicorn) that "we" have the ability to exist in an in-between space, where distinctions of hierarchy need not continue to immobilize us. Focusing on the dispositions of diverse worldviews and consciousness of frequent self-evaluation, as the frame suggests, is made more powerful when applied to Lorde's disposition of a focus on survival.

This distinction of Lorde's work as a librarian, compared to her societal contributions as a mother/poet/revolutionary, locates her efforts and identities inside of an imagined space, a library space, thereby creating a new paradigm for understanding and interpretation. This chapter's imagining, to *reference Lorde,* is to imagine her as a librarian during her years inside the public and school library, to remember her actions as an educator inside the classroom, and to recall her facilitation inside conferences and workshops populated by a community of lesbians and writers. In consideration for how to enact a reference interaction that promotes social justice, referencing Lorde will mean seeking refuge in an in-between space, as if our survival depended on it, and fleeing traditional library/patron dichotomous behavior, beyond silence.

---

28 American Library Association, "Framework for Information Literacy for Higher Education," Text, *Association of College & Research Libraries (ACRL),* (February 9, 2015), http://www.ala.org/acrl/standards/ilframework.

29 Ibid.

30 Ibid.

Works Cited

American Library Association. "Framework for Information Literacy for Higher Education." *Association of College & Research Libraries (ACRL)*, February 9, 2015. http://www.ala.org/acrl/standards/ilframework.

Bales, Stephen E. "The Academic Library as Crypto-Temple: A Marxian Analysis." In *Class and Librarianship: Essays at the Intersection of Information, Labor and Capital*, edited by Erik Sean Estep and Nathaniel F. Enright, 5–24. Sacramento, CA: Library Juice Press, 2016.

de jesus, nina. "Locating the Library in Institutional Oppression." *In the Library with the Lead Pipe*, September 24, 2014. http://www.inthelibrarywiththeleadpipe.org/2014/locating-the-library-in-institutional-oppression/.

Gumbs, Alexis Pauline. "'But We Are Not the Same': Generating a Critical Poetics of Diaspora." In *Audre Lorde's Transnational Legacies*, edited by Sabine Broeck and Stella Bolaki, 163–76. Boston: University of Massachusetts Press, 2015.

Hathcock, April. "White Librarianship in Blackface: Diversity Initiatives in LIS." *In the Library with the Lead Pipe*, October 7, 2015. http://www.inthelibrarywiththeleadpipe.org/2015/lis-diversity/.

Higashida, Cheryl. "Audre Lorde Revisited: Nationalism and Second-Wave Black Feminism." In *Black Internationalist Feminism: Women Writers of the Black Left, 1945–1995*, 134–57. Urbana: University of Illinois Press, 2011.

Lesbian Herstory Archives. "1979–1983." *Special Collections: A Guide to Lesbian Herstory Archives' Special Collections*, July 24, 2012. https://herstoryspecialcollections.wordpress.com/1979-1983/.

Lorde, Audre. "A Litany for Survival." In *The Black Unicorn: Poems*, 31–32. New York: Norton, 1978.

———. *Conflicts in the Black Lesbian Community, Brooklyn NY, Organized by the Committee on the Visibility of the Other Black Woman (Tape 2 of 3)*. Committee for the Visibility of the Other Black Woman, 1980. Herstories: Audio/Visual Collections of the LHA. Accessed December 13, 2016. http://herstories.prattinfoschool.nyc/omeka/document/SPW1163.

———. "I Am Your Sister: Black Women Organizing Across Sexualities." In *A Burst of Light: Essays*, 19–26. Ithaca, N.Y.: Firebrand Books, 1988.

———. "The Transformation of Silence into Language and Action." In *Sister Outsider: Essays and Speeches*, 40–44. Trumansburg, NY: Crossing Press, 1984.

Lorde, Audre, and Adrienne Rich. "An Interview with Audre Lorde." *Signs* 6, no. 4 (1981): 713–36.

Parker, Pat. *The Complete Works of Pat Parker.* Edited by Julie R. Enszer. First edition. Sapphic Classics 102. Brookville, NY: A Midsummer Nights Press; Dover, FL: Sinister Wisdom, Inc., 2016.

Seattle Art Museum, Fowler Museum at UCLA, and Brooklyn Museum. *Disguise: Masks and Global African Art*, 2015.

Smith, Shawn(ta) D. "Patricia's Child, Patrick's Penis & the Sex of Reference: A Lesbian Librarian's Log of Perverse Patronage." In *Out behind the Desk: Workplace Issues for LGBTQ Librarians*, edited by Tracy Marie Nectoux. Series on Gender and Sexuality in Librarianship, no. 1, 241–53. Duluth, MN: Library Juice Press, 2011.

Smith-Cruz, Shawn(ta) D. "Tape-by-Tape: Digital Practices and Cataloging Rituals at the Lesbian Herstory Archives." In *Queers Online: LGBT Digital Practices in Libraries, Archives, and Museums*, edited by Rachel Wexelbaum, 85–110. Sacramento, CA: Litwin Books, 2015.

Whitmire, Ethelene. "The Audre Lorde Was a Librarian Project: Audre Lorde, Black Lesbian Feminist Mother Poet Warrior, Was a Librarian." *The Audre Lorde Was a Librarian Project*, April 9, 2013. http://theaudrelordelibrarianproject.blogspot.com/2013/04/audre-lorde-black-lesbian-feminist.html.

Winter, Nina. "Audre Lorde." In *Conversations with Audre Lorde*, edited by Audre Lorde and Joan Wylie Hall, 9–17. Jackson: University Press of Mississippi, 2004.

Lesbian Librarianship for All: A Manifesto

Shawn(ta) Smith-Cruz

Coming Out with the L-Word

In March 2015, I gave a talk at Pratt Institute School of Information and Library Science at a student-led event called Feminism in Libraries. Although I felt internal pressure for my lack of direct identification as a feminist, I reassured myself that feminism as a topic to be explored, and not as an identity, was what I could contribute to the panel. The concept for "Lesbian Librarianship for All" was derived from that mantra I walked with while giving the talk. Suffering from the internal dialog as to whether or not I ought to "come out" as "not a feminist," I developed a coping mechanism that was in direct response to any assumption of nomenclature as central. Seven months later, to my surprise, Pratt's *School of Information and Library Science* changed its name to *Pratt School of Information*, relinquishing itself of what seemed to be a weight or burden of the L-Word. This shift felt strangely connected to other parts of my life, where I am asked to participate because of my identity. In the Pratt talk I developed a malleable concept of being a Lesbian Librarian, one that can be extended to include all librarians, regardless of sexual orientation. One can "be a lesbian librarian" without needing to actually be a lesbian. I began to walk with this concept, wondering if all lesbians could be librarians for their communities, without actually having the MLS. Determining if this were possible, connecting these L-words, "lesbian" with "librarian," was something that required further exploration.

To indulge this inquiry, I asked myself two questions: what does it mean to be a lesbian? And, what does it mean to be a librarian? How do the two overlap and intersect, and how might they meet in marginality, struggle, and implication for silence. Do both require an active movement toward justice? At the time of the writing of this essay, lesbian identity is synonymous to many in the queer community as outdated, regressive, and trans-misogynistic.[1] Similarly, shifts in the word "library" to the library profession, or the role of librarians in academic environments, has made many professionals shy of the word, needing often to "come out" as library affiliates when among other faculty colleagues.

This essay intends to bridge the gap between two under-appreciated communities by committing to ways that each enhances the other. The complications for being a lesbian librarian outlined here may be applied to any librarian or any lesbian, with a goal to supersede the prevalence of waning value to our communities. I intend for this chapter to act as a type of manifesto: the ever-puzzling autobiographical manifesto, coupled with an invitation for others to stake a claim as lesbian librarian. Referencing lesbian writer Cherríe Moraga's autobiographical narrative, scholar Sidonie Smith critiques a function of the autobiographical manifesto as a form which may result in a transformation of knowledge from the public performance of marginal perspectives. "To bring things 'into the light of day,' to make manifest a perspective on identity and experience, affects an epistemological breakage in repetition: it asserts the legitimacy of a new or alternative 'knowledge' located in the experience of the margins."[2]

---

1   Bonnie J Morris, *The Disappearing L: Erasure of Lesbian Spaces and Culture* (NY: SUNY Press, 2017). I co-presented with Bonnie Morris and others at an historic conference celebrating 40 years since the publication of Jonathan Ned Katz's *Gay American history: lesbians and gay men in the U.S.A.: a documentary history.* The single panel on lesbian identity was riddled with this concern and ended quite tragically. Morris presented findings on her 2017 publication for which I think is apt to summarize with this citation, especially since she has been barred and uninvited to present on the book since its publication, out of community fears of transphobic material, despite its focus of lesbian erasure, the book then, being evidence to its title.

2   Sidonie Smith, "The Autobiographical Manifesto: Identities, Temporalities, Politics," *Prose Studies Prose Studies* 14, no. 2 (1991): 191.

To bring into the light of day this alternative knowledge, I find it helpful to use a simple analogy, beginning with what I assume the readers of this collection to be the most familiar:

Librarian is to _____ *as Lesbian is to* _____ .

Let us begin.

Marginality in Librarianship

Chattel slavery was enforced in the United States until 1865. It should then be no surprise to any migrant or immigrant or descendant of slaves that our encroachment on indigenous land is inconsistent with human rights, mutual respect, and justice. In a nation built on blood, upholding this capitalist structure is the primary function of any institution. As a result, the promotion of institutional practices that honor a vision of social justice has, at best, an inherent contradiction. Public Services librarians grapple with this capitalist-focused/justice-seeking contradiction at the very core of our points of service: The aim to uphold national values, through referencing the canon, promoting academic publishers, assisting teaching faculty, assigning access policies, and other practices, reify a systemic flaw of our profession in an attainment for justice.

To remedy implications of capitalist collusion, librarians must locate themselves as simultaneously marginal as well as in positions of power, first, before the ability to effect change is enacted. Although tribalistic, association of oneself as a librarian-as-identity, may implicate a possible world where librarians are at the center, thereby standing between a spectrum of two opposing forces of power. In the case of some academic librarians, for example, the constant struggle to secure tenure is often at odds with both recognition as faculty by colleagues of neighboring departments, and the daily requirements of service work for which library colleagues are equally measured. If centered, the librarian may see herself holding power over her patrons on one end, and yet, beneath faculty and colleagues on the other. This centering may equate a feeling of marginalization when focused in the capitalist, hierarchy-driven ethos of our institutions. Scholar Lisa Sloniowski details this struggle by stating, "there is a ceiling for care workers in the university because we are viewed not as professionals or scholars, but as support and administrative workers."[3] She goes on to say,

> We struggle to find time to research and write because our service work is considered more useful to the corporate goals of the university, and university administrators are often unsupportive of our research goals when they take our limited time and bodies away from serving library users and their various anxieties. Simultaneously, the rise of digital humanities has opened doors for librarians and programmers to be more involved in academic projects, but nonetheless such projects are generally managed and funded within traditional academic-labor hierarchies, with professors directing the work of librarians and other alt-academics whose intellectual contributions are devalued as merely service work or project management.[4]

Measuring struggle is a route toward locating an "ongoing invisibilization," or, if in the context of manifesto, identifying marginality within the librarian profession for academic librarians.[5]

At the end of 2015, during a large-scale campaign to demand faculty of color be targeted as potential employees at the Graduate Center (City University of New York), a list of demands was presented to the University President and the Provost office. A comprehensive overview of the numbers of appointed faculty of color listed a paltry handful of women appointed by the University Provost, demanding more. Of course I was pressed to sign the letter until I saw that my own name was not counted. Immediately, I contacted the committee alerting them of the good fortune that indeed another female faculty of color was on the core faculty line, at the University, inside the library, and that person was me! It was a pleasure to greet them, yet again, as their faculty library liaison. The response was thoughtful despite its flaw. The committee representative thanked me for my attention, but explained they would not add my name:

---

3   Lisa Sloniowski, "Affective Labor, Resistance, and the Academic Librarian," *Library Trends* 64, no. 4 (September 13, 2016): 645–66, doi:10.1353/lib.2016.0013.

4   Ibid.

5   Ibid.

Also, as to identifying central line faculty in particular, as I understand it, the idea was to try to throw into relief by focusing specifically on the GC as a college, and speaking as a college, the white maleness of the building. It'd be great if other cohorts would organize to speak to these matters as well.[6]

It is a difficult feeling to recall the impact that erasure brings when it is directed by those advocating for your existence. Despite my campus committee service, or assigned research leave time to write essays such as this one, or ultimately, despite the faculty appointment letter signed by both the Provost and President sitting in a file folder, in a cabinet beneath three shelves lined with layers of thank you cards from students and colleagues, I continued to support the efforts of female faculty of color, while cradling myself with resolve in my positioning as a *sister outsider*. From this position I understood that this fight wasn't about me, the faculty librarian; it was about the destruction of white maleness in the building among faculty "in the college." The skewed nature of the target, as so often occurs in social justice initiatives that push for diversity, has a flaw of dismissing the very people it aims to claim allegiance and advocacy.

I've found refuge in marginal positions as a librarian in librarian of color writers like April Hathcock, or lesbian of color faculty like Sara Ahmed. One notable instance I recall is from Sara Ahmed's blog, *Feminist Killjoy*, where she used her posts to document the development of her 2017 publication, *Living a Lesbian Life*. She posted the transcript of her Keynote of the 2015 Lesbian Lives conference. Ahmed, although not a librarian, made an interesting comparison to diversity work and lesbian life, which I found to be very librarian, in its focus on data.

> Living a lesbian life is data collection; we collect information about the institutions that govern the reproduction of life: it is almost too much data; we don't have time to interpret all the material we collect. If living a lesbian life generates data, then lesbian feminism provides the tools to help us interpret that data.

---

6   From email correspondence of the author. Clarification on how the perception of the library as not a part of "the college" was never sought, however the assumption is a distinction between the Graduate School and the University Center, holding administrative offices and departments as not a part of the college-proper.

> And by data I am referring to walls. I first began thinking about
> walls when completing a research project on racism and diversity
> within institutions. Diversity practitioners would talk of how the
> very institutions that appointed them would block their efforts...
> And what I learnt from doing this research was that unless you came
> up against the walls, they did not appear... .[7]

Social justice work, at its essence, is not meant to act only in the service
of the marginalized or those silenced into corners of exclusion, but to ensure that all people "come up against the walls." This can happen, I believe,
when analogous manifestos such as this one are claimed by those who
wouldn't ordinarily implicate their connections to other groups. Commu-
nal exchange through ownership is one idealized goal that this manifesto aims toward.

The continual dilemma of librarians as faculty is one that inhibits
equal participation in the academy as well as compromises scholarly output outside of the academy. Librarians are marginal as a result of our enduring values, which are at times at odds with our dual administrative and
faculty positions. This positioning is similar to lesbianism and its position
in a larger community of peers for which their significance is measured
and at times challenged.

Or simply put: *Librarian is to* __Faculty__ *as Lesbian is to* _____ .

Marginality in Lesbianism

In Summer 2016, I was asked to deliver a keynote to an international
LGBTQ conference on archiving, librarianship, museums, and special libraries (LGBTQ ALMS). At this conference my talk on black lesbian community organizing in New York City in the 1970s and early 80s led to audience questions solely about the inclusion of trans-women, most of which
was irrelevant to the talk on specific lesbian women of the aforementioned
time. I was unprepared to answer questions unrelated to the talk, and

---

7   Sara Ahmed, "Living a Lesbian Life," *Feministkilljoys*, February 26, 2015,
    https://feministkilljoys.com/2015/02/26/living-a-lesbian-life/.

wondered why similar questions weren't presented to other speakers whose work focused mainly on gay men.

Later that year, I was asked to participate in a documentary on lesbian identity as a result of my role as co-editor of a special issue of *Sinister Wisdom, a Multicultural Lesbian Literary and Art Journal* on Celebrating the Michigan Womyn's Music Festival—a forty-year-old annual festival for "women-born-women," a claim newly established and also the reason for its ending. The festival was an iconic space worthy of an entire journal issue, as it touched the lives of thousands of women internationally, many of whom identified as lesbian. I was contacted as co-editor to present a historical timeline of lesbian identity, similar to my Keynote, but to focus on Michfest, as opposed to black lesbian organizing. Similar to other requests I've had throughout the years due to my affiliation with the Lesbian Herstory Archives and likely my role as lesbian librarian of color, fulfilling in these instances the mix of representation and professional legitimacy, I responded to these inquiries as a faculty reference librarian would.

This interview stood out to me as an example of lesbian librarianship because the interviewee, MJ Corey, was a young lesbian who expressed concern for the recurring and gripping fear that she experiences, when coming out as lesbian in a queer world. This fear led to none other than silence—a burden that she carried as an out and proud lesbian, not within mainstream straight communities, but when among the queer world. Although the connections of her story to the attendees and lovers of *Michfest* were apparent, I couldn't help but to equate her silence among other queers with the silence that I felt as a librarian among other faculty.

So to complete the analogy:

Librarian is to _____Faculty_____ *as Lesbian is to* _____Queer_____ .

Spring and Fall 1977 featured publication of the first issues of *Sinister Wisdom: a Journal of Words and Pictures for the Lesbian Imagination in All Women*, now titled, *Sinister Wisdom, A Multicultural Lesbian Literary and Art Journal*. Now one of the longest-running lesbian cultural, art, and literary publications, its very existence and archive cites a pronounced definition for the concept, term, and cultural underpinnings of the word "lesbian." The cover of the third issue features a print by lesbian photographer, Tee Corrine. The cover frames a two-toned photographic-negative of a couple tussling in bed: one reclining nude is played like a guitar in the arms of her lover. One arm clutches a neck to meet lips; the other arm, an arrow between open thighs. The entirety of a hand disappears into a contoured darkness. Wisps of layered cropped hair dance at the lightest sections of the horizontal negative exposure. I claim this Tee Corrine print and its 1977 *Sinister Wisdom* debut as cover image, known to be of two different-ly-abled women, as a timestamp of lesbian culture, representing a quest for visibility.[8] This same issue features an article by poet Adrienne Rich titled, "It is the lesbian in us… ." Rich writes, "The word 'lesbian' must be affirmed because to discard it is to collaborate with silence and lying about our very existence, the closet-game, the creation of the *unspeakable.*"[9] Both Corrine's photographic print, highlighting differently abled bodies, and Rich's essay on language, speak to a modern-day divisiveness that exists within the queer community, where politics of gender-identities challenges any claim to the term "lesbian." In a world where gender is a variable that must remain fluid, sexual identities that are perceived to rely on the stability of gender have implications of transphobia or gender-essentialism. This challenging concept of lesbian-centered culture and identity as antiquated has silenced dykes who manifest claims to lesbian-centered identities.

After the interview with the young lesbian documentarian, I put on my librarian hat and sent her links to the very first issues of *Sinister Wisdom* where she could source originations of lesbian political consciousness—one in particular is described by Harriet Desmoines in the first issue of Sinister Wisdom. In a piece titled, "Who-o-o-o is a Lesbian?" Desmoines states, "everytime a woman draws a circle around her psyche, saying 'this is a room of *my own*' and then writes from within that 'room,' she is inhabiting a lesbian consciousness."[10] In Desmoines' interpretation of consciousness, I attest that this room can be an ephemeral space, a library space, a writer's space, a researcher's space, or any conceptual space where a self-affirming idea may be transformed into action.

---

8   Shawn(ta) Smith-Cruz, "Graphic Activism: Lesbian Archival Library Display," in *Gender Issues and the Library: Case Studies of Innovative Programs and Resources*, ed. Carol Smallwood and Lura Sanborn (McFarland, 2017). A similar description of the Tee Corrine print is also included in the Graphic Activism book chapter to reference the Lesbian Herstory Archives display at the CUNY Graduate Center. The iconic Sinister Wisdom cover is highlighted in this book chapter as well as in a Sinister Wisdom post-card series to celebrate an upcoming fifty years.

9   Adrienne Rich, "It Is the Lesbian in Us… ," *Sinister Wisdom* 1, no. 3 (Spring 1977): 6–9.

10   Harriet Desmoines and Catherine Nicholson, *Sinister Wisdom*, vol. 1, 1977.

The Convergence: The Lesbian Librarian

For ultimate clarity in this comparison, "Librarian is to <u>Faculty</u> as Lesbian is to <u>Queer</u>" for the purpose of this manifesto, it is the case that librarians are faculty just as lesbians are queer. Although there are librarians who within the capitalist structure, supply reference work, conduct research, provide technical services, and contribute to scholarly communication, but are not faculty, there are also lesbians who live their lives as women who love other women but are not, and choose to not identify with the reclaimed term "queer." Despite the existence of these multiple groups, in order to rely on the convergence ahead, let's remain focused on the communities where all things are true: Lesbians who are Queer and Librarians who are Faculty. Once we are clear in this instance, the remainder of this chapter will denote, even further, that one need only be a lesbian or a librarian to be a lesbian librarian.

Nomenclature in Lesbianism and Librarianship

The two identities shall meet with reference service as the adhesive. The term "lesbian" does not only describe a sexual orientation; lesbian is also a constructed political identity. As a result of a current political climate in which gender fluidity has precedence over gender essentialism, choosing lesbian identity is, similar to as it had been during the birth of the radical lesbian feminist movement, beyond sexual behavior.[11] During its beginnings, women who did not have sex with women identified as lesbian to prove their allegiance to ending patriarchy, by withholding access of their bodies from men. Over time, a lesbian identity was applied to anyone who choose to define herself as such, the necessary factors including, but not limited to, identification as a woman who also loves other women.

The American Library Association's Committee on Accreditation (COA) adopted the Standards for Accreditation in 1972.[12] However, iden-

---

11   This refers to terms such as "old gay" and "new gay" which distinguished between women who were out pre and post the radical women's movement. Some new gays were considered non-sexual lesbians who identified with a political affiliation, with the premise that patriarchy could only be ended by absolute exclusion from men.

12   William R. Eshelman, "The Erosion of Library Education," *Library Journal* 108, no. 13 (1983): 1309.

tification as a librarian predates accreditation of a master's degree in library and information studies, the current standard. In addition, similar to the 2015 name change by Pratt University from *School of Information and Library Science* to *School of Information*, of the sixty schools listed under the ALA database of accredited programs, twelve, or 20%, of programs do not have the name "library" in their granted degree.[13] The degree names listed below have the number of institutions who hold the degree, with no library-titled degree alternative, in parenthesis:

- Master of Science (5)
- Master of Information Studies (2)
- Master of Science in Information (1)
- Master of Science in Information Science (1)
- Master of Information Studies (1)
- Master of Science in Information Studies (1)
- Master of Information (1)

Furthermore, like Pratt Institute, schools that do supply degrees with "library" in the name of the degree granted are close to 50% less likely to have "library" in the name of the school. Twenty-seven out of sixty, or 45%, of schools accredited by the COA do not have "library" in the name of the school or department.[14]

    Variation in the use of the word "library" in library school programs, departments, degrees (and although not discussed here, also position titles), make clear that the word "library" is a disappearing indicator for identifying librarians. "The word library is important—or should be…" but is increasingly removed from the mouths of practitioners in the name of legitimacy and innovation.[15]

---

13   Pratt Institute School of Information actually does supply a Master of Science in Library and Information Science.

14   American Library Association and Committee on Accreditation, "Directory of Institutions Offering ALA-Accredited Master's Programs in Library and Information Studies," Database, (April 26, 2017), www.ala.org/accreditation.

15   Connie Van Fleet and Danny P. Wallace, "The I-Word: Semantics and Substance in Library and Information Studies Education," *Reference & User Services Quarterly* 42, no. 2 (Winter 2002): 104–9.

Being a Lesbian Librarian

Now that we've got naming out of the way, understand that naming one-self a lesbian or a librarian will be contested by those who have remained loyal to the title(s) and hold the "authority" to name themselves as such: Lesbians who actually have relationships with women will grow confused if non-lesbians begin to adopt the title; similarly, librarians will often test others with a talk of library school, to ensure to rid the room of any im-posters.[16] Nevertheless, these methods may be applied in the following in-stances with the clear understanding that one does not have to be attract-ed to women or have an MLS to be a "lesbian librarian."

Lesbian Librarianship for Librarians

- If living life as a man, then your affiliation as a lesbian librarian may be akin to subject specialty, as would be the case for a white-bodied per-son to be the Africana Librarian or an abled-bodied person to the Dis-abilities Librarian. It is extremely important to question your reasons for wanting to be a lesbian librarian and be prepared to describe these reasons when asked.

- If living life as a woman, but not a lesbian, then your affiliation may be the same as a lesbian studies subject specialty, but it would be extreme-ly important to consider every moment when you experience the need to "come out" as "not a lesbian" by sexual orientation, and the hetero-centric predisposition of these needs.

Lesbian Librarianship for Lesbians

- If without an MLS or its equivalent, then respond to inquiries on les-bianism as a librarian would, using reference style communication, sourcing references, and providing community assistance.

- If with an MLS, or its equivalent (or plainly put, Lesbian Librarianship For Lesbian Librarians)—this is not enough. A lesbian with an MLS must also be equipped with the same material as non-lesbian MLS holders in regard to lesbian history, political analysis, literature, archi-val material, and other aspects of lesbian studies.

---

16   Maia Ramnath, "Authority," ed. Kelly Fritsch, Clare O'Connor, and A. K Thompson, *Keywords for Radicals: The Contested Vocabulary of Late-Capitalist Struggle*, 2016.

Expectations of a Lesbian Librarian

If we are to use my career trajectory as an example, my undergraduate degree in Queer Women's Studies led me to work with leading institutions in NYC, namely, the Lesbian Herstory Archives, and the Center for Lesbian and Gay Studies. I also had hands-on experiential work with non-profits, various academic institutions, women's studies departments and youth organizations throughout New York. However, my access to on-the-ground lesbianism was due to my being an actual lesbian. Prior to college, I co-founded a non-profit that employed young women living in the street economies, *Sister Outsider*, and was also a co-founding member of FIERCE, an LGBT youth activist organization. The goal in my listing community affiliations is to allow for non-lesbians to understand the possibility of a life of community affiliations. In the case where my upbringing is atypical, say in the instance of non-activist-affiliated lesbians living outside of city-centers, the ways to make up for lack of community access and experience is to use reference resources.

Harboring the knowledge of lesbian feminism, lesbian separatism, and lesbian herstory in general are the tools required to supply adequate lesbian librarianship and is far more impacting than exhibiting traits of same-sex-female sexual attraction. Ultimately, all lesbians, by sexual orientation alone, may not be equipped to be librarians with a lesbian subject specialty, or "lesbian librarians," even if she holds an MLS.

Referencing Lesbians

To equip both lesbians and librarians with the tools to adequately supply lesbian reference service, I recommend enrollment in professional development courses at local institutions where lesbian herstory is taught from a community perspective. One such example of this is in New York City at the Lesbian Herstory Archives (LHA), the oldest and largest volunteer-run lesbian archive in the world. *Lesbian Lives* is the course that is the programmatic center of the Lesbian Lives Institute at LHA. Founded in 2013 by art historian, Flavia Rando, PhD., Lesbian Lives utilizes archival collections to apply an historical framework to archival materials for researchers, lesbians, and other community members with interest in LHA collections in particular, and lesbian herstory in general. Offered as a ten-week course on-site at the herstoric limestone building in Park Slope, Brooklyn, this course allows for hands-on implementation of personal projects into its curriculum.

A lesbian librarian approach to reference aims to quote, cite, and refer other lesbians when responding to research questions. This includes the necessary application of language for identities synonymous to lesbian throughout time and location: dyke, bull-dagger, queer, same-gender-loving, afrekete, masculine-of-center, etc. Use of LGBTQ databases and archival material will help to direct resources away from large generalities to specifications in lesbian communities. It is also important to keep in mind L-word erasure when sourcing LGBTQ materials—that the search will likely yield results that are not lesbian, unless lesbian is specifically sought.

Lastly, since lesbian is a political identity, it is apt to end this manifesto by referencing lesbian librarian, Audre Lorde. As described in the preceding chapter, referencing Audre Lorde may mean to connect with our patrons, faculty colleagues, and community members in ways that allow for acknowledgement, mutual stretching, and resource sharing. To become a lesbian librarian, one must constantly hold internal awareness of our own societal positions in regard to class, race, sexual orientation, gender, age, religion, and physical ability in respect to the demographic breakdown of those who utilize the library, including the faculty, students, colleagues, and other public patrons. For me, I'd say: I am a salaried Assistant Professor, black/Hispanic, lesbian, woman (and assigned so at birth), mid-thirties, etc. As a result of my identities, I am singled out by students of color, placed on diversity committees, and chosen as representative for the library in outward facing programming. Acknowledgment of how many identities are reflected in this world, a world where librarians and lesbians are continuously silenced, is key to moving forward on a roadmap to justice.

Works Cited

Ahmed, Sara. "Living a Lesbian Life." *Feministkilljoys*, February 26, 2015.
https://feministkilljoys.com/2015/02/26/living-a-lesbian-life/.

American Library Association, and Committee on Accreditation. "Directory of
Institutions Offering ALA-Accredited Master's Programs in Library and
Information Studies." Database, April 26, 2017. http://www.ala.org/accreditation.

Desmoines, Harriet, and Catherine Nicholson. *Sinister Wisdom*. Vol. 1, 1977.

Eshelman, William R. "The Erosion of Library Education." *Library Journal* 108, no. 13
(1983): 1309.

Morris, Bonnie J. *The Disappearing L: Erasure of Lesbian Spaces and Culture*.
NY: SUNY Press, 2017.

Ramnath, Maia. "Authority." Edited by Kelly Fritsch, Clare O'Connor, and A. K
Thompson. *Keywords for Radicals: The Contested Vocabulary of Late-Capitalist
Struggle*, 2016.

Rich, Adrienne. "It Is the Lesbian in Us…" *Sinister Wisdom* 1, no. 3 (Spring 1977): 6–9.

Sloniowski, Lisa. "Affective Labor, Resistance, and the Academic Librarian." *Library
Trends* 64, no. 4 (September 13, 2016): 645–66. doi:10.1353/lib.2016.0013.

Smith, Sidonie. "The Autobiographical Manifesto: Identities, Temporalities, Politics."
Prose Studies Prose Studies 14, no. 2 (1991): 186–212.

Smith-Cruz, Shawn(ta). "Graphic Activism: Lesbian Archival Library Display." In *Gender
Issues and the Library: Case Studies of Innovative Programs and Resources*, edited by
Carol Smallwood and Lura Sanborn. McFarland, 2017.

Van Fleet, Connie, and Danny P. Wallace. "The I-Word: Semantics and Substance in
Library and Information Studies Education." *Reference & User Services Quarterly*
42, no. 2 (Winter 2002): 104–9.

Author Biographies

Maria T. Accardi is Librarian and Coordinator of Instruction and Reference at Indiana University Southeast, a regional campus of Indiana University located in New Albany, Indiana. Maria holds a BA in English from Northern Kentucky University, an MA in English from the University of Louisville, and an MLIS from the University of Pittsburgh. She served as a co-editor of and contributor to *Critical Library Instruction: Theories and Methods* (Library Juice Press, 2010), and is the author of *Feminist Pedagogy for Library Instruction* (Library Juice Press, 2013), for which she received the ACRL Women and Gender Studies Section Award for Significant Achievement in Women and Gender Studies Librarianship in 2014. She is also the editor of *The Feminist Reference Desk: Concepts, Critiques, and Conversations* (Library Juice Press, 2017). She lives in Louisville, Kentucky.

Kate Adler is the Director of Library Services at Metropolitan College of New York, where, among other things, she oversees the information literacy and reference programs and has developed special collections focused on the history of poverty in New York and on community organizing. Her research interests pivot around the intersection of libraries, social justice and community empowerment and engage critical theories of race, gender, class, geography, disability, affect and biopower, and histories of poverty, labor and social movements. She has written and presented on these topics and on Critical Reference. She received her MLIS from Queens College, CUNY and her MA in Liberal Studies from the CUNY Graduate Center.

Veronica Arellano Douglas is Instruction Coordinator at the University of Houston Libraries. She received her MLS from the University of North Texas and is an ALA Spectrum Scholar. Her research interests include relational-cultural theory, gendered labor in librarianship, and critical librarianship and information literacy. She blogs at veronicaarellanodouglas.com.

Ian Beilin is Humanities Research Services Librarian at Columbia University. Ian serves on the editorial boards of the open access, open peer-reviewed journal *In the Library with the Lead Pipe* and of the open access journal *Canadian Journal of Academic Librarianship*. He has presented and published on topics in critical librarianship, critical library instruction, and critical information literacy. He is also a historian of modern Germany. He received his PhD in history from Columbia University and his MSIS from The University at Albany (SUNY).

Danielle Ball is a former librarian at California Department of Corrections and Rehabilitation. She received a Master of Library and Information Science from University of California, Los Angeles and a Bachelor of Science in Psychology from California Polytechnic State University, San Luis Obispo. While in graduate school, Danielle gained experience in academic libraries and completed fieldwork at the Yosemite National Park archives. She is currently a public librarian in a large metropolitan system. In her free time, Danielle is involved in political organizing and voter engagement at the local level.

Jennifer Bowers (MLS, MA), Professor, is the Social Sciences librarian at the University of Denver. She is coeditor of the fifteen-volume Rowman and Littlefield series, *Literary Research: Strategies and Sources*, and the coauthor of three volumes in the series. She is also the coeditor, with Carrie Forbes, of *Rethinking Reference for Academic Libraries: Innovative Developments and Future Trends* and coauthor of the *Collection Management* article, "'If You Want the History of a White Man, You Go to the Library:' Critiquing Our Legacy, Addressing our Library Collections Gaps." Bowers' current research focuses on critical approaches to teaching with archival materials in the social sciences, collaborative research consultations, and popular press reception of the pioneering archaeologist, Harriet Boyd Hawes.

Megan Browndorf is East European Studies Liaison & Reference Librarian at Georgetown University. She holds an MA in Russian and East European Studies and an MLS from Indiana University. Her interests include Soviet library history, instruction, and area studies librarianship.

Iyra S. Buenrostro (BLIS 2005, cum laude; MLIS 2010) is a Ph.D. Candidate in Information Studies from Wee Kim Wee School of Communication and Information, Nanyang Technological University in Singapore. Her current research involves photographs and memories of Martial Law in the Philippines. Iyra is also a faculty member (on study leave) of the School of Library and Information Studies, University of the Philippines Diliman.

Johann Frederick A. Cabbab (BLS 1994; MLS 1999) is a full time faculty member and former Dean of the UP School of Library and Information Studies. He was managing editor, writer and graphic artist for several children and young adult publications prior to rejoining the academe in 2007. He is currently pursuing his Doctor of Literature and Philosophy in Information Science (DLitt et Phil) via distance mode at the University of South Africa (Universiteit van Suid-Afrika).

Rachael Dreyer is the Head of Research Services for the Eberly Family Special Collections Library at the Pennsylvania State University's University Park campus. She worked previously as a reference archivist at the American Heritage Center at the University of Wyoming and as a reference librarian at the Chelsea District Library in Chelsea, Michigan. She holds a Master of Science in Information from the University of Michigan's School of Information. Her professional interests include increasing access to special collections and archives, creating user-focused archival service points, and building more diverse and inclusive archival holdings.

Joshua Finnell is the Head of Research & Instruction and an Associate Professor in the University Libraries at Colgate University in Hamilton, NY. His work has appeared in *Library Philosophy and Practice*, *Journal for the Study of Radicalism*, *International Information & Library Review*, and *New Library Review*. He is also the co-founder of the Awesome Foundation Libraries Chapter and associate editor of *Global Knowledge, Memory and Communication*.

Carrie Forbes (MLS, MA), Associate Professor and Associate Dean, oversees the University of Denver Libraries' public services including research support, instruction, outreach/programming, and borrowing and lending services. She co-edited, along with Jennifer Bowers, *Rethinking Reference for Academic Libraries: Innovative Developments and Future Trends* published by Roman & Littlefield in 2014. Other recent publications include a co-authored chapter in *Academic Librarianship Today* on reference and instruction models and a co-written article in *College & Research Libraries* on "Expanding Support for Graduate Students: Library Workshops on Research Funding Opportunities." She is currently working on an edited volume on academic outreach initiatives to be published by Roman & Littlefield in late 2018.

Marisa Hernandez is a 2016–2018 National Diversity Scholar for the Association of Research Libraries, a 2018 Smithsonian Institute Libraries Minority Awards Program intern at the Hirshhorn Museum and Sculpture Garden Library, and the 2017 recipient of Yale University's Beinecke Rare Book & Manuscript Library Professional Fellowship. Her experience includes work with the County of Los Angeles Public Library, serving the East Los Angeles community as a Jill-of-all-library-trades and master storyteller. Additionally, Ms. Hernandez taught high school special education classes at Los Angeles Job Corps to formerly incarcerated young adults. Ms. Hernandez holds a Master of Management in Library and Information Science from the University of Southern California and a Bachelor of Arts in American Studies from the University of California at Santa Cruz, where she completed her thesis under the advisement of the History of Consciousness graduate program.

Jeff Hirschy is currently a PhD student at the University of Alabama in Tuscaloosa, Alabama. His personal interests revolve around cats, reading, and Star Trek. His professional interests focus around the relationship between collecting institutions, public history, and social justice.

Emily Jacobson is the Correctional Services Librarian at The New York Public Library, where she provides library services to people on Rikers Island. In 2016, she helped create the first permanent library space on Rikers at the Rose M. Singer Center. She also coordinates reference correspondence with people who are incarcerated across the country. In the future, she would like to collaborate with other library systems who do similar reference work.

Hannah Lee focuses on the future developments of information systems and technology. In a time that facing a crossroads where we need information professionals, Hannah is able to understand how we communicate with each other, what types of information infrastructure is needed, and how to organize information. Some of her interests include copyright, intellectual property, cybernetics, book arts, mentoring, and volunteering for non-profit organizations.

Julia Marden is a data librarian and consultant, with a decade of experience working at the intersection of civic technology, education, and community engagement. With her firm, Tiny Panther Consulting, she brings data librarian services to the public, teaching data literacy workshops and helping socially-minded organizations collect and analyze data with the communities they serve. Julia commutes around NYC on a glitter purple bicycle, on a quest to demystify data and upset the balance of power in data-driven research.

Stephanie Osorio is the first in her family to earn undergraduate and graduate degrees. In August 2017, she completed her Master of Management in Library and Information Science from the University of Southern California. Ms. Osorio recently completed an internship at the Library of Congress as a Program Support Assistant. She currently works as a Library Associate for the Los Angeles Law Library. .

Erin Rivero is a Reference Librarian at Chapman University and Torrance Public Library. Previously, Ms. Rivero offered digital asset management for the Los Angeles Philharmonic, managed an early childhood education library for the Los Angeles County Office of Education, and served as an incarcerated adult literacy educator at a Southern California correctional facility. Ms. Rivero holds a Master of Management in Library and Information Science from the University of Southern California, as well as a Master of Arts in International Studies, a Master of Arts in Teaching, and a Bachelor of Music in Music Education from Chapman University.

Shawn(ta) Smith-Cruz is Assistant Professor and Head of Reference at the Graduate Center Library of the City University of New York.

Her work has appeared in *Sinister Wisdom: A Multicultural Lesbian Literary and Art Journal, Journal of Lesbian Studies, Frontiers: A Journal of Women's Studies*, multiple Library Juice Press publications, and others. Shawn is a board member for the Center for LGBTQ Studies/CLAGS where she chairs the archives committee, and speaks internationally on Black Lesbian archival narrative sourcing the work from collections of the Lesbian Herstory Archives, where she has been a volunteer Coordinator for ten years. From Queens College, CUNY she received her MLS with an archival certification and her MFA in Creative Writing with a focus on Fiction.

Eamon Tewell is Reference & Instruction Librarian at Long Island University Brooklyn. He received his MLIS from Drexel University and his MA in Media Studies from LIU Brooklyn. Eamon has published and presented on the topics of critical information literacy, popular media and active learning in library instruction, and televisual representations of libraries.

Vanessa Villarreal is the first in her family to attend college and graduate school. She received her BA in History with a minor in Ancient Greece and Rome Studies at Lake Forest College in Lake Forest, IL. She is currently studying to receive her MMLIS at the University of Southern California. Her library service includes recent work as a Bilingual Bookmobile Associate, Reference Desk Assistant, and Children's Reference Desk Assistant for Cook Memorial Library in Libertyville, IL. She has a passion for travel, knowledge, and experience.

Haruko Yamauchi is the library teaching coordinator and liaison to college transition programs at Eugenio María de Hostos Community College (CUNY). Her current research interests include urban public library history, and exploring challenges of/opportunities for supporting and empowering students new to research as they strengthen their critical research and analysis skills. A lesson plan of hers was published in the 2016 ACRL publication *Critical Library Pedagogy Handbook* (vol. 2). In 2016, she also chaired the planning committee of the ACRL/NY Annual Symposium: *Money and Power.*

Index

CPSIA information can be obtained
at www.ICGtesting.com
Printed in the USA
BVHW041435241219
567674BV00006B/45/P